D1610201

ARTHURIAN STUDIES XXXIV

# CHIVALRY IN TWELFTH-CENTURY GERMANY
## The Works of Hartmann von Aue

Hartmann von Aue is a major figure in medieval German literature; his works are important in the history of chivalry, highlighting its key features at an important phase of transition and consolidation. His unusual position as an educated knight gave him access to the worlds of clerical learning and spirituality as well as secular aristocracy, and he draws on all these sources to provide a complex and revealing vernacular self-interpretation of knighthood. This book is the first full-scale enquiry into the presentation and the role of knighthood and chivalric values across the full range of Hartmann's poems; the author considers chivalry and its social and ideological dimensions in Hartmann's works, and in the historical context. The various strands of influence that informed the developing ideology of chivalry in the late twelfth-century are explored, fruitfully combining literary, linguistic and historical approaches.

The opening chapter places Hartmann's works in the broader perspective of Arthurian literature and of kingship and chivalry in the twelfth century, while the second examines the historical reality of knighthood as a military and a social order in twelfth-century Germany. Further chapters are devoted to each of Hartmann's works, *Erec*, *Gregorius*, the *Klage* and his lyrics, *Der arme Heinrich* and *Iwein*, which are interpreted with a historical perspective, and in the light of Hartmann's French sources.

This study links up to current debates on both the historical study of chivalry and the literary interpretation of Hartmann's poems. It sheds fresh light on the relation of aesthetic stylization and social function in these works, and contributes to an understanding of the history of aristocratic self-consciousness by analyzing the social, ideological and literary dimensions of chivalry in the works of an educated and thinking knightly author.

Dr W.H. JACKSON is Senior Lecturer in the Department of German at the University of St Andrews.

# ARTHURIAN STUDIES

ISSN 0261-9814

Previously published volumes in the series
are listed at the back of this book

# CHIVALRY IN TWELFTH-CENTURY GERMANY

## The Works of Hartmann von Aue

W. H. Jackson

D. S. BREWER

First published 1994
D. S. Brewer, Cambridge


ISBN 0 85991 431 3


D. S. Brewer is an imprint of Boydell & Brewer Ltd
PO Box 9, Woodbridge, Suffolk IP12 3DF, UK
and of Boydell & Brewer Inc.
PO Box 41026, Rochester, NY 14604-4126, USA


British Library Cataloguing-in-Publication Data
Chivalry in Twelfth-century Germany: Works of
Hartmann von Aue. - (Arthurian Studies, ISSN
0261-9814; Vol. 34)
I. Jackson, W. H. II. Series
831.2
ISBN 0-85991-431-3

Library of Congress Cataloging-in-Publication Data
Jackson, W. H.
    Chivalry in twelfth-century Germany : the works of Hartmann
von Aue / W.H. Jackson.
        p.   cm. – (Arthurian studies, ISSN 0261-9814 ; 34)
    Includes bibliographical references and index.
    ISBN 0-85991-431-3 (alk. paper)
    1. Hartmann, von Aue, 12th cent. – Criticism and interpretation.
2. Arthurian romances – History and criticism. 3. Chivalry in
literature. 4. Knights and knighthood in literature.
I. Title. II. Series.
PT1535.J33    1994
831'.2–dc20                                                     94-19696

Printed in Great Britain by
St Edmundsbury Press Ltd, Bury St Edmunds, Suffolk

# Contents

# Acknowledgements

It is a pleasure to acknowledge the various debts of gratitude I have incurred in writing this book. The Alexander von Humboldt-Stiftung and the Deutscher Akademischer Austauschdienst have provided financial support which made possible extended periods of research in Germany. The Deutsches Seminar of the Georg-August-Universität Göttingen and the Max-Planck-Institut für Geschichte in Göttingen have provided excellent working facilities and heartening support for this project over many years. In Britain, the Strawberry Hill conferences on medieval knighthood have been an invaluable source of information and stimulus for a literary scholar working with historical evidence.

These institutions, as well as providing a framework for research, have also been a focus for many personal discussions which have greatly helped my work on knighthood, on the historical and the literary side. My thanks go to all the individuals involved in these discussions. I would, however, like to express particularly warm and personal thanks to two friends and colleagues, Jeffrey Ashcroft and Martin Jones. They have given generously of their time and wisdom in reading and commenting on a draft of this book, the final version of which has benefited considerably from their advice.

Finally, I acknowledge my gratitude to Richard Barber for his encouragement during the years I have worked on this book, and to the staff at Boydell and Brewer for their helpful efficiency in its production.

*St Andrews*                                                          W.H.J.
*July 1994*

# Preface

The second half of the twelfth century was a key period for the social and ideological history of knighthood, and for the rise and spread of vernacular literature in Germany. The developments of this period had a profound influence on the social culture of large parts of medieval Europe, they express and in turn shaped the self-understanding of the aristocracy in a lengthy history of change. The works of Hartmann von Aue, produced in south-west Germany at the end of the century, incapsulate some of the main energies which informed these broader social, ideological and literary processes. Hartmann describes himself, in his works, as an educated knight. This was an unusual combination of qualities for this time in the German empire, but one which allowed him to tap the cultural resources of clerical learning and of the secular aristocracy in a historically symptomatic way. Further, whilst knights, *ritter*, had appeared in German literature for a century before Hartmann, it was not until the works of Hartmann himself that the concept of knighthood achieved a breakthrough to dominance in the literary sphere, a breakthrough which also marks an enhancement of prestige for knighthood in broader social and cultural terms.

In view of Hartmann's authorial status, and the importance of knighthood in his works, it is not surprising that knighthood and chivalric values have received attention in Hartmann scholarship for over a century. However, in earlier work on Hartmann the historical dimension and meaning of knighthood was largely taken for granted, in a way that would not stand up to critical scrutiny in the light of recent historical studies, whilst in recent years the topic of knighthood has usually been treated in connection with more specific, or more general lines of enquiry, notably with discussions of the *ministeriales*, or of Hartmann's works as adaptations of the romances of Chrétien de Troyes. Meanwhile, no large-scale study of knighthood across the full range of Hartmann's works has yet been produced, although the advances which have been made over the past thirty years in research into knighthood as a historical phenomenon, and which have called into question many older views on the relation of the literary portrayal of knighthood to social reality in Germany around 1200, mark the need for such an undertaking.

The following study tries to meet this need. It considers the role of knighthood and of chivalric values in Hartmann's works, which are presented, so far as the evidence allows, in chronological sequence, and in their relation to the historical context. The opening chapter, on Arthur's kingship and the rise of knighthood in the twelfth century, places Hartmann in a broader European perspective. The second chapter considers knighthood as a matter of social status in twelfth-century German history and in Hartmann's *Erec*. The third outlines the chief components of chivalry as an ideology, or a complex of ethical ideals and behavioural patterns, and moves into more sustained literary analysis of *Erec*. Chapters 4 and 6 are devoted to the religious narratives *Gregorius* and *Der arme Heinrich*, Chapter 5 to Hartmann's treatment of love in the *Klage*, and to the chronologically problematical matter of his lyric poetry, and Chapters 7 and 8 to his last romance, *Iwein*. Chapter 9 draws some of the main threads of the study together in an essay of synthesis.

This disposition of the textual material of Hartmann's works raises two open questions, or rather complexes of questions, in Hartmann scholarship. First, some uncertainty attaches to both the relative and the absolute chronology of Hartmann's works. For his narrative works, the sequence *Erec – Gregorius – Der arme Heinrich – Iwein* is accepted as established, save that the relative priority of the last two works is not certain. The time-frame of the works as a whole is the period from ca. 1180 to ca. 1203. However, whilst it is widely accepted that Hartmann's literary activity began in the 1180s, it is not at all clear whether his earliest work, or works, should be placed early or later in that decade, nor is it clear whether his last work was completed in the 1190s or in the early years of the thirteenth century. Unclear, too, is the chronological span of Hartmann's lyric poetry, whether it was concentrated in a short, early phase, or whether it stretched over more of his creative life. The present study follows the judiciously flexible account of the chronology of Hartmann's works in the current standard introduction to the author.[1] This places the *Klage* and *Erec* somewhere in the period 1180–1190, and *Der arme Heinrich* and *Iwein* somewhere in the decade leading up to ca. 1203, with *Gregorius* appearing after *Erec* and before *Der arme Heinrich*. Some at least of the lyric poetry may be taken as early work, and the crusading songs may be linked either to the crusade of 1189 or to that of 1197.

Whilst the uncertainty of up to ten years or so sets limits on the interpretative conclusions that can be drawn in relating Hartmann's

[1]  Cormeau / Störmer, *Hartmann von Aue*, pp. 25–32, 241–43.

works to their immediate context, the framework of no more than about twenty years, and perhaps less, for the entire *œuvre*, and its setting at an important time of transition provide much firm ground for interpreting Hartmann's works in the broader context of the social and ideological history of chivalry. Similarly, whilst the exact geographical location of Hartmann's literary activity, and the identity of any patron, or patrons, who may have encouraged his work, remain uncertain, the accepted general location in Swabia, in south-west Germany, provides, together with the relatively specific time-frame, more purchase for historical analysis than is often the case with medieval works. These are topics we shall return to at various points in the following chapters.

The second set of uncertainties is specific to Hartmann's first romance, *Erec*. It involves the reliability of the manuscript evidence as a guide to Hartmann's own text, and the relation of Hartmann's work to the *Erec et Enide* of Chrétien de Troyes. These questions have been opened up again by the discovery of further manuscript fragments of *Erec* in the Herzog August Bibliothek in Wolfenbüttel. The new fragments contain a version of two episodes which differs from that in the *Ambraser Heldenbuch*, the compilation of texts, written between 1504 and 1515/16 by Hans Ried for Emperor Maximilian I, which contains the only (near) complete version of Hartmann's *Erec*.[2] With regard to the German *Erec*, the new fragments pose the question of how reliable the Ambras manuscript is as a record of Hartmann's own version, and with regard to the relation of the German and French versions, they raise again the old question of whether Hartmann's *Erec* is an adaptation directly from Chrétien's text, or from some other, lost version, or whether Hartmann used another source beside Chrétien. More work is needed before we can have greater certainty on these issues. It is sufficient here to take it as our starting point that, on present evidence, the Ambras manuscript is probably a reliable guide to Hartmann's own text, and that Hartmann's *Erec* was a free adaptation of the *Erec et Enide* of Chrétien de Troyes, albeit with the possibility that Hartmann drew on other oral traditions for some name-forms.[3] Indeed, the close similarities which the following chapters will show in the treatment of knighthood in *Erec*, as it is recorded in the *Ambraser Heldenbuch*, and Hartmann's other works, perhaps especially *Gregorius*, tend to support the view that the Ambras manuscript has, after all, preserved much of Hartmann's voice for us.

The approach taken in the following study is comparative in several senses. The consideration of all Hartmann's works provides a comparative view of knighthood across different literary genres, and allows an

---

2  The recently discovered fragments are printed and discussed in Gärtner, 'Der Text der Wolfenbütteler Erec-Fragmente', and Nellmann, 'Ein zweiter Erec-Roman?'.
3  On these points see Cormeau / Störmer, *Hartmann von Aue*, pp. 19, 168f.

interplay of coherence and diversity to emerge which is characteristic of
Hartmann's *œuvre*. In the case of Hartmann's *Erec*, *Gregorius*, and *Iwein*,
where the French source is available which Hartmann adapted into
German, I have consulted this source so as to arrive at a comparative
view of knighthood as presented by the German author and his French
predecessors. This line of comparison, as we shall see, goes well beyond
merely linguistic differences to bring into sharper focus both the specific
qualities of Hartmann's works, and the broader similarities and
differences between the French and German cultural areas, and
between authors of different social status, with regard to knighthood.
Finally, in every chapter, and with reference to each and all of
Hartmann's works, the study draws on historical evidence of various
kinds and views the literary texts in a historical perspective. There is a
high degree of literary stylization in the presentation of knighthood and
chivalric values in Hartmann's works, and it would be deeply
misleading to treat them as if they were faithful, passive mirrors of the
social reality of knighthood. However, these works were also connected
to this reality in a variety of ways, ranging from the surface realism of
descriptions of up-to-date armour to the literary processing of tensions
inherent in the aristocratic society of the day. The literary exploration of
knighthood, which was undertaken in a pioneering way by Chrétien de
Troyes in France and by Hartmann von Aue in Germany, was also part
of the broader social and ideological history of the medieval aristocracy,
and just as the use of historical evidence can illuminate works of
literature, so the study of literature can contribute to an understanding
of historical reality precisely in the field of knighthood. The following
chapters will try to define more closely this dialectic of literary
stylization and social gearing which pervades Hartmann's presentation
of knighthood.

# Abbreviations

Note: Works of Hartmann von Aue are referred to with the abbreviations AH = *Der arme Heinrich*, Er = *Erec*, Gr = *Gregorius*, Iw = *Iwein*, Kl = *Die Klage*. The most frequently cited works of Chrétien de Troyes are referred to with the abbreviations EeE = *Erec et Enide*, Yv = *Yvain*. For the editions used, see the Bibliography.

| | |
|---|---|
| *Annales ESC* | *Annales: Economies, Sociétés, Civilisations* |
| ATB | Altdeutsche Textbibliothek |
| *BBSIA* | *Bulletin bibliographique de la Société Internationale Arthurienne* |
| BDNL | Bibliothek der gesamten deutschen Nationalliteratur |
| BLVS | Bibliothek des litterarischen Vereins in Stuttgart |
| *CCM* | *Cahiers de Civilisation Médiévale* |
| *DA* | *Deutsches Archiv für Erforschung des Mittelalters* |
| DTM | Deutsche Texte des Mittelalters |
| *DU* | *Der Deutschunterricht* |
| *DVLG* | *Deutsche Vierteljahrsschrift für Literaturwissenschaft und Geistesgeschichte* |
| FGädL | Forschungen zur Geschichte der älteren deutschen Literatur |
| FSGA | Freiherr vom Stein-Gedächtnisausgabe. A. Ausgewählte Quellen zur deutschen Geschichte des Mittelalters |
| *FMLS* | *Forum for Modern Language Studies* |
| GAG | Göppinger Arbeiten zur Germanistik |
| *GLL* | *German Life and Letters* |
| *GR* | *Germanic Review* |
| *GRM* | *Germanisch-Romanische Monatsschrift* |
| HRB | Geoffrey of Monmouth, *Historia Regum Britanniae* |
| *HRG* | A. Erler and E. Kaufmann, *Handwörterbuch zur deutschen Rechtsgeschichte*, vols I–IV (Berlin, 1971ff.) |
| *LiLi* | *Zeitschrift für Literaturwissenschaft und Linguistik* |
| MF | *Des Minnesangs Frühling* (see Bibliography) |

| | |
|---|---|
| MGH | Monumenta Germaniae Historica |
| MGH Const. | MGH Constitutiones et acta publica imperatorum et regum, vols I–III |
| *MLN* | *Modern Language Notes* |
| *MLR* | *Modern Language Review* |
| MPL | J. P. Migne, *Patrologiae cursus completus. Series Latina* |
| MTU | Münchener Texte und Untersuchungen zur deutschen Literatur des Mittelalters |
| *OGS* | *Oxford German Studies* |
| *PBB* | *Paul und Braunes Beiträge zur Geschichte der deutschen Sprache und Literatur* |
| PhStQ | Philologische Studien und Quellen |
| QF | Quellen und Forschungen zur Sprach- und Culturgeschichte der germanischen Völker |
| SGAK | Studien zur Germanistik, Anglistik und Komparatistik |
| TLF | Textes Littéraires Français |
| VMPIG | Veröffentlichungen des Max-Planck-Instituts für Geschichte |
| WdF | Wege der Forschung |
| *WW* | *Wirkendes Wort* |
| *ZfdA* | *Zeitschrift für deutsches Altertum* |
| *ZfdPh* | *Zeitschrift für deutsche Philologie* |
| *ZfrPh* | *Zeitschrift für romanische Philologie* |

# 1

# King Arthur and
# the Rise of Knighthood

*Arthur's kingship and the rise of knighthood in the twelfth century*

The literature which grew up and proliferated around the figure of King Arthur and his court is a major cultural expression of the developing ideology of knighthood from the twelfth century through to the chivalric revivalist movements of the Renaissance. And Arthurian literature is particularly closely meshed with the history of knighthood in the formative period of the twelfth century.

Knighthood, as a military function, a mark of social status, and a complex of ethical and behavioural values, has roots that stretch back in various directions and to different depths in history.[1] Whatever older views are subject to revision in recent work on the social and ideological dimensions of knighthood, there remains general agreement that its origins rest in the military sphere. In a centuries-long interaction of warrior class, Church and secular rulers, the military function became associated with concepts of protection and ethical obligation, a process which is discernible as early as the Carolingian ninth century, and which received fresh impetus in connection with the peace movements and the crusades of the eleventh and twelfth centuries. In terms of social status the bearing of knightly arms, having for long been the birthright of high men and a means of upward social movement for lesser men, came increasingly to be viewed in the twelfth century as a mark of aristocracy which set even the lesser knights off from the vast majority of the population in a process whereby the old, open warrior class gradually

---

[1] For recent work on knighthood see Bumke, *Ritterbegriff*; Borst (ed.), *Rittertum*; Fenske et al. (eds), *Festschrift Fleckenstein*, pp. 549–726; Keen, *Chivalry*; Arnold, *German Knighthood*; Flori, *L'idéologie*; id., *L'essor*.

evolved into a more closed aristocracy and ultimately into a landed gentry. Finally social intercourse in the lordly households, which were experiencing more stable conditions from the twelfth century onwards, furthered increasingly cultivated patterns of peacetime behaviour in the developing model of chivalry, patterns which received expression in the literary association of knighthood with love and courtliness.

Each of these strands will be documented and discussed in the course of this study. What is important to note here is that it was the twelfth century that saw the decisive social and ideological ascent of knighthood, and that this process was most marked in Anglo-Norman England, in the great French feudal houses of the Plantagenets and of Champagne and Flanders, and in the German empire, whilst the heartland of the Capetian kings of France played a relatively minor role.[2] These areas favourable to the ascent of *chevalerie* were also the main growth points of Arthurian literature in this same period. Geoffrey of Monmouth's *Historia Regum Britanniae*, written in England, begun before 1135 and completed in 1138, brings the earliest extensive portrayal of Arthur and his *milites*. This work also sprang from an Anglo-Norman cultural context in which there was an early association of royal lineage with the rising terminology of knighthood, as is witnessed by the fact that one of the earliest references to a prince being 'knighted', in a Germanic formulation, is on Anglo-Norman soil, in a passage in the *Anglo-Saxon Chronicle* that was probably copied about 1121 from an earlier archetype, with the statement that William I 'dubbade his sunu Henric to ridere'.[3] A generation after Geoffrey's controversial and immensely influential work, Arthur and his court play a key part in the romances of Chrétien de Troyes, whose *Erec* established Arthurian romance as a poetic genre, and whose work shows links with the Plantagenet dynasty and more distinctly with the northern French feudal houses of Champagne and Flanders – all focal points for the growing prestige of knighthood. With Hartmann von Aue's adaptations of two of Chrétien's romances we move to the German empire, where the concept of knighthood was acquiring greater social and ideological prominence in the second half of the twelfth century, and where Hartmann's own works provided the decisive breakthrough for this concept in vernacular literature. Moreover, and importantly, Hartmann was himself a knight, a *ritter*, and his works break new ground by providing an unprecedentedly nuanced view of knighthood as seen from the inside, by a member of the group.

The figure of Arthur has particular importance for the history of knighthood since Arthur is presented in medieval literature primarily in

[2]   Flori, *L'essor*, pp. 249–330.
[3]   *The Peterborough Chronicle*, p. 9. On the dating see Clark, 'Studies', p. 67; on the rise of knightly terminology in princely arming ceremonies see below, pp. 69–71.

relation to his knights, the *milites, chevaliers, ritter* of the texts. In this chapter I shall consider the changing status and function of King Arthur in the works of these three authors, Geoffrey of Monmouth, Chrétien de Troyes and Hartmann von Aue, each of whom was of major innovatory importance in his own context. This comparative approach aims to place Hartmann himself in a broader European perspective, and to shed light on some of the historical forces at work in the rise of knighthood in twelfth-century literature and society by treating the portrayal of kingship and the relation of royal authority to knighthood in each of these authors.

## *Geoffrey of Monmouth's* Historia Regum Britanniae

Historiography was in vogue in the cultural sphere of the Norman kings, and Geoffrey of Monmouth is much indebted to the earlier histories of William of Malmesbury and Henry of Huntingdon in a formal sense. However, unlike these he allowed himself considerable inventive freedom and independence from factual record.[4] His work is pseudo-history, so shot through with fiction that the critical historian William of Newburgh could dismiss it as fabulous invention,[5] but it is sufficiently close to authentic history in its form to give Arthur's kingship authoritative status in later, more overtly poetic treatments of the material, and even to be cited by kings of England as proof of their claims to sovereignty.[6]

Following the dominant trend of secular historiography at the time, Geoffrey presents the history of Britain as the story of its rulers, just as in the German *Kaiserchronik*, a few decades later, history is seen as a succession of kings and emperors. Arthur's rule occupies a fifth of the *Historia* (HRB, cc. 143-78; Thorpe, IX, 1-XI, 2),[7] far more space than is justified by its time span. It forms the narrative climax of the work and the period of greatest British achievement. Arthur himself embodies the author's main racial and political intentions, his desire to glorify the British past and to exalt the strong king as symbol and guarantor of national unity.[8] Arthur's rule is that part of the *Historia* which has most

---

[4] See Hanning, *The Vision of History*, pp. 135f.

[5] *Historia Rerum Anglicarum*, pp. 11–13; compare Brooke, 'Geoffrey of Monmouth', p. 78: 'There has scarcely, if ever, been a historian more mendacious than Geoffrey of Monmouth'.

[6] Giffin, 'Cadwalader, Arthur and Britain', passim; Parry and Caldwell, 'Geoffrey of Monmouth', pp. 88f.

[7] HRB refers to Wright's edition of Geoffrey's *Historia*, Thorpe to the translation by Lewis Thorpe; the double form of reference facilitates the use of other editions.

[8] On Geoffrey's motives in writing the *Historia* see Tatlock, *The Legendary History*, pp. 422–32; Wright, introduction to HRB, p. xix; Gillingham, 'The Context and Purposes', passim; on the king as symbol of the *regnum* in the *Historia* see Pähler, *Strukturuntersuchungen*, p. 97.

contemporary traits, as Geoffrey projects concerns, attitudes and manners of his own time into the narrative at the point where it has the greatest exemplary value; and this projection is flattering to the Norman kings of England. Arthur's crown-wearing echoes ceremonial practices of the Anglo-Norman kings, his court is modelled on their household, and his conquest of England echoes the course of events in William's campaign of 1066, which founded the Anglo-Norman royal house.[9] By aligning Arthur's dominion with the Norman achievement Geoffrey's *Historia* acts as something of a pseudo-historical legitimatory precedent for Norman rule over England, a counter-product to the emerging cult of Charlemagne, whom the Capetian kings of France deployed as a precedent to legitimize their rule.[10] This view receives support from the fact that the three men to whom Geoffrey wrote dedications of the *Historia* (Robert of Gloucester, Waleran of Meulan and King Stephen) were all Norman magnates who were at least close to the crown.

However, Arthur remains a Briton, not a Norman, and Geoffrey has Merlin prophesy that Normandy will lose the British isles and the Britons will be restored (HRB, c. 115,18; Thorpe, VII, 3), which may suggest that his commitment to specifically Norman rule was not wholehearted.[11] The *Historia* has been illuminatingly interpreted as containing Geoffrey's warning to the contemporary ruling class in England which was, after the death of Henry I in 1135, divided in its allegiance between Henry's daughter, the ex-empress Matilda, and his nephew Stephen, who had seized the crown on his uncle's death.[12] The end of Arthur's reign, brought about by the treachery of Arthur's nephew Mordred, thus reads as a comment on the contemporary situation in England, and a warning against dissension. Indeed, what emerges more strongly from the *Historia* than propaganda specifically for a Norman dynasty is a general plea for unity under royal rule, from which any ruler of England could draw encouragement.

As a product of racial and political wishful thinking on Geoffrey's part Arthur acquires a nimbus of glory that he will preserve in the continental romances. But in contrast to his frequently reduced political role in the later romances, Geoffrey presents him as an energetic and powerful king, seen almost exclusively in affairs of state, extending his territories, distributing fiefs and benefices, gathering mercenaries and

[9] Tatlock, *The Legendary History*, pp. 271–73, 293, 308.
[10] See Gerould, 'King Arthur and Politics', pp. 40–51; Knight, *Arthurian Literature*, pp. 44f.
[11] See Faral, *La Légende arthurienne*, II, p. 391; Gillingham also warns against exaggerating Geoffrey's commitment to the Anglo-Norman élite, and he sees a pro-Welsh tendency as part of the complex, ambiguous pattern of sympathies in the *Historia* ('The Context and Purposes', passim).
[12] Schirmer, *Die frühen Darstellungen*, pp. 24–28; Pähler, *Strukturuntersuchungen*, pp. 133–44.

feudal levies, and securing peace in his kingdom. Above all Geoffrey's Arthur is a young warrior king (he is aged fifteen when he comes to rule, HRB, c. 143; Thorpe, IX, 1) whose conquests reflect the military expansiveness of the Norman warrior stock – it is not only modern historians who see a particularly powerful dynamic in the Norman conquests in Italy and England in the late eleventh century,[13] for already Bishop Otto of Freising, commenting on these events from the perspective of the German empire, with its ancient kingship, wrote wonderingly of the conquering Normans as 'gens inquietissima' (*Chronica*, VI, 33, p. 486). In our context, three aspects of Arthur's warrior kingship call for particular comment: its political focus, the composition of Arthur's retinue, and the style of fighting.

The contrasting climaxes to Arthur's military career are revealing of the political perspective in which Geoffrey views his kingship. At the height of his power Arthur is called to account by the senate of Rome for the injuries he has done to the Roman empire (HRB, c. 158; Thorpe, IX, 15). He launches an attack on the empire itself and seems near to glorious success when his nephew Mordred's usurpation of the crown forces him to return to Britain and launch the campaign which leads to Mordred's death and to Arthur's enigmatic mortal wound (HRB, c. 178; Thorpe, XI, 2). Although Arthur is, from the standpoint of Rome, a rebel king who has refused tribute and seized a province of the empire by force, Geoffrey passes no critical judgement on him, but when the noble Mordred seizes the crown and disturbs the peace within Britain, Geoffrey roundly condemns his tyranny and treachery (HRB, c. 176: 'per tyrannidem et proditionem'; Thorpe, X, 13). Mordred's adultery with Guinevere and his blood relationship to Arthur only compound his political crime. Indeed Geoffrey's contrasting evaluation of Arthur's uprising against the Roman empire and Mordred's rebellion against Arthur suggest the royalist (and emerging nationalist) standpoint of an author who is prepared to contemplate the overthrow of the Roman emperor by a British king, but who shrinks in horror from what was in twelfth-century historical reality the far more real possibility of baronial rebellion against the king. War, in Geoffrey's eyes, should be waged by the king and under tight military discipline, not as an independent activity of ambitious nobles.

Arthur's military power is based on the use of allies, subject lands, and the warriors in his own retinue, his *familia* (HRB, cc. 143, 154; Thorpe, IX, 1; IX, 11). Arthur is twice shown expanding his warrior retinue, first by distributing material wealth (the king's 'largitas', HRB, c. 143, is here still clearly a means of augmenting military power), later

---

[13] See for example Douglas, *William the Conqueror*, pp. 6f.; Allen Brown, *The Normans*, pp. 15–19.

by attracting *milites* by his fame as well (HRB, c. 154; Thorpe, IX, 11). This phenomenon of the *familia*, the household or retinue, is of the utmost importance for the historical development of knighthood,[14] and Geoffrey's account of how the great lord increased his military entourage by dispensing wealth, then using the retinue to make war and gain booty to reward his retainers, is an idealizing, abbreviating reflection of the formation of military retinues in historical reality in western Europe and in the German empire.

The late eleventh and early twelfth centuries were an important period for the formation, expansion and consolidation of such retinues in various parts of Europe. The last third of the eleventh century saw a volume of military activity in Europe that was not to be surpassed until the fourteenth century.[15] At the same time a quickening of economic activity and the gradual formation of larger lordships were providing a framework for the maintenance of the retinues which were needed for larger scale warfare and also (for instance in post-conquest England) to secure conquered territory – military activity and the cementing of lordships were often not far apart in the eleventh and twelfth centuries.[16] Evidence of great lords attracting knights into their retinues is ample during this period. In Germany the troubled times of Henry IV's reign in the late eleventh century witnessed a proliferation of bands of *milites* around the nobles involved in warfare for or against the king, and in Lampert of Hersfeld's *Annales*, as in Geoffrey's *Historia*, such *milites* are often described as 'young men', *iuvenes* or collectively *iuventus*.[17] Georges Duby has shown the importance of the large number of knights in northern France who sought their fortunes by attaching themselves as warriors to men of greater substance;[18] and he has drawn attention to the important part played by the courts of rulers as focal points for the activities of these *iuvenes*.[19] In England, Walter Map tells of Henry I enrolling young men from the continent in his retinue,[20] and later in the century the Young King Henry, son of Henry II, supported a large retinue of *milites* as his companions, 'commilitones'.[21] The warrior

[14]  On the *familia* see Arnold, German *Knighthood*, pp. 100–03 and often; below, pp. 47–49.
[15]  Leyser, 'Early Medieval Canon Law', p. 564.
[16]  For a useful discussion of the factors leading to more extensive retinues of knights in the eleventh century see Arnold, *German Knighthood*, pp. 17–29.
[17]  *Annales*, pp. 208,24; 228,16; 288,15; 290,28; 356,12; 366,27; HRB, cc. 143, 155; Thorpe, IX, 1; IX, 11. The anonymous *Vita Heinrici IV imperatoris* has an interesting account of the dismay of *milites* at the disbanding of warrior retinues in Germany after the declaration of an imperial peace by Henry IV in 1103 (c. 8).
[18]  Duby, 'Les "jeunes" ', pp. 837–39.
[19]  Duby, 'La vulgarisation des modèles culturels', pp. 306–08.
[20]  *De Nugis curialium*, V, 6, p. 470 and compare V, 5, p. 438; see Tatlock, *The Legendary History*, p. 294.
[21]  *La Chronique de Gislebert de Mons*, p. 83,14; compare p. 97,8ff. for the tourneying retinue of the young Baldwin (V) of Hainault after his knighting.

retinues raise two matters which are of fundamental importance for the history of knighthood, and which will be discussed at various points later in this study. First, the period of greatest expansion of these retinues, the late eleventh and early twelfth centuries, was also the period of greatest expansion of knighthood in general, a time when the rise from lower levels was most feasible, whilst the period from the later twelfth century onwards was characterized socially by a strengthening of restrictive, aristocratic tendencies in knighthood and a loosening of the bonds of military obligation in favour of inherited land-ownership. The history of the *familia* thus shows the gradual evolution of knighthood from a warrior function to a mark of inherited nobility. And second, the role of warrior retinues in establishing and securing larger lordships shows an interplay of self-assertive violence (the warrior function) and increasing social control (the consolidation of lordships) which is central to the history of knighthood.

Arthur's rule is also the most up-to-date part of the *Historia* in military techniques, for there is little mention of cavalry in the early parts of the work, where fighting seems to be on foot, whilst Arthur follows the latest military practice by using cavalry widely and as a matter of course.[22] The word *miles*, which originally meant 'soldier' in general, appears in the *Historia* in the restricted, 'knightly' sense of 'mounted warrior' when Geoffrey sets *milites* off, as cavalry, from the foot-soldiers, *pedites* (HRB, cc. 143, 162; Thorpe, IX, 1; IX, 19). It would be difficult to overestimate the importance of equestrian combat for the rise of knighthood. Already in the eleventh century, continental sources commonly distinguish between *milites* and *pedites*, and the high cost of equipment for the mounted men even in this early period ensured a *de facto* social as well as a military gap between cavalry and foot-soldiers.[23] Mounted combat received a notable stimulus with the development of the couched lance charge in the eleventh century, which enhanced the dominance of mounted troops and called for further specialization of equipment and training, which in turn contributed to the rising prestige of the mounted warrior.[24] At the same time the proliferation of warfare in western Europe in the late eleventh century created an enhanced need for specialist cavalry and offered opportunites of social advance-ment or enrichment through military service. All these factors furthered the gradual crystallization of a chivalric group consciousness based on an élite military function. The expansion of mounted warfare in the later eleventh century was especially marked in the heartlands of Carolingian and Ottonian Europe, that is to say in France, southern Germany,

[22] Tatlock, *The Legendary History*, pp. 328–31.
[23] See Johrendt, *'Milites' und 'militia'*, pp. 24–32.
[24] See Keen, *Chivalry*, pp. 23–27.

Saxony, along the Rhine and in northern Italy.[25] Still in the eleventh century, fighting on foot seems to have enjoyed a higher prestige amongst the aristocratic thegns of England than was the case with their continental counterparts.[26] However, even here equestrian combat received a considerable impetus after the Norman conquest; and the Arthurian section of Geoffrey's *Historia* has cavalry in the fully modern sense of mounted men using the lance as a thrusting weapon to unhorse the opponent.[27] The lance charge, with its connotations of material wealth, power and control will remain one of the most potent expressions of chivalric class consciousness throughout the Middle Ages. In addition, Geoffrey's comment that Ireland, Iceland, Gotland, the Orkneys, Norway and Denmark did not yet use cavalry and sent only foot-soldiers to Arthur's army (HRB, c. 162; Thorpe, IX, 19) suggests the perspective of Geoffrey's own day, or the recent past, when mounted combat, which is crucial to knighthood as a military phenomenon, had not yet spread from its continental heartland to the outlying regions of Europe.

The two periods of peace in Arthur's reign (HRB, cc. 154, 156f.; Thorpe, IX, 11–14) show Britain at its cultural peak, surpassing all other realms in affluence and civilization. Especially at the king's great Whitsun feast, which dominates the second period of peace, Arthur's court shows new traits of modern chivalry that will loom large in the later Arthurian tradition. Such festivities were an important feature of lordly display in actual life in the Middle Ages, and they rapidly became a stock feature in poetic narratives. Indeed the motif of the feast is one of the closest points of contact between literature and real life in the twelfth and thirteenth centuries.[28] Feasts were a valuable focus for the social interaction of knights away from the battlefield and thus an important element in the development of a broader chivalric mentality. Geoffrey's acount of the feast introduces two important new elements in the transition from a simpler warrior mentality to a knightly ideology, as the knights' practice of wearing distinctive colours (HRB, c. 157; Thorpe, IX, 13) shows an early stage in the development of heraldry, whilst the reference to women refusing to give their love to any man who had not proven himself three times in battle (loc. cit.) establishes a connection between love and military prowess which was novel in the early twelfth century and merely episodic in the *Historia*, but which was to be of

[25] Leyser, 'Early Medieval Canon Law', p. 565.
[26] Brooks, 'Arms, Status and Warfare', pp. 96f.
[27] See HRB, c. 155; Thorpe, IX, 11 for Arthur unhorsing Frollo in a lance charge such as will be repeated countless times by the literary knights of romance; on the lance as a weapon of collision in the 'modern' parts of the *Historia* see also Tatlock, *The Legendary History*, p. 328.
[28] See Bumke, *Höfische Kultur*, I, pp. 12f. and 276–317.

central importance in the fully articulated secular ideology of chivalry by the end of the century.

Geoffrey briefly illustrates a connection between erotic stimulus and military activity by telling how women spurred the knights on in the 'imitation battle' (HRB, c. 157: 'simulachrum prelii'; Thorpe, IX, 14) which formed part of the Whitsun festivities. It may be doubted whether Geoffrey has in mind here the full scale tourneys which were developing especially in northern France in his day, and which were such a threat to order that they were banned by the Church and often by secular rulers.[29] In historical reality tournaments were often a threat to public order and an expression of baronial independence from, even opposition to, the king.[30] But in the *Historia* the 'simulachrum prelii' remains firmly under royal control, as only one of many sporting competitions, with Arthur himself distributing a prize to each winner; and as the great Whitsun feast is the starting point not for the adventures of an individual knight (as will often be the case in later romances), but for the collective campaign against the Roman empire, and under Arthur's leadership, it is clear that the activities of the knights remain, in the *Historia*, harnessed to the will of the king. Arthurian knighthood, which will be one of the most persistent literary manifestations of chivalry throughout the Middle Ages, receives its first broad-ranging expression as obedient service rendered to a powerful warrior king.

## The Arthurian romances of Chrétien de Troyes

Chrétien's romances show a decisive development in the conception and role of Arthur, as the image of an energetic warrior king providing a flattering precedent for the actual rulers of England recedes to give way to the enigmatic portrayal of a more passive figurehead who is characterized by a certain human weakness and political ambiguity, a portrayal which opens up the way for Arthur's complex and shifting role in later medieval romance.

Geoffrey's *Historia* was adapted into the vernacular by the Norman clerk Wace, who completed his *Roman de Brut* in 1155. Wace made a number of alterations to the *Historia*, notably expanding the Arthurian section and introducing the seminal motif of the Round Table (9747ff., 10285f., 13269f.).[31] His work is gentler, less heroic in style than Geoffrey's *Historia*, but he retains Geoffrey's historical narrative with its

---

[29] On tournament prohibitions see below, pp. 17, 105.
[30] See Denholm-Young, 'The Tournament', p. 241; Barber and Barker, *Tournaments*, pp. 146–49.
[31] On the Round Table see Morris, *The Character of King Arthur*, pp. 124–26.

glorification of the king. Wace does not speak of a patron in his *Brut*, but the English poet Lawman states that Wace gave a copy of his *Brut* to Queen Eleanor, wife of Henry II, who succeeded to the English crown in 1154. Wace himself in his *Roman de Rou* (written between 1160 and ca. 1174) speaks of material benefits he has received from Henry II, and there is reason to believe that he wrote the *Brut* partly in order to invite Henry's favour by making the substance of Geoffrey's *Historia* more widely accessible to the Norman ruling class.[32]

Through Wace's *Brut*, if not directly from Geoffrey's *Historia*, Chrétien de Troyes had access to the image of Arthur created by Geoffrey, and in Chrétien's early romances *Erec* and *Cligés* Arthur preserves many of the traits he acquired in the *Historia*. He is lord over a vast feudal empire, with kings, dukes and counts owing allegiance to him (EeE 6559–63, 6645–55) and none daring to disregard a summons to court (EeE 1923–28). Erec's own kingdom forms part of this empire, as he receives his land from Arthur on the death of his father (EeE 6544f.). Arthur is a mighty and generous king (EeE 6667), he has more fine cities, beautiful palaces and strong castles than any other king or emperor (EeE 3883–89), and his generosity exceeds that of Alexander, Caesar and all the rulers named in the *chansons de geste* (EeE 6673–85). In *Cligés* Arthur also appears as a stern general (though he is not described in combat) who exacts harsh retribution from traitors (*Cligés* 1499–503), and he is described by the narrator without reservation as 'the best king who ever was or will be' (*Cligés* 310f.). Indeed in these two early romances Chrétien places Arthur briefly, but pointedly and repeatedly, in a universal context, raising him above the rulers of antiquity and of the French heroic tradition.

However, Chrétien's romances also show some change in the political substance of Arthur's kingship in comparison with Geoffrey of Monmouth. Historians of political thought have shown how theocratic and feudal principles interacted in the conceptions and practice of kingship in the Middle Ages.[33] As a theocratic sovereign the king ruled by the grace of God and stood outside and above the people. According to this 'descending' notion of government, law was an emanation of the king's will, in the making of which the king acted as God's vice-regent and had theoretically no obligation to consult the people. However, this extreme position, which was to provide a metaphysical foundation for later absolutism, was modified in the practice of government by the king's role as feudal suzerain, for as feudal overlord the king was

---

[32] On Wace and patronage see Tatlock, *The Legendary History*, pp. 466–68; Broich, 'Heinrich II. als Patron der Literatur', pp. 65–70.

[33] See F. Kern, *Gottesgnadentum und Widerstandsrecht*, passim; Ullmann, *The Individual and Society*, pp. 18–98; id., *Medieval Political Thought*, pp. 130–45. In what follows I take 'ascending' and 'descending' themes of government from Ullmann.

himself a member of the community, not placed outside and above it, and was bound by the reciprocal loyalty of lord and vassal to attend to the vassals' interests and listen to their counsel. The feudal nexus thus provided an 'ascending' notion of government capable of limiting the king's theocratic power – the Magna Carta thrust upon King John by his barons, and so often invoked as the fount of British liberty, was in this sense a thoroughly feudal document. As regards law, the king in his capacity as feudal lord could make it only with the consent of his tenants-in-chief.[34] The ambivalence in the sources and nature of royal authority expressed in the interplay of theocratic and feudal ideas is evident in theoretical writings and in the actual conduct of kings and nobles throughout Europe in the twelfth century, as time and again criticisms were launched from the standpoint of nobles against the king on the grounds that he had neglected his feudal duty by curtailing their customary rights or failing to consult them,[35] whilst in the other direction kings sought to strengthen their position by emphasizing the theocratic nature of their authority.[36] Chrétien does not wholly neglect the theocratic aspect of rule, for he points to the sacred character of kingship in Erec's coronation (EeE 6856–69).[37] But it is significant that this potentially absolutist mystique of royalty is not brought to life to justify royal actions in the narrative. Rather the kingship of Arthur, and of other rulers, is given a certain limited, feudal quality in Chrétien's romances, as time and again the ruler is seen in the community of his barons (eg. EeE 1523, 1836, 2125, 6419, 6515; Cligés 151, 319, 390, 421, 424, 2395, 2450; Lancelot 38, 51, 3856; Yv 653, 676, 2148, 2796, 6315; Perceval 1208, 4605).

Of all Chrétien's works, Erec et Enide is the most intimately concerned with kingship.[38] The opening episode of the work – the hunt for the white stag – is a literary processing of central concerns of contemporary kingship: the relation of king to barons, to counsel and to law; and the main body of the narrative exhibits the young hero's fitness to rule, culminating in the great coronation scene in which chivalry and kingship merge at the end of the work. Here it is the opening episode that concerns us as a paradigm of kingship in action. Unusually for Chrétien's romances, Arthur himself sets the action in motion by calling a hunt for the white stag, this not as an expression of innovatory

---

[34] Ullmann, Medieval Political Thought, pp. 146–52.
[35] For England see Warren, Henry II, pp. 380ff.; similar examples from German literature below, p. 24.
[36] See Ullmann, Medieval Political Thought, pp. 132f.; id., The Individual and Society, pp. 68–70; for the idea that the king, ruling by the grace of God ('divina gratia'), stood above human law see Otto of Freising, Chronica, p. 2 (addressing Frederick Barbarossa).
[37] Misrahi, 'More light?', p. 94.
[38] For an interpretation of Erec as Chrétien's exploration of a complete cycle of kingship see Maddox, Structure and Sacring, passim.

sovereign will, but to revive an old custom (EeE 38: 'Por la costume ressaucier'). The topic of counsel is personalized in the figures of Gawain and Guinevere. In Geoffrey's *Historia* Gawain ('Gualguanus', HRB, cc. 152, 154, 166, 168, 173, 177) figures only in a military capacity. Already in Wace's *Brut* he comes more to the fore as an advocate of peaceful and harmonious social relations.[39] In the opening episode of *Erec* Chrétien develops Wace's image to present Gawain as a wise, independently-minded counsellor and critic,[40] who warns Arthur of the threat of combats among the knights in connection with the sensitive issue of the successful huntsman bestowing a kiss on the most beautiful maiden at court (EeE 41–58, 302–06), and who takes part in the council of the 'mellors barons de la cort' (EeE 312) which Arthur calls to deal with the incipient commotion. Guinevere's role too is expanded as we move from Geoffrey's *Historia* to Chrétien's romances. Geoffrey makes passing references to Arthur's marriage (HRB, c. 152; Thorpe, IX, 9), to Guinevere's presence at the plenary court (HRB, c. 157; Thorpe, IX, 13) and to her adultery with Mordred and her subsequent taking of the veil (HRB, cc. 176f.; Thorpe, X, 13f.). The queen is seen more often in Chrétien's romances, a development which may reflect the growing importance of women as patrons or readers of the new style of imaginative courtly poetry, and which may, in the case of Chrétien's *Erec*, be a bow specifically towards Queen Eleanor of Aquitaine, wife of Henry II of England. In the episode of the white stag the queen's role parallels that of Gawain as a counsellor, for she takes part in the 'consoil' (EeE 311) and provides the crucial suggestion proposing a postponement of the kiss until Erec returns from his pursuit of Yder (EeE 335–39). Significantly she makes her proposal conditional upon the agreement of the other, baronial counsellors (EeE 337: 'Se cist baron loent mon dit'), which anticipates Arthur's asking the assembled court's approval for his choice of Enide as the most beautiful woman (EeE 1780–92, 1815–20). Indeed one metaphorical dimension of the hunt in *Erec* is the pursuit of proper behaviour in knight and ruler, and one of the political messages of this opening episode is the point favourable to a limited view of kingship, that rulers should listen carefully to advice, as Arthur himself states with the maxim that it is wise to accept counsel: 'Qui croit consoil, n'est mie fos' (EeE 1225).

A sense of the limitations as well as the high office of kingship also underlies the great address on the duties of the king with which Arthur prefaces his request for baronial approval of his choice of lady (EeE 1793–1814). This is a veritable *miroir de princes*, a rare point in Chrétien's

---

[39] See Nitze, 'The Character of Gauvain', p. 222.
[40] See also Nitze, loc. cit.; Foulon, 'Le rôle de Gauvain', pp. 150f.; Busby, *Gauvain in Old French Literature*, p. 51.

works where matters of political conduct, which one so often senses as a subtext of his narrative, are openly discussed. However the speech is remarkable for its narrow focus, for it is almost exclusively concerned with the relation of the ruler to law, to 'loi' (1798, 1809), 'justise' (1799) 'droiture' (1796), 'costume' (1805, 1809) and 'usage' (1805, 1811). Further, the task of kingship in Arthur's speech seems to consist almost exclusively in preserving established custom. As Erich Köhler has shown, the courtly romance here, and often subsequently, holds to a traditionalist, feudal view of the ruler (he is the 'leal roi', EeE 1797) as the guardian of customary law, a view which contrasts with the tendencies of the emerging national monarchies to strike out beyond a mere feudal overlordship towards a less limited concept of sovereignty.[41] On this point too Chrétien's romances differ in their political implications from the more monarchist tendency of Geoffrey's *Historia*, for whereas Chrétien's Arthur consults his barons and sets his face against making new laws (EeE 1807–14), Geoffrey of Monmouth shows much admiration for kings as makers of law, for instance praising Dunvallo Molmutius as a great law-maker (HRB, c. 34; Thorpe, II, 17) and Arvirargus for his confirmation of laws and his making of new ones (HRB, c. 69: 'leges etiam ueteris traditionis confirmare, nouas etiam inuenire'; Thorpe, IV, 16). Moreover, in his reference to the legislative activities of kings, Geoffrey disregards the consent of the great magnates of the realm, which suggests that he had little desire to press the claims of the feudal nobility to a powerful voice in government. Geoffrey's attitude towards the law is 'a very strong example of his monarchic and Norman sympathies',[42] whilst Chrétien's romances tend towards a more limited, feudal concept of kingship.

*Lancelot* or *Le Chevalier de la Charrette*, which has been described as 'a landmark in Chrétien's work',[43] introduces new and portentous negative traits into the portrayal of Arthur. None of Chrétien's later romances shows as much interest in kingship as does *Erec et Enide*, and none shows Arthur in the role of stern and punitive overlord which is his in the early part of *Cligés*. In the later romances Arthur preserves the high fame he enjoyed in *Erec* and in *Cligés*, but moments of weakness, ineffectiveness, and voices of criticism from those around him are increasingly present, especially in the first scene at Arthur's court in each romance. It is as if Chrétien were seeking to make his audience reflect critically on kingship by opening the Arthurian action with a surprise contrast between past high fame and present deficiency. *Lancelot* opens with the image of a king who is powerless to aid the

---

41  Köhler, *Ideal und Wirklichkeit*, pp. 9–11.
42  Tatlock, *The Legendary History*, p. 283.
43  Topsfield, *Chrétien de Troyes*, p. 105.

captive knights and ladies of his household (*Lancelot* 52–65), and who shows a humiliating dependence on the seneschal Kay when he asks the queen to throw herself at his feet if necessary in order to dissuade him from leaving his (Arthur's) service (*Lancelot* 118–29).[44] This inadequacy of the king in the face of a threat to his court contrasts not only with Arthur's spirited response to the summons of the Roman senate in Geoffrey's *Historia* (HRB, c. 159; Thorpe, IX, 16), but also with the way Arthur effectively handles potential strife at the beginning of *Erec*, and treachery in the early stages of *Cligés*. Further, by contrast with Geoffrey's clear condemnation of Guinevere's adultery with Mordred in the *Historia*, the enigmatic idealization of Lancelot's and Guinevere's love in Chrétien's romance casts a dubious light on Arthur, and indeed lays the seeds of the inner dissension that will destroy the Arthurian world in the later romance tradition.[45] In the opening scene of *Yvain* knights are critical of the king's retiring to his bed on such a high feast-day (Yv 42–52). In *Perceval* Arthur appears inert and passive, unable to defend his sovereignty against the Red Knight (*Perceval* 907–67). He seems to be an ageing figure in contrast with the young, vigorous, impetuous Perceval; and in the course of the romance the Grail world begins to emerge as a realm spiritually superior to the declining Arthurian world.

These signs of deterioration in the image of Arthur show Chrétien leaving the inheritance of Geoffrey's *Historia* behind to create a more flexible world of romance for which he may well have been drawing more heavily on material of Celtic origin. The change also suggests a shift in the political focus of Chrétien's art. There is broad agreement that *Erec* contains at least a compliment to the contemporary King Henry II of England, who by virtue of his English sovereignty and his feudal holdings in France ruled over an empire which stretched from the Pyrenees to Wales and Ireland. The climactic scene of Erec's crowning links the fictive world of Chrétien's romance to the actual, contemporary Plantagenet empire, as the guests at the coronation feast (EeE 6641–55) come from areas subject in the early 1170s to Henry's lordship; and the location of the coronation at Nantes, and some of its circumstances, seem to echo Henry's holding court at Nantes on Christmas Day 1169 to receive, with his son Geoffrey, the homage of the barons of Brittany.[46]

[44] Kay is portrayed in a more negative (boastful and quarrelsome) light by Chrétien than in earlier traditions. This shift probably reflects aristocratic suspicion about the power and influence of royal seneschals in the historical reality of twelfth-century courts (see Haupt, *Der Truchseß Keie*, pp. 70–72; Knight, *Arthurian Literature*, pp. 78f.).

[45] See also Morris, *The Character of King Arthur*, pp. 98f.

[46] The evidence linking *Erec* to the court of Henry II is marshalled in Schmolke-Hasselmann, *Der arthurische Versroman*, pp. 190–201; see also Fourrier, 'Encore la chronologie', pp. 70–74. For a historical account of Henry II's relations with the Breton barons in the years leading up to 1169 see Warren, *Henry II*, pp. 99–101, 106, 108–11.

Chrétien may also have had in mind the crowning of Henry II's eldest son, the Young King Henry, in Westminster Abbey in June 1170.[47] The (for Chrétien) unusually forceful manner in which Arthur acts in punishing rebellion in *Cligés* has been compared to the political firmness of Henry II,[48] and may contain an echo of Henry's handling of the rebellion of 1173. Some attentiveness to the Plantagenet sphere of interest is also suggested by the fact that *Erec* and *Cligés* contain far more English place-names than do Chrétien's later romances.[49] As Arthur acquires more negative traits, these later romances also betray less desire to please a contemporary king of England. One thus senses a certain pro-Plantagenet strand in Chrétien's *Erec* and perhaps still in *Cligés*, which seems to fade in his later romances. The pragmatic context of this development is not fully reconstructable on present evidence. It has been suggested that Chrétien may actually have written *Erec* with the court of Henry II and Eleanor of Aquitaine in mind, that he was a well-informed observer of the events in Brittany in 1169, perhaps as a guest at court, perhaps even as a member of Eleanor's entourage, and that the echoes of the great feast of 1169 in Chrétien's description of the unusual and politically suggestive Arthurian court at Nantes in *Erec* may have been intended at least in part as support for Henry II's rule in Brittany.[50] At the latest with *Lancelot*, Chrétien had the court of Champagne in mind, for he refers to the countess of Champagne as his patroness (*Lancelot* 1–30), and later he addressed his Grail romance to Philip, count of Flanders (*Perceval* 7–68). It is thus possible that the increasingly negative traits in Arthur reflect a change in patronage and target audience in Chrétien's works, from the Plantagenet court of Henry II and Eleanor to the non-royal households of Champagne and Flanders.

This hypothesis has an appealing neatness. However, Chrétien may have been associated with the court of Champagne from the beginning of his career.[51] There was a close connection between Champagne and the Plantagenet house when Chrétien was writing, for Marie, countess of Champagne was the daughter of Eleanor of Aquitaine by her first marriage (to Louis VII of France). Chrétien could have had contact with the sphere of influence of Henry II and Eleanor through this channel. What is of prime importance is that the only patrons Chrétien refers to are of baronial, not royal status. They belong to the great feudal houses of northern France, and this matches the change in the political texture

---

47  See Topsfield, *Chrétien de Troyes*, p. 58.
48  Ibid., p. 93.
49  Schmolke-Hasselmann, *Der arthurische Versroman*, pp. 199f.
50  See Pernoud, *Aliénor d'Aquitaine*, p. 161; Laurie, *Two Studies*, pp. 16–20, 40; Schmolke-Hasselmann, *Der arthurische Versroman*, pp. 191f.
51  See e.g. Hofer, *Chrétien de Troyes*, pp. 49f.; Frappier, *Chrétien de Troyes*, pp. 8f., 56.

of Arthur's kingship that we noted already in Chrétien's *Erec* in comparison with Geoffrey's *Historia*. More than in the *Historia*, Arthur's kingship is viewed in Chrétien's romances through baronial eyes, both in a positive sense, when Arthur himself expresses an ideal of limited, feudal kingship in *Erec*, and in a more negative light in *Lancelot*, *Yvain*, and *Perceval*, when Arthur's royal authority is undercut by traits of indecision and human weakness. Seen in this perspective, the strange combination of high reputation and passivity, even weakness, which is a dominant feature of Arthur's kingship in Chrétien's works, reflects a tension in baronial feelings about kingship – on the one hand a sense of the necessity and value of kingship for the maintenance of the feudal hierarchy, and on the other hand fear of the actual power of the king and a desire to limit it.[52]

The relation of kingship and knighthood also undergoes a significant shift in the transition from Geoffrey's *Historia* to Chrétien's romances. In the prologue to *Cligés* Chrétien sketches a broad historical view of the transmission of culture from ancient Greece to the present day in which two points command our interest. First, Chrétien presents contemporary 'France' (*Cligés* 35) as the peak of culture, thus implicitly setting off 'France' against 'Angleterre' (*Cligés* 16).[53] And second, he presents the transmission of culture from Greece through Rome to present-day France in terms of 'chevalerie' and 'clergie' (*Cligés* 31f.) rather than empire or kingship. Geoffrey of Monmouth's conception of history as the story of rulers, in which the *milites* play a part chiefly as instruments of royal power, has given place to a view of history in which the values of chivalry and learning are the guarantors of a people's honour (*Cligés* 39: 'enors'). With this shift the Arthurian material could grow beyond the specific racial and dynastic concerns which dominated Geoffrey's *Historia* and become a broader expression of the developing consciousness of knighthood as a social grouping. The new mode of courtly, vernacular literature had an important part to play in this sense of French cultural pride, as a vehicle for the harmonizing of *chevalerie* and *clergie*.

*Chevalerie* should not be seen as too abstract a concept in Chrétien's works, for it still has the concrete sense of 'mounted combat'. Moreover, the history of the tournament provides a parallel in the outside world to Chrétien's literary praise of France as the peak of *chevalerie*. The tournament is of prime importance for an understanding of the evolving mentality of the knightly class from the beginning of the tournament in the late eleventh or the early twelfth century, when its bellicose early form expressed the disposition of a knighthood that was still very much

---

[52] See Köhler, *Ideal und Wirklichkeit*, pp. 7, 21f.; Knight, *Arthurian Literature*, p. 78.
[53] On the meaning of 'France' in the prologue to *Cligés* see *Chanson de Geste und höfischer Roman*, pp. 31f.

a warrior grouping, through to the closed aristocratic tournaments of the fifteenth century which reflect the social evolution of knighthood to a nobility of birth, or special promotion by the ruler.[54] The tournament was still close in style to feud warfare in the twelfth century, involving a *mêlée* on open ground between fully armed, mounted combatants, and with prisoners being taken for ransom and booty seized, primarily in the shape of the warhorses of unseated participants. The tournament developed chiefly in northern France, whence it radiated out in the twelfth and thirteenth centuries to other parts of Europe. Historical evidence indicates that the 1170s and 1180s were a period of particularly frequent tourneying in northern France and the adjacent Low Countries.[55] Further, there is clear evidence of royal distrust of the practice in England and in France at this time. In England Henry II, like Henry I before him, prohibited tournaments as a threat to public order, so that knights wishing to take part in them had to travel abroad.[56] The chronicler Roger of Hoveden comments that Henry's three oldest sons, Henry, Richard and Geoffrey, all sought tournaments as practice for real warfare, and particularly the Young King Henry appears in the history of William Marshal as one of the leading figures on the tournament circuit in northern France in the late 1170s.[57] It is indeed one of the ironies of chivalric literature (and perhaps a deliberate one on Chrétien's part) that precisely during the reign of Henry II, when Chrétien was presenting Arthurian Britain as a place *par excellence* of knight errantry, to which knights flocked in pursuit of glory, the real England of the day seems to have been instead a place which young nobles left in order to seek such glory in tournaments in France.

[54] On the history and the social and political dimensions of the tournament see Fleckenstein (ed.), *Das ritterliche Turnier*; Barber and Barker, *Tournaments*.
[55] The main sources for this period are *La Chronique de Gislebert de Mons*, pp. 95, 97, 101, 108, 116f., 123f., 127, 133, 144; Lambert of Ardres, *Historia Comitum Ghisnensium*, p. 604, cc. 91f. (this work shows an interesting combination of tourneying interests and reception of Arthurian stories at the court of Guines, see Holmes, 'The Arthurian Tradition'); *L'Histoire de Guillaume le Maréchal*, 2471–5044. For the focus on the 1170s and 1180s see also Duby, *Le dimanche de Bouvines*, pp. 150f.
[56] William of Newburgh, *Historia Rerum Anglicarum*, p. 422; Barker, *The Tournament*, p. 7.
[57] Roger of Hoveden, *Chronica*, II, pp. 166f.; *L'Histoire de Guillaume le Maréchal*, 2443–4970. On the passage in Roger of Hoveden's chronicle as a document of the importance of tourneying in preparing knights psychologically for real warfare see Keen, *Chivalry*, p. 88; Fenske, 'Der Knappe', pp. 68–70; Jones, 'Chrétien, Hartmann and the Knight', p. 103. On the regional spread of tourneying, Barker (*The Tournament*, p. 9) suggests that Henry II may have allowed some tourneying in England. However, there cannot have been much, for no authenticated tourneying venue is known for England in Henry's reign. Moreover the main source for Barker's surmise, *L'Histoire de Guillaume le Maréchal*, refers only once to the Young King Henry's passing his time tourneying in England during an enforced stay, without naming a place (2394); and this is an exceptional passage, for England is described elsewhere in this work as a poor place for active knights, and is compared unfavourably with Britanny and Normandy, where tourneys were frequent (1526–50). All this is in line with the testimony of William of Newburgh.

In France there is no evidence of royal patronage of the tournament in the twelfth century; rather the Capetian kings seem to have considered tourneying, quite apart from its physical danger, to be incompatible with the religious dignity of kingship.[58] It was the great crown vassals of northern France and the Low Countries, including the comital houses of Champagne and Flanders, with which Chrétien's works are connected, who promoted the tournament in Chrétien's day.[59] Regionally, chronologically and in terms of known patronage, the rise of the tournament thus shows a remarkable alignment with the works of Chrétien de Troyes; put in another way, the emergence of Arthurian romance and the spread of the tournament are twin expressions of a decisive phase in the socio-cultural history of knighthood. Chrétien himself provides in *Erec* what may be the earliest description of a tournament, and tournaments continue to figure in one way or another in his later romances.[60] The evidence of the tournament confirms that Chrétien's works are indeed northern French in character, and the motif of the tournament again suggests that Chrétien was attentive to the practices and interests of the contemporary French feudal aristocracy rather than the Capetian king.

The shift of historical perspective also has an important impact on Arthur's role as we move from Geoffrey's *Historia*, in which the exercise of royal power was at the centre of interest, to Chrétien's romances, in which the values of *chevalerie* come more sharply to the fore. In terms of narrative theme this shift involves a reduction in the scope of Arthur's role and an enhancement of that of the individual knight. Chrétien's heroes are sons of kings, but for most of the narrative they are presented in their capacity as *chevaliers*, knights who could command identification across the aristocratic hierarchy, from the sons of kings and princes down to the lesser knighthood. The knightly hero is at once more individualist and broader in his social reference than was Geoffrey's Arthur. Much of the energy of Chrétien's narrative is concerned with the exploration of this strand of individualism, and with ways of reintegrating it into a communal framework in a dialectic which again involves an interplay of self-assertive violence and social control in the sword-bearing function of knighthood. The literary processing of this

---

58   See Duby, *Le dimanche de Bouvines*, p. 156.

59   Henry the Liberal, count of Champagne 1152–1181, arranged a tournament as early as 1149 which attracted the criticism of Bernard of Clairvaux (MPL, 182, col. 581; see also Henry's letter to Suger in connection with the same tourney, in Bouquet, *Receuil des Historiens des Gaules*, 15, p. 511). Henry the Liberal's son, Henry (b. 1166), appears in the 1180s as a tourneying companion of Arnold of Guines (Lambert of Ardres, *Historia Comitum Ghisnensium*, cc. 91f.; see also Duby, 'Les "jeunes" ', p. 838). On the tourneying activities of Philip of Flanders see *La Chronique de Gislebert de Mons*, p. 97; *L'Histoire de Guillaume le Maréchal* 2667ff., 2713ff., 3242ff., 3684ff.

60   See Benson, 'The Tournament', passim.

tension between self-assertion and social control will be discussed later, when we turn to the knight's use of military force in Hartmann's adaptations of Chrétien's *Erec* and *Yvain*.[61] With regard to the place of Arthur in Chrétien's works, whilst he is still extolled as a renowned king and lord over a mighty empire, he is rarely shown active in this capacity, and his role diminishes in narrative autonomy in comparison with Geoffrey's *Historia* and becomes largely contributory to that of the knightly hero, whose configuration now carries the main thematic and ideological thrust of the narrative. This reduction of Arthur's role will be carried further in Hartmann's adaptations of Chrétien's romances, but not always along the lines that have led from Geoffrey of Monmouth to Chrétien de Troyes.

## Hartmann's adaptations of Erec and Yvain

There are wide divergences of view on the status and evaluation of King Arthur in Hartmann's adaptations of Chrétien's *Erec et Enide* and *Yvain*. On the one hand it is widely maintained that Arthur is subject to criticism in one way or another. Those taking this line usually distinguish between an intact view of Arthur in Hartmann's *Erec* and a stronger thread of criticism in *Iwein*, but Peter Wiehl for instance sees negative traits in Arthur already in Hartmann's first romance.[62] As regards *Iwein*, it was noted in an article published in 1976 that almost all current scholarship assumed an implicit criticism of Arthur.[63] Recently Volker Mertens, to whom we are indebted for major contributions to Hartmann studies, still refers without qualification to 'die Artuskritik' in *Iwein*.[64] Yet other scholars see Hartmann presenting Arthur in an exemplary light even in *Iwein*, or at least they express doubt about the critical line of interpretation.[65]

This variety of responses is in part provoked by the multi-layered image of Arthur in Hartmann's works. Already Chrétien's romances presented a secondary (and changing) Arthur who combined power and glory inherited from the Anglo-Norman monarchy with the counter-pointing traits of passivity, even weakness, which he acquired in the context of the non-royal courts of northern France; and Hartmann's adaptations of Chrétien's romances into German now add a third layer to the palimpsest. To enquire after the one 'essential' Arthur in

---

61  See below, Chapters 3 and 8.
62  Wiehl, *Redeszene*, p. 110.
63  Selbmann, 'Strukturschema', p. 82.
64  Mertens, 'Das literarische Mäzenatentum', p. 131.
65  See Gürttler, *Künec Artûs*, pp. 59–87; Zutt, *König Artus*, pp. 4–15; Voß , *Artusepik*, p. 146; Pérennec, *Recherches*, I, p. 201; Hunt, 'Beginnings, Middles, and Ends', pp. 88–90.

Hartmann's works is to disregard the fact of this narrative complexity. However, by studying Hartmann's adaptations of Chrétien we learn much about the view of kingship which the German author sought to put across, and this is valuable historical information. In his adaptations, Hartmann remains broadly faithful to Chrétien's story-line, but he allows himself considerable freedom in presentation (especially in *Erec*) and in details of motivation. As regards Arthur, Hartmann makes many changes of detail and emphasis to Chrétien's romances, changes which subtly modify Arthur's narrative and political status, including his relations to the hero and to the knights at court.[66] In broadest terms Hartmann plays down the concept of Arthur as a majestic ruler, but he also omits the direct criticisms of Arthur found in Chrétien, and moreover he reduces the impression of a powerful, independent baronage around Arthur. It is usually a question of detailed modifications, but it is not sufficiently widely recognized in Hartmann criticism how consistent – and complex – a pattern of reactions these modifications form. Further, the attitude towards kingship implied in Hartmann's portrayal of Arthur and in other aspects of his work deserves fresh consideration in the current debate about the social context of Hartmann's work.

Hartmann draws even less attention than Chrétien does to Arthur's regal power, glory and dominions. He typically omits the reference in Chrétien's *Erec* to Arthur's having greater dominions than any other king or emperor (EeE 3886–89; contrast Er 4535–40), and he lacks the scene of the coronation at Nantes, in which Chrétien's Arthur appears in his greatest regal dignity. There is less Arthurian regal glory in Chrétien's *Yvain* than in his *Erec*, but still in *Yvain* Arthur is greeted on his entry into Laudine's realm as 'li rois et li sire / Des rois et des seignors del monde' (Yv 2370f.); and Hartmann again cuts this royal eulogy and the ceremonial greeting, bringing instead a discourse on hospitality and friendship (Iw 2683–716). Throughout his romances Hartmann avoids raising Arthur above the level of past or present kings or emperors in their specific capacity as rulers. This is a suggestive political constellation – it is as if Hartmann, while preserving a nimbus of glory around Arthur, wished to protect the German notion of *imperium* (according to which it was the German kings who renewed the glory of the Roman empire), and to avoid any slight on the contemporary German king and emperor.

By playing down the imperial aspect of Arthur, Hartmann continues in the direction taken by Chrétien de Troyes in contrast with Geoffrey of Monmouth. However, whereas Chrétien differs from Geoffrey by

---

[66] The fullest study of these changes is by Gürttler, *Künec Artûs*, pp. 13–90, with whose findings I am in basic agreement.

showing signs of weakness in Arthur and recording valid criticisms of his actions, Hartmann on this point takes the different line of cutting these critical aspects in his adaptation. *Iwein* is here, of course, the crucial text. In the opening episode of *Iwein* Hartmann preserves the motif of Arthur's sleep, which is necessary for the action, but he cuts the expressions of surprise and criticism on the occasion of Arthur's withdrawal (Yv 42–48; contrast Iw 77–85) and supplies a positive motivation by telling how Arthur and the queen retired more out of companionship than because of indolence (Iw 83f.: 'mê durch geselle-schaft [. . ..]/ dan durch deheine trâkheit'). Nor can we assume that a contemporary audience would see irony here and be critical of Arthur without the narrator's prompting, for there are other medieval texts in which the ruler retires for a rest after a meal.[67] The narrative situation in itself could be worked either way – the fact of having eaten could justify a retiral, the fact that it was a high feast day could justify criticism. The audience's response is dependent on the narrator's signals, and it is typical of Hartmann that he gives a positive signal, thus preserving an action of Arthur's which shows the king in a poor light in Chrétien, but remotivating it so as to remove the negative connotations.[68]

A similar tendency is evident in Hartmann's treatment of the (for Arthur) awkward affair of Guinevere's abduction. Chrétien exploits this motif at the beginning of his *Lancelot* in such a way as to show Arthur in a negative light because of his extreme dependence on the seneschal Kay, in whose ineffective guardianship he allows the queen to depart. Gauvain criticizes Arthur for his foolishness (*Lancelot* 228: 'mout grant anfance'), and in the later plot Guinevere's abduction is interwoven with the fateful matter of her love for Lancelot, which casts a further shadow over the portrayal of Arthur. Chrétien refers again to Guinevere's abduction in *Yvain*, twice having characters echo Gauvain's criticism, with the comment that 'li rois fist que fors del san' (Yv 3708) and that he was foolish, 'fos' (Yv 3926). Hartmann preserves both these speeches in which characters refer to the queen's abduction, but in each case he omits the critical comment on Arthur (Iw 4290–302, 4520ff.). Hartmann introduces a full account of the abduction into his *Iwein* in order to flesh out what would otherwise have been a puzzling blind

---

[67] Rudolf von Ems refers, without criticism, to the king of England's taking a nap with his beloved queen (*Willehalm von Orlens* 3658–62); see also Schultz, *Das höfische Leben*, I, p. 362.
[68] See also Gürttler, *Künec Artûs*, p. 62; Ruh, *Höfische Epik*, I, p. 143. Pütz, 'Artus-Kritik', p. 193 maintains that Hartmann's direct criticism of Kay's sleeping (Iw 74–76) also implies criticism of Arthur; but this interpretation disregards the differences of subjective motivation and of etiquette between the two acts, for Kay lies down out of laziness (Iw 76: 'ze gemache ân êre stuont sîn sin'), and in the presence of the other knights, whilst Arthur retires to a private room (Iw 81: 'kemenâte') and does so out of 'geselleschaft'. In a narrative so attentive to ethical intentions and the niceties of social behaviour as Hartmann's, these are crucial differences.

motif for a German audience with no knowledge of Chrétien's *Lancelot*. It is not clear how Hartmann came by his version of the abduction.[69] But it is significant that in his version, quite unlike Chrétien's, little if any critical light falls on Arthur himself. Hartmann has the strange knight Melegeant request a boon of Arthur, and Arthur shows sound judgement by at first refusing to grant the request unless it is a seemly one, which the knight should specify in advance (Iw 4544–46). This the knight refuses to do, and he questions the substance of Arthur's generosity (Iw 4558–65). In response the knights of the Round Table with one voice urge Arthur to grant the request as a matter of honour (Iw 4569–78). Arthur follows their advice, only to regret it when Melegeant requests permission to lead Guinevere away from court. Now Arthur realises that the advice of his knights has led him into a trap (Iw 4591f.: 'die disen rât tâten, / die hânt mich verrâten'), but he keeps his word and allows the queen to leave.

In Hartmann's version of Guinevere's abduction the main critical light falls on the knights of the Round Table, who seem too ready to trust a fellow knight, whilst Arthur first shows sound, sceptical judgement, then is caught, through no fault of his own, in a position of conflicting loyalties, his agreement to Guinevere's departure being prompted by two qualities which are more positive than negative: listening to advice and keeping one's word. It would seem that even in this delicate matter of Guinevere's abduction, Hartmann was more willing to allow a critical light to fall on Arthur's retinue than on the king himself.[70] If a political moral were to be drawn from Hartmann's version of the abduction, it would be that a king should stick by his own judgement and not be moved even by the collective voice of his nobles – a message more favourable to royal independence than to a limited, baronial view of kingship.

The relation of king and barons involves another shift in the portrayal of Arthur's kingship in Hartmann's adaptations. Chrétien presented Arthur as a feudal suzerain ruling over lands held from him by great vassals, and presiding over a court at which he was surrounded by a powerful baronage. However, Hartmann cuts precisely those aspects of Chrétien's romances which bear on the feudal, legal and political relationship of Arthur and the great vassals, and he eliminates in his adaptations the baronial elements which limit Arthur's independence in Chrétien.[71]

---

[69] See Shaw, 'Die Ginoverentführung', pp. 38–40; Brandt, 'Die Entführungsepisode', pp. 323f.

[70] See also Zutt, *König Artus*, pp. 11f.; Lofmark, 'The Advisor's Guilt', p. 5. Pütz's view ('Artus-Kritik', p. 195) that Hartmann shows Arthur to be more at fault in this episode than Chrétien does rests on too narrow a view of the evidence.

[71] See also Kaiser, *Textauslegung*, pp. 53f.; Gürttler, *Künec Artûs*, pp. 23, 43–51.

This tendency is exemplified in Hartmann's treatment of the hunt for the white stag in *Erec*. Hartmann follows Chrétien by referring to a competition (Er 1751: 'den ritterlîchen strît'), but he cuts all the references to threats of combat, and he omits the baronial council summoned by Chrétien's Arthur to deal with the problem. Consequently Gawein no longer appears as a baron who is critical of the king. Also Guinevere's proposal to defer the kiss, which was part of the council of barons and dependent on their consent in Chrétien's work, is remotivated by Hartmann, who has the queen make the proposal as a personal request, a 'bete' (Er 1150), which she puts to her husband using the familiar 'dû' form of address (Er 1142–47; contrast the polite form in Chrétien, as befits the formal council, EeE 335–39), and which the king grants out of his own power, without any reference to consultation. Nor does Hartmann take up Arthur's address on the duties of the ruler, with its politically sensitive formulation of a limited ideal of kingship in relation to law, rather he merely has Arthur bestow the kiss without direct speech (Er 1784–96). In short, whereas Chrétien's version of the hunt for the white stag raises matters of political concern in the relationship of king and barons (consultation, counsel, the king's attitude towards law) and envisages the possibility of armed opposition to a royal decision, Hartmann remotivates the episode to eliminate all these points which restrict the king's independence and indicate a powerful, potentially fractious baronage, and instead he presents Arthur's court as a place of unruffled harmony between king and knights.

The playing down of a sense of baronial opposition, or independence, continues in Hartmann's adaptation of *Yvain*. We have noted Hartmann's silencing of the voices at court that were critical of Arthur's withdrawal to sleep. Later in Chrétien's romance Yvain and Gauvain, returning from a tournament, decide not to visit Arthur's court in Chester, instead they pitch camp and hold court themselves outside the city, so that Arthur has to come and visit them (Yv 2685–93). Stephen Knight cites this interlude as a 'clear anti-royal element' in *Yvain*, a reflection of 'the hostility between king and barons in late twelfth-century France', and he is surely right to criticize a narrowly moral reading of the situation.[72] Hartmann unerringly senses the pointed baronial stance and the diplomatic slight on the king here, and he characteristically remotivates, omitting Chrétien's references to the pair's 'not wishing to enter the city' and to their 'holding court', instead commenting that they pitched camp 'in order to rest' (Iw 3069: 'durch ir gemach'). Arthur then visits the 'German' Iwein and Gawein no longer as a king whose court has been upstaged by that of two baronial young

---

[72] Knight, *Arthurian Literature*, pp. 77f.

bloods, but as a respected ruler who wishes to congratulate the knights of his court for their good work done (Iw 3075–79). Such differences between Chrétien and Hartmann show the German author attentive to the diplomatic signals of Chrétien's narrative, and eager to eliminate anti-royal implications even in the detail of social intercourse.

These modifications in the portrayal of Arthur are typical of a general pattern in Hartmann's works, that is to say that Hartmann tends not to show kings in an unfavourable light (whether as tyrants, aggressors or weaklings), and not to develop a sense of baronial opposition to the king. In general the viewpoint of the tenants-in-chief, the great feudal princes, seems less strongly present in Hartmann than it is in Chrétien or indeed in a number of other German works of the period. The crown vassals, as imperial princes, are often referred to in twelfth-century German sources as *vürsten*.[73] This term *vürsten* plays an important part in German works which articulate a baronial standpoint, and which show the king (or emperor) in the context of his *vürsten* much as French works present the king in relation to his barons. In the *Kaiserchronik* it is the mark of a tyrant king that he tries to rule without the advice and consent of the 'vursten' (12813–24, 16551ff.). The motif of princes defending their rights against royal tyranny or infringement is also developed in works close in genre and time to Hartmann's romances: in Ulrich von Zatzikhoven's *Lanzelet*, King Pant is a tyrant whose nobles rebel against him, whilst later the 'fürsten' of the land (*Lanzelet* 8162, 8199) welcome Pant's son as rightful king on condition that he will treat them better than his father did (*Lanzelet* 8210f.: 'ob er uns baz triutet / dan sîn vater der künic Pant');[74] and in Wolfram's *Parzival*, Landgrave Kingrimursel gives a classic expression of the vassalic right of resistance against a king who has failed in his duty when he warns King Vergulaht that, if he (the king) fails to treat the princes as befits their status, then they will trouble the crown: 'kunnet ir niht fürsten schônen, / wir krenken ouch die krônen' (*Parzival* 415,21f.).

It is particularly interesting to compare this situation in Wolfram's *Parzival* with Hartmann's adaptations of Chrétien's romances, for Wolfram's romance is also based on one of Chrétien's works (*Perceval*), but whereas Hartmann plays down conflict between king and vassal, Wolfram in this episode intensifies the conflict between the two and clearly places the vassal Kingrimursel morally in the right against the unprincipled action of a king. As Wolfgang Mohr has shown, Wolfram

---

[73] On the *Reichsfürsten* and the developments in their relation to the German crown in the twelfth century see Mitteis, *Der Staat des hohen Mittelalters*, pp. 257–60; Ganshof, *Feudalism*, pp. 147–49; Munz, *Frederick Barbarossa*, pp. 335–57; Arnold, *Princes and Territories*, passim.
[74] On the relation of king and magnates in Ulrich's *Lanzelet* and in the historical context see W.H. Jackson, 'Ulrich von Zatzikhoven's *Lanzelet*', passim; Roßbacher, '*Lanzelet*', passim.

is here surely reflecting a political stance at the court of his patron, Landgrave Hermann of Thuringia, in criticism of the Hohenstaufen king, Philip.[75] Nowhere in Hartmann's works is there a remotely comparable justification of vassalic resistance to royal power, or such a sharply profiled assertion of a baronial standpoint against the king. Indeed Hartmann seems little interested in the political sphere of the imperial princes, for he uses the term *vürste* on only six occasions in his entire *œuvre*, and never in a politically charged sense.[76]

Whereas Hartmann plays down the political themes of imperial power and the relation of king and barons in portraying Arthur, he develops and expands the theme of *chevalerie*. Even more than with Chrétien, this is where Hartmann's main interest lies. Thus he expands on Chrétien's portrayal of Arthur's court as a place where knights can win honour, for instance when he adds to Chrétien's *Erec* the information that the knight Cadoc was travelling to Arthur's court to gain recognition (Er 5649–53), and when he has Erec praise Arthur's court as the supreme source of glory for a knight (Er 5681–87). Typically, Hartmann retouches the Cadoc episode so as to reduce a sense of Arthur's royal presence and enhance the image of his court and retinue as a focus for chivalric glory. In general, Hartmann goes even further than Chrétien in reducing the narrative autonomy of Arthur and his court and making their role relative to that of the hero. More specifically Arthur and his court mark the hero's progress as a knight, and particularly his acquisition of *êre* – prestige, honour.

This tendency is apparent in Hartmann's *Erec* at each of the three stages of the romance where Erec appears at Arthur's court. Hartmann's elimination of the politically sensitive issues concerning the attitude of the king towards his barons and to law brings a reduction of narrative suspense within Arthur's court in the opening stages of the romance.[77] However, Hartmann compensates for this by heightening the narrative tension around Erec, for whereas Chrétien introduces Erec as a proven 'chevaliers' who has already won great fame (EeE 81–92), he is for Hartmann youthful and inexperienced at the beginning of the romance. Time and again in the early stages of Hartmann's romance, narrator and characters evoke Erec's youth by referring to him as a *jungelinc*, or by applying the adjective *junc* to him (18, 145, 708, 757, 930, 1138, 1264, 2255, 2285, 2324, 2331). In Hartmann's version, quite unlike Chrétien's, Erec's combat with Iders is his first chivalric deed (Er 1266), and the

---

[75] Mohr, 'Landgraf Kingrimursel', pp. 33–37. On Wolfram's relations with Hermann of Thuringia see Bumke, *Mäzene*, pp. 164f.

[76] Four occurrences relate to the guests summoned by Arthur to Erec's wedding feast (Er 1896, 1903, 2012, 2213), one to Gregorius (Gr 3036), one (in the form of a comparison) to Heinrich (AH 43).

[77] See also Wiehl, *Redeszene*, p. 150.

tournament is the first one he has ever taken part in (Er 2252–53). There is also a greater sense of self-consciousness and anxious reflectiveness about Hartmann's youthful hero, as he ponders about how to do well the things which Chrétien's more experienced hero achieves with seemingly effortless confidence.[78] Stripped of its internal tensions, Arthur's court becomes more static and unproblematical in Hartmann's *Erec* than it was in Chrétien's work, whilst the hero is presented more dynamically and inwardly in his self-conscious passage from untried youth to warrior manhood; and Arthur marks the initial stage in this passage by calling on his knights to reward the young Erec with 'êre' (Er 1285–92) for his success in his first combat. Arthur, the queen and the whole retinue again show Erec great 'êre' when he pays an unwilling visit to the court during his journey in pursuit of *âventiure* (Er 5085–88). In a seminal study of Hartmann's *Erec*, Ernst Scheunemann showed, by comparing this scene of Erec's unwilling visit to the court in Chrétien and Hartmann, the extent to which Hartmann's portrayal of Arthur's court is conditioned by the inner state of the hero, for just as Hartmann's Erec is here wounded, tired and lacking in the joy a knight should bring to court (Er 5052–67), so Hartmann tones down the joyfulness of the court in adapting Chrétien at this point.[79] When Erec makes his last visit to Arthur's court he has won glory by restoring joy to the court of Brandigan, hence Arthur's court is again seen in a state of joy, 'wünne' (Er 9948), and again, this time climactically, Arthur praises Erec, and the whole court grants him the 'crown of honour' (Er 9891: 'der êren krône'). Indeed Arthur's court appears in Hartmann's *Erec* largely as a projection of the hero's state of mind and an embodiment of knightly prestige.

On only one occasion does Hartmann significantly expand Arthur's role in adapting Chrétien's *Erec*, and this is in his account of the tournament. The tournament episode in Hartmann's *Erec* is probably the earliest description of such an event in German literature, and it is indicative of Hartmann's preoccupation with the latest chivalric practices that he expands Chrétien's account of the tournament to over four times its original length (EeE 2126–270; compare Er 2222–2851), adding much new material concerning the *realia* and the ethos of the tournament. The tournament has little narrative importance in Chrétien's *Erec*, but Hartmann gives it a more substantial and integral place in his more dynamic, biographical presentation of the hero by making it into an important learning experience for Erec.[80] The tournament episode also shows a significant difference between

---

78    See e.g. Erec's self-conscious preparations for the tournament (Er 2248–61, 2378–90) – a projection of youthful earnestness by Hartmann which has no parallel in Chrétien.
79    Scheunemann, *Artushof und Abenteuer*, pp. 71f.
80    See below, pp. 104f.

Chrétien and Hartmann in the relationship of Arthur and Erec in material terms.[81] Chrétien's Erec appears as an independent prince at Arthur's court, having his own retinue and his own considerable material resources, sending his own knights and men-at-arms with gifts to his father-in-law (EeE 1845-76). In adapting this passage Hartmann states that Erec received the rich gifts for Enite's father from Arthur (Er 1806-19). Chrétien makes no reference to Arthur's equipping Erec for the tournament, but Hartmann states at length that Erec, as a guest at Arthur's court, and far from his homeland, lacked material resources and had to be given tourneying equipment (armour, weapons, warhorses) by the king (Er 2262ff.). Hartmann's account of Arthur's equipping the young Erec shows the German author independently developing an image of King Arthur as a poetic fulfilment of the hopes of many poorer knights in historical reality that they might find an equally lavish patron to provide the costly equipment needed for the knightly lifestyle. Hartmann extends this image of Arthur as Erec's chivalric patron by departing from Chrétien's version to have Arthur attend the tournament (Er 2368-71) and learn of Erec's success (Er 2516-22). Arthur's court will keep its association with tourneying in *Iwein*, but its role as a focus of chivalric activity will be more problematical in this romance, and will be discussed in a later chapter.[82]

In the light of the actual functioning of kingship in the historical reality of the twelfth century, the path that leads from Geoffrey's *Historia* through Chrétien's romances to Hartmann's adaptations shows a certain depoliticization, a progressive narrowing of political interest in Arthur's role. In the transition from Geoffrey of Monmouth to Chrétien the dimension of active warrior monarchy fades. In Hartmann's adaptations of Chrétien it is rather the impression of Arthur's relation to an independent and powerful baronage that fades, to leave a suggestive constellation of harmony linking king and knight. In narrative terms, King Arthur has become subordinate to the hero knight, even more than was the case in Chrétien's romances. However, this is not to say that the Arthurian court has in Hartmann's works lost touch with contemporary social reality and become a purely poetic, ahistorical realm. Rather Hartmann's portrayal of Arthur's court links up with the actual social practice whereby young nobles spent a period of military and broader social training in the household of a lord with whom they had ties of a family or political (feudal) nature.

Historical sources in the narrow sense usually provide only meagre information about the upbringing of young nobles in secular life, but it is clear in general outline that throughout medieval Europe it was an

---

[81] See also Kaiser, *Textauslegung*, pp. 50–52.
[82] See below, pp. 270–76.

important function of lordly households to provide placements of varying duration for youths, who in this way gained a broader experience than was accessible to them on the often remote manors which formed the main economic basis of noble life.[83] Fosterage in lordly households can be traced back many centuries. It was an important factor in the military training of youths, especially with the development of the more elaborate forms of mounted combat that characterize chivalric warfare; and such an upbringing was a potent social force in that it helped to further a sense of communality, of shared lifestyle and group consciousness linking young knights of various regional origins and social degrees.[84] From the twelfth century onwards there is increasing evidence of the acquisition of courtly forms of behaviour beside the military training function of such periods of residence.[85] Indeed the rapid growth and diffusion in the twelfth century of new forms of vernacular literature which contain much prescriptive detail about forms of behaviour appropriate to the court are part of this broad social stream. The practice of sending young nobles to a great court for their social education is well documented for twelfth-century Germany.[86] There is every possibility that something of this kind figured in Hartmann's own life, and several of his alterations to Chrétien's *Erec* suggest that he saw Arthur's court largely in this light.

That Hartmann took it for granted that the social education of nobles was acquired at a court is indicated in the way he has Erec, independently of Chrétien's text, reproach Count Galoain[87] for his uncouthness, with the comment that he must have been 'brought up at a poor court' (Er 4202: 'ir sît an swachem hove erzogen'). Hartmann also points up the fostering and educative aspects of Erec's relation to Arthur's court. Thus it was frequently a maternal uncle who took the young noble into his household for training,[88] and Hartmann departs from Chrétien's version to make Erec into Arthur's 'neve' (Er 1794, 9944), a family relationship which he exploits by having Arthur and Guinevere adopt a more parental attitude of concern and relief towards Erec than was the case in Chrétien (e.g. Er 144–47, 1137–40, 1260–69). In general there is in Hartmann's portrayal of Erec's attitude towards Arthur's court much of a child who seeks the approval of his parents.

---

83   See Orme, *From Childhood to Chivalry*, pp. 44–58; Fenske, 'Der Knappe', pp. 70–77, 82–95; Ashcroft, '*Als ein wilder valk erzogen*', pp. 61–63.
84   See also Keen, *Chivalry*, p. 26.
85   See Bumke, *Höfische Kultur*, II, pp. 434f.
86   Examples in Bumke, *Höfische Kultur*, II, pp. 433f. include evidence from two of the great courts with which Hartmann may have had contacts: the Welf and Hohenstaufen households (see *Historia Welforum*, p. 22 and *La Chronique de Gislebert de Mons*, p. 234).
87   The name 'Galoain' appears only in Chrétien's *Erec et Enide* (3129), but I use it throughout this study to refer also to the corresponding figure in Hartmann's *Erec*.
88   Flori, *L'essor*, p. 52.

Chrétien's Erec says he has been at Arthur's court for three years (EeE 653f.), but Hartmann's version suggests a longer period of residence, since childhood (Er 1275: 'von kinde'; compare 2865-69, where Hartmann's Erec has not been back to his father's land since he was 'ein kindelîn'), and, as we have seen, Hartmann repeatedly draws attention to Erec's youth and inexperience in the opening episode, presenting Arthur's court as the base for Erec's military education, the point of departure for his first chivalric combat (Er 1266) and his first tournament (Er 2252f.). A contemporary audience would see here quite naturally a sojourn of noble fostering, with King Arthur as the lordly relative under whose guidance and patronage (expressed in the parental concern and the gift of tourneying equipment) Erec makes the transition from youth to chivalric manhood.

Finally, the difference between Hartmann and Chrétien in the social and political conception of Arthur's court is sufficient to account for the different treatment of Arthur and his court at the end of their respective versions of *Erec*. Just as Hartmann emphasizes Erec's youth in the early stage of the romance, so he intensifies the biographical dimension of the hero's progress by omitting Chrétien's account of the magnificent crowning at Arthur's court and taking Erec at the end of the romance away from Arthur's realm to assume the duties of kingship in his homeland (Er 9971ff.). Earlier scholars attached such a generally ideal function to Arthur's court in Hartmann's thinking that they found it hard to believe that he should have thus reduced its role at the end by making it not the final goal but a stage in the narrative. Consequently it was argued that Hartmann did not himself invent Erec's final return to his homeland, but took it from a postulated secondary source;[89] or that he used a version of Chrétien's *Erec* which differed from the one which has been transmitted to us, and which corresponded more closely to Hartmann's text.[90] These are unnecessarily speculative interpretations which rest on too abstract a conception of Arthur's role in *Erec* and which fail to do justice to Hartmann's (*vis-à-vis* Chrétien) subtly and consistently modified view of Arthur. Erec's crowning at Nantes and his receiving of his lands from Arthur are in keeping with Chrétien's attentiveness to the relation of king and high vassal in his presentation of Arthur. However, from the beginning of *Erec* Hartmann has reduced this aspect in his portrayal of Arthur, and he has presented Arthur's court primarily in its relation to Erec's knighthood, as a measure of his strictly knightly achievement. Once the period of Erec's education and testing as a knight is at an end and Erec gives up his errant existence to succeed his father as king (Er 9971-76, 10064ff.), Arthur's role as Erec's

[89] Sparnaay, *Hartmann von Aue*, I, p. 111.
[90] Scheunemann, *Artushof und Abenteuer*, p. 106, n. 322.

patron in chivalry, and that of his court, is also played out in Hartmann's romance, as surely as, in historical reality, the fostering role of the lordly household in which a young noble has been trained is played out when the noble enters his own inheritance and himself assumes the duties of lordship.

## King Arthur and the social context of Hartmann's works

What light does the portrayal of Arthur throw on the social context of Hartmann's works? Linguistic and other evidence places Hartmann in the south-west of Germany, in the old duchy of Swabia.[91] The tenor of his works suggests a secular court as his target audience. However, unlike Geoffrey of Monmouth and Chrétien de Troyes, Hartmann never mentions a patron or dedicatee, and it is impossible to assess what – if any – constraints of sponsorship he was working under, though his own utterances point in the direction of freedom rather than limitation in his handling of material.[92] As regards the court, or courts, which provided encouragement and (in whatever form) sponsorship for Hartmann, scholars have recently looked variously to the three most powerful families in Swabia, each of whom had a sufficiently highly developed lordship to act as a focus for major literary activity: the dukes of Zähringen (Berthold IV died 1186, Berthold V ca. 1160–1218),[93] the Altdorf branch of the Welfs (Welf VI, duke of Spoleto, 1115/1116–1191),[94] and the Hohenstaufen imperial family.[95]

It must be said that in all three cases the evidence is wholly circumstantial. The hypothesis of Zähringen patronage currently enjoys much favour. One of the main planks in this argument is the view, put forward most firmly by Volker Mertens, that Hartmann's romances are biased decidedly towards the territorial princes rather than the king, that especially *Iwein* shows Arthur's kingship in a critical light, and that this stance argues strongly against sponsorship by the Hohenstaufen ruling dynasty.[96] In support of this view Mertens refers to Köhler's interpretation of Chrétien's romances, where indeed there is a combination of non-royal patronage and some critical distance from the figure

---

[91] See Cormeau/Störmer, *Hartmann von Aue*, pp. 32–36.
[92] See below, pp. 196f.
[93] Ruh, *Höfische Epik*, I, pp. 104f.; Mertens, *Gregorius Eremita*, pp. 32–37; id., *Laudine*, pp. 95, 97–99; id., 'Das literarische Mäzenatentum', pp. 121–31.
[94] Thum, 'Politische Probleme', pp. 67–70; Bayer, *Hartmann von Aue*, pp. 90–99.
[95] Jungbluth, 'Das dritte Kreuzlied Hartmanns', pp. 156–62; Schweikle, 'Der Stauferhof', pp. 255–59.
[96] Mertens, *Gregorius Eremita*, pp. 32f.; id., 'Das literarische Mäzenatentum', pp. 124, 131.

of the king.[97] However, since Hartmann, in adapting Chrétien, tones down the anti-royal traits, the independent, self-assertive baronial viewpoint, and the criticisms of Arthur, it must seriously be questioned whether Köhler's reading of Chrétien's work can be applied without modification to Hartmann. A similar question is provoked by Klaus Schmidt's view that the German Arthurian romance as a genre shows a general ideological standpoint of the non-royal territorial princes.[98] Schmidt rightly sees this standpoint expressed in Wolfram's *Parzival*, a work known to be connected with the non-royal court of Landgrave Hermann of Thuringia.[99] However, Wolfram's position of baronial assertiveness against the king, as we have seen, lacks parallels in Hartmann's works, so it is unwise to generalize about the ideological stance of the genre as a whole on this point. Indeed, is it merely coincidence that, on the one occasion when Wolfram refers to Hartmann by name, he does so in a challengingly ironical manner and describes King Arthur as Hartmann's lord, 'iwer hêrre' (*Parzival* 143,23)? Or is Wolfram here, from the standpoint of a non-royal court, mocking what he sees as a Hohenstaufen, royalist tendency in Hartmann?

The particular combination of Hartmann's cutting the negative, critical aspects of Chrétien's portrayal of Arthur, but also eliminating the references to Arthur as being greater than other kings and emperors suggests that Hartmann may have been working with a social context in mind that was favourably disposed to the Hohenstaufen ruling family, or at least that he was aware of the German royal sphere of influence and did not wish to develop an oppositional stance towards kingship in general, or to speak of a former king of Britain in terms that could be construed as a slight on the contemporary king of Germany. This attitude could be compatible with his working within a Zähringen, an Altdorf Welf or a Hohenstaufen environment.

There was certainly territorial and political rivalry at times between the Zähringen and the Hohenstaufen families in Swabia. But Berthold IV of Zähringen was also a loyal supporter of Frederick Barbarossa in the 1180s,[100] which formed the early period of Hartmann's literary activity, and Hartmann could have had access to Hohenstaufen affairs through this channel. Berthold V seems to have kept a more sceptical distance from the imperial court, and he joined the Saxon and Rhenish alliance of anti-Hohenstaufen forces against Emperor Henry VI in 1192. But he was close to the emperor in 1195 and 1196, and in 1198 a party even sought

---

[97] See also Thomas, who argues that Hartmann's *Erec* occupies a similar political position in German literature to that of Chrétien's works in French literature ('Matière de Rome – matière de Bretagne', pp. 99f.).

[98] Schmidt, 'Das Herrscherbild', pp. 191–94.

[99] Ibid., p. 193.

[100] Heyck, *Geschichte der Herzöge von Zähringen*, pp. 412–17.

his candidature for the crown after Henry's death.[101] With the benefit of hindsight it is tempting, but misleading, to construct too general an opposition of interests between the German territorial princes and the crown, and in the cut and thrust of political and dynastic developments in Swabia in Hartmann's day, a poet might well have found it prudent to present kingship in a favourable light even if writing with an eye on the Zähringen court, for who could predict how the next alliance might turn out? If Hartmann was working in the Altdorf Welf context a favourable attitude towards Hohenstaufen rule is quite unproblematical, since in the late 1170s Welf VI, after the death of his own son, designated his nephew, Emperor Frederick I, and his (Frederick's) sons as his heirs, and on his death in 1191 his Swabian lands became part of the Hohenstaufen patrimony.[102] There is no direct evidence of sponsorship of vernacular narrative literature by the imperial court in Hartmann's day, but this court seems to have been a focus for the courtly lyric, and Hartmann's songs, especially his crusading songs, are often adduced as evidence of his contact with the Hohenstaufen sphere of influence.[103] Bruno Boesch has surmised that Hartmann's œuvre as a whole seems to fit a pro-Hohenstaufen environment;[104] and in a study that is highly important for our purposes, René Pérennec has raised the possibility of a connection between Hartmann and the imperial court on the basis of affinities between Hartmann's romances and Barbarossa's policies in the promotion of knighthood.[105]

Any attempt to place Hartmann's works in a social context must attach considerable weight to the related phenomena of knighthood and the court. And here a difference of politico-cultural focus emerges between northern France and the German empire, for whereas in northern France it was chiefly the great non-royal courts that furthered the practices and ideology of chivalry in the second half of the twelfth century, in Germany precisely the Hohenstaufen imperial court seems to have been active in defining and promoting the status and values of knighthood in this period.[106] Military values played a decisive part in

---

101   Ibid., pp. 439–41, 444f.
102   *Historia Welforum*, p. 70; Jordan, *Henry the Lion*, pp. 156, 163, 194; Bradler, *Studien zur Geschichte der Ministerialität*, pp. 427–29.
103   See above, p. 30, n. 95; below, pp. 186f.
104   Boesch, 'Mittelhochdeutsche Dichtung am Oberrhein', p. 91.
105   Pérennec, *Recherches*, I, pp. 168–70.
106   See Fleckenstein, 'Friedrich Barbarossa und das Rittertum', passim; W.H. Jackson, 'Knighthood and the Hohenstaufen Imperial Court', passim. Heinz Thomas has a more sceptical view of the role of chivalric interests at the Hohenstaufen court. He agrees that the new style of chivalric, aristocratic culture was promoted by Barbarossa in the 1180s, but he also sees conservative opposition to this new chivalry in and around Hohenstaufen circles ('Ordo equestris – ornamentum Imperii', pp. 348–50). Elsewhere ('Matière de Rome – matière de Bretagne', p. 94) he doubts whether the association of emperor and knighthood

Frederick Barbarossa's own life and in his family history, as is well documented in Otto of Freising's *Gesta Frederici*. Barbarossa's grandfather, Frederick, count of Swabia, was raised to the status of duke and received the hand of Emperor Henry IV's daughter because of his loyal military service (*Gesta Frederici*, I, 8, p. 144). His son Duke Frederick II of Swabia attracted many *milites* into his service by his generosity (ibid., I, 12, p. 152), and the earliest reference to a 'tournament' on German soil relates to an event in a military campaign undertaken by this Frederick (who was Barbarossa's father) and his brother Conrad in 1127 (ibid., I, 18, p. 158: 'tyrocinium, quod vulgo nunc turnoimentum dicitur'). It is not clear just what form this 'turnoimentum' took.[107] But it was held under the aegis of Frederick Barbarossa's father and uncle, and Otto of Freising does not condemn them (though as a bishop, and writing in the late 1150s, he must have been well aware of the Church's hostility to the tournament), rather the 'turnoimentum' appears as further evidence of the Hohenstaufen family's good warrior stock. Otto tells us nothing about the boyhood and youth of Duke Frederick II's son, the future emperor Barbarossa, until he is old enough to bear arms – this is a mark of the importance of initiation into warrior manhood in the life of the twelfth-century noble. Then we hear that he received the belt of knighthood and was trained, as was customary for the nobility, in military sports (ibid., I, 27, p. 180: 'educatus, ut assolet, ludis militaribus'), before undertaking feud warfare. As an ageing ruler he issued invitations to a tournament which was to be held at Ingelheim following the knighting of his sons Henry and Frederick at Whitsun in 1184 in Mainz.[108] This tournament was in fact cancelled, but its very planning in connection with a state occasion in the imperial heartlands suggests a less hostile attitude in Barbarossa towards this still controversial manifestation of military chivalry than was usual in rulers of the twelfth century. Indeed there is no evidence of a royal prohibition of tourneying in twelfth-century Germany, the early history of the tournament is associated with the Hohenstaufen family, and Barbarossa's own participation in the great equestrian display which actually

was so pervasive in the 1180s as Fleckenstein has maintained; and he also points out that, despite the chivalric interests evidenced at the imperial court in the late twelfth century, this court did not assert itself as a focus for chivalric culture in the long run, rather from the thirteenth century onwards the accent in Germany shifted increasingly towards the territorial princes in this matter as in larger constitutional developments ('Nationale Elemente', pp. 350–61). Even in Thomas's challenging and sceptical view, the last decades of the twelfth century remain a key period for the reception of chivalric forms in the German empire, and the Hohenstaufen family are seen as playing some part in this process.

[107] It was probably a serious military action, see Fleckenstein, 'Das Turnier als höfisches Fest', p. 230; Barber and Barker, *Tournaments*, p. 19.

[108] *La Chronique de Gislebert de Mons*, pp. 151f.; see Fleckenstein, 'Das Turnier als höfisches Fest', pp. 236–38.

accompanied his sons' knighting[109] shows a continuing self-identification with knightly practice.

Military chivalry also played an important part at a high political level in the imperial ideology whereby Barbarossa presented his rule as a renewal of the glory of the Roman empire, for in this context the contemporary knighthood of the Hohenstaufen empire appeared as the inheritors of the prowess and discipline of the 'equestris ordo' of ancient Rome.[110] Categories of military and social order inherited from Roman antiquity and reinterpreted to suit the contemporary reality were influential in shaping the concept of knighthood in the twelfth century, and the Hohenstaufen concern with a renewal of empire provided a prestigious framework for this process. Thus on the question of social hierarchy the chronicle of Ebersheimmünster in the 1160s derived the status of the German princes ('principes') and the lesser knights ('minores milites') from that of the senators and citizens of Rome under Julius Caesar.[111] This myth of the origins of the German aristocratic hierarchy reflects a standpoint favourable to the Hohenstaufen imperial court and to the lesser knighthood, the *ministeriales*, who are seen as having an important part to play in Hohenstaufen rule.[112] We shall see later that imperial legislation during Barbarossa's reign (1152–1190) was also attentive to the contemporary knighthood as regards both social status and military discipline.[113] The cultivation of knighthood offered pragmatic advantages, was indeed in one way or another a political necessity for the imperial court in Hartmann's day, for the German emperor was heavily dependent on the knights, especially the imperial *ministeriales*, for the government of far-flung lands, and by enhancing their prestige and acknowledging their social forms he might hope to tie them more closely to service of the crown. The promotion of knighthood could also serve imperial interests by encouraging some ideological integration of greater and lesser men in the *militia* under Hohenstaufen rule, whilst the imperial legislation in Barbarossa's reign (as we shall see) favoured the knighthood by sanctioning certain aristocratic class privileges and also sought to extend the peace by promulgating a more disciplined code of feuding.

To a large extent the Hohenstaufen imperial court was, with the increased prominence of knightly interests, simply reflecting a broader development of the second half of the twelfth century. We are better informed about the Hohenstaufen court in this period than about other lordly households in Germany, and the general tendencies which are

[109]  *La Chronique de Gislebert de Mons*, p. 157.
[110]  *Gesta Frederici*, II, 32, p. 346; see Thomas, 'Nationale Elemente', pp. 350–52.
[111]  MGH Scriptores, 23, p. 432; see also Keen, *Chivalry*, pp. 35f.
[112]  See Bosl, *Die Grundlagen*, pp. 199–201.
[113]  See below, pp. 72, 88–92.

documented in Hohenstaufen circles may have been typical of other lordships too. Certainly, knightly concerns are evident elsewhere in the German historical sources at this time. For instance in the Welf family chronicle, Duke Welf VI appears as a lord who holds lavish feasts and shows great generosity to the knights of his court and their colleagues ('curiae suae militibus et consociis') by giving them fine armour and clothes.[114] Though the gesture is far too generalized to permit a specific link, the historical Welf, with whose sphere of influence Hartmann may have been connected, appears here, like Hartmann's Arthur, as a lordly patron of knighthood.

The question of the precise location of Hartmann's literary activity remains unanswered. However, the harmony between king and knight which characterizes Hartmann's adaptations of Chrétien's romances (and which contrasts with Wolfram's greater readiness to adopt an oppositional stance) is sufficiently analogous to the association of emperor and knighthood in the German historical sources of Barbarossa's reign to justify the hypothesis that Hartmann may have been writing with a court in mind that was favourably disposed to Hohenstaufen rule. Even leaving the question of patronage on one side as an open problem, it is illuminating, in discussing the topic of knighthood in Hartmann's works, to draw on historical evidence relating to the *milites* in Hohenstaufen sources, because this evidence shows, at the very least, that knighthood was not only an imported literary concern, but also a phenomenon of considerable, complex and developing importance in the German social reality of Hartmann's day.

Finally it is important for an intrinsic interpretation of Hartmann's works, and for an understanding of their relation to a social context, that, when Hartmann provides information about his social status in his later works *Iwein* and *Der arme Heinrich*, he presents himself as a knight, a *ritter* (AH 1, Iw 21). Unfortunately the prologue to *Erec*, which might have furnished similar information about the author, has not been preserved. In his comments as narrator in *Erec*, Hartmann twice refers to himself as a *tumber kneht* (Er 1603, 7480). The word *kneht* could at this time mean 'squire' in the sense of a youth or young man of knightly birth who had not yet been knighted.[115] Consequently some early scholars looking for biographical clues concluded that Hartmann had not yet become a knight, that he was still a young squire awaiting the time of his knighting, when he composed his *Erec*. Against this view

114 *Historia Welforum*, p. 72. On social life at the court of Welf VI see Schreiner, ' "Hof" (*curia*)', pp. 69–71; unfortunately the social life of the Zähringen household is far (or rather: even) less well documented than that of the Welfs and Hohenstaufen (see Heyck, *Geschichte der Herzöge von Zähringen*, p. iv), so we can only surmise about chivalric practices there.
115 See below, p. 51.

Schwietering has rightly pointed out that the term *kneht* is used in these two passages in opposition not to *ritter*, but to figures of authorial experience ('manec wîser munt', Er 1595; 'meister [. . ..] Umbrîz', Er 7470); the designation *kneht* is, in this position, especially in connection with the adjective *tump*, a formula of modesty, by means of which Hartmann indicates his own lack of experience as author in this early work, and the term consequently does not provide evidence as to whether Hartmann was, in his biographically real life, still a squire.[116] However, whether Hartmann was already a knight when he was working on *Erec*, or whether he was still a young squire who had not yet been knighted, he stands as narrator inside the knightly world.

Moreover, whilst Hartmann makes no reference to the prompting of a patron, his works convey an unusually strong sense of authorial personality. Hartmann names himself in his works with unusual frequency, he has a remarkably explicit mediating presence as narrator and an exceptionally strong awareness of the audience, and he shows a high degree of identification with his knightly protagonist, especially in his early works. Thus Hartmann's knightly status is not a merely external autobiographical fact but part of the mental structure of his works. In contrast with the more objective, clerkly style of Geoffrey's *Historia*, and still to some extent (though in a different manner) of Chrétien's romances, Hartmann's works are a more subjective self-presentation of knighthood; and in *Erec*, Hartmann appears as an inexperienced, but talented and eager young author and narrator who, in his authorial modifications to Chrétien's text, and in his own style of narration, shows particular involvement with the learning experiences of knightly youth.

We shall follow the modulations of this knightly perspective through Hartmann's works, according to chronology and genre. Here it is enough to point out that King Arthur, having emerged in Geoffrey of Monmouth's work as an embodiment of the author's racial and dynastic inclinations, has been appropriated into Hartmann's knightly perspective as a projection of the German author's ideal of a chivalric patron. However, the nature and the implications of this 'knightly perspective' remain to be defined, for the question of the social status and reality of knighthood in Germany in Hartmann's day is currently a matter of controversy which will be discussed in the next chapter.

---

[116] See the discussion of this self-reference in Schwietering, *Demutsformel*, p. 37.

# 2

# Knighthood and Social Status in Twelfth-Century Germany and in Hartmann's *Erec*

*Preliminary sketch*

The figure of the knight and the social and ethical values of chivalry are of central importance for a study of Hartmann's works, and for an understanding of the place of these works in the culture of Hartmann's own time. Hence the use of historical evidence is essential for a full literary appreciation of Hartmann's *œuvre*. The literary works of this period also have evidential value for the historian, for at a time when historical sources in the narrow sense were written predominantly in Latin and by clerical authors, vernacular literature, for all its fictive stylization, provides insight into material details and mental structures that fall outside the scope of Latin historical sources. Vernacular writings also give direct information about the actual means of verbal communication of the vast majority of the population, without the problems of translation posed by Latin sources. Knighthood is a particularly rewarding topic for co-operation between historical and philological disciplines. However, precisely this topic is the subject of controversy and divergence of view in recent work on the German material in our period.

Joachim Bumke's *Studien zum Ritterbegriff im 12. und 13. Jahrhundert*, first published in 1964, is a landmark of research in this field because of its wealth of documentation from poetic works, and the often controversial vigour of its main propositions. Bumke has amply demonstrated that, in German poetic works up to 1250, the men described as *ritter*, 'knights', do not all form a unified stratum of social equals. Against an older view, prevalent in German literary scholarship,

37

which linked knighthood primarily with nobility and lordship, Bumke sees service as the nucleus of the concept of chivalry.[1] Further, against a naive reading of the poetic texts as unbroken reflections of social reality he tends to detach the literary portrayal of chivalry from this reality, seeing it as belonging more to the realm of ideas than to that of social history.[2] Bumke's study could not be a definitive account of chivalry because he draws only incidentally on Latin historical sources. Hans Georg Reuter has complemented Bumke's work by considering Latin historiography as well as poetic sources in German.[3] Like Bumke, Reuter concludes that the knights did not form a homogeneous, unified class in the German empire in the twelfth and thirteenth centuries. Indeed, Reuter seems almost to work on the principle that nothing is like anything else, and the gist of his iconoclastic study is that practically 'nothing useful may be said about the social status of knights in the period under discussion'.[4] The usefulness of Reuter's study is limited by the scope of his question, for he restricts himself to asking whether or not the knights formed a unified, corporate class or status-group ('Stand'), without paying due attention to the common features which coexisted with the elements of social heterogeneity for which he has such a sharp eye. The status of knights is a complex problem of historical research and of terminology, and in a sociological discussion of 'knighthood', 'la chevalerie', 'das Rittertum', 'die Ritterschaft' or 'der Ritterstand' (the plurality of terms in current German research is indicative of the variety of views) it is essential to give due weight to the features of identity or communality which motivate the common name, as well as to the legal, hierarchical and economic differences which run through this chunk of society. In studying the phenomenon of knighthood, the choice is not necessarily one between isolated individuals and a totally homogeneous, hermetically sealed-off group; and so heavy has been the fire directed by Bumke and Reuter against the notion of a unified 'Ritterstand' that it seems timely to warn against the danger of an excessively fragmented view of the knights that might be as far from the historical reality of the twelfth century as the excessively corporate view rejected by these scholars.

Bumke's work has attracted justified criticism on the grounds that, in his intentness on demolishing the myth of a unified noble class of knights, he has underplayed the importance of knighthood as an actual social grouping and placed the knights of his texts, especially in the period up to about 1180, in an unduly modest social condition.[5]

1   Bumke, *Ritterbegriff*, p. 68.
2   Ibid., p. 147.
3   Reuter, *Ritterstand*, passim.
4   Hunt, 'The Emergence of the Knight', p. 16, n. 18.
5   See W. Schröder, 'Zum *ritter*-Bild', passim; Brogsitter, '*Miles*', p. 429.

However, no large-scale new study of the literary evidence about knighthood has replaced Bumke's and Reuter's work,[6] and recent studies of German literature around 1200 often show hesitancy or outright disagreement on the usefulness of the concept of knighthood as a tool for social analysis. Thus at times 'die Ritterwelt' is still seen as a meaningful concept for categorizing the upper part of the lay hierarchy,[7] and 'die ritterliche Gesellschaft' is described as a historically real form of integration of feudal society,[8] whilst elsewhere knighthood is confidently detached from social groupings: 'Above all the concept of a distinct social class or order of knights in twelfth-century Germany, a class related in some way either with an old aristocracy or with the fairly new social category of the *ministeriales*, must be abandoned: it was based on a naive and outmoded tendency to view medieval literature as a faithful reflection of reality. No evidence from that century indicates that the words *ritter* and *miles* were employed to designate members of a real social group, distinguished by legal or social criteria'.[9]

Against this last, extreme pronouncement, which is based on Bumke's and Reuter's work, not on independent historical research, it should be emphasized that, over the past twenty years, a number of major studies, drawing on a wide range of historical sources (especially the use of the terms *miles* and *ministerialis*), have been devoted precisely to the historical reality, the social grouping and the legal connotations of knighthood in Germany from the eleventh to the thirteenth century.[10] From these studies a broad outline emerges of the rise of knighthood as a phenomenon of social history in Germany in this period which may be summarized here, with further discussion of key points to follow later in the chapter.

In the German sources, as elsewhere, knighthood has its roots in military soil, in the practice of mounted warfare: the early knight was a warrior trained to fight on horseback. Eleventh-century sources show an early stage in the formation of chivalry, with the word *miles* referring to the professional warrior vassal, who is often explicitly distinguished

---

[6] Useful commentaries and illustrative texts, however, in Arentzen and Ruberg, *Ritteridee*; also Bumke himself draws heavily on literary texts to provide in many ways a fuller account of knighthood in his *Höfische Kultur* than he did in his earlier *Ritterbegriff*.

[7] Voß, *Artusepik*, p. 108.

[8] Fischer, *Ehre*, p. 189.

[9] Clifton-Everest, *'Ritter* as "rider" ', p. 151. On the unsureness of literary scholars about the referential value of the literary portrayal of knighthood see Schupp, 'Kritische Anmerkungen', p. 408; compare Bumke, *Höfische Kultur*, I, p. 64: 'Wie die Realität des Rittertums zu erfassen und zu interpretieren ist, darüber ist [. . .] noch keine Übereinstimmung erzielt worden'.

[10] See especially Arnold, *German Knighthood*; the work of Fleckenstein listed in the bibliography; and various contributions to Fenske et al. (eds.), *Festschrift Fleckenstein*, especially pp. 549–726. Useful recent comments on Germany in a broader context in Keen, *Chivalry* and Flori, *L'essor*.

from foot-soldiers (*pedites*). The *milites* did not yet form a closed, sharply defined legal class. However, the cost of knightly equipment presupposed considerable inherited wealth, or lordly patronage, and the *milites* of eleventh-century Germany were already an upper layer of society, including nobles, for whom the exercise of military power was a longstanding tradition, and men of lesser birth who made their way up by the use of arms. Knighthood remained primarily a military function during the twelfth century in Germany, but it also acquired more complex social and ideological associations, largely due to the growing importance of social interaction at the lordly courts and to the spread of Christian concepts of military office. In the twelfth century there was still considerable economic and social layering within knighthood, with men of various degrees of birth appearing as *milites*; but the sheer expense of equipment and the need for collective training, together with social interaction at the courts and the Church's preaching of ethical duties common to all *milites*, of whatever status of birth, were also factors that cut across this layering and contributed to a degree of group consciousness. At the same time legislative pronouncements sharpened the class distinctions between *milites* and other groups, especially the peasants, who formed the mass of the population, so that what had been emerging as a *de facto* situation already in the eleventh century (the social superiority of the *milites*, as specialist warriors, over the peasantry) became a legal norm. Lastly, the second half of the twelfth century witnessed an increased penetration of aristocratic principles into the status of knighthood, as great nobles increasingly adopted the title of *miles* in formal knighting ceremonies, and towards the end of the century the socially exclusive tendencies in chivalry were boosted when the granting of knighthood to the sons of peasants and priests was forbidden by law – a move that marked an important stage in the gradual transformation of the originally open military status of knighthood into an inherited nobility.

With regard to south-west Germany, the general area of Hartmann's literary activity, Josef Fleckenstein has traced the social reality and the expansion of the *militia* from the eleventh into the first half of the twelfth century, drawing mainly on the informative chronicles of the monasteries of St Gallen and Zwiefalten.[11] The Zwiefalten chronicles of Ortlieb and Berthold present the knights (*milites, ministeriales*) of the early twelfth century as turbulent warrior vassals seeking to further their own interests by military force.[12] Even the lesser knightly status of *minister-*

---

11  Fleckenstein, 'Vom Rittertum der Stauferzeit am Oberrhein'.
12  See *Zwiefalter Chroniken*, pp. 154f., where the *milites* are described as the main threat to the peace of monasteries, because of their quarrels and their usurpation of monastic property; for ministerial knights usurping (or appropriating) lands of the monastery of Reichenau see Borst, *Mönche am Bodensee*, p. 175.

*ialis* enjoyed considerable social prestige in the early twelfth century, as lower men tried to better their social position by acquiring the rights and dignity associated with knightly arms and the status of 'clientes sive ministeriales'.[13] Fleckenstein also shows how the common military profession and the disciplinary and ethical prescriptions of secular lords and the Church had an integrating effect on the various levels of *milites* to produce, during the twelfth century, 'a consolidated knightly society which is a verifiable historical phenomenon'.[14]

Working in a broader European perspective, Jean Flori also points to the growing prestige of the term *miles* in Latin sources in Germany during the twelfth century.[15] However, citing Bumke and Reuter, he adds that in this period 'le mot *Ritter* n'a le plus souvent aucune signification sociale'.[16] A gap thus exists between historical research based on Latin sources, which points to knighthood as a distinct (if complex) social reality in twelfth-century Germany, and a strand of literary and linguistic research based on vernacular sources, that is to say on the language actually used in everyday life, which seems to attribute far less social reality and content to knighthood. This state of affairs calls for a fresh look at the vernacular evidence in the light of historians' work over the past twenty years. In the rest of this chapter I shall look at the term *ritter*, and at knighthood as a mark of social status, particularly in Hartmann's *Erec*, in the light of the historical evidence; and it will be shown that the vernacular terminology of knighthood, when viewed in the light of historical evidence, is imbued with more social meaning than has sometimes been suggested.

Hartmann's *Erec* and *Iwein* are adaptations of French romances in which the knight was already a central figure. However, the rise of the word *ritter* in German literature during the hundred years before Hartmann's activity indicates that knighthood was not a sudden and purely literary import from France in the late twelfth century, but has roots in German society (though this is not to underestimate the importance of French influence on the development of chivalry in Germany, in a literary and a broader social and cultural sense). Reference has been made to the increased need for specialist mounted warriors in the troubled times of the eleventh century.[17] It is in keeping with this that the German word *ritter* seems to have been a new coining

---

13 *Zwiefalter Chroniken*, p. 48.
14 Fleckenstein, 'Vom Rittertum der Stauferzeit am Oberrhein', p. 39: 'So ist es kein Zufall, daß aus den unterschiedlichen Gruppen eine geschlossene ritterliche Gesellschaft zusammengewachsen ist. Sie ist als solche nicht bestritten und stellt auch ein nachprüfbares historisches Faktum dar.'
15 Flori, *L'essor*, pp. 224, 246f.
16 Ibid., p. 225.
17 See above, pp. 6–8.

of about this time, first appearing in a German text of 1060/1065.[18] From its first appearance the word competed with the older warrior terms *helt*, *degen*, *wîgant*, *recke* and *guoter kneht*. Up to the middle of the twelfth century the word appears seldom, due partly to the religious subject matter of the literature of this period. The generation up to about 1180 shows a marked increase in frequency, then the word proliferates in use from the last two decades of the twelfth century onwards. This increase is evident in the changing relation of the word *ritter* to the older heroic terms, as well as in the rise in absolute numbers of occurrences of *ritter*, and the increase appears in indigenous works such as the epic *Nibelungenlied* as well as in works based on French sources.

The increased frequency of the word *ritter* in poetic texts of the second half of the twelfth century shows a striking chronological alignment with the tendencies towards an ideological integration of the various levels of the *milites*, and with the sharpening of social, even legal, class distinctions between the *milites* and other social groups which are evident in Latin historical sources in the same period in Germany. Various points concerning the social status and the terminology of knighthood in Germany before the time of Hartmann's activity will be considered later in this chapter. Suffice it here to say that when Hartmann embarked on his adaptation of Chrétien's *Erec et Enide*, he did so in a German context in which knighthood was a complex and developing social reality, and in which the figure of the knight was gaining in importance in literature, but still awaited a decisive breakthrough.

This breakthrough came with Hartmann's *Erec*. The word *ritter* occurs more often, both absolutely and relative to the length of the work, in *Erec* than in any earlier German work: the period from about 1060 to about 1180 brings in all some 180 occurrences of the word *ritter* in literary works, whilst Hartmann's *Erec* alone has 134 occurrences.[19] Hartmann also, throughout his works, makes little or no use of the ancient warrior terms which had dominated over *ritter* in earlier literature, and which still led a vigorous life beside *ritter* in the works of many other poets well into the thirteenth century: against 134 occurrences of *ritter*, Hartmann's *Erec* has one of *helt*, eleven of *degen*, none of *wîgant*, and none of *recke*; and his other works show a similar pattern.[20] This preference of *ritter*

---

[18]  See Bumke, *Ritterbegriff*, pp. 21–8; for the following quantitative points see the table of frequencies, ibid., pp. 29–34.

[19]  Ibid., pp. 28, 33.

[20]  See ibid., p. 33. The recently discovered Wolfenbüttel *Erec*-fragments include one occurrence of the word *wîgant* (Er, p. 137, W II, 13: '[die] snellin wig*ande*'). Hartmann's avoidance of *wîgant* elsewhere (noted also by Nellmann, 'Ein zweiter Erec-Roman?', p. 64) would tend to argue against the hypothesis that this fragment represents Hartmann's own work, though too much weight should not be placed on one word. For a discussion of the various hypotheses concerning the Wolfenbüttel fragments see Gärtner, 'Der Text der

over the old warrior terminology has a programmatic quality, and it suggests that Hartmann was far less interested in an ancient concept of warrior heroism than in a modern and evolving social and cultural concept of knighthood. The word *ritter* is also applied more freely to great nobles in *Erec* than in any earlier work, as well as applying still to the lesser serving knights, so that the knightly terminology permeates the aristocratic hierarchy more fully here than ever before in German literature. Finally, the main protagonist is also described as a *ritter* more often in *Erec* than in any earlier work. Quantitatively and qualitatively the term *ritter* thus assumes a centrality in Hartmann's *Erec* which surpasses earlier German literature, but which will be more character-istic of the following generations. Hartmann's first romance holds a key position in the rise of the word *ritter* in German literature, and is indeed an important document in the broader social and ideological history of knighthood.

## Knighthood and military function

It is a feature of Hartmann's style that he presents individual phenomena in relation to general norms more frequently than Chrétien does. As René Pérennec has observed, this tendency is particularly marked in Hartmann's use of the term *ritter*,[21] and this allows us to observe what Hartmann viewed as military, social, behavioural and ethical norms of chivalry.

For both Chrétien and Hartmann knighthood (*chevalerie, ritterschaft*) is still a military function. Knights are men who normally fight on horseback, wearing armour and using lance and sword. The German noun *ritter* derives from the verb *rîten*, 'to ride', and thus shows the intimate connection of knighthood with the equestrian sphere, as does the French word *chevalier*.[22] Particularly in his first romance Hartmann delights in descriptions of chivalric accoutrements. His account of Erec's preparation for the tournament (Er 2285–354) is the most detailed description of knightly equipment in his works, and a revealing indication of what he himself saw as equipment fit for a young princely knight, since he adds it independently of Chrétien's text. Erec takes to the tournament three shields and matching pennants, all with one device but in different colours. A lady's sleeve attached to each shield is a mark of love-service, and the love-motif is developed in the painting of a lady on the inside of the shield. He has five Spanish warhorses. His

Wolfenbütteler Erec-Fragmente', pp. 424–29. On Hartmann's use of the term guoter kneht, see below, pp. 53–55.
21 Pérennec, *Recherches*, I, p. 65.
22 See also Brogsitter, '*Miles*', pp. 429–32; Bumke, *Höfische Kultur*, I, p. 66.

body armour comprises helm, decorated with an angel and a golden crown (Er 2336–38 – an emblem of his future kingship and obedience to God's will), hauberk of mail and mail chausses (Er 2330: 'îserkolzen'). He wears a surcoat over his armour (Er 2339: 'wâpenroc') and his horse has a matching cover, a trapper (Er 2339: 'kovertiure'). He has ten painted lances for each horse. These are transported to the tournament in advance, by cart. His sword is not mentioned in this description but is taken for granted as an essential weapon. He is attended for the tournament by fifteen lightly armed squires (Er 2344: 'knaben'). This equipment is not merely generally of the twelfth century, but is well in advance of that in Geoffrey of Monmouth's *Historia* and fully up to the moment of the last two decades of the century.[23] For instance the horse-cover first appears, according to historians, about 1190,[24] and Hartmann's *Erec* provides the earliest German references (Er 738, 2339, 10025).

Hartmann's interest in recent developments in arms and armour is further documented when he departs from Chrétien to make a contrast between the modern equipment of Iders and the old-fashioned arms which Erec has to borrow from Enite's father, the ageing Coralus (Er 732–50). Mail hauberk, helm and shield remained the chief defensive armour for the knight throughout the twelfth century and beyond. But particularly from the late twelfth century onwards the body armour underwent much change in that it became more comprehensive in its protection, with added cover for legs, hands and face, which in turn allowed for a reduction in the size and weight of the old Norman kite-shaped shield.[25] Protection for the horse also increased from the late twelfth century, for the new decorative horse-cover also had the practical purpose of protecting the horse, particularly when it was placed over mail horse armour, of which there is evidence before the end of the twelfth century.[26] Hartmann encapsulates these important developments in a few lines when he comments that Iders is equipped as a knight should be for combat, with fine armour, surcoat and horse-cover (Er 736–45), whilst Erec and his horse are only imperfectly protected (Er 749: 'halp er und daz ros blôz'), and his shield is old,

---

[23] For developments in knightly equipment in this period see Schultz, *Höfisches Leben*, II, pp. 1–105; Blair, *European Armour*, pp. 19–36; Gamber, 'Bewaffnung'; Bumke, *Höfische Kultur*, I, pp. 210–27.
[24] Gamber, 'Bewaffnung', p. 116.
[25] Blair, *European Armour*, pp. 28–30; Gamber, 'Bewaffnung', pp. 114–16.
[26] *La Chronique de Gislebert de Mons*, p. 197: 'equos ferreis cooperturis ornatos haberent' (s.a. 1187); Ulrich von Zatzikhoven, *Lanzelet* 4414: 'mit einer îsern kovertiure'. See also Blair, *European Armour*, p. 184; Bumke, *Höfische Kultur*, I, pp. 223f.; Davis, *Warhorse*, p. 21. Davis refers to King Richard I's capture of 200 horses from the French in 1198, of which 140 were 'clad in iron' (Roger of Hoveden, *Chronica*, IV, pp. 58f.: 'cooperti de ferro'). The references thus seem to cluster suddenly from the 1180s on.

heavy, long and broad (Er 747: 'sin schilt was alt swære lanc und breit').[27] Hartmann here links one of his favourite literary motifs (the victory of the good man despite physical disadvantage) with a contrast of generations in knightly equipment that would be immediately evident to a contemporary audience.

Hartmann's interest in the functioning of knightly equipment is attested by many other practical details which he adds independently of Chrétien, for instance the knights having their chainmail cleaned and re-strapped before the tournament (Er 2409f.), Erec's pretence that his helm is badly fitting and needs the straps adjusted (Er 3071–76), and the reference to the completeness of Erec's armour as a reason why he fails to see or hear approaching danger (Er 4150–59).[28] The episodes containing these passages (Erec's first combat, the tournament, his departure from his father's court, his journeying with Enite) are all rich in ethical and psychological associations, but each of these situations combines metaphorical connotations with practical military detail in a way which is characteristic of Hartmann's insider treatment of knighthood.

The mere appearance of a mounted man in full armour is sufficient for him to be referred to as a *ritter* in Hartmann's world, even if nothing else is known of his status (e.g. Er 10, 14–17, 3210, 4337). In combat, hauberk, helm, shield, lance and sword form the minimum normal chivalric equipment. When a *ritter* is involved in combat with less than this equipment, Hartmann refers to special factors, as when Galoain and his *ritter* (Er 4244) are in too much of a hurry to put on full defensive armour when pursuing Erec (Er 4107–09, 4213) – a deficit which leads to the count getting a severe side-wound. Figures who use less than this equipment are not normally called *ritter*. The two giants who wear no armour and fight with cudgels (Er 5381–90) are not described as *ritter*, and the fifteen attendants who accompany Erec to the tournament and wear light defensive armour of 'panzier' and 'îsenhuot' (Er 2349) are simply called squires (Er 2344: 'knaben'). This light, evidently sub-chivalric defensive armour of *panzier* and *îsenhuot* is also worn by the robbers whom Enite once refers to as 'ritter' (Er 3186) but whom the narrator calls 'roubære' (Er 3116, 3190, 3229).[29] These are interesting

---

27. On Hartmann's modernity here see also Schultz, *Höfisches Leben*, II, p. 88; Bumke, *Höfische Kultur*, I, p. 218.

28. This last reference presupposes the new style of helm which began to appear towards the end of the twelfth century and provided more complete face covering than the old Norman nasal helm, at the expense of diminished vision and hearing (see Schultz, *Höfisches Leben*, II, pp. 64f., 80); for literary consequences of this and other developments in armour around 1200 see Green, *Recognition*, pp. 264–73.

29. The *îsenhuot* is the 'chapel de fer' or 'kettle-hat', which 'was, above all, the headpiece of the common soldier' (Blair, *European Armour*, p. 32). It should not be confused with the chainmail hood, or coif (Er 952, 2640, 6988, 8966: *hüetelîn* – this appears in German also as *hersenier*) worn by knights under the helm (see Blair, pp. 24, 27f.), or with the helm itself (Er 848 and often: *helm*), both of which are part of prestigious knightly equipment. The

figures on the fringe of the knightly world, and we shall return to them.[30]

The sheer material cost of knightly equipment combined with the connotations of power that were associated with the use of force to ensure that the military function of knighthood was in itself a mark of social prominence. Reliable statistical information is notoriously difficult to gather for the social history of the Middle Ages. Nevertheless, it seems clear that even the basic equipment of the knight as early as the eleventh and early twelfth centuries presupposed a degree of material wealth that surpassed that of the mass of the peasantry.[31] Further, the material cost of equipping and attending a knight rose markedly during the twelfth century as knightly equipment became more elaborate.[32] This involved not only a greater expense of acquisition, but also an added need for support personnel, the squires and servants who become ever more noticeable in attendance on knights the further forward one moves from the eleventh century through to the thirteenth.[33] The amount of land needed to support a knight consequently increased. In England there were knights holding as little as about 1–2 hides in the late eleventh century, but by the late twelfth century 5 hides were deemed necessary to make a knight's fee.[34] In Germany the minimum endowment for a lesser knight was about 3–5 hides in the early twelfth century, but this had risen to four or five times as much a hundred years later.[35]

The increase in the material cost of knighthood seems to accelerate in various parts of Europe from around the middle of the twelfth century, and it contributed powerfully to two tendencies that are important for the sociology of courtly literature. First, as the cost of equipping a knight rose, the numbers of actual knights declined.[36] The greatest expansion of

panzier is defence for the trunk, also worn less by knights than by lightly armed personnel (Schultz, Höfisches Leben, II, p. 49). Hartmann introduces these sub-knightly pieces independently of Chrétien, thus emphasizing the special nature of the knight even as a military figure.

[30] See below, pp. 109–11.

[31] Johrendt, 'Milites' und 'militia', p. 119 estimates the cost of equipment for a knight, including warhorse, in the eleventh century at 250–300 solidi, which was equivalent to ca. 25–30 oxen.

[32] See Harvey, 'The Knight', p. 39. At 5 marks of silver, the cost of a warhorse alone almost equalled the average value of a one-hide peasant farm in twelfth-century Germany (Rösener, 'Ritterliche Wirtschaftsverhältnisse', p. 303).

[33] See Fleckenstein, 'Das Rittertum der Stauferzeit', pp. 103f.; Davis, Warhorse, pp. 23–26. The knight of romance who rides alone, without assistants or spare mounts, is, of course, a literary stylization, not a reflection of military reality.

[34] Harvey, 'The Knight', pp. 14f., 30–36.

[35] Rösener, 'Ritterliche Wirtschaftsverhältnisse', pp. 303–06, 321.

[36] This was a general European phenomenon, see Oman, Art of War, I, p. 372. For England, see the estimates in Denholm-Young, 'Feudal Society', passim; on the decline in the number of knightly families documented in German charters between the twelfth and the late thirteenth century see Rösener, 'Ritterliche Wirtschaftsverhältnisse', p. 335. It has

the *militia* in Germany seems to have been in the late eleventh and early twelfth centuries, while the following generations (which saw the rise of courtly literature) were a period of static or declining numbers of knights, when it was more a matter of knightly families protecting established positions. And second, the rising cost of the knightly lifestyle, and the consequent enlargement of the economic base needed to support it, enhanced the social prestige of knighthood and contributed decisively to the transformation of the knight from a purely professional warrior into a more aristocratic figure.[37] These developments are suggested in Hartmann's descriptions of knightly equipment and in his presentation of knights in social settings in *Erec*.

## Knights in lordly retinues: ritter *and* knehte, ritter *and* vrouwen

As well as being a military function, knighthood had strong connotations of service in the twelfth century. Indeed the military function of knighthood was predominantly a form of service, the service owed by free knights and *ministeriales* to a lord in return for a fief. Institutionally the knight's service of a lord is often expressed in historical sources in terms of his belonging to the lord's *familia*. Benjamin Arnold, writing illuminatingly about the role of knights in the *familia*, points out: 'Familia had no very precise definition, and can inelegantly be translated as household, or retinue, or aggregate dependents of a lord. Used without qualification, *familia* might [. . .] include kindred, friends, and advisers, as well as military retainers of whatever status, clerics high and low, and all those in some way bound or obliged to a lord and protected by him, including the mass of serfs.'[38] The knights formed the military establishment of the *familia*, they were enfeoffed with lands, castles, revenues and offices, had the right to give counsel to the lord, and they performed military service in garrison duties and as cavalry in the field.[39] Key features of this social structure are reflected in Hartmann's *Erec* in an abbreviated and stylized way, as throughout the work *ritter* appear in attendance at courts, in some kind of (usually unspecified) dependence on the lord, as part of his household. The native German term for *familia*

---

been calculated that the total number of those living a knightly life-style in Germany in the twelfth and thirteenth centuries can only have made up about 1% of the population as a whole (Fuhrmann, *Deutsche Geschichte*, p. 197); thus in discussions of the hierarchical levels within knighthood, it should always be remembered that even the lesser knights formed part of an exceedingly narrow upper stratum of German society, which lived off the labour of the vast mass of serfs and peasants.

[37] See also Harvey, 'The Knight', p. 42; Rösener, 'Ritterliche Wirtschaftsverhältnisse', p. 337.
[38] Arnold, *German Knighthood*, pp. 100f.
[39] Ibid., pp. 110f.

was *gesinde* (e.g. Er 1478) or *ingesinde* (e.g. Er 1274), and this term was joined in the late twelfth century by *massenîe* (e.g. Er 1517, 2066), one of a host of borrowings from French at this time relating to chivalry and the court.

Kurt Gärtner has recently studied the French loanwords in Hartmann's *Erec* in an article which makes a number of points that are of particular interest in our context.[40] First, drawing on earlier research, Gärtner observes that the high point in borrowings from French was in the years around 1200, when German literary works based on French sources reflect the great influence of the French language on German, especially in matters relating to aristocratic culture (pp. 76f.). Second, he shows, by a detailed comparison of tournament vocabulary, that the French loanwords in Hartmann's *Erec* are, for the most part, not drawn from Chrétien's work, rather they must have been known to Hartmann and his German audience as borrowings from French into German in the spoken language; in other words, most of the French loanwords in *Erec* show social contact between the aristocracies of France and Germany across linguistic boundaries, and they were probably known in the spoken language of Hartmann's German, aristocratic public even before they appeared in the manuscripts of such romances as *Erec* (pp. 85–88). The finding that the loanwords taken into German from French were often not purely literary borrowings, but known in the spoken language of the German aristocracy, gives further support to one of the main contentions of our study: that Hartmann's concern with knighthood was not a merely literary reception of French chivalry, but was also part of broader social and cultural processes in the actual life of the German aristocracy. The study of courtly and chivalric vocabulary also provides further evidence of the key importance of the last decades of the twelfth century for the development of a knightly ideology and its forms of expression. A final point of interest concerns a difference between Hartmann's two romances, as Gärtner points out (p. 77) that Hartmann's *Iwein* contains far fewer French loanwords than his *Erec* (35 as against 71); it may be added that the fashionable new loanword *massenîe*, which prompted this look at Hartmann's use of borrowings from French, occurs in both works, but only once in *Iwein* (6897) as against eleven times in *Erec*. This retreat of French loanwords in *Iwein* is again symptomatic, it suggests an enthusiasm on Hartmann's part for the latest manifestations of western chivalric culture in his early years, which gives way to a more reserved attitude in his later works.

If we turn to the composition of the *familia*, knights are an important

---

[40] Gärtner, 'Stammen die Lehnwörter Hartmanns aus Chrétien?'. For a general survey of the impact of French vocabulary on German in the Middle Ages, see Öhmann, 'Der romanische Einfluß'.

feature of Arthur's household (Er 1285, 1390, 2129, 5117, 5254, 10078). The knights at Erec's court see him as 'their lord' (Er 3086; compare 2998); knights help 'their lord' (Er 4245), Count Galoain, to pursue Erec; King Guivreiz summons his knights to arms in order to help Erec (Er 6852–55); Count Oringles takes counsel (Er 6194, 6206, 6212: 'rât') with his knights (Er 6183: 'ritter') about marrying; knights accompany their lord for some unspecified purpose (Er 6125–32) or on a hunting party (Er 4629.6ff.), and greet a wounded fellow-knight (Er 5116ff.). Thus in *Erec*, as in the historical reality of Germany in Hartmann's day, there are knights resident at the courts of great lords (for what duration we are not told) who can be mustered as a military force at short notice, and who are involved in counsel and broader social interaction with the lord. The respect enjoyed by knights in lordly retinues is indicated in the fact that they are also referred to as the lord's 'companions' (Er 6186: 'gesellen'), which indicates a fraternal element in the relationship as well as one of superior and inferior.[41]

With regard to the statistics of knighthood, it is worth noting that Hartmann reduces the numbers of knights in attendance on lords in adapting *Erec et Enide*. In Chrétien's text there are 500 noble maidens at Arthur's court, each of whom has a valiant knight as a friend (EeE 50–58), Galoain bursts into Erec's lodging with 100 armed knights (EeE 3523), and Guivret rides to Erec's aid with 1,000 knights and men-at-arms (EeE 4960: 'Serjanz et chevaliers ot mil'), whilst Hartmann tones these figures down to 140 knights at Arthur's Round Table (Er 1697), 19 knights accompanying Galoain (Er 4042) and 30 knights in Guivreiz's party (Er 6855). Too much should not be made of these shifts, but they are consistent, and it is likely, given that Hartmann's numbers are smaller and less conventional than Chrétien's, that Hartmann was deliberately altering Chrétien in the direction of realism, stating in each case numbers that might have seemed plausible in the contemporary reality in contrast with the inflated numbers of knights which are characteristic of the hyperbolic style of the epic tradition and the *romans d'antiquité*, and which still show through to some extent in Chrétien's *Erec*.[42]

It is crucial for an understanding of the social connotations of knighthood in twelfth-century Germany that, even as a term of service, the concept *ritter* enjoyed considerable social prestige, the knights formed an upper level of the lordly household, and the socially

---

[41] The vernacular term *geselle* corresponds to the designation of *milites* as *commilitones* of their lord in Latin chronicles (e.g. *La Chronique de Gislebert de Mons*, pp. 97, 328).

[42] On large numbers of knights in literary works (up to 200,000) see Bumke, *Ritterbegriff*, pp. 59f.; on these numbers as expressions of the past glories of Greece, Rome and the Carolingian period rather than indications of the insignificance of knights in the twelfth-century reality see W. H. Jackson, 'The Concept of Knighthood', pp. 40f.

prestigious connotations of knighthood became increasingly marked in vernacular sources in the second half of the twelfth century. Some light is thrown on this process by the new pairings *ritter unde vrouwen* and *ritter unde knehte*. Edward Schröder observed that the emergence of these new pairings reflected linguistically the consolidation of knighthood as a social status or class (a 'Ritterstand'), and an enhanced social prestige of the word *ritter* from about the middle of the twelfth century onwards.[43] Bumke is less inclined to see a prestigious social demarcation of knighthood in these groupings.[44] However, a fresh look at the vernacular usage in the light of historical evidence suggests that Schröder's view has much to recommend it.

The relation of the words *ritter* and *kneht* is a complex and dynamic one that touches on central points in the terminological and social history of knighthood.[45] The word *kneht*, English *cniht*, is of obscure origin, and common to the West Germanic languages. Its earliest attestations in Old English and Old High German point to 'boy', 'youth', 'lad' as a primary meaning, but the word was quickly associated with service, as 'servant', 'attendant', and specifically with military service. In England *cniht* took a socially upward semantic path, for it was used after the Conquest as an equivalent of the French *chevalier*, and the word *cniht* then acquired aristocratic connotations, along with the Latin *miles* and the continental vernacular terms *chevalier* and *ritter*, so that its original humbler and more junior senses had to be taken over by other words. There seems to have been some competition between *cniht* and *ridere* for the sense of 'knight' in early twelfth-century English, for both terms appear in the *Anglo-Saxon Chronicle*.[46] There was semantic competition in German too between *kneht* and *ritter* in the emerging terminology of knighthood, for the German word *kneht* occasionally appears in the general sense of 'warrior' or 'knight' in the late eleventh and early twelfth centuries.[47] However, already in this period the sense of 'warrior' or 'knight' is conveyed less often by *kneht* standing alone than by *kneht* in combination with a eulogizing adjective, usually the adjective *guot*. This use of an emphatic adjective is not merely a poetic adornment, but also a reflection of the social climate of the war-ridden late eleventh century, when the armed warrior already commanded a privileged position in lordly retinues. He was not merely an 'ordinary' youth or retainer, but a 'good' or 'select' one.

It is essential for an understanding of the further development of the

---

[43]   E. Schröder, 'Datierung', pp. 295f.
[44]   Bumke, *Ritterbegriff*, pp. 37, 55, 63f.
[45]   See W.H. Jackson, 'Verhältnis von *ritter* und *kneht*', with further bibliography.
[46]   *The Peterborough Chronicle*, pp. 9, 21; see Clark, 'Studies', p. 84; Flori, *L'essor*, pp. 59–61.
[47]   *Annolied* 20,7; *Vorauer Alexander* 1453f.; see also Bumke, *Ritterbegriff*, p. 88.

words *ritter* and *kneht* in the later twelfth and into the thirteenth century to distinguish firmly between the simple noun *kneht* and the adjective-noun combination *guoter kneht*. For whereas even great lords in manhood are referred to as *guote knehte* still into the thirteenth century, it is only in very exceptional circumstances, such as in relation to God, that such men are described simply as *knehte*.[48] As regards the relation of *kneht* and *ritter*, the German development follows a quite different course from the English one after the early twelfth century. Whereas the English *cniht* acquired more prestigious connotations, leaving *ridere* ultimately with the purely functional sense of 'rider', in German it was *ritter* that took the higher road and acquired the prestigious, 'knightly' senses, while *kneht* was held down to senses of subordination or tutelage. Already during the twelfth century the words *ritter* and *kneht* became increasingly distinct from each other, for just as *kneht* had for long, as a term of subordination, been distinct from *herre* ('lord'), so it became distinct from and subordinated to the new word *ritter*. A functional hierarchy thus emerged in the twelfth century, with *ritter* establishing itself in a higher position, as the fully armed, mounted warrior, an upper figure in lordly retinues, and the noble who has undergone a knighting ritual, whilst *kneht* remained connected with subjugation in its opposition to *herre*, and now to *ritter*, having the senses of boy, lad, male servant or attendant, and, in the aristocratic sphere, the sense of youth of knightly birth who has not yet been knighted. With this combination of humble and aristocratic elements, the German word *kneht* shares a fundamental similarity with the terms for 'squire' in other parts of Europe in the twelfth and thirteenth centuries,[49] terms which are notoriously difficult to render without distortion by present-day words.

Hartmann is typical of his time in distinguishing between *ritter* and *knehte* and in according less honourable, more menial tasks to the latter than the former. For instance in *Erec* two *knehte* administer a beating at Erec's command (Er 1065), a *kneht* (Er 3522, 3542, 3546, 3558) carries food and water for a washing of hands, Oringles's *knehte* (Er 6309) cut branches for a bier, Guivreiz's *knehte* (Er 7080) prepare bivouacs for Erec, Enite, Guivreiz and the knights accompanying them, and time and again the tending of horses appears as the task of a *kneht* (Er 350–65, 3272–76, 3431f., 3454–59, 4002f., 4103f., 7364f.). By contrast, *ritter* ride independently across the lands (Er 5ff., 5649ff.), accompany ladies on social visits of an evening (Er 1389ff.), appear as guests at a prince's wedding feast (Er 2129), and fight in armour,

---

[48]  See also Bumke, *Ritterbegriff*, pp. 88f.; W.H. Jackson, 'Verhältnis von *ritter* und *kneht*', pp. 24–26.
[49]  On these see Bennet, 'The Status of the Squire'; Paterson, 'The Occitan Squire'.

using the aristocratic weapons of sword and lance in serious combats (e.g. Er 732–950, 4378–438, 9070–315) and in the tournament (Er 2413–807), at which *knaben*, 'squires' appear carrying clubs in a subordinate capacity (Er 2344–50).

This constellation of *ritter* and *kneht* in Hartmann's work corresponds to the elevation of *chevalier* above *serjant* and *escuiier* in Chrétien's *Erec et Enide*. Indeed, Hartmann's reference to 'ritter unde knehte' at Erec's court (Er 2975) is based on Chrétien's comment: 'Tant fu blasmez de totes janz, / De chevaliers et de serjanz' (EeE 2463f.); and Galoain's servant, or squire, who is referred to in Hartmann's text as a *kneht* (Er 3522, 3542, 3546, 3558) and as a *knabe* (Er 3491, 3499, 3510, 3541, 3575) and whom Erec addresses as 'knabe' (Er 3559, 3590, 3599) appears in Chrétien's text as an *escuiiers* (EeE 3124, 3131, 3168, 3170, 3179, 3209, 3216) and a *serjanz* (EeE 3165, 3233), and is clearly in neither author's view a knight. Moreover, this correspondence of Hartmann and Chrétien on the hierarchy of *ritter* and *kneht* does not indicate that we are dealing solely with a literary borrowing from France, or with a social gradation that would have seemed foreign to Hartmann's German audience, for historical sources in twelfth century Germany also raise the knights, that is to say *milites* or *ministeriales*, above *servi*, *famuli*, *armigeri* – all terms which correspond to the vernacular *kneht*. As early as 1084 a Saxon peace-edict distinguishes between the three categories 'nobilis', 'liber aut ministerialis', 'servus'.[50] A few decades later Honorius Augustodunensis distinguishes between 'liberi', 'milites' and 'servi';[51] and in the 1160s the chronicle of Ebersheimmünster states that the service owed by the 'minores milites' is of an honourable nature and raises them above the servile tasks of 'servi ac famuli'.[52] The disciplinary measures for Barbarossa's army in 1158 distinguish between 'miles' and 'servus' in the type of punishment,[53] and his peace-edict of 1186 excludes the 'servus' from knightly privileges.[54] In narrative sources too, *servi* appear as subordinate to the *milites*. In Barbarossa's march on Milan in July 1158 the 'milites' lead the way, whilst the 'servi' bring along the knights' baggage in the company of the 'pedites'.[55] Later the 'milites' arm themselves, whilst 'servi' prepare dry wood to make fire.[56] And in the account of a military engagement in 1164 Helmold of Bosau tells how 'servi', who are also called 'armigeri' and 'pueri', tend the horses and are protected from attack by their lords ('domini'), the

---

50  MGH Const., I, no. 426, cc. 2, 6 (p. 608).
51  *De imagine mundi*, MPL, 172, col. 166.
52  MGH Scriptores, 33, p. 432.
53  Otto of Freising and Rahewin, *Gesta Frederici*, III, 31, pp. 456, 458.
54  MGH Const., I, no. 318, c. 20 (p. 452): 'servus autem omni iure milicie privetur'.
55  Otto of Freising and Rahewin, *Gesta Frederici*, III, 38, p. 474.
56  Ibid., III, 42, p. 480.

'milites'.[57] Latin chronicles and normative legal sources thus confirm and flesh out what the German vernacular texts say about the relation of *ritter* and *knehte* in the twelfth century. The chronological parallel is perhaps even closer, for the distinction between *miles* and *servus* seems to be made with particular sharpness and frequency in the second half of the century. This coincides with the sharper demarcation of *ritter* and *kneht* in the vernacular texts, and again suggests the development of an enhanced sense of prestige amongst the knights in this period.

Whereas Hartmann thus distinguishes *ritter* from *kneht*, he nevertheless applies the term *guoter kneht* precisely to knights. Indeed all the named persons whom Hartmann describes as *guote knehte* are also described as *ritter*, so that the term *guoter kneht* appears in his works as an alternative expression for *ritter*, 'knight'.[58] This use of *guoter kneht* throws light on the developing vocabulary of knighthood in Hartmann's day. It has been suggested that the use of *guoter kneht* beside the privileged term *ritter* perhaps introduces a certain vagueness into the socially referential quality of Hartmann's knightly terminology.[59] However, a more satisfactory explanation is probably that the conjoint use of *ritter* and *guoter kneht*, rather than indicating some social imprecision of the term *ritter*, shows that *guoter kneht* has become quite detached from the simple (and less elevated) noun *kneht*. Further, *guoter kneht* was in any case becoming less frequently used, was becoming an archaism already in Hartmann's day. These points deserve some elaboration.

From the earliest occurrences of the word *ritter*, it competed with *guoter kneht* in the developing semantic field of knighthood. For about a century, up to the 1170s, available statistical evidence suggests a slight but consistent preponderance of *guoter kneht*, with a *ritter* : *guoter kneht* ratio averaging 0.7 : 1.[60] Then in the decades from about 1170/1180 onwards, *guoter kneht* retreats sharply relative to *ritter*, with the period ca. 1170–ca. 1200 producing a *ritter* : *guoter kneht* ratio of 7.9 : 1, and the period ca. 1200–ca. 1220 a further slide to 35.7 : 1. Later in the thirteenth century *guoter kneht* figures only rarely, *ritter* over a hundred times more often. Significantly, *guoter kneht* behaves quite differently from the other heroic terms in relation to *ritter*, for once *ritter* has gained the upper hand over *guoter kneht* in the later twelfth century, *guoter kneht* becomes a rarity even in works in which the older heroic terms, especially *helt* and *degen*, continue to appear frequently. This suggests that we are

---

[57] Helmold of Bosau, *Chronica Slavorum*, p. 350; for *servi* as the Latin equivalent of *knehte* or *knappen* who serve a knight, see Arnold of Lübeck's Latin translation of Hartmann's *Gregorius*, where *knehte* is translated as *servi* (see critical apparatus to line 1723 in the Paul / Wachinger edition of *Gregorius*).

[58] See also Pérennec, *Recherches*, I, p. 68.

[59] Ibid., I, pp. 69–71.

[60] Evidence based on lists of occurrences in Bumke, *Ritterbegriff*, pp. 32–34; the following *ritter* : *guoter kneht* ratios are tabulated in more detail in W.H. Jackson, 'Aspects', p. 54.

witnessing not so much an undifferentiated competition between *ritter* and the old heroic terms in general, but specifically one between *ritter* and *guoter kneht*, in which *guoter kneht* goes into a fairly sudden and consistent decline when *ritter* makes its sharp ascent in literary works in the last decades of the twelfth century.

Hartmann's *œuvre* reflects the key transitional stage in this process, for the distribution of the 25 occurrences of *guoter kneht* in Hartmann shows that he himself used the term less with the passage of time. Here again Hartmann's works give us a detailed insight into the terminology of knighthood at an important stage in its development. Already in *Erec* Hartmann uses *guoter kneht* less often, relative to *ritter*, than was the practice of authors earlier in the century, the *ritter* : *guoter kneht* ratio of 6.7 : 1 in *Erec* (134 *ritter*, 20 *guoter kneht*) closely matching the average of 7.9 : 1 for the period ca. 1170–ca. 1200. *Guoter kneht* figures even less often in Hartmann's later works, never in *Gregorius* and *Der arme Heinrich*, and only five times in *Iwein*, where the *ritter* : *guoter kneht* ratio has slipped to 16.6 : 1 (83 ritter, 5 *guoter kneht*). Thus 80% of the occurrences of *guoter kneht* in Hartmann's works figure in his first romance, *Erec*. Further, of the 20 occurences in *Erec*, 10 appear in the first quarter of the work (Er 17, 700, 835, 903, 1502, 1615, 1629, 1790, 2070, 2384); of the 25 occurences of *guoter kneht* in Hartmann's work as a whole, 23 are in the rhyme, and the only two internally in the line (and thus without a possible technical motivation) are in the first third of *Erec* (Er 17, 3112). We thus have a clear pattern of Hartmann using the term *guoter kneht* more often in the opening stages of his first romance than he ever does later. This higher frequency of *guoter kneht* in the early stages of *Erec* surely shows that here Hartmann is still finding his feet stylistically, he is still drawing on an older stylistic tradition to use quite frequently a term which was already on the retreat and which he himself will use less often later in the very same work. The appearance of *guoter kneht* in a rhyming position in all its occurrences in Hartmann after line 3112 of *Erec* indicates a major reason why this term survived as long as it did, i.e. its convenience in providing a rhyme (especially with *reht*). Conversely *ritter* is extremely difficult to accommodate in a rhyme,[61] and its prolific use in rhymed poetry from the last decades of the twelfth century onwards despite this encumbrance testifies to the strength of the socio-cultural impetus that was driving this word.

Whereas the relation of the terms *ritter* and *kneht* shows knighthood acquiring an increasingly prestigious social sense by a hierarchical opposition, the pairing *ritter unde vrouwen* shows the same development

---

[61] Hartmann rhymes *ritter* only once (with *bitter*, Gr 1503f.), Wolfram von Eschenbach, Gottfried von Straßburg and Rudolf von Ems never (Wießner / Burger, 'Die höfische Blütezeit', pp. 216f.).

in a hierarchical association. The word *vrouwe* still belonged in an elevated social sphere in the twelfth century, denoting 'lady' or 'mistress', whilst the generic term for 'woman', and the term used for humbler women, was *wîp*. Hartmann himself plays on the difference of social level between *vrouwe* and *wîp*, with a critical view of the arrogance of the aristocratic *vrouwe*, in a well-known song.[62] Chrétien frequently associates *chevalier* and *dame* (e.g. EeE 1295, 1436, 2745, 4743, 5541, 6913). However, the pairing *ritter unde vrouwen* first appears, about the middle of the twelfth century, in German texts which were not based on French sources (*Kaiserchronik* 4209, 5765; *König Rother* 278), so that here again we are dealing not merely with a foreign import, but with a usage that also relates to the German reality. In Hartmann's *Erec*, 'ritter unde vrouwen' are onlookers whom combatants seek to impress (Er 651), guests at feasts to celebrate Erec's victory (Er 1390) and his crowning (Er 10078), and friends at Arthur's court who visit the wounded hero (Er 5254) and bid him and Enite a tearful farewell (Er 5278). This deployment of *ritter unde vrouwen* as a stock phrase in *Erec* is typical of the German usage of Hartmann's day, and shows that the word *ritter* was reaching out beyond the military sense of 'mounted warrior' to indicate a more general social status that commanded respect at court and was associated with the leisure activities of aristocratic life.[63]

Translated into terms of social history, the semantic relations of *ritter* to *kneht* and to *vrouwe* in Hartmann's *Erec* and in other literary works of the late twelfth century, far from suggesting a lack of social content and reference, indicate rather an enrichment of social meaning and an enhancement of social prestige in the term *ritter* and in the institution of knighthood. Moreover, the fact that the older warrior terms *helt*, *degen*, *recke*, and *wîgant* did not establish themselves in stock phrases linked with words for other social categories (such as *kneht* and *vrouwe*) indicates that they were restricted primarily to the military, heroic sphere and lacked the contemporary social connotations which underpinned the rise of the word *ritter*. Finally, the retreat of *guoter kneht* in Hartmann's works, like his comments on obsolete armour, show Hartmann as an accurate reflector of contemporary developments in chivalric forms.

### Knighthood and social differentiation in the twelfth century: ritters name

The findings of the last section were based on the position of knights in lordly retinues. These can now be expanded by a consideration of the

---

[62]  MF 216,29ff; see below, pp. 181f.
[63]  On the pairing of *ritter* and *vrouwen* as evidence of an elevated status of knighthood in poetry before Hartmann, see W. Schröder, 'Zum *ritter*-Bild', pp. 343–46, 349f.

expression *ritters name*, which allows us to view knighthood in relation to other social groups in the broader perspective of the population at large.

The expression *ritters name* provides useful information about social and ethical norms of knighthood in Hartmann's works and elsewhere in the literature of the period. In the two occurrences of the term in Hartmann's *Erec*, it is the notion of privileged treatment for the knight that is uppermost (Er 4201, 5468). The second of these occurrences is in the account of Cadoc's captivity, an episode which is revealing for the social ideology of the work, since it shows programmatically a knight being ill-treated by two non-knightly figures (the giants) and rescued by the hero-knight (Erec), who sends Cadoc on his way to Arthur's court, the place *par excellence* of knightly honour. The giants are shown mercilessly whipping Cadoc as he rides bound and naked before them (Er 5378–428). Already Chrétien's Erec reproves the giants for treating a knight (EeE 4413: 'chevalier') so basely (EeE 4415: 'si vilainnemant'). Hartmann takes up this point by commenting that the giants offended against chivalric norms (Er 5412: 'ritters reht') by treating a knight in this way, and like Chrétien he has Erec admonish the giants for failing to show the respect due to a knight (Er 5468–70: 'hât dirre man ritters namen, / so möhtet ir iuch immer schamen / daz er des niht geniuzet'). Indeed this episode seems calculated not only, perhaps not even primarily, as a criticism of brutality against a human being in general, but specifically to make the point that it is a breach of civilized norms to strip and beat someone who belongs to the category 'knight'.

Knighthood is thus associated in Chrétien's and Hartmann's accounts with a norm of more respectful treatment than can be expected by other persons, and this is in itself a kind of social demarcation and categorization.[64] Further, when Chrétien and Hartmann present it as particularly humiliating that a knight should suffer the indignity as well as the pain of being whipped, their implied norms correspond to those of contemporary society, for time and again corporal punishments with lash or rod appear in historical sources as dishonouring, servile punishments, 'Knechtesstrafen'.[65] For instance in the disciplinary measures for Barbarossa's army in 1158, a breach of camp discipline is punishable by the forfeiture of arms and exclusion from the army in the case of a knight ('miles'), whilst a subordinate 'servus' (who would be called a *kneht* in the vernacular) may be shorn, flogged and branded on the cheek.[66] Thus the line of dignity which is drawn in Hartmann's *Erec*

---

[64] On the socially demarcating function of *ritters name* and *ritters reht* in this episode see also Voß, *Artusepik*, pp. 107f.; Pérennec, *Recherches*, I, pp. 65–68.

[65] Schnelbögl, *Bayerische Landfrieden*, p. 133.

[66] Otto of Freising and Rahewin, *Gesta Frederici*, III, 31, p. 456. The thrashing dealt out to Iders's dwarf on Erec's instruction is typical of this kind of punishment (Er 1064–77).

between knights and non-knights is not a merely poetic matter, but has its parallel in the sober language of legal sources.

The first occurrence of *ritters name* (Er 4201) comes in a heated exchange of words between Erec and Count Galoain (Er 4166-204), and is all the more revealing for the German context because this exchange is Hartmann's own composition, it has no precedent in Chrétien's text. Also, Hartmann leads up to the exchange differently from Chrétien by having Enite tell the count a fabricated story, that Erec is her social inferior who abducted her as a young girl from the court of her noble father, and who in consequence has been outlawed from his homeland and now leads an errant existence, all the while ill-treating her (Er 3865f.) – Hartmann seems fascinated by social parities and disparities, a point we shall return to in this and in later chapters. In Hartmann's version, the count thus believes Erec to be an upstart adventurer who has criminally abducted a noble girl, and he addresses him brusquely, as a common thief (Er 4172: 'arger diep') who is trying to escape under cover of darkness (Er 4183f.). Nevertheless, Galoain says that because Erec is a knight, he will not hang him for his crime but let him go if he will hand over Enite (Er 4179–81: 'wan daz ir geniezet / daz ir ritter sît genant, / ich hieze iuch hâhen hie zehant'). There can be no question of the term *ritters name* referring to ethical norms of chivalry here, for Galoain firmly believes Erec to be a felon; rather the mere fact of being a knight, in this case even supposedly a criminal abductor, gives a man a greater degree of privilege than the count would grant to a non-knight. Precisely the absence of an ethical dimension in the count's attitude throws the privilege of knighthood into sharp relief here as a matter of social status. And just as the giants' cruelty is presented as a crime specifically against the social category of knights, so Erec, in his response to Galoain, reproves the count specifically for his insulting and offensive behaviour towards a knight (Er 4199–201: 'von wem habet ir die lêre / daz ir scheltet einen man / der ie ritters namen gewan?'). Erec is surely speaking for Hartmann here. In Hartmann's eyes, a proper social education evidently involves learning to be polite to men who are called 'knights', and this insight into the forms of social communication again endows knighthood with a distinct social presence.

Even Bumke, who is sceptical about the social distinctiveness of knighthood, concedes that there is always something distinctive and prestigious about the term *ritters name*.[67] This view is born out by the two German literary works in which the term appears prior to Hartmann's *Erec* – the adventure epic *König Rother* (ca. 1150/1160) and the verse chronicle, the *Kaiserchronik* (completed between 1147 and ca. 1165). In *König Rother*, when the eponymous hero shows his generosity towards

---

67 Bumke, *Ritterbegriff*, pp. 130f.

needy folk, he singles out those who have 'ritaris namen', i.e. knights, and treats them with special favour, giving them warhorses and other equipment (Rother 1331–46).[68] This is a typical gesture of wealthy lordship towards knighthood in twelfth-century poetic and historical sources,[69] and it indicates that even in the scale of lordly largesse, knights occupied a privileged place among the laity. The comment that the knights were 'separated out' from other folk (Rother 1332: 'Die sundirte man dan') is a sociologically revealing gesture of selection and privilege or favour, such as one meets often in connection with knights in German poetic texts of the twelfth and thirteenth centuries – knights tend to be favoured by magnates and included in the exercise of lordship.

The Kaiserchronik throws more detailed light on social ties and social groupings in the middle of the twelfth century in southern Germany, and the work has two revealing occurrences of ritters name. On the first occasion the term is associated with a reference to feudal tenure, when the Bavarian duke Adelger orders his people to support him in the shame that has been done to him by the Roman emperor (Kaiserchronik 6796–806). Unfortunately the precise sense of the passage is obscure, for in the formulation 'swelhe lêhenreht wolten haben / oder ritteres namen' (ibid. 6800f.) it is not clear whether the 'oder' has a linking or a separating function, and thus not clear whether the granting of knighthood is co-terminous with the granting of a fief, or something separate.[70] But whichever way the passage is interpreted, it is clear that those called 'knights' are figures of leading importance in the Bavarian ducal lordship. In the second occurrence the knights, those who have 'rîteres namen' (ibid. 8104), are associated with dukes and counts and share with them the privilege of wielding the sword and the attendant duty of protecting Christendom (ibid. 8096–110). This warrior group is also distinguished from the other lay groups of 'bûliute' and 'choufman' (ibid. 8112), that is to say from the peasants, who formed the vast mass of the population in twelfth-century Germany, and merchants, who with the economic expansion of the time were becoming sufficiently numerous and important in the body politic to be recognized as a distinct social category. Later in the Kaiserchronik (14791–814) it is recorded that peasants should wear only modest clothes, black or grey in colour, and should be forbidden from carrying the sword, which earlier (ibid. 8106) was defined as the privilege of knightly status.

In the Kaiserchronik the definition of the duties of military status, and the attendant categorization of lay society into knights, peasants and

---

68  See also W. Schröder, 'Zum ritter-Bild', p. 350.
69  See above, pp. 5f., 27, 35.
70  See the discussion of this unclarity in Bumke, Ritterbegriff, p. 48, n. 41.

merchants, are projected back into the past and seen in a great two-stage historical movement, first as the emperor Constantine's reform of Roman society by legal decree (*Kaiserchronik* 8099: 'phahte'), and then as Charlemagne's renewal of this 'pfahte Constantînî' (ibid. 14783), which had supposedly fallen into disuse. However, in a way that is typical of the twelfth century, the author of the *Kaiserchronik* is in fact revising Roman and Carolingian history in the light of contemporary notions of Christian chivalry and social organization, and seeking 'mythical historical prototypes for contemporary institutions and ideals'.[71] The *Kaiserchronik* here captures a process of social differentiation which is of the utmost importance in the history of knighthood. From the late eleventh century onwards, legal and other historical sources show knighthood and peasantry becoming ever more sharply differentiated from each other, and acquiring increasingly well-defined social and juridical class characteristics.[72] The material cost of knightly equipment, as we have seen, outstripped the economic means of the mass of the peasantry; and with the growing importance of mounted warfare the knights acquired class characteristics, first in a military sense, as specialist warriors, then gradually also in broader social and legal senses. This process, which coincides chronologically with the emergence and spread of the word *ritter* in German poetic sources from the late eleventh century onwards, is reflected in legal texts in the gradual displacement of the older, early medieval distinction between *liber* and *servus* (freeman and serf) in favour of the new opposition of *miles* and *rusticus* (knight and peasant). Already the Saxon peace edict of 1084 has the new opposition *miles* and *rusticus* beside that of *liber* and *servus*.[73] This text thus bears early witness to a new tendency to categorize lay society into 'knights' and 'peasants' rather than 'freemen' and 'serfs', though the older system continued for long to run beside the new. Then Barbarossa's peace edict *De pace tenenda* of 1152, the first year of his reign, distinguishes between knight ('miles'), peasant ('rusticus') and merchant ('mercator'), with knights and peasants being subject to different legal procedures (to the disadvantage of the peasants), and peasants and merchants subject to more stringent restrictions than knights in the carrying of arms.[74] It is a matter of debate whether the passages in the *Kaiserchronik* relating to the distinction of knights from peasants (and from merchants) derive from this edict of 1152, or perhaps

---

[71] Ashcroft, '*Miles Dei – gotes ritter*', p. 56; compare the mythical account of the Roman origins of the German *principes* and *minores milites* in the Ebersheimmünster chronicle (see above, p. 34).

[72] See Fleckenstein, 'Zur Frage der Abgrenzung von Bauer und Ritter', passim; Rösener, 'Bauer und Ritter', passim.

[73] MGH Const., I, no. 426, cc. 6, 10 (pp. 608f.).

[74] MGH Const., I, no. 140, cc. 10, 12, 13 (pp. 197f.); see Otto, 'Abschließung', pp. 20–23.

from a lost local Bavarian law based on this edict, or whether the *Kaiserchronik* precedes Barbarossa's legislation.[75]

What is clear is that the decades around the middle of the twelfth century were a period of increasingly marked social differentiation according to Latin and vernacular sources. Precisely in the legislation of Barbarossa's reign (1152–1190), which was also a key period in the formation of vernacular courtly literature, considerations of social status ('ständerechtliche Gesichtspunkte') came sharply to the fore, particularly with the aim of establishing a sharp distinction between knighthood and peasantry.[76] Further, there is a historically symptomatic parallel between Barbarossa's edict of 1152 and the prescriptions on social organization attributed in the *Kaiserchronik* to Constantine and Charlemagne, for in both cases the ordering of society is decreed by the king (or emperor-elect) working within a Christian, metaphysical framework – the preface to Barbarossa's *De pace tenenda* speaks of the emperor's intention to fortify 'divine and human laws',[77] and in the *Kaiserchronik* each of the reforming emperor-kings, Constantine and Charlemagne, works in harmony with the pope (*Kaiserchronik* 8084–134, 14779–90).[78] A complex of ideas thus emerges in the middle of the twelfth century in Germany in which the contemporary Hohenstaufen emperor, Frederick I, could be seen as renewing the ancient imperial decrees of Constantine and Charlemagne, not least of all as regards the status of knighthood.

These factors indicate that the formation of a knightly class (a *Ritterstand*), the contours of which were emerging with ever greater clarity by the middle of the twelfth century, was a complex development involving the self-assertive drive of a specialist warrior class (whose military function presupposed access to a considerable material base), and the efforts of secular rulers and the Church to harness this drive. Only at the intersection of these lines of force can the development of a social ideology of chivalry be fully understood. Further, the historical evidence shows that the rise of knighthood in twelfth-century Germany, far from being purely a poetic or abstract cultural matter, was part of a broad process of social differentiation involving economic, military, legal, political, cultural and religious factors. The linguistic expression of this social differentiation is that, just as Latin sources set *milites* apart from *servi*, *rustici* and *mercatores*, so German vernacular texts from the middle of the twelfth century onwards, as a matter of course, set *ritter* off from *knehte*, *bûliute / gebûre* and *koufman*. Thus the usage of the

---

[75]   Possibilities discussed by Schnell, *ZfdPh* 99 (1980), 436.
[76]   Gernhuber, *Landfriedensbewegung*, p. 136.
[77]   MGH Const., I, no. 140, p. 195: 'tam divinas quam humanas leges'.
[78]   On the cooperation of emperor and pope in the *Kaiserchronik* see Wattenbach / Schmale, *Geschichtsquellen*, I, pp. 44f.

*Kaiserchronik* points the way to the future. For instance a collection of sermons in a manuscript dating probably from the beginning of the second half of the twelfth century contains a sermon addressed to the various social estates of 'riter', 'chouflute' and 'bulute'.[79] In his adaptation of the French *Roman d'Eneas*, Heinrich von Veldeke independently lists as distinct categories 'riddere ende gebure, / knechte ende koufman' (*Eneide* 9250f.). Some time between 1190 and 1217, Herbort von Fritzlar refers in his adaptation of the *Roman de Troie* to 'knecht', 'gebur' and 'koufman' as not being of knightly status, not 'ritters genoz' (*Liet von Troye* 9856-59). And the moralist and commentator on contemporary German society, Thomasin von Zerklaere, writing ca. 1215/1216 lists as lay social groups 'ritter', 'kneht', 'gebûr', 'koufman' and 'wercman' (*Der wälsche Gast* 2639-58), thus adding to the by now familiar list of knights, peasants and merchants the further lay category of artisans.

From the late eleventh century onwards, and with increasing vigour from the middle of the twelfth century, Latin and vernacular historical and literary sources of the most varied kinds (imperial laws, regional laws, chronicles, poetico-historical works, sermons) thus distinguish in Germany between knights and persons belonging to other social groups. This suggests that in Hartmann's view, and on the horizon of expectation of his audience, knights formed an actual social category that was distinct from other social categories even in legal status, and that was (as we shall see in more detail in the next section) becoming more exclusive as a matter of legal norm. The expression *ritters name*, and such related terms as *ritters ambet*, *ritters reht*, *ritters leben* often have ethical connotations, referring to chivalry as an ethical task.[80] Hartmann himself will use *ritters name* in a strongly ethical sense in *Iwein*.[81] But these terms were also indicators of social status in twelfth-century Germany, and in so far as they are ethically or ideologically loaded terms, they denote standards of behaviour which were linked as ideal desiderata to that social status. In other words the ethical duties of chivalry were connected with a social group. The ethical dimension of the expression *ritters name*, and of knightly terminology in general, presupposes – and reinforces ideologically – the existence of a social category and cannot properly be understood in isolation from that category.

It is true that *ritter* are not as explicitly distinguished from persons belonging to other categories, for instance peasants and merchants, in

---

[79] *Speculum ecclesiae*, no. 60, pp. 138-43; on 'die Ritterschaft als Stand' in this sermon see Brogsitter, 'Miles', p. 430.
[80] See Bumke, *Ritterbegriff*, pp. 131f.
[81] See below, pp. 229-32.

Hartmann's *Erec* as in many other works of the period.[82] However, this does not suggest that there is, after all, some vagueness in the social reference of the term *ritter* in *Erec*, but is due to the fact that this romance has a narrower angle of social vision than the other texts we have just considered. Barbarossa's peace laws take into consideration the entire population, as do the sermon on the social estates in the *Speculum ecclesiae*, and Thomasin von Zerklaere's comments on this subject. The historical perspectives of the *Kaiserchronik*, Veldeke's *Eneide* and Herbort's *Liet von Troye* too are broad enough to allow at least marginal reference to peasants and merchants. Hartmann's *Erec* has a narrower social perspective, focussing intensely on the knightly hero and his partner, and if knights are not explicitly set off against peasants and merchants, it is simply because these groups are never mentioned in this work.

Already Chrétien's *Erec et Enide* concentrates on the hero and his partner, and Hartmann goes even further in limiting the narrative perspective to the knightly world. For instance when Erec returns to his homeland of Carnant, Chrétien conjures up a flourishing town and castle with its surrounding forests and fertile vineyards, fields and gardens (EeE 2318–21), and a broad social spectrum of elegant clerks freely spending their incomes (EeE 2324f.: 'De jantis clers bien afeitiez, / Qui bien despandoient lor rantes'; compare EeE 2334, 2340), and wealthy burghers (EeE 2327: 'borjois posteïz'; compare EeE 2345, 2389) beside the ladies and knights (EeE 2322: 'dames et chevaliers'; compare EeE 2334, 2345, 2389). Chrétien may have had in mind here an actual princely residence such as that of the counts of Champagne in the prosperous trading town of Troyes. Be that as it may, this passage conveys the sense of a broad social perspective which is rarely made so explicit in Chrétien's *Erec*, but which one senses more often at an implicit level. At the corresponding point in his adaptation, Hartmann passes over the mass reception for Erec and Enite in a few lines (Er 2892–903), referring only briefly and generally to King Lac's kinsfolk and vassals (Er 2894: 'mâge unde man'), and omitting Chrétien's evocation of non-knightly groups.

Hartmann's abbreviation of the social spectrum is here all the more striking because he has, just before this passage, massively expanded Chrétien's account of the tournament, which is a central feature of the knightly experience,[83] and straight after his abbreviated rendering of Erec's reception, he will show a much more expansive interest in the next stage of the theme of knighthood, Erec's neglect of active chivalry for the marital bed, and his departure in pursuit of *âventiure* (Er 2924–

---

[82] Pérennec, *Recherches*, I, p. 75.
[83] See above, p. 26.

3092). This is a characteristic shift of accent in Hartmann's adaptation of Chrétien's *Erec et Enide*, and, as Karl Bertau has seen, the difference between Chrétien's and Hartmann's approaches has a sociological aspect, for Chrétien's presentation of chivalric culture probably betrays the perspective of an author who is not himself a knight, but a clerically trained court poet looking at knighthood from the outside, with a more detached viewpoint, while Hartmann presents in his depiction of knighthood a poetic stylization of the profession and values of his own social class from more of an inside perspective.[84] This inside perspective is sustained with particular coherence in Hartmann's first romance, in which work the young author's enthusiasm for the ethos and practice of knighthood was probably at its peak.

## Knighthood and nobility in historical sources

Although knights formed a distinct category in German society in the second half of the twelfth century, this category was by no means homogeneous in the economic or juridical status or in the condition of birth of its members. The references to 'poor knights' in historical and literary sources[85] suffice, when compared with the sumptuous equipment of a princely *ritter* such as Erec, to indicate wide differences of material resources amongst knights. An interplay of group identity and heterogeneity also emerges at the juridical level, for example in the imperial peace edict of 1152. Here the knight ('miles') is distinguished from peasant and merchant, and for the weighty purpose of a judicial duel a further distinction is made between the 'legitimus miles', that is to say the *miles* stemming from a knightly family, and other knights.[86] These other knights must have been men of non-knightly parentage, who had nevertheless made the crossing, in some cases from upper peasant families, into the status of knight. In refusing these *arriviste* knights the right of judicial combat against 'legitimate' knights, Barbarossa's law at once recognizes the ascent from lower social levels into knighthood, and also limits the rights of these upwardly mobile knights until such time as their descendants are able, with the passage of generations, to identify themselves as being of knightly stock.[87]

The layering within the ranks of those called knight is particularly evident in the relation of knighthood and nobility as matters of social

---

[84] Bertau, *Deutsche Literatur*, I, p. 436; Jaeger, *The Origins of Courtliness*, pp. 242f., also sees the transition from Chrétien to Hartmann in sociological terms, as one from a cleric to 'the knightly class'. One wonders whether Chrétien's reference to the well-heeled clerks at King Lac's court (EeE 2324f.) might be a nudge to a patron?

[85] See Mohr, *'arme ritter'*, passim; W.H. Jackson, *'prison et croisié'*, passim.

[86] MGH Const., I, no. 140, c. 10 (p. 197).

[87] Otto, 'Abschließung', pp. 21f.; Fleckenstein, 'Zum Problem der Abschließung', p. 266.

status. A guiding principle of work in this field over the past thirty years has been the recognition that nobility is more ancient than knighthood. A further crucial difference is that nobility as a social status was, in the predominant medieval view, inherited from one's parents, whilst knighthood was, in its origins and its early history, a matter of function: the early knight was a professional warrior, often explicitly a serving vassal, irrespective of his birth. However, from the eleventh century onwards, the term *miles* acquired increasingly aristocratic connotations in historical sources, a development which reflects some adjustment of even the lesser knights towards the old nobility, and a consequent gradual redefinition of knighthood as being no longer solely an occupation, but also a mark of nobility. This process is observable throughout feudal Europe, but it shows marked chronological and regional differences in the decisive period from the eleventh century through to the thirteenth. Georges Duby has concluded that, as early as the eleventh century, the term *miles* embraced an aristocratic society in the Mâcon area in which there were gradations of power and wealth, but in which the great lords were not regarded as 'more noble' than other *milites*, and in which the terms 'noble' and 'knight' seem interchangeable.[88] Further north, there were many non-noble knights in Picardy still in the middle of the twelfth century,[89] and in Flanders in the thirteenth century,[90] whilst it was common practice for sources using juridically exact terms to list knights as a category distinct from nobles in the German empire throughout the twelfth and into the thirteenth century.[91] Indeed, the testimony of historical sources suggests that the lesser *milites* became recognized as noblemen earlier in the French than the German areas, but also that this process was under way even in the German empire by the time of Hartmann's literary activity.

It is essential for an understanding of the relation of knighthood to nobility in the German empire to consider the position of the German knights who were called *ministeriales*, and whose juridical status differed from that of the French knighthood on the matter of 'freedom'.[92] The bearing of arms was a traditional right of the old, free nobility in the German areas from earliest times. Then frequent internal warfare, and the economic and demographic expansion of the eleventh and twelfth centuries, created a need, and the resources, for larger retinues of warriors in the service of greater lords (again it should be emphasized

88   G. Duby, 'Lignage', p. 822.
89   Fossier, *La terre et les hommes*, I, pp. 537ff.
90   Warlop, *The Flemish Nobility*, Part 1, vol. I, p. 333.
91   Duby, 'Les origines de la chevalerie', pp. 329f.
92   For recent work on the *ministeriales* see Arnold, *German Knighthood*, passim; Fleckenstein (ed.), *Herrschaft und Stand*, pp. 23-27, 35-39, 51-58, 109-36 and often; Freed, 'The Origins of the European Nobility', passim; Kaiser, *Textauslegung*, pp. 56-100; Cormeau / Störmer, *Hartmann von Aue*, pp. 40-79 (all with further bibliography).

that the rise of knighthood and the gradual emergence of stronger territorial lordships are intimately related phenomena). The warrior vassals in these retinues are often referred to in Latin documents in Germany, especially from the eleventh to the thirteenth century, as *ministeriales*, that is to say unfree knights; and they played a key part in the social, political and constitutional history of the Hohenstaufen period. It is a matter of debate, and due to the patchiness of evidence probably not ascertainable, to just what extent this new category of *ministeriales* was drawn from the free men of earlier generations who became *ministeriales* out of necessity, or in pursuit of material advantage in the shape of the fief which was the normal material basis for ministerial service, or was composed of men of servile origins who grasped the profession of arms as a means of social advancement in turbulent times. The *ministeriales* are also referred to at times as *milites*, and they appear in vernacular texts as *dienestman* and as *ritter*. Until well into the thirteenth century the term *dienestman* appears in formulaic status lists as the lowest category of important men in the lay, feudal hierarchy, after kings (*künege*), princes (*vürsten*), lords (*herren*), dukes (*herzogen*), counts (*grâven*) and free men (*vrîen*).[93] This usage corresponds to the distinction that continued to be made in Latin sources throughout the Hohenstaufen period between *ministeriales* and free-born nobles.[94]

There seems to have been a considerable influx of men into the status of *ministeriales* in the late eleventh and early twelfth centuries, so that the *ministeriales* formed the majority of German knights in the twelfth century, probably outnumbering the remaining free vassals by the order of about three or four to one.[95] The numerical preponderance of *ministeriales* in German knighthood makes an understanding of their position essential for a proper grasp of the social context of German literature around 1200. This is doubly true for Hartmann's works, since Hartmann describes himself as a 'ritter' and 'dienstman' (AH 1–5), and consequently historical evidence about the *dienestman* can throw light on the social contours of Hartmann's position as author and narrator. Two connected aspects of the complex question of the social status of the German *ministeriales* are particularly relevant to the theme of knighthood in Hartmann's works: the comparative position of German *ministeriales* and the French knighthood; and the relation of *ministeriales* within the German empire respectively to serfs and to free-born nobles.

In his *Livre des Manières*, written probably between 1174 and 1178, Etienne de Fougères, bishop of Rennes, assumed that a knight was a

---

93 Examples in Bumke, *Ritterbegriff*, p. 137.
94 Arnold, *German Knighthood*, p. 70.
95 Fleckenstein, 'Vom Rittertum der Stauferzeit am Oberrhein', p. 26.

free man, born of a free mother (589: 'Franc home de franche mere nez').[96] This general condition was normal for France at this time, but would have been invalid for the German empire, where the knights who were *ministeriales* were precisely not reckoned to be of 'free' stock, although this did not diminish their knighthood. It is the hereditary obligation to serve a lord that is the distinguishing feature of German ministerial knighthood – knights in France were free men whose vassalic service of a lord was a contract freely entered into, whilst the service of the German *ministeriales* was a hereditary duty owed to a lord into whose ownership they had been born.[97]

However, several factors reduce the apparent sharpness of this distinction, and qualify the nature of the German lord's hereditary power over his *ministeriales*. First, the obligation on the *ministerialis* to serve was dependent upon the lord's grant of a fief, and increasingly with the passage of time, the grant of a fief was regarded as a hereditary kindred right of the *ministeriales*.[98] Consequently service as a *ministerialis* was less a burdensome yoke than a means of social advancement, in that it granted access to the knightly lifestyle and the security of hereditary land tenure. Second, and consequently, some custumals explicitly state that, if no fief was available, the *ministerialis* was free to leave the retinue and serve another lord. Thus the most detailed surviving statement of the rights and duties of *ministeriales*, the custumal drawn up around 1165 by Archbishop Rainald of Cologne, confirms the hereditary right of fiefs and offices for the eldest sons of ministerial families, and adds that younger brothers who take up knighthood are allowed to leave the archbishop's service and enter another retinue if he does not offer them a fief.[99] Third, the technically involuntary ascription of the *ministerialis* to a particular lord was eroded from the twelfth century onwards by the development and spread of the practice of multiple allegiance, as many knights established ministerial allegiances to more than one lord, and also held fiefs by real homage beside the fiefs held by their hereditary ascription to a lord.[100] As a result of this development, the contrast between different types of fief became eroded in Germany. Consequently, even the technical difference between the free vassals of France and the *ministeriales* of the German empire became even less marked during the course of the twelfth century, and all the while the German

---

[96] On Etienne's concept of knighthood see Painter, *French Chivalry*, pp.72f.; Flori, *L'essor*, pp. 315–19.

[97] Arnold, *German Knighthood*, p. 18.

[98] Ibid., p. 97.

[99] Text in Weinrich, *Quellen*, pp. 266–78 (here pp. 276–78); see Arnold, *German Knighthood*, p. 83. This important principle of mobility was established already in the earliest surviving written list of ministerial rights, the Bamberg custumal of ca. 1060 (Weinrich, *Quellen*, p. 120; Arnold, *German Knighthood*, p. 80).

[100] Arnold, *German Knighthood*, pp. 103–16.

*ministeriales* shared the same knightly lifestyle as the French knighthood. Nor was the social status of the German *ministeriales* in general somehow more modest than that of knights elsewhere, for the material wealth and political influence of the *ministeriales* varied enormously. Many were petty knights living on small manors with revenues that held them near to the better-off peasants. At the other extreme most *ministeriales* holding direct from the emperor had retinues of their own knights.[101] The famous imperial *ministerialis* Wernher of Bolanden had seventeen castles of his own and received 1100 knightly homages,[102] which placed him far above the mass of French knights in his actual social condition.

Nor does the 'unfreedom' of the German ministerial knights mean that they were in the same legal category as serfs. Recent historians have criticized the use of the term 'serf-knight', or 'chevalier-serf', by modern scholars as a designation for the *ministeriales*, rightly pointing out that German society knew many levels below that of the free-born nobility, and that the unfreedom of the *ministeriales*, connected as it was with knighthood and the grant of a fief in return for service, was in practice akin to vassalic service of the French type, and quite unlike the unfreedom of serfs.[103] The special social position of the *ministeriales* is indicated in the fact that they rank below the nobility but also above the mass of serfs in juridical status. As early as 1084 a Saxon peace edict places the *ministeriales* below the nobles, but on a par with free men and above bondmen and serfs in the level of punishments.[104] This hierarchy corresponds closely to the *Vorauer Moses* (written ca. 1130/1140), which lists 'edele', 'frige lute' and 'dinestman' as the three upper social categories, and adds 'chnehte' as a further, subordinate group (15,1–7).[105] An instance of the *miles / ritter* terminology standing in for *ministerialis / dienestman* in this juridical position between free nobles and serfs is Honorius Augustodunensis's division of the human race into the three categories 'liberi', 'milites', 'servi', a triplet which then appears in the German *Lucidarius* towards the end of the twelfth century as 'frigen', 'ritere', 'eigin lúte'.[106]

---

101  Ibid., p. 130.
102  *La Chronique de Gislebert de Mons*, p. 162.
103  Parisse, *Noblesse Lorraine*, pp. 246, 266; Keen, *Chivalry*, pp. 34f.; Arnold, *German Knighthood*, pp. 54f.
104  MGH Const., I, no. 426, c. 6 (pp. 608f.): 'nobilis' / 'liber aut ministerialis' / 'lito aut servus'. It is a punishable offence in this edict to give protection to a runaway serf ('fugitivum servum', c. 9); compare the similar provision in Barbarossa's disciplinary measures for the army in 1158 regarding the 'servum qui sine domino est' (Otto of Freising and Rahewin, *Gesta Frederici*, III, 31, p. 460). Evidently serfs had far less freedom of movement than *ministeriales* from the eleventh century onwards.
105  See Grubmüller, 'Nôes Fluch', pp. 107–09.
106  *De imagine mundi*, MPL, 172, col. 166; *Lucidarius*, p. 8. See Bumke, *Ritterbegriff*, p. 137; Grubmüller, 'Nôes Fluch', p. 106; Flori, *L'essor*, p. 231.

The use of the adjective *eigen* in vernacular texts throws further light on the hierarchical value of the terms *dienestman* and *ritter*. The term *eigen* is closely connected with servitude, and is often used with *kneht* or *man* to mean 'serf' or 'bondman'.[107] However, as a legal term, *eigen man* is distinct from *dienestman*.[108] The word *ritter*, 'knight', also seems to resist a connection with the adjective of servitude *eigen* in the twelfth century. In his useful list of knightly attributes up to the middle of the thirteenth century, Bumke provides over a hundred instances of the adjective *edel*, 'noble', linked with *ritter*, but only one occurrence of the expression *eigen ritter*.[109] Further, this one occurrence is in the metaphorical context of a knight's love-service of a lady, and it throws no light on the socially real juridical status of knighthood.[110] Indeed, the use of the terms *ritter*, *dienestman*, *eigen* and *kneht* in vernacular sources confirms the findings based on Latin charters, custumals and legal and narrative sources, namely that the ministerial knighthood of the German empire in the twelfth century ranked distinctly above serfdom in juridical status as well as in style of life. The convergence of vernacular literary texts and Latin historical sources on this important point is a further indication that the German literature of the Hohenstaufen period is in closer tune with real life than has sometimes been suggested in recent work.

Although *ministeriales* were legally unfree persons who remained juridically distinct from free-born nobles, they nevertheless came to be accepted themselves as noblemen during the twelfth century.[111] A key factor in this development was the fact that *ministeriales* shared the prestige of the knightly function with the old, free nobility, so that there was some merging of lifestyle between these legally distinct layers of the upper reaches of German lay society long before the juridical distinctions faded. The development of multiple allegiances in the twelfth century, especially the tendency for *ministeriales* to accept fiefs by real homage ('echte Lehen') beside their ministerial fiefs ('Dienstlehen'), further eroded the difference between ministerial and free-born knights.[112] The heritability of fiefs encouraged the development of an aristocratic sense of knightly family amongst the *ministeriales*, as did the legal separation of knights from peasants, which was evident in Barbarossa's peace of 1152. The constitution against arsonists of 1186 went a step further in this direction by forbidding the granting of the

[107] See W.H. Jackson, 'Verhältnis von *ritter* und *kneht*', pp. 23f.
[108] Hennig, 'Herr und Mann', p. 182.
[109] Bumke, *Ritterbegriff*, pp. 119f.
[110] Ulrich von Lichtenstein, *Frauendienst*, 65,5.
[111] See Arnold, *German Knighthood*, pp. 69–75; Fleckenstein, 'Entstehung des niederen Adels', p. 30.
[112] Fleckenstein, 'Entstehung des niederen Adels', p. 30.

belt of knighthood to sons of priests, deacons and peasants.[113] Barbarossa's peaces of 1152 and 1186 thus express, as legal norms, developments observable in other sources: first the crystallization of knighthood as a socio-professional category already distinct in status from the majority of the population; and then, towards the end of the twelfth century, the strengthening of attempts to restrict access to knighthood according to a principle of nobility: that of birth.[114]

In fact, sons of wealthy peasants did continue to make their way into the ranks of knighthood (though in what numbers is not known) despite these attempts at exclusion.[115] But this does not alter the fact that, as a matter of social norm, even the lesser knighthood was, in the late twelfth century, acquiring more exclusive, aristocratic connotations relating to birth as well as to military function. At the same time, in the second half of the twelfth century, the adjective *nobilis* became applied to individual *ministeriales*, and this usage was widespread by the end of the century.[116] Thus Hartmann's literary activity took place during a period when there were shifts in the German aristocracy, shifts which give early signs of a socio-political development that becomes much clearer in the course of the thirteenth century: the crystallization of a lesser nobility, a 'niederer Adel' based on the principle of knightly birth.[117]

Whilst these developments in the *ministeriales* show aristocratic principles percolating down into the lower ranks of knighthood in the second half of the twelfth century, even the greatest German nobles were increasingly associating themselves with the forms and decorations of knighthood in this period. This process is illustrated in changes in the terminology used to describe the initiatory arming of

---

113 MGH Const., I, no. 318, c. 20 (pp. 451f.).
114 See also Otto, 'Abschließung', pp. 34–39; Fleckenstein, 'Zum Problem der Abschließung', pp. 266–68; Flori, 'Les origines de l'adoubement', p. 248.
115 Rösener, 'Bauer und Ritter', pp. 680f. The reciprocal social mobility between peasantry and knighthood is a fascinating chapter of social history in later medieval Germany (though difficult to research due to the scattered nature of the evidence), as wealthier peasant families managed some social rise, whilst economic pressures caused decline of status in some knightly families. On movement through the grey area linking the upper level of peasantry to the lesser knighthood in the thirteenth century see Schindele, 'Helmbrecht', pp. 163–75 and passim; Dopsch, 'Probleme ständischer Wandlung', pp. 235, 249f.; Rösener, 'Bauer und Ritter', pp. 686–90; Fenske, 'Soziale Genese', pp. 721f.; W.H. Jackson, 'Verhältnis von *ritter* und *kneht*', pp. 31–35.
116 Arnold, *German Knighthood*, p. 71.
117 For an overall view of this structural change, and detailed studies of various regions (Baden, Worms, Jülich, Halberstadt, Austria, Styria, Salzburg, Brandenburg) see Fleckenstein (ed.), *Herrschaft und Stand*. On the twelfth-century roots of the process see also Feldbauer, *Herren und Ritter*, pp. 42ff., 99ff.; Thum, *Aufbruch und Verweigerung*, p. 458. Van Winter, 'Ritterschaft als "classe sociale" ', especially pp. 377–87, sees knighthood and nobility as separate legal estates in the German empire in the twelfth century, which then merged to form the social class of knights in the later Middle Ages.

young nobles. Jean Flori has shown how these ceremonies were usually described in the Carolingian period with the words for sword (*gladius*, *ensis*), belt (*cingulum*) or arms in general (*arma*), and whilst the terms *militia* and *militaris* do appear in this early period, it was not until the tenth century that a new terminology emerged involving the use of the word *miles*, with the notion of 'becoming' or 'being made' a *miles*.[118] This new terminiology, with the expressions *miles fieri*, *miles factus*, *miles effectus* and the like, appears first in France in the tenth century, then in the Anglo-Norman domains in the eleventh century, and in Flanders and the German empire in the twelfth century, the new expressions being used more frequently relative to the older style in France and Flanders than in the German empire in the twelfth century.[119] Flori is surely justified in seeing this terminological shift in arming rituals as an expression of the rise in prestige of the *milites* as a social category, with which even the sons of rulers showed some affinity by 'becoming *milites*'.

Moreover, the instances which Flori cites as the earliest applications of the new, knightly terminology to the arming of princes in Latin sources in the German empire appear in contexts close to Frederick Barbarossa. The first is Otto of Freising's account, written in 1157 or 1158, of the arming of the young King Geisa of Hungary.[120] The second is Rahewin's account of how Barbarossa gave permission at Würzburg in 1157 for the young Duke Frederick of Swabia, to be 'girded with the sword and declared a knight'.[121] The third and fourth are sources in the 1190s which apply the terminology of 'becoming a knight' to the *Schwertleite* of Barbarossa's sons Henry and Frederick at the famous Mainz court of 1184.[122] These factors suggest that the new, western terminology of noble knighthood was received with favour in Hohenstaufen circles, and that the Hohenstaufen court was a point of access for this terminology into the German-speaking world.

This view receives some backing from another event in the (for our topic) important decade of the 1180s. Early in 1189, Count Baldwin V of Hainault sent his son Baldwin (VI) to stay at the court of Barbarossa's son, the young King Henry, and Henry ordained the young Baldwin a knight with great honour in the city of Speier at Whitsun in that year

---

[118] Flori, 'Les origines de l'adoubement', pp. 240f.

[119] Ibid., p. 269.

[120] *Gesta Frederici*, I, 34, p. 196; for this and the occurrences in the next two footnotes see Flori, 'Les origines de l'adoubement', p. 241.

[121] *Gesta Frederici*, III, 6, p. 404.

[122] *Annales Aquenses*, p. 39: 'duo filii imperatoris facti sunt milites, rex Heinricus et dux Fridericus'; *La Chronique de Gislebert de Mons*, p. 156: 'dominus Henricus rex Romanorum et Fredericus dux Suevorum, domini Frederici Romanorum imperatoris filii, novi ordinati sunt milites'. On the Hohenstaufen tendency of the *Annales Aquensis* (= Aachen) see Wattenbach and Schmale, *Geschichtsquellen*, I, pp. 371–73.

(exactly five years after Henry's own *Schwertleite*).[123] Baldwin hailed from a French-speaking area in which the new terminology for knighthood was well established in the noble sphere.[124] Since one of the purposes of his stay at the Hohenstaufen court was to cement the new concord between his house and the German emperor by learning the German language and the ways of the imperial court,[125] there must have been bilingual discussions about his *Schwertleite* which can only have helped the rise of the western expressions for 'knighting' in Hohenstaufen circles. This occasion provides an unusually specific insight into the kind of interchange between the German aristocracy (in this case, the Hohenstaufen court) and their western counterparts, which furthered the spread of knightly forms and of French chivalric vocabulary in German aristocratic circles. That the new terminology for the *Schwertleite* did indeed have a specifically 'knightly' ring is indicated by the fact that the corresponding vernacular expressions use the modern word *ritter* (and never one of the older heroic terms), in the phrases *ritter werden* and *(ze) ritter machen*. The new vernacular expressions for 'knighting' also first appear in the princely sphere in German literary works from the late twelfth century onwards, so that on this point too there is a close correspondence of vernacular literature and other historical evidence in the development of chivalric forms.[126]

In conclusion, four points deserve special emphasis in the relation of knighthood and nobility. First, the historical evidence shows time and again that knighthood was a status shared by juridically distinct groups in twelfth-century Germany, not to speak of the great differences of wealth and social influence within the different juridical categories. Only by studying the features which these groups had in common, and the features which distinguished them from each other, can we approach a proper understanding of the social context in and for which the chivalric literature of the period was produced. Second, the twelfth century was a period of key developments in the structure of the German aristocracy, which involved some *rapprochement* of lesser and higher men in the larger status-group of knighthood. Benjamin Arnold comments: 'The high nobility, the free knights, and the *ministeriales* were often viewed as belonging to one knighthood, "the order of knights" as a charter of 1139 put it, including in this *ordo* a duke, two

---

[123] *La Chronique de Gislebert de Mons*, p. 237.
[124] See W.H. Jackson, 'Knighthood and Nobility', pp. 799, 805.
[125] *La Chronique de Gislebert de Mons*, p. 234: 'ad discendam linguam theutonicam et mores curie'.
[126] Heinrich von Veldeke, *Eneide*, 6164f.: 'Der ist noch ritter worden niht. / Deme wil ich morgen geben swert', following the *Roman d'Eneas*, 4763: 'demain lo ferai chevalier' (King Evander speaking of his son, Pallas). The *Nibelungenlied*, treating native German traditions ca. 1200, uses *riters namen gewinnen* and *riter werden* in connection with the *Schwertleite* of Siegfried (a king's son) and his 400 companions (31,4; 33,3).

counts, and five prominent *ministeriales* belonging to the archbishop of Cologne'; and 'twelfth-century chroniclers also assumed that free and unfree knights belonged to one military and social community'.[127] These conclusions, which establish the notion of a knightly *ordo* as an actual social community in twelfth-century Germany, are all the more valuable for students of literature because they are drawn from non-literary sources and therefore free of the taint of circularity when used as a basis for interpreting literary works. Third, the common features linking the various hierarchical levels of knights came to the fore in various ways during the second half, more particularly the last third of the twelfth century. This was the period when aristocratic principles were infusing the lesser knighthood, and when the higher nobility were increasingly adopting knightly forms. Further, there was active Hohenstaufen involvement in these developments, for the new knightly forms seem to have been welcomed in Hohenstaufen circles at the level of the princely *Schwertleite*. Also, the growing sense of lineage amongst the lesser knights was actively encouraged by the imperial court in the class-defining legal provisions of 1152 and 1186.[128] And the imperial *Hoftage* at Mainz in 1184 and 1188 acted as a focus for these integrative tendencies, as accounts at times refer to the participants generically as *milites*, or as the *militia*.[129] Thus the history of social forms at the imperial court suggests an attention to knighthood as a quality common to *ministeriales* and free nobles in the same period as the term *ritter* made its decisive breakthrough in German vernacular poetry. Finally, as regards a comparison of Germany and France, even the German *ministeriales* shared the same style of life as the French knighthood, apart from the difference of hereditary ascription to a lord as opposed to formal freedom – a difference which was fading in importance precisely in the late twelfth century. This communality of lifestyle between German *ministeriales* and French vassalic knighthood, involving knight service, an expensive military status, familiarity with mounted combat, higher social prestige and greater social privilege than the mass of the peasantry, and much in the way of shared social and ideological values with the high nobility, is an important factor in Hartmann's reception of Chrétien's romances, indeed in the reception of French chivalric poetry in general in the decades around 1200. These are not only fascinating inner-literary developments, but part of a broader process of the German aristocracy's drawing on French culture to further its own self-understanding at a time of transition.

---

[127] Arnold, *German Knighthood*, pp. 111, 112; similarly Fleckenstein, 'Entstehung des niederen Adels', pp. 27–31; Keen, *Chivalry*, pp. 36f.
[128] See also Arnold, *German Knighthood*, pp. 136f.
[129] Fleckenstein, 'Friedrich Barbarossa und das Rittertum', pp. 1028f.

*Knighthood and nobility in Hartmann's* Erec

On the topic of knighthood and nobility, as in the other major aspects of the social status of knighthood, Hartmann's *Erec*, although it is an adaptation from the French of a story relating to Arthurian Britain, is closely in tune with the contemporary German reality, for the work shows (and this at times in alterations which Hartmann makes to Chrétien's text) an interplay of communality and stratification within the ranks of knighthood which has clear affinities with the structure of German society around 1200, as it is reflected in Latin historical sources. In *Erec*, as in the historical record, the profession of arms, and the privileges that set knights off from other social groups, provide for some cohesion within the *ordo militaris*, but this order also includes men of widely differing hereditary and hierarchical status.

The word *ritter* stretches to the topmost level of the hierarchy in *Erec*, as great nobles, even sons of kings, are described as *ritter* more often than in any earlier German work.[130] The knights at Arthur's court are referred to generally as 'diu ritterschaft' (Er 1168), 'ritter' (Er 1285, 1390) and 'guote knehte' (Er 1615, 1790), and the list of their names includes many sons of kings, and other men identified by patronymics (Er 1629–95). This corresponds to the use of *milites* and *militia* as generic terms for the participants (including great nobles) at the Mainz courts of 1184 and 1188.[131] In *Erec* great nobles are also referred to individually as *ritter*. Erec, the son of a king, is often described as a 'ritter' (e.g. Er 3634, 4201, 4230, 5007, 5023, 5288, 5776, 6135, 6844, 8590, 8813); five young kings invited to Erec's wedding feast are described by the narrator as 'diu junge ritterschaft' (Er 1978); Erec addresses King Guivreiz as 'edel ritter' (Er 8030); Keii refers to Arthur's nephew Gawein as 'der edel ritter Gâwein' (Er 4785); and Mabonagrin, nephew of King Ivreins, is also referred to as a 'ritter' (Er 8012, 8476, 8757, 8788, 9636). The precise social degree is not explicit in the case of the 'ritter' Iders (e.g. Er 778, 817, 825), Brien (Er 1640) and Keii (Er 5014). However, Iders's fine armour (Er 732–45) and the fact that he is identified with a patronymic (Er 677: 'Îdêrs fil Niut'), Brien's place at the Round Table (Er 1616), and Keii's office as Arthur's seneschal (Er 1153: 'der truhsæze Keiîn') suggest in each case a person of substance.

These noble knights match the use of the word *chevalier* in Chrétien's romance. However, there is at times almost a propagandistic thrust in the use of the word *ritter* in Hartmann's *Erec*. This emerges, for instance, in the use of the appellation *der ritter N*. This formulation is attested, but

---

[130] See also Bumke, *Ritterbegriff*, p. 92.
[131] See above, p. 72, n. 129.

rare, before and after Hartmann's *Erec*.[132] Here the phrase is used twelve times – of Iders (Er 778), Brien (Er 1640), Keii (Er 5014), Mabonagrin (Er 9636), Gawein (Er 4785: 'der edel ritter Gâwein'), and especially of Erec (Er 3634, 4230, 5007, 5023, 5288, 6135, 8590). As has been shown, this formulation places the word *ritter* in a linguistic position otherwise often occupied by terms of elevated social status such as *künec* (king), *herzoge* (duke), *herre* (lord), and by the laudatory heroic terms *helt, degen, recke* and *wîgant*, with the effect that the concept of knighthood is given a proud ring and is promoted, as a combination of social status and military or ethical merit, beyond its use by earlier authors.[133] Hartmann's frequent exploitation of this unusual appellation thus reflects the same ideological drive as his programmatic use of the concept *ritters name*. He seems fascinated by the very word 'knight' in *Erec*.

However, it should be noted that the word *ritter* is not freely interchangeable with such titles of lordship as 'king', 'duke', and 'count'. More precisely Hartmann tends not to designate as *ritter* those high men who are referred to as actually exercising lordly functions, but to give them their more specific title of lordship. Thus the kings Arthur, Lac and Ivreins, the duke Imain, and the counts Galoain and Oringles are never referred to by the word *ritter*. Throughout Hartmann's works, the word *ritter* refers usually to nobles who are still young, and who are seen actually or potentially in a martial capacity, or attending at court. We shall return to this association of knighthood with 'youth', and its sociological implications, later.[134]

At the lower end of the knightly hierarchy, the unnamed *ritter* in the retinues of lords in *Erec* (e.g. Er 3722, 4244, 6132, 6302), while of too little narrative importance for us to be given much detail about them, were probably associated in the minds of Hartmann and his audience with the *ministeriales* who formed the main body of German knightly retinues in the twelfth century. Indeed Hartmann refers to 'dienestman' in the retinue of Count Oringles (Er 6278, 6332, 6361). The term *dienestman* deserves attention, for it throws light on a striking difference in the vocabulary of knighthood between vernacular texts and the Latin sources, as these latter have been presented by Benjamin Arnold. Arnold points out that the German scribal preference for the term *ministerialis* overwhelmed other words for knight in the twelfth century: 'In the Latin sources for the Hohenstaufen age, *ministerialis* is the prevalent term for knight in Germany. The word referred not to his most characteristic function, that of fighting on horseback, but to his

---

132  Bumke, *Ritterbegriff*, p. 93, n. 19; Pérennec, *Recherches*, I, pp. 83, 86f.
133  Pérennec, *Recherches*, I, pp. 82–100; Pérennec rejects as unlikely the view that this formulation *der ritter N.* may be due more to a later scribe than to Hartmann himself (pp. 87f.).
134  See below, pp. 219–21.

hereditary status, and was therefore applicable to his womenfolk, children, and relatives in holy orders. In other words, *ministeriales* look like a social class, with the hereditary profession or function of knightly cavalrymen'.[135] And he adds: 'As *ministerialis* became the ascendant scribal word, the vernacular found its equivalent in *dienestman*, which contained the essential meaning of service, like the Anglo-Saxon equivalent, *cniht* or knight'.[136] German *ministeriales* were frequently also called *milites*, since both words indicated the same type of knightly duty, and this practice spread during the thirteenth century, when the term *ministerialis* receded considerably in the sources, to be replaced by *miles*.[137] The Latin legal language thus shows *ministerialis* and *miles* used for the same category of person, with *ministerialis* dominating from the early twelfth into the thirteenth century, and *miles* then gaining the upper hand, so that the legal Latin terminology of knighthood in Germany catches up with the rest of Christendom after its special 'detour' through the *ministerialis* phase.

The equivalent vernacular terms for *ministerialis* and *miles* are *dienestman* and *ritter*.[138] However, the vernacular literary texts differ from what one would expect on the basis of Latin legal usage in that here *ritter*, not *dienestman*, is the prevalent term for knight already in the twelfth century. Hartmann's works have in all 236 occurrences of *ritter* as against only eight of *dienestman*. Three occurrences of *dienestman* relate to the knights in Oringles's retinue (Er 6278, 6332, 6361), one to vassals mentioned beside kinsfolk at the court of King Ivreins (Er 9762: 'des küneges mâge und dienestman'), one to a mixed ducal *familia* in *Gregorius* (Gr 201: 'mâge man und dienestman'). The occurrences in the *Klage* (1568) and *Iwein* (7477) are in metaphorical contexts of love or chivalric friendship. Finally Hartmann describes himself as a 'ritter' and 'dienstman [. . .] z'Ouwe' in *Der arme Heinrich* (1,5). When he introduces himself in *Iwein*, he describes himself only as a 'rîter' (Iw 21), which suggests that of the two pieces of information about his social position (ministerial status and knighthood), it is knighthood that he attaches most importance to in his self-stylization as author. This preponderance of *ritter* over *dienestman* is not peculiar to Hartmann, but characteristic of German vernacular texts from the second half of the twelfth century onwards, and it runs through different types of work (adaptations from French courtly literature, native German epic poetry, didactic literature) and author (clerical or lay, named or unnamed).[139]

---

135 Arnold, *German Knighthood*, p. 24.
136 Ibid., p. 37.
137 Ibid., p. 26; Bumke, *Höfische Kultur*, I, p. 70.
138 See also Bumke, *Ritterbegriff*, pp. 70ff.
139 Sample frequencies of *ritter* / *dienestman* in literary texts, mid-twelfth to early thirteenth century, according to Bumke, *Ritterbegriff*, pp. 32–34f., 71f.: *Rother* 28/0; *Kaiserchronik* 10/17; Veldeke, *Eneide* 59/0; Hartmann von Aue 236/8; Ulrich von

What light does this discrepancy between Latin legal usage and vernacular literature throw on the dynamics of knighthood in the twelfth century? One reason for the infrequency of *dienestman* in literary works around 1200 is simply that the main characters are themselves princes. But this is not a sufficient explanation, for even when knights appear in anonymous groups, they are still referred to as *ritter* more often than as *dienestman*. And modesty of social status in itself can hardly explain the infrequency of *dienestman*, for the word *kneht* has decidedly unprestigious connotations and yet appears far more often than *dienestman*. A key factor is surely that, once the word *dienestman* had become the equivalent of the legal term *ministerialis*, it became felt as a rather narrow, juridically specific term relating to the particular hereditary status of the knights concerned, whereas *ritter*, whilst indicating the social function of fighting on horseback, was less juridically narrow than *dienestman* (for it could apply to other legal categories, such as free nobles), and was consequently more appropriate for wider use.[140] In other words, *ministerialis* and *dienestman* were primarily matters of technical, legal language, the stuff of charters, witness lists and legal history, whereas *miles* and *ritter* were more flexible matters of social function and social history.

The testimony of vernacular literature makes it likely that *ritter*, rather than *dienestman*, was the prevalent term for 'knight' (and thus the equivalent of French *chevalier* and English *cniht*) in Hohenstaufen Germany in everyday speech. Certainly the dominance of *ritter* over *dienestman* in verse cannot be explained by the exigencies of rhyme, for *dienestman* is as easy to place in the rhyme as *ritter* is difficult (seven of the eight occurrences of *dienestman* in Hartmann are in the rhyme). Seen in this light the literary works of twelfth-century Germany are of much interest to the historian, for despite all their aesthetic stylization, they take us in some ways closer to the actual forms of communication of lay folk than does the technical language of legal Latin. And they suggest that the appellation *ritter* was more frequent for 'knight' than was *dienestman* in everyday life. That is to say that the fading of *ministerialis* (vernacular *dienestman*) in favour of *miles* (vernacular *ritter*) in thirteenth century charters is to some extent a catching-up process within Germany, as the legal terminology followed a custom which was widespread in vernacular literature (and probably in everyday language) already a few decades earlier.

Moreover, since the word *ritter* referred primarily to the characteristic function of mounted combat rather than to hereditary status (though

Zatzikhoven, *Lanzelet* 208/3; Herbort von Fritzlar, *Liet von Troye* 113/8; *Nibelungenlied* 170/0; Wolfram von Eschenbach, *Parzival* 372/5, *Willehalm* 89/2; Gottfried von Straßburg, *Tristan* 64/4; Wirnt von Gravenberg, *Wigalois* 335/6.
140 Similarly Bumke, *Ritterbegriff*, pp. 72f.

this element was coming to the fore, in an aristocratic sense, in the second half of the twelfth century), and since it was applicable to free nobles as well as to *ministeriales*, its widespread use suggests that the concept of hereditary unfreedom was losing ground already in the twelfth century as a social determinant, and giving place to the criterion of knightly status and knightly lifestyle, a criterion which in turn was acquiring increasingly hereditary coloration by the end of the twelfth century. Thus the use of the word *ritter* in vernacular texts again suggests that the shifts in the German aristocracy which led to the gradual transformation of the *ministeriales* into a lesser nobility were indeed well under way in the twelfth century, as 'the prestige of the knightly function conferred upon the *ministeriales* the quality of nobility',[141] even though they were still juridically distinct from the free-born nobles.

The fact that the status of being a *ritter* is shared by serving knights and great lords in *Erec* does not, however, mean that Hartmann after all presents the sword-bearing aristocracy as an egalitarian group in which the least *dienestman* is on a par with the greatest prince. Rather it is again a matter of weighing up factors of communality and factors of diversity; and despite the integrative tendencies of the *ordo militaris* (which are reflected in the wide use of the term *ritter*), the social structure of the German aristocracy was still, in Hartmann's day, more complex, with a keener sense of hierarchical differentiation, than was the case in France.[142] Here again, Chrétien and Hartmann reflect basic features of their respective societies, for aristocratic society seems indeed more nearly homogeneous, or at least less hierarchically stratified in a juridical sense, in Chrétien's *Erec* than it is in Hartmann's adaptation.[143] Hartmann's characters repeatedly express concern about parities or disparities of social status, especially in situations which would, in real life, be dynastically sensitive, for instance in connection with marriage and with surrender. Each of these acts involves (actually or potentially) a transformation in the hierarchical status of the individual(s) concerned, with possible consequences for an entire lineage. They are consequently situations of great importance for an author who is sensitive to social status, and it is no coincidence that on three occasions involving these acts, Hartmann alters Chrétien's text so as to show an independent interest in the question of 'nobility'.[144]

In Chrétien's work, Enide's father is a 'povre vavassor' (EeE 1559; compare 375, 384, 397, 485, 556). Vavassors were sub-vassals (*vassus*

---

141 Arnold, *German Knighthood*, p. 70.
142 See also Borst, 'Das Rittertum im Hochmittelalter', p. 222.
143 See also Pérennec, 'Adaptation', pp. 300f.
144 Various interpretations of this complex in Hartmann's *Erec* in Zink, '*Geburt*', pp. 26f., 29; Borck, 'Adel', pp. 441f.; Kaiser, *Textauslegung*, pp. 103–06; Pérennec, 'Adaptation', pp. 297–303; id., *Recherches*, especially I, pp. 107–11; Voß, *Artusepik*, pp. 170f.

*vassorum*), that is to say at 'the lowest grade among the holders of military fiefs'.[145] Just as seneschals, largely because of their influence as lordly officials, generated an unfavourable stereotype in courtly literature, so vavassors, as a low nobility, living often in modest conditions, receive a more sympathetic treatment in French literature.[146] And the marriage of Erec, the son of a king, to Enide, the daughter of a vavassor, has a programmatic value in Chrétien's romance, showing that the extreme poles of the feudal, knightly hierarchy can come together even in such a dynastically momentous institution as marriage; for Enide's father, though a poor vavassor, yet has the essential quality of nobility: freedom (EeE 1561: 'Ses peres est frans et cortois'). In the German feudal arrangements, the position equivalent to that of the French vavassors, at the lower end of the sword-bearing hierarchy, was held by the lesser *ministeriales*. However, as we have seen, these did not count as free men. Furthermore, marriage between a free-born noble and the daughter of a *ministerialis* would have been a *mésalliance* in Hartmann's day, with any offspring taking the legal status of the mother.[147] It is probably for this reason (i.e. to avoid any hint of a *mésalliance*) that Hartmann, while making Enite's family even more impoverished than they were in Chrétien's romance, raises her father to the status of a once mighty count (Er 402: 'er was ein grâve rîche') who has been unjustly ousted from his inheritance by war (Er 400–13).[148] Hartmann also points up the nobility of the family by using the terms 'edel' (Er 289, 432, 1831) and 'adel' (Er 1837) and by emphasizing Enite's high birth (Er 439: 'ir geburt was âne schande'). Hartmann's alteration to Chrétien's text thus responds to the German society of his day, in which precisely marriage practices were constrained by the divisions of juridical rank that continued to separate the lesser knights from the free-born nobles in the *ordo militaris*.

There is some flexibility, even ambivalence, in the concept of nobility in Hartmann's *Erec* which is revealing for this time of transition in the German aristocracy. As we have seen, Mâcon sources show as early as the eleventh century a juridically homogeneous aristocratic society, in which the great lords were not 'more noble' than the lesser knights.[149] But still at the end of the twelfth century, Hartmann's *Erec* exhibits the German characteristic of a more heterogeneous aristocracy. For instance, when Erec insists (independently of Chrétien) that he is 'more

---

[145] M. Bloch, *Feudal Society*, I, p. 177.
[146] Woledge, 'Bons vavasseurs', passim.
[147] Schulte, *Adel*, pp. 24–7; Beyerle, 'Der *Arme Heinrich*', pp. 33f.
[148] Cramer, 'Soziale Motivation', pp. 102f. rightly sees this alteration as a mark of Hartmann's attention to matters of social status in adapting Chrétien (though this is not to agree with Cramer's further interpretation of Enite's role); see also Cormeau / Störmer, *Hartmann von Aue*, p. 222.
[149] See above, p. 64.

noble' than Galoain (Er 4204: 'ich bin edeler dan ir sît'), it is clear that the social mentality of the German work permits various degrees of nobility; and if Erec is 'more noble' than the count, how much higher must he rank above the knights in Galoain's retinue? Hartmann's use of the expression *edel ritter*, 'noble knight' indicates a certain ambivalence in the term *edel*. When the man so addressed, or referred to, is known to the speaker as a king, as is the case when Erec addresses Guivreiz (Er 8030), or the nephew of a king, as when Keii refers to Gawein (Er 4785), the adjective *edel* could be motivated by knowledge of the man's noble ancestry. But this form of address is also used when the speaker does not yet know the identity of the knight he is addressing (Er 898, 957, 9325). The last of these occurrences is a surrender scene where Mabonagrin, having addressed the victorious Erec as 'edel ritter' (Er 9325) then goes on to enquire after Erec's parentage, and to say that he would sooner die than surrender to someone who is not a nobleman (Er 9349: 'hâtz ein unadels man getân, / so enwolde ich durch niemen leben'). Already in Chrétien's version, Mabonagrain raises the question of social parity (EeE 6010–23), but it is Hartmann who makes it an issue specifically of nobility, and a matter of life and death, so that here again the German text conveys the sense of a cleavage that runs across the knightly hierarchy, a continuing sense of hierarchical difference between noble and non-noble knights, or between knights who are, as it were, truly noble (i.e. free-born), and others who are only 'noble' in a looser sense.

Two senses of the term 'noble' thus emerge in connection with knighthood in the German work. On the one hand the adjective *edel* can be applied, as a matter of polite usage, to any knight, even when his parentage is unknown; and on the other hand the adjective also has the more specific sense of applying only to men of 'true' (i.e. free) noble birth. This dual usage of the vernacular *edel* corresponds interestingly to the trend in Latin historical sources in Germany, where the adjective *nobilis* came increasingly to be applied to the *ministeriales* in the late twelfth century, because they were regarded as noble by their style of life, but was still used in the narrow, technical sense of the free-born nobility, who remained juridically distinct from the *ministeriales*.[150]

An ambivalence of chivalric nobility is expressed even more clearly when the knightly King Guivreiz surrenders to Erec. Both Chrétien and Hartmann have Guivreiz ask for mercy (EeE 3843–48; Er 4442–59.). But in this passage Hartmann departs from Chrétien to have Guivreiz make

---

150  On the Latin usage see Arnold, *German Knighthood*, pp. 69–72. The ambivalent usage of *edel* in *Erec* well illustrates the important historical development, that precisely in the twelfth century '[the] social meaning [of nobility] was widened as it was transferred to the knightly but unfree social order of German ministeriales' (Arnold, *Princes and Territories*, pp. 12f.).

utterances on the relation of nobility, knightly prowess and status of birth which show the German author reflecting independently of his source on a matter of importance to the German knighthood of his day. Guivreiz offers himself as Erec's vassal, commenting that he does not care who Erec's father was, for Erec is 'ennobled' by his own achievement (Er 4456–59: 'sus ist ez mir unmære: / swer dîn vater wære, / sô edelet dich dîn tugent sô / daz ich dîn bin ze herren vrô'). In deriving the victor's nobility from his prowess, not his parentage, Guivreiz draws on an ancient moral tradition. The rival claims of virtue and descent, achievement and blood, as the true key to nobility were discussed throughout the Middle Ages, not least in connection with knighthood, which combined demonstrations of prowess with inherited aristocracy.[151] The concept of a nobility of virtue, or achievement, as against the inherited nobility of blood reaches back to classical antiquity. This concept, and the related postulate that those of inherited noble stock should justify their status by good deeds, were expounded by churchmen with renewed vigour during the reform movements of the eleventh and twelfth centuries, when the Church sought to instil a greater sense of ethical purpose into the lay aristocracy.[152] Hartmann draws on this moral discussion of *nobilitas* and *virtus* for the formulation of Guivreiz's praise of Erec (Er 4458: 'edelet' and 'tugent'). Further, the idea that a knight might rise to nobility and lordship on the basis of the specific merit of military prowess (Er 4452: 'manheit'), a quality towards which clerical writers often had a sceptical attitude, suggests that the old moral tradition is also being exploited in Guivreiz's words in a way sympathetic to the aspirations of the lesser, ministerial knights, who were not of the old, free-born nobility, but who were seeking to establish themselves as an aristocracy in Hartmann's day by virtue of their profession of arms.[153] Indeed, before Erec reveals his high noble lineage to Guivreiz, Hartmann sketches an idyllic picture of comradeship based on the profession of arms that brought the extreme poles of the *ordo militaris* together, as the battle-weary combatants bind each other's wounds with makeshift bandages and take each other by the hand (Er 4481–97).

However, Hartmann's discussion of the nature of nobility in this episode does not end with this idyll of social homogeneity, for Guivreiz goes on to ask, with some circumstance, about Erec's social status, and whether he is indeed a nobleman (Er 4533: 'ein edel man'). And now nobility is seen in more conventional, aristocratic terms, as a matter of lineage, kin and birth (Er 4523: 'geslehte'; 4536: 'künne'; 4538: 'geburt').

---

[151]   Keen, *Chivalry*, pp. 156–61; on nobility of virtue and nobility of blood in Hartmann's day, see also Borck, 'Adel', pp. 423–43.

[152]   On the Church's ideals of the *militia* see below, pp. 85–88, 185, 192f., 255–58.

[153]   See also Kaiser, *Textauslegung*, pp. 103–06.

The very diplomatic carefulness of Guivreiz's approach to the question of Erec's parentage (Er 4514–34 can be paraphrased thus: 'Don't take offence at what I'm going to ask, and of course your prowess forced my surrender. But if it turned out that indeed your lineage was of a quality to match your prowess, then my honour would be all the greater; and I shall be eternally happy at this, my first defeat, if a nobleman has bested me.') suggests the complex mentality of a society in which preoccupation with precise conditions of birth existed side by side with the recognition of new men who had made their way up to a position of *de facto* aristocracy which outstripped their juridically inferior status. Moreover, having opened the door to a concept of nobility based on merit, Guivreiz seems tactfully to close it again and present nobility, after all, as a matter of birth.

The two concepts of nobility uttered by Guivreiz (a nobility based on merit, and a nobility based on parentage) are logically incompatible, but were nevertheless closely intertwined in the mentality of the medieval aristocracy. They also articulate in an unusually pointed way a tension between two strands of thinking that run through Hartmann's works, as he exhibits on the one hand an anxious concern with parities of social rank, a static, conservative respect for the established hierarchy based on condition of birth, and on the other hand a preoccupation with moral effort, and achievement by merit, which intimates a rather different, more dynamic set of values – that it is not only the unalterable fact of birth, but also the processes of merit and achievement that determine a person's worth, and that might even justify an enhancement of social status.[154]

What light does this fluidity in Hartmann's concept of nobility throw on the theme of knighthood? Gert Kaiser has interpreted the themes of knightly achievement and nobility in Hartmann's *Erec* as a poetic legitimation of the upward social thrust of the ministeriales.[155] There is much to agree with in this view, for the unprecedented cultural dignity given to the word *ritter* and to the condition of knighthood in Hartmann's Erec constitutes an enhancement of prestige for the historically real *ordo militaris* as a whole, most of whose members were technically ministerial knights. However, the respect which Hartmann exhibits for parities of social status also indicates that he was reaching out to the old, free-born nobility with his concept of knighthood. As we have seen, the word *miles*, 'knight', was applied to nobles in historical sources in the late twelfth century, and this speaks somewhat against the view that, by using the word *ritter* in the high noble sphere,

---

[154] See also Zink, 'Geburt', pp. 29–31; more fully Pérennec, *Recherches*, especially I, pp. 108–11.
[155] Kaiser, *Textauslegung*, pp. 103–26.

Hartmann was departing from contemporary social reality to express a programmatically ministerial ideology.[156] The ideal of knightly service in Hartmann's romances, connected as it is with defence of justice and the oppressed, links up to socio-ethical duties which applied as much to rulers as to lesser knights.[157] Further, commenting on the courtly romance in general, Ursula Liebertz-Grün rightly points out that the literary portrayal of chivalry could relate to and represent, in a selective, stylized, idealized way, the reality and the aspirations of the highest nobility.[158] On the other hand, the interest of the 'high nobility' is perhaps pressed too exclusively with the surmise that the great magnates, as literary patrons, were probably not concerned to see the lifestyle and the dreams of the lesser nobility expressed in literary form.[159]

With regard to Hartmann's works, we do not know who Hartmann's patron was, or indeed to what extent his works were conditioned by the desire to please a (hypothetical) lordly patron. But Hartmann describes himself as a serving knight (AH 1–5), and we can safely take it that the audience he had in mind in composing his works contained knights of various juridical categories. Even if we postulate a great magnate as Hartmann's patron, the total social field of force operative in his work (author, audience, patron) still stretched from great lordship to lesser ministerial knighthood. We shall see a certain sympathy on Hartmann's part for the perspective of lesser knighthood again in other works.[160] Moreover, if this perspective is relativized from above by an affirmation of the old nobility of birth in *Erec*, there is also a Christian thrust to Hartmann's thinking about the relationship of moral worth and social status which will lead him in *Der arme Heinrich* to see high moral worth right outside the knightly world.[161] Indeed, the literary project of chivalry in Hartmann's works, like the rise and crystallization of knighthood as a social and ideological phenomenon in general in the twelfth century cannot adequately be understood by reference to the *ministeriales* or to the free-born nobility alone, but is a product of interaction and merging between these sections of the sword-bearing class, and a product too of the interface that linked the lay aristocracy with the world of clerical learning and with Christian ideals of military function. Just as the prestige of the knightly function conferred the social quality of nobility on the German *ministeriales*, as it had earlier on

---

[156] See also W.H. Jackson, 'Knighthood and Nobility', pp. 806–09. For further reservations about Kaiser's ministerial thesis, see Peters, 'Artusroman und Fürstenhof', pp. 177–90; Schupp, 'Kritische Anmerkungen', pp. 407–21.

[157] See also Schupp, 'Kritische Anmerkungen', p. 421.

[158] Liebertz-Grün, *Zur Soziologie des 'amour courtois'*, pp. 106f., 182 n. 565.

[159] Ibid., p. 182 n. 565.

[160] See below, pp. 157f., 177f.

[161] See below, pp. 202–08.

the knighthood of France, so the old, free-born nobility had good reason to accept and promote knightly forms. The mounted knight was, beyond all the nice juridical distinctions in different parts of Europe in the twelfth century, everywhere the most potent expression of the martial power and the social pre-eminence which the free nobility saw as its birthright. In addition, the socially protective ideals of the *militia*, and the new, sophisticated patterns of feeling and social discourse around the figure of the knight, to which we shall turn in later chapters, were welcome ethical and cultural legitimations of the nobility's privileged status. In short, there were good pragmatic and ideological reasons for the spread of chivalric forms at all levels of the aristocracy in Germany in Hartmann's day, from the lesser *ministeriales* up to the greatest magnates.

The sword-bearing function of the *ordo militaris* was an integrative factor in the twelfth century, embracing *ministeriales* and free-born nobles. But juridical and material distinctions remained alive within the class. Further, there were signs, already in the twelfth century, of the growing importance of the aristocratic principle of birth and lineage in knighthood, which led to the gradual formation of a lesser nobility on the basis of knightly birth. Hartmann does not explicitly thematize this complex and shifting structure of the German aristocracy (indeed he can only have been at most dimly aware of the changes which are evident to us with the benefit of hindsight), but it forms an important undercurrent in his work. Hartmann's preoccupation with parities and disparities of social status, and with the justification of social position through merit and achievement, may have personal, autobiographical roots which we cannot uncover. However, this feature is also an appropriate expression of a time of change, when old and new patterns overlapped; and in his manner of adapting Chrétien, Hartmann processes key elements in the changing situation of the contemporary German aristocracy, as his unprecedentedly frequent and emphatic use of the term *ritter* presents knighthood as an overarching social status and as an ideology with which lesser *ministeriales* and great nobles in his audience could identify, while the ambivalence of the concept of nobility in *Erec* reflects the continuing social distinctions, even tensions, within the *ordo militaris*, and warns us against too harmonizing a view of the integration of greater and lesser men in German knighthood at the end of the twelfth century.

# 3

# Knighthood and the Ethics of Force in *Erec*

*Peace movements, the court and the development of knightly ethics*

Although the aristocratic principle of birth was gaining ground even amongst the lesser knights in Hartmann's day, the military function remained an essential factor common to the various hierarchical levels of knighthood. Knights were that (upper) section of society which bore sword and lance, and which exercised armed force as of right. The profession of arms continued to be central to the knight's social identity, whether he was by hereditary status a *ministerialis* or a free-born noble. It formed a target for clerical criticism, and a legitimizing base for the knights' social prestige. It was as the exercisers of force, potential or actual, that the mass of the population, still for the most part tied to the soil, experienced the armed and mounted knights. On the use of force, Hartmann's *Erec* is again a literary stylization of central concerns of the contemporary society, for the critical presentation of destructive violence and the delineation of exemplary patterns of knightly behaviour are essential to the thematic and mental structure of the work. Further, the twelfth century was as important for debate about the military function of knighthood as it was for developments in the social status of the *milites*. By the end of the century an ideology of chivalry had emerged which was different from earlier warrior patterns, and Hartmann's *Erec* brings an unprecedentedly full elaboration of this ideology. However, before we turn to this key aspect of Hartmann's first romance, we must first briefly consider the broader historical perspective so as to understand the complex, even conflicting, norms that bore on the knight's use of force at this time.

In sketching the origins and formation of the values that make up the chivalric ideology of the central Middle Ages, it should be emphasized from the outset that the knight of the twelfth century, as a figure in

84

social reality and as an idealized pattern in literature, was also the linear descendant of the warrior of earlier centuries by virtue of his martial function. This function was not created by the Church, or by any other force outside the lay aristocracy. It provided a continuity linking the Germanic warrior to the later knight, and it remained of decisive importance in the self-understanding of medieval knighthood. The warrior status generated from within itself an ethic based on the pursuit of praise and recognition by military prowess, an ethic that was already a step beyond unbridled violence, but which was often openly attacked by voices within the Church. The pursuit of honour remained an important constituent of the modern, knightly mentality of the decades around 1200.[1] It is a recurrent theme, in various configurations of affirmation and criticism, in Hartmann's works.

However, in a centuries-long interaction with secular powers and the Church, the concept of exemplary warriordom became modified in the direction of a greater channelling and suppression, a harnessing of warrior energy to notions of protection, justice and even peace. As early as the ninth century, Carolingian church councils sought to adjust the exercise of armed force to ideas of ethical obligation by prescribing that, for grave crimes, the offender should be removed from the warrior profession.[2] Such pronouncements form an early stage in the long process whereby ecclesiastical and lay authorities tried to contain warrior activity, to subject warfare to Christian, ethical notions, and to extend peace in a society in which the feud was still regarded, by the lay aristocracy, as a proper legal process and an inborn right.[3] The related processes of promulgation of the peace and a christianization of warfare accelerated markedly in the period from the late tenth to the early thirteenth century in the associated developments of the Peace and Truce of God, the crusades, and peace ordinances stemming from secular authorities. These developments were responses to a considerable disintegration of public, especially royal, authority in post-Carolingian Europe. The disintegration was particularly pronounced in France in the tenth and eleventh centuries, where it promoted the formation of local warrior allegiances (the growth of feudalism), and led to a proliferation of feuding, which often entailed disorderly violence and the devastation of lay and church lands.[4] The ravages of feuding in turn called forth attempts at restraining measures from church and lay sources, and it was in this lengthy interplay of violence and the desire

---

[1] On the importance of honour in medieval knighthood see Barber, *The Knight*, pp. 44f.; Keen, *Chivalry*, pp. 55, 162ff., 198f. and often.
[2] Leyser, 'Early Medieval Canon Law', p. 555.
[3] On the legal and constitutional implications of the feud see Brunner, *Land und Herrschaft*, pp. 1–110.
[4] Cowdrey, 'The Peace and the Truce of God', p. 47.

for restraint that the earlier warrior ethos gave place to the knightly values of the central Middle Ages.

The Peace of God (*Pax Dei*) was first pronounced in Burgundy and Aquitaine in the late tenth century, and the Truce of God (*Treuga Dei*) first appeared there some decades later.[5] The Peace of God placed under protection certain categories of persons (especially monks, priests and the poor) and certain material things (especially church property and the peasants' means of livelihood). The Truce of God was a further development which called for the cessation of all armed violence on certain days (especially Sunday), thus attempting to create periods of peace during the conduct of feuds. What is of general importance for our topic is that the Peace and Truce of God were promulgated by councils at which bishops enlisted the aid of the lay aristocracy in trying to secure peace and justice.[6] Thus the peace movements, from their earliest stage, brought the Church and the warrior class, the *milites*, together in discussions about the function and duty of the warrior. The peace movements were instrumental in identifying the *milites* as a social category distinct from, and more powerful than, the *rustici*; and by ascribing ethical duties to the *milites*, they also contributed to the formation of a class ideology for emerging knighthood.[7]

The tenth century also brought the first literary manifestations of a new ethic of Christian life for the laity, originating in the Cluniac reform. For instance in Odo of Cluny's life of Count Gerald of Aurillac, and then in the mid-eleventh-century Latin *Ruodlieb* (composed in south Germany), the heroes are shown as living exemplary Christian lives even in the secular world, and both works reject vengeance and the pursuit of personal glory in warfare, advocating instead humility and mercy in the victor.[8] The conception that the military life, if properly ordered, could be pleasing to God, was developed by churchmen in various parts of Europe during the twelfth century, alongside clerical criticisms of the violence and the thirst for booty and glory of contemporary knights. For instance in Germany, Gerhoh of Reichersberg (provost 1132–1169), while condemning those who took up arms to rob the poor, or to exact vengeance, also saw the knight as fulfilling a mission pleasing to God if he loyally served the civil authority.[9] This clerical voice within Germany anticipates a key feature of the socio-

---

[5]  Ibid., p. 42; compare Hoffmann, *Gottesfriede und Treuga Dei*, pp. 16–23; 70ff.
[6]  Cowdrey, 'The Peace and the Truce of God', p. 43.
[7]  Duby, 'Les laïcs et la paix de Dieu', pp. 237f.
[8]  Braun, *Studien zum Ruodlieb*, pp. 19–38; Bumke, *Höfische Kultur*, II, pp. 400f.; on *Ruodlieb* see also below, pp. 114f.
[9]  On Gerhoh's view of the social and religious role of the *militia* see Flori, *L'essor*, pp. 257–63; on his criticism of the German *ministeriales* see Arnold, *German Knighthood*, pp. 47, 116, 231f.

religious legitimation of chivalry which Hartmann will undertake in his adaptation of French works, and again indicates that chivalric values were not merely foreign imports from France at the end of the twelfth century.

An important feature of the interaction of Church and warriors is that the Church sought to instil a sense of ethical purpose by extending to the sword-bearing class in general the ethical obligation to protect the weak, and defend peace and justice, which had previously been regarded primarily as tasks of the ruler. This extension is documented in the rise of liturgical formulae to accompany the arming ceremonies of young nobles, for the formulae drew on existing texts used for royal coronations.[10] When these blessings arose, in the tenth century, they may have been reserved for the sons of rulers, but they became more generalized in the course of time, stretching ultimately to the knighthood as a whole. The addition of the phrase 'ad faciendos novos milites' to the text of such a blessing in a manuscript of Klosterneuburg in the late twelfth century indicates that this generalization was operative in southern Germany in Hartmann's day.[11] The elaboration of an ethical code of chivalry in ecclesiastical circles thus shows knighthood inheriting some of the ethical prestige of kingship.

The interpenetration of Christian and secular values in the developing ethic of chivalry received a powerful stimulus in the crusading movement from the late eleventh century on. It is currently a matter of debate just how decisive a turning point the crusade marked in the history of chivalry, and just what contribution crusading ideology made to the rising prestige of knighthood. Recently Maurice Keen has modified the novelty of the interweaving of Christian and warrior strands in crusading thought by pointing to antecedents in earlier German and Anglo-Saxon traditions; and Jean Flori (perhaps too sceptically) doubts whether the preaching of the first crusade (launched at Clermont in 1095), and Bernard of Clairvaux's writings, made any positive contribution to the enhancement of knighthood beyond its narrow role in the service of the church.[12] Moreover we shall see that the impact of the crusading movement on the rise of knightly terminology in the German vernacular is not at all clear.[13] However, neither should the ideological contribution of the crusades to chivalry be underestimated. In particular, the appeals to crusade which followed Pope Urban II's proclamation at Clermont on 27. November 1095, and which were reiterated and elaborated throughout the twelfth century, provided two

---

10  Erdmann, *Entstehung*, pp. 76f.; Flori, *L'essor*, pp. 81–96, 319–29.
11  Flori, *L'essor*, pp. 322f.; Bumke, *Höfische Kultur*, II, pp. 402f.
12  Keen, *Chivalry*, pp. 49–57; Flori, *L'essor*, pp. 191–214.
13  See below, pp. 182–84.

related and powerfully suggestive concepts for the development of ideals of chivalry in secular literature. First, the Church's presentation of the crusade as a means whereby 'the order of knights [. . .] might find a new way of gaining salvation', without abandoning secular affairs,[14] provided a new sanction for military prowess as a means of winning eternal life, and this in turn opened up the way for poets to endow the knight's armed questing in romance with metaphysical significance. And second, the contrast of the old (evil) and the new (virtuous) *militia*, and the appeal to inner conversion in crusading propaganda,[15] provided a concept of knighthood as a moral process, which, with greater or lesser degrees of secularization, contributed to new ways of presenting the knight as protagonist in vernacular literature.

The promulgation of peace at an official level took a somewhat different chronological and political course in Germany than in France, and one that throws light on the social context of Hartmann's literary concern with knightly ethics. Royal authority remained more intact in Germany than in France during the tenth and early eleventh centuries. Consequently the ecclesiastical peace movement did not penetrate Germany in this period. Later, the spread of civil war and feuding in the reign of Henry IV (1056–1106) did produce conditions in Germany similar to those which had given rise to the peace movement in southern France a century earlier, and now German bishops followed the French example by proclaiming the Peace of God in the empire at councils in Liège (1082), Cologne (1083) and Mainz (1085).[16] The ecclesiastical Peace and Truce of God played only a brief part in Germany, for here peace legislation was quickly taken over by the secular authorities, who gathered assemblies to proclaim general territorial peaces (*Landfrieden*) from the end of the eleventh century onwards. The earliest *Landfrieden* were promulgated at a regional (ducal) level in Swabia and Bavaria. Then, in 1103, Henry IV declared a peace valid for the whole empire. This was the first in a long series of imperial and provincial peaces, which reached to the *Ewiger Landfriede* ('Eternal Peace') of 1495, when the feud was finally banned for all time. From the accession of Lothar of Supplinburg (1125) to the fifteenth century, it was customary for each new king of Germany to declare a peace as a kind of government programme.[17] Peaces were also declared in mid-reign. The period from

---

[14]  Guibert of Nogent, *Gesta Dei per Francos*, p. 124; quoted by Riley-Smith, *The Crusades*, p. 9.
[15]  See for instance Bernard of Clairvaux's contrast of the vainglorious secular knighthood and the virtuous new knighthood of the Templars (*De laude novae militiae*, cols 921–27), and Otto of Freising's reference to the 'sudden and unusual change of heart' which led violent plunderers to take the cross for the crusade in 1147 (*Gesta Frederici*, I, 43, p. 210: 'hanc tam subitam quam insolitam mutationem').
[16]  Cowdrey, 'The Peace and the Truce of God', pp. 64f.
[17]  Angermeier, 'Landfriedenspolitik', p. 167.

1103 to 1235 was particularly active, with some 28 known peace ordinances (though not all the texts have survived).[18] This certainly sufficed to ensure that the provisions of these *Landfrieden* were constantly being re-stated, and in some cases modified in the light of experience and changing circumstances.

The *Landfrieden* are the chief sources for legislation about criminal justice in Germany in the twelfth century, from which time they 'became a cardinal feature of imperial and aristocratic politics'.[19] They form a valuable normative record, and they throw light on chivalric ethics by providing public criteria by which to judge the use of force. The *Landfrieden* drew on various sources, including the earlier Peace and Truce of God, and customary law. Their provisions are of a mixed nature, including, for instance, prescriptions about the amount of fodder a traveller may take from the wayside for his horse.[20] However, the overwhelmingly dominant concern of the ordinances was with violations of the peace. Up to the early decades of the thirteenth century the peaces were concerned mainly with the conduct of knights in feuds. Then the emphasis changed, and from the middle of the thirteenth century peace legislation became more concerned with peasants, sub-knightly armed men, and townsfolk.[21] This development shows knights as the main source of violence up to the early thirteenth century, and the rising importance of other groups in this respect in later generations – a trend which has its literary reflection in Wernher der Gartenaere's *Helmbrecht*. The *Landfrieden* took over the main tenets of the Peace and Truce of God. A typical instance is the Rhenish Franconian peace of 1179, which placed priests, monks, women, peasants and merchants under protection, granted safety to objects and places essential for agrarian production (ploughs, mills, villages), and allowed the conduct of armed hostilities only on Mondays, Tuesdays and Wednesdays.[22] In general, recurrent provisions of the peace laws deal with robbery, bodily injury, abduction, rape, homicide and (especially in the decades around 1200) with specific feud actions such as the declaration of hostility, pursuit of the enemy, arson and the holding of captives.

Since peace legislation called on knights to give up ancient practices in the interests of peace, it was in some conflict with the martial aspect of knighthood. However, it would be a misunderstanding of the *Landfrieden* of Hartmann's time to see in them only this element of conflict, as if they were essentially at odds with knighthood and imposed entirely from outside. For one thing, even the lesser knights, the *ministeriales*,

18  See the useful chronology of peaces in Gernhuber, *Landfriedensbewegung*, p. XII.
19  Arnold, *Princes and Territories*, p. 43; compare Gernhuber, *Landfriedensbewegung*, p. 62.
20  MGH Const., I, no. 140, c. 20 (p. 198); no. 277, c. 13 (p. 382).
21  See also Schnelbögl, *Bayerische Landfrieden*, p. 58.
22  MGH Const., I, no. 277, cc. 1–3 (p. 381).

were by this time a hereditary landowning order.[23] Consequently they too had some interest in the more stable conditions of life and the protection of the agrarian economy sought by the peace laws. Further, the *Landfrieden* of the twelfth century were not expressions of the ruler's unlimited power, but were usually promulgated in express consultation with the lay aristocracy. For instance the two peaces which, by virtue of their date, give the best evidence of norms with which Hartmann must have been familiar (the Rhenish Franconian peace of 1179 and the constitution against arsonists of 1186), were declared by the emperor in consultation with the princes, the nobles and the *ministeriales*.[24] Thus at the time when the *ritter* and *dienestman* Hartmann von Aue was elaborating a new concept of knighthood in literature, German knights in historical reality were co-operating with the emperor in legislation to regulate their own military activity. In their content too the *Landfrieden* show a pro-knightly bias precisely in the second half of the twelfth century. As we have seen, the ordinances of 1152 and 1186 sanctioned class privileges of the *milites* and encouraged the sense of exclusivity and noble family in knighthood.[25] This tendency of peace legislation corresponds to the literary development of the same period, in which the knight became an increasingly central figure in poetic texts, and increasingly distinct in his mode of behaviour from other social groups.

The provisions regulating the use of armed force point in a similar, pro-knightly direction. In his first imperial peace of 1152, Barbarossa tried to take a tough line by defining all killing, save in self-defence, as a capital offence.[26] This amounted to the declaration of an all-embracing king's peace and a ban on feuding, which would have dramatically curtailed a traditional right of the military aristocracy. However, it is significant that this ordinance of 1152, which tried to assert royal authority so energetically against customary aristocratic rights, is highly unusual in the history of the *Landfrieden* in that it was promulgated in the name of the king alone, with no reference to the consent of the magnates.[27] Such an attempt at an extreme pacification proved fruitless against the continuing insistence of the German knighthood on settling quarrels by military means, and the peace laws of the later period of Barbarossa's reign (the Rhenish Franconian peace of 1179 and the constitution against arsonists of 1186) took a different, less radical line by recognizing the right of feud and now trying to regulate its conduct. Thus the peace of 1179 structures the conduct of hostilities by placing

---

23  Arnold, *German Knighthood*, p. 21.
24  MGH Const., I, no. 277 (p. 381); no. 318 (p. 449).
25  See above, pp. 68f.
26  MGH Const., I, no. 140, c. 1 (p. 195).
27  See the preamble to the *Constitutio de pace tenenda* of 1152 (MGH Const., I, no. 140, p. 195); and Gernhuber, *Landfriedensbewegung*, p. 94.

certain persons and objects under protection, and by limiting hostilities to certain days of the week.[28] This law also adds interesting prescriptions about the manner of pursuit, stating that an enemy may be pursued across open country, but shall have peace if he takes refuge beside a plough, or in a mill or village; and if he is taken prisoner he is to be brought forthwith ('statim') before the competent judge.[29] Clearly, these measures sought to protect non-combatants, especially the rural population, and to work against the holding of captives to ransom – a practice which caused much friction. The proper feud was to be itself a legal process, not merely the winning of material goods, or the inflicting of unmerited human damage.[30] The constitution against arsonists sought to limit the feuder's practice of destroying his enemy's lands by fire, and also decrees that anyone wishing to attack an enemy shall give at least three days' notice, and the messenger carrying the defiance shall have complete immunity from injury.[31]

The peace ordinances of 1179 and 1186 are novel in the detail of their prescriptions about the conduct of feuds. Indeed, in the span of the peace movements from the late eleventh century to the mid-thirteenth century in Germany, it is the peaces of the decades around 1200 (1179, 1186, 1221 and 1224) that form the most intensive phase in the legislative battle to bring order into the conduct of feuds.[32] Moreover, in formulating restraints on violence in this period, the peace edicts drew not only on earlier ecclesiastical provisions, but also to an unprecedented extent on the unwritten customary laws of feuding which had grown up within the military aristocracy. The provisions about an advance declaration of intent to attack, and about the treatment of messengers, did not create new law, but gave imperial sanction to what was already regarded as honourable practice.[33] In other words the imperial peace legislation is here influenced by concepts of good practice from within knighthood. On this point there is a remarkable convergence of developments in the *Landfrieden* and in German poetic literature in the decades around 1200. For just as the peace laws of Barbarossa's last decade took up knightly norms from the custom of feuding, so the same period saw a decisive stage in the transformation of an earlier, more violent warrior model into the restrained, ethically oriented figure of the knight as a defender of justice in the new literary genre of Arthurian romance. We shall see that Hartmann's *Erec* and

---

[28]  MGH Const., I, no. 277, cc. 1, 3 (p. 381).
[29]  Ibid., c. 2 (p.381).
[30]  On the legal dimensions of the feud see Brunner, *Land und Herrschaft*, pp. 41–110; Asmus, *Rechtsprobleme*, passim.
[31]  MGH Const., I, no. 318, cc. 17–19 (p. 451).
[32]  Gernhuber, *Landfriedensbewegung*, p. 222.
[33]  Otto, 'Abschließung', pp. 38f.

*Iwein* are key documents of this transformation. Finally, the mixture of religious and secular punishments in the constitution against arsonists[34] is analogous to the amalgam of secular and religious values that we shall also see in Hartmann's portrayal of exemplary chivalry.

Beside the Church's teaching, and peace ordinances of secular rulers, a social institution of major importance remains to be considered in the regulation of violence in Hartmann's day: the court. As an important institution of lordly rule, the court was intimately connected with concepts of justice and peace from early times. In the Carolingian period the court was still reserved to the king or emperor. Then from the eleventh, and more from the twelfth century onwards, non-royal lords spiritual and temporal developed their households into courts (*curiae*) after the royal pattern, so that the concept of a court, and a courtly style of life became more widely diffused.[35] This process was only one expression of the increased concentration of wealth generated in the more stable (though by no means completely pacified) conditions which characterized much of the twelfth century after the widespread warfare of the eleventh century. The economic improvement allowed the construction of more expansive castles which, beside their continuing military function, also acted as centres of administration and social activity, and permitted a greater ease than their forerunners (though the comfort even of these later castles should not be exaggerated).[36] The lordly courts provided military and social instruction for youths connected with the lord's family. In this, and in other ways, they formed an important matrix for the developing values of chivalry.

Since knighthood had its origins in the warrior sphere, while the court was connected with peace and justice, there was potential tension between the two. However, there are signs especially by the mid-twelfth century of a growing accommodation of knighthood and the court. Thus the developing vocabulary of 'courtliness' shows chronological and sociological parallels with that of knighthood.[37] The rise of the Latin terms *curialis* and *curialitas* in clerical writers of the eleventh and twelfth centuries expresses a widening social and cultural range of the court. The vernacular followed somewhat later, and the German words *hövesch* and *hövescheit* first appear in the mid-twelfth century. These terms are first attested in the *Kaiserchronik* (4351, 4614: 'hovesc') and *König Rother* (3776: 'houisheit') – two works which also show the rise of the term

---

34   On this mixture see Otto, 'Abschließung', pp. 36–39.
35   Schreiner, ' "Hof" (*curia*)', pp. 68–73; Bumke, *Höfische Kultur*, I, pp. 71–82.
36   Anderson, *Castles*, pp. 74, 152f., 159; Bumke, *Höfische Kultur*, I, pp. 143–61.
37   On the vocabulary of 'courtliness' see Schrader, *Studien*, passim (useful collection of material, but the interpretation is unreliably idealizing and schematic); Jaeger, *The Origins of Courtliness*, especially pp. 129–75; Bumke, *Höfische Kultur*, I, pp. 78–82; Ganz, '*curialis / hövesch*', passim; Fleckenstein (ed.), *Curialitas*, pp. 15–54.

*ritter.*[38] These early occurrences link the warrior world with that of women,[39] and although the concept of courtliness rapidly broadened, this remained a frequent connotation. Further, the evaluative terminology of courtliness parallels the growing social distinctiveness of knighthood, in that both sets of terms developed in opposition to the peasant sphere. The opposition of *miles* and *ritter* to *rusticus* and *gebûr*, which became ever more marked in the twelfth century, is paralleled in the sphere of the court by the opposition of *curialis* and *hövesch* to terms from the peasant sphere, such as *rusticus, rusticitas* and *dörperlich.*[40] Thus the courtly form of life, like knighthood, was socially defined by being set off, at its lower end, from the peasantry.

Particularly towards the end of the twelfth century we hear more of knights at court: Duke Welf VI gave lavish gifts to the 'militibus [. . .] curiae suae';[41] and the lady of the Tegernsee Liebesbriefe (ca. 1160–1180) even describes the *milites* as arbiters of *curialitas.*[42] However, this is a rather one-sided view, for clerics were important figures at courts too. Indeed the court was a prime focus for interaction between the world of the secular, military aristocracy and that of the Church and clerical learning. The courts were also the social matrix for the new developments of romance and courtly lyric, which were to be the main genres for the poetic exploration and self-expression of knighthood. Indeed the elaboration of a style of behaviour appropriate for the court in German literature from the late twelfth century onwards had a class function in that it gave a cultural backing to the social differentiation that set knights off from other social groups. Finally, courtly culture had a strong international dimension, which facilitated the reception of French literature in German aristocratic circles around 1200, and which, in a

---

[38] See above, pp. 57f.

[39] In *Rother* the courageous hero is said to have won the emperor's daughter by his 'courtliness' (3776). In the *Kaiserchronik* 'courtly' ladies are mentioned together with 'knightly sports' (4350f.), and the love of women is said to make a man 'courtly and brave' (4609–15). These links are reminiscent of the well-known passage in Geoffrey of Monmouth's *Historia*, in which knights compete in imitation battle and are spurred on by the flirtatious behaviour of the watching womenfolk (HRB, c. 157; Thorpe, IX, 13). Clearly, it was not only in the genre of Arthurian romance that this new, 'courtly' interaction of love and military prowess was received into the German sphere.

[40] On this latter opposition see Jaeger, *The Origins of Courtliness*, p. 115; Bumke, *Höfische Kultur*, I, pp. 79f.

[41] *Historia Welforum*, p. 72. The phrase *milites curiae* emphasizes the connection of knights to the court as an institution, relegating personal bonds to the background (see Schreiner, ' "Hof" (*curia*)', p. 70); the crystallization of the court as an institution, which is reflected in the emergence of this type of phrase in Latin historical sources in the twelfth century, has its poetic counterpart in the increasing importance of the court, and the protagonists' sense of belonging to the court as a collective, in the new genre of romance from the late twelfth century onwards. On the role of knights in the Hohenstaufen imperial court in the 1180s see Fleckenstein, 'Friedrich Barbarossa und das Rittertum', passim.

[42] See Ganz, *'curialis / hövesch'*, p. 46.

broader sense, promoted chivalry as an ideology that ranged across political and linguistic boundaries.[43]

What light do the peace movements and the emergence of 'courtliness' throw on the development of knightly ethics in the twelfth century? On the subject of knighthood and violence, the development of courts as social institutions, and the emergence of an ideology of courtly behaviour, were an important context for the transition from an earlier warrior mentality to the knightly ethics of the central Middle Ages, for social interaction at courts, and the patterns of polite behaviour and emotional introspection propagated in the new poetry of the courts provided, beside the battlefield, an additional, physically less aggressive centre of values which was favourable to the emergence of the gentler aspects of chivalry. Norbert Elias is surely right to see the court society of the twelfth and thirteenth centuries as an important stage in the 'Verhöflichung der Krieger', the process of 'civilizing' which involved greater restraint in the expression of violence.[44]

However, it is not clear just how substantial the mental and behavioural changes were that Elias postulates, and just what psychological, social and cultural factors were operative in these changes in the medieval period. In Elias's view, the mechanisms of moderation and restraint in knighthood sprang from within the changing structure of feudal society itself, as the greater centralization of authority, and the elaboration of larger networks of competition and interdependence at the emerging courts led to some channelling and disciplining of the warriors' aggressive instincts, even though this process did not yet reach as far as it was to do under later absolutist rule.[45] Recently Stephen Jaeger has modified Elias's theory of the dynamics of 'civilizing' in knighthood. Jaeger agrees with Elias that the court was an institution of leading importance in this development. But against the widespread view that the more civilized, courtly ethic of chivalry of the period around 1200 arose within knighthood, as an evolutionary product of changing social circumstances, Jaeger maintains that this ethic first arose outside the warrior class, in the world of courtier clerics who were educated in statesmanship and in the social arts needed in proximity to the ruler. This ideal of the courtier was then passed on from the clerical sphere to that of the warrior.[46] Jaeger lays far more emphasis than Elias does on education as a motor of the 'civilizing' process.[47] He sees chivalric values as a product of education by clerics, and the courtly

---

[43] Writing about courtly culture, Ganz, '*hövesch / hövescheit*', p. 54, speaks of 'die wesentliche Einheit dieser internationalen ritterlichen Subkultur'.
[44] Elias, *Prozeß der Zivilisation*, II, pp. 351–69.
[45] Ibid., pp. 88–121 and often.
[46] Jaeger, *The Origins of Courtliness*, pp. 101f. and often.
[47] Ibid., p. 259 and often.

romance as a means of instruction: 'The architects of chivalry were clerics functioning in their capacity as educators; their most efficient pedagogic instrument was the courtly romance'.[48] The romance itself is seen not as an expression of pre-existing values of the secular nobility, but as a poetic means of establishing new values: 'In short, romance does not mirror the chivalric values of the feudal nobility; it creates them'.[49]

There is much to agree with in Jaeger's important and challenging study. We shall see that Hartmann's works support Jaeger's view of the moral, 'civilizing' intention of romance. However, Jaeger surely goes too far in playing down the importance of 'the real social-political circumstances of the lay nobility' in the formation of chivalric ideals;[50] and his study does not devote enough attention to the warrior and aristocratic mentality of knighthood, or to the ideological role of love, to be a fully satisfying account of chivalric ethics and their social framework. Jaeger sees the socio-cultural situation of knighthood (and of the courtly romance) at the end of the twelfth century as one in which 'this class of rough-cut and boorish warriors'[51] submitted itself to the civilizing influence of clerics. This view falls well short of the whole truth. Jaeger aptly draws on Thomasin von Zerklaere for evidence of the important role of clerics in the education of young nobles.[52] Thomasin was himself a cleric, and his work is a revealing compendium of forms of behaviour deemed appropriate for the court around 1200, ranging from table manners to the duties of lordship. Thomasin urges lords to engage learned teachers (*Der wälsche Gast* 9252: 'meister wol gelêrt') to educate their children in ethics and courtesy. But he also urges noble youths to follow the example of 'good knights' at court (ibid. 346: 'der rîter guot'). In Thomasin's disquisition, knights are thus involved in the education of young nobles at court, as role models, as well as the clerics who provide education in a narrower sense. This surely reflects actual social practice. The military education of young nobles was in the hands of knights, for that was their profession. Moreover, this military education

---

[48] Ibid., p. 213.
[49] Ibid., p. 209.
[50] Ibid., p. 207. Jaeger's emphasis on the clerical, educative input leads him to support the view that 'the ideals of the courtly chivalric ethic derived ultimately from classical antiquity' (p. 114). This begs some important questions. Curtius, 'Das "ritterliche Tugendsystem" ', pp. 142–45, and Rocher, 'Lateinische Tradition', pp. 467–77, argue cogently for a more pluralist and differentiated view of knightly ethics, with stronger reference to the reality of twelfth-century society; and Hempel, *Übermuot diu alte*, pp. 183f., maintains that the self-assertive ethic of knighthood was essentially native (Germanic) in origin, and only coloured in a secondary way by classical ethics. The deployment of material from classical antiquity in medieval thinking about the *militia* deserves fresh study in the light of recent research on knighthood as a historical phenomenon.
[51] *The Origins of Courtliness*, p. 207. Such a broad and stereotype description is hardly more conducive to a proper historical understanding than the one-sidedly idealizing view of knighthood against which Jaeger rightly reacts.
[52] Ibid., pp. 219f.

also involved some inculcation of broader social values concerned with honour, and with the customary and sanctioned ways of using arms in combat and feud. These values were generated within the knighthood as a military class, they had an impact even on the imperial laws of Hartmann's day, and they must be taken into account in any full consideration of chivalric ethics, for they were of immediate importance in shaping the mentality and the practical morality of knighthood.

In short, what is striking is the heterogeneity of factors involved in the development of chivalric ethics in the key period of the late twelfth century: the warrior pursuit of honour; a claim to armed force as a legitimate means of redress; concepts of the *militia* as an ethical obligation and an instrument of law and protection; a strand of humility stemming from the lay piety of the Christian reform; a tendency to restraint and moderation in behaviour arising from the social culture of the courts. All these factors are evident in Hartmann's treatment of the knight's use of force in *Erec*, and in his presentation of knighthood in general, which is culturally far more complex than has at times been suggested.

## The role of combats in the composition of Erec

The heterogeneity of values which characterizes the cultural situation of the aristocracy around 1200 is expressed in the very structure of Hartmann's *Erec* and its French source, in that the themes of love and the exercise of force are interwoven throughout the work, whilst the crisis of the hero's neglect of military activity for the marital bed brings into conflict two central components of chivalric ideology: the ancient military base and the new concern with love. The central crisis of the work thus has a timely public resonance as well as a personal, emotional dimension; and the heterogeneity of values is especially marked in Hartmann's adaptation as he gives the religious dimension increased prominence beside the secular strands of knighthood.

The theme of love is a major innovation of secular, literary projections of the *militia* in the late twelfth century, as against religious conceptions of chivalry emanating from the Church. In sociological terms, love was a welcome value for the secular aristocracy to cultivate at a time when it was seeking broader forms of cultural legitimacy than the purely military. From the late twelfth century onwards, love, or the service of ladies, remained central to the secular model of chivalry, forming an almost obligatory element in poetic treatments of knighthood and a recurrent motif even in chronicles treating historically real persons.[53]

---

[53] On the appropriation of love and 'Frauendienst' as supports for the ideology of aristocratic lordship in thirteenth-century German chronicles see Wenzel, *Höfische Geschichte*, pp. 122–27, 147; Ashcroft, 'Fürstlicher Sex-Appeal', p. 94.

However, the military function remained essential to knighthood still in Hartmann's day, and the interplay of martial and amatory values is expressed in *Erec* in the interweaving of love and combat as the principal elements of plot. A schematic representation of Erec's combats by reference to his opponents reveals an expressive pattern in the romance (see p. 98). Indeed, these combats, far from forming a random sequence, are part of the meaningful compositional symmetry of this pathbreaking romance, to which attention has often been drawn since the important interpretation of Chrétien's *Erec* by Bezzola and of Hartmann's adaptation by Kuhn.[54] The romance as a whole presents a double initiation of the hero (and of the partnership between Erec and Enite) into the prestige and responsibilities of lordship, with the first initiation ending in failure (Erec's neglect of chivalry), and the second, longer initiation echoing and expanding motifs from the first, and ending with Erec newly integrated into society as an exemplary ruler.

The combat situations form an essential part of this overarching dual symmetry, and they show in many details the compositional principle of repetition modified by variation along an ascending line which is central to the work as a whole. For instance the main sequence of encounters (section II) opens with Erec meeting a group of three robbers, then immediately afterwards a group of five robbers. This doubling of a motif with a numerical increase is a signal to the audience to be on the lookout for intensifying repetitions in the rest of the work.[55] The main sequence of encounters is made up of two co-ordinated strands which are separated by the burlesque incident of Erec unseating the unfortunate Keii with the butt of his lance. Each of these strands (II A 1–3 and II B 1–3) has an ascending line in the social dignity of Erec's opponents, starting with non-courtly figures (robbers, giants) and progressing to a count and a king. The two(!) giants with whom series II B begins are related to the two(!) bands of robbers in that in each case these opponents are marauders who waylay innocent travellers; Oringles echoes Galoain in that each is a count and lord of a castle and a knightly retinue, and each covets Enite; and affinity between opponents gives way to identity when Erec twice meets King Guivreiz. The opening and closing combats (sections I and III), as well as having some links with other combat scenes, share features which mark them out as being especially closely related to each other. Each is a formal challenge combat in which Erec is pitted against a finely equipped knight who has the advantage of better armour and greater experience (Iders) or greater size and experience (Mabonagrin); in each case both combatants champion a lady; on each occasion Erec spares the life of his opponent;

54 Bezzola, *Le sens de l'aventure et de l'amour*; Kuhn, 'Erec'.
55 See also Kuhn, 'Erec', p. 143.

# The Composition of Hartmann's *Erec*

I    THE OPENING SECTION

    1.   The knight Iders

    2.   The tournament

    (Return to Arthur's court, then to Karnant)


II    THE MAIN SEQUENCE OF ADVENTURES

  A    1a.   Three robbers

      1b.   Five robbers

      2.   Count Galoain

      3.   King Guivreiz

      4.   Burlesque encounter with Keii

      (Unwilling visit to Arthur's court)

  B    1.   Two giants

      2.   Count Oringles

      3.   King Guivreiz


III    THE CLIMACTIC ADVENTURE: 'JOIE DE LA CURT'

    1.   The knight Mabonagrin

    (Return to Arthur's court, then to Karnant)

and after each combat the defeated opponent becomes a member of a court (Iders joins Arthur's retinue, and Mabonagrin returns to the court of Brandigan), and Erec returns with Enite to be acclaimed at Arthur's court.

The formal symmetry of Chrétien's and Hartmann's *Erec* has considerable emotional, ethical and social expressive power. Both works present a pattern of integration into aristocratic society of the potentially destructive, or excessively self-seeking, forces of sex and violence, which are refined into socially creative forms of love and combat. In both works the presentation of combats along an ascending line gives the narrative an enquiring, self-reflecting, self-correcting dynamic. Moreover, Hartmann intensifies the pattern of progression in his adaptation by making Erec, who was a proven knight at the beginning of Chrétien's work, into an inexperienced youth in his opening adventure, and by taking him at the end of the work away from Arthur's court and back to his homeland to take up the duties of kingship. Hartmann's hero progresses from being an untried youth, a *jungelinc*, through a crisis and a series of testing and learning situations as a knight, a *ritter*, to emerge in the closing stages of the romance as a king, *der künec Êrec*. Hartmann thus alters Chrétien's work by accentuating the theme of Erec's personal progress,[56] which allows the German author to touch on aspects of socialization from apprentice knighthood through to the duties of kingship.

The integration of combat into a broader view of the hero and of his relation to the world is symptomatic of a fundamental tendency in Hartmann's works, which is as evident at the microstructural level of descriptive detail as it is at the macrostructural level of the arrangement of episodes in the narrative as a whole: Hartmann is concerned less with combat for its own sake than with combat as an expression of moral and social values. We have seen how Hartmann's interest in the realia of equipment links his romance with the real world of military chivalry.[57] However, the knight's solitary questing in Hartmann's romances is also unrealistic in a military sense, it is a selective literary stylization which draws the military encounters into the direction of metaphor or metonomy, that is to say that they become a vehicle for the demonstration of social and moral values, a means whereby aristocratic society reflects on and seeks to legitimize its own existence. The ideological character of literary combats is especially evident in the motif of the knightly single combat.[58]

---

[56] On Hartmann's alterations to Chrétien in this direction see also Kellermann, 'L'adaptation', pp. 512f.
[57] See above, pp. 43–45.
[58] See also Bumke, *Höfische Kultur*, I, pp. 227–36; Haferland, *Höfische Interaktion*, pp. 125–36.

Chivalry was not yet, in the last decades of the twelfth century, a static, codified set of rules, but a complex and dynamic response on the part of the secular aristocracy to a changing world. In this situation the use of armed force, which was the distinctive class prerogative of knighthood, was a central issue in the Church's propaganda, in legislation, in poetry – and no doubt in the actual life of the secular aristocracy to which all these related. The following sections of this chapter will bring an interpretative reading of the combat situations in Hartmann's Erec as documentations of an educated knight's response to this question of the legitimacy of armed force, and as expressions of a knightly mentality at a time of cultural change. In this reading more attention will be paid than is often done in Hartmann studies to the motives and actions of Erec's opponents. For just as Hartmann presents predominantly (though by no means exclusively) exemplary patterns of behaviour in the knightly hero, so he presents predominantly (though not exclusively) deficient patterns in his opponents, so that the portrayal of these opponents forms a critical examination of the unjust and destructive exercise of force in the actual life of his own day. The legitimation of contemporary aristocratic society is combined in Hartmann's works with a persistent note of criticism, and this note sounds nowhere more clearly than in Hartmann's portrayal of the hero's opponents.

## Iders: combat and the restoration of order

Erec's first combat introduces a recurrent theme of Hartmann's Arthurian romances: the exercise of destructive violence which is followed by retribution and the hero-knight's restoration of order by a deed of arms.

In this opening episode the unjust violence takes three forms. First is the petty violence of the dwarf Maliclisier, who strikes Guinevere's lady and the unarmed Erec with a whip (Er 52–58, 95–98), and who is punished, justly in the eyes of narrator and onlookers (Er 1064: 'ze rehte'; 1075: 'gar rehte'), with the rod (Er 1064–70). Such beatings were a typically dishonouring punishment, prescribed in German law mainly for serfs and menials.[59] Second, the knight Iders is presented as a figure of arrogance (Er 1230: 'unrehter hôchmuot'; 980: 'hôchvart'; 983: 'übermuot') who has twice taken the prize of a sparrowhawk at Duke Imain's festival 'by force' (Er 215: 'mit gewalte'). The term *gewalt* is here, as often in this period, in opposition to justice, and later Erec indeed

[59] See above, p. 56.

tells Iders that he has taken the prize 'âne reht' (Er 701). This arrogance finds a just punishment with Iders's defeat at Erec's hands (Er 965–85). Erec's victory also restores a proper order of things in the custom of the festival, as the prize now does go to the woman who is unsurpassed in beauty – to Enite (Er 1253–59, 1763–83). Finally Enite's father appears as an innocent victim of petty warfare such as was endemic in Germany in Hartmann's day, for he has been deprived of his lands by oppressors commanding superior military force (Er 396–413). Here again Erec restores order by giving to Koralus two castles as his own property (Er 1826). Erec's knightly generosity (Er 1807: 'vil ritterlîche') thus restores Koralus to the lordly lifestyle, marked by wealth and free, allodial property, which was deemed appropriate for the free nobility in German aristocratic society.[60]

Hartmann takes over the general pattern of restoration of order from Chrétien in this episode. But he also makes significant changes in presenting the ethical psychology of the knight's use of force, and he shows considerable and independent interest in this issue. For example Chrétien tells us that Enide's father was impoverished through having sold and mortgaged his lands to pay for the wars he has spent his life waging (EeE 515–17). We are given no indication of the justice of these wars, rather it is as if warfare were the natural, unquestioned content of life for Enide's father. Hartmann, however, explicitly states that Koralus was the innocent victim of oppression (Er 402–10). Enite's aged father enjoys Hartmann's sympathy, and the German poet is anxious to shield such a sympathetic figure from any suspicion that he may have waged war without good cause. A similar concern underlies Hartmann's treatment of Erec himself. When Chrétien's Erec asks for a loan of arms he bases his request simply on the fact of his enmity towards Yder, which he reports with unceremonious abruptness: 'Cel chevalier, je ne l'aim pas' (EeE 602). The mere fact of an affective hostility seems sufficient in the mind of Chrétien's Erec to justify a passage of arms. Hartmann at the same point has Erec carefully explain the insult paid to him by Iders's dwarf, and that this is the reason for his seeking combat: to gain satisfaction for the insult and injury he has suffered (Er 476–94). These alterations are characteristic of an important tendency in Hartmann's adaptation of Chrétien's work, namely that the German, knightly author pays greater (or more explicit) attention than Chrétien does to the ethical grounds for combat. Serious combat, where it is a matter of life and death, is never, in Hartmann's view, fully justified solely by reference to an affective will, to military prowess or to the pursuit of personal glory (which is a different matter from the legitimate defence of threatened honour). Hartmann discusses the grounds for the

---

60  On allods see Mortimer, 'Knights and Knighthood', p. 89.

use of force more explicitly than Chrétien does, and he repeatedly places passages of arms in a more explicitly ethical framework. In terms of Elias's model of the process of civilization, Hartmann's knightly protagonist is further than Chrétien's along the road that leads away from a spontaneously aggressive warrior ethos towards greater restraint, he is more 'civilized' in that his lust for combat is less directly expressed, his instinctive urge more regulated, he feels the need to explain and justify the assertive warrior drive to which Chrétien's hero gives a more spontaneous, unquestioning expression.

Iders also experiences the combat in more moral terms in Hartmann's than in Chrétien's work. It is true that Chrétien's Erec describes Yder's defeat as a just punishment for his 'orguel' (EeE 1021). But there is no indication that Yder himself draws a personal, moral consequence from his defeat, and when he hands himself into the queen's power he merely reports his defeat without giving a moral interpretation of it (EeE 1187–97). Hartmann, however, has Iders explain in a much longer speech (Er 1214–59) that his defeat was a just punishment for his pride, his 'unrehter hôchmuot' (Er 1230). So morally self-accusing is Hartmann's Iders that for most of his speech (Er 1214–43) he attributes his defeat to his own folly and arrogance, making it seem that his true enemy was his own inner weakness, his 'tumbez herze' (Er 1224). He only briefly mentions, after this self-indictment, that it was actually Erec who defeated him (Er 1244–47), and even here he describes Erec as exacting a just punishment for his 'wâriu schulde' (Er 1247), thus again internalizing the cause of his defeat. With his insistence on Iders's 'übermuot' (Er 970, 983), 'hôchvart' (Er 980) and 'hôchmuot' (Er 1230) Hartmann may be drawing independently on a clerical tradition as well as on Chrétien's reference to 'orguel', for the church regarded pride as the characteristic sin of secular knighthood.[61] Indeed, the affinity between Iders's self-criticism and the Church's language of penitential discipline indicates a recurrent tendency on Hartmann's part to raise the moral prestige of secular knighthood in Erec by drawing on religious patterns of thought.[62]

Erec's defeat of Iders is an act of vengeance (Er 135–37, 167–69, 480–91). The association of this act of vengeance with the restoration of order suggests affirmation of the knighthood's right to settle their quarrels by force of arms, so that the whole episode has an ideological function of justifying the knighthood's privilege of carrying arms. But Hartmann's attention to the proper grounds for combat, and his concern for justice and order, also suggest a cultural situation in which this privilege needed careful legitimation. Vengeance is here the enactment of

---

[61] See Hempel, *Übermuot diu alte*, pp. 115f., 183–86 and often; Flori, *L'essor*, p. 216.
[62] See also below, pp. 106, 115f., 119, 125, 131–33.

justice.[63] Hartmann is not advocating an anarchical right of the strongest (a position adopted rather by Iders, who has to see the error of his ways), but suggesting that the truly legitimate use of arms should be linked with other considerations of appropriateness, need and justice. This position is central to Hartmann's concept of military chivalry, and it will be expressed time and again, with modifications, throughout his two Arthurian romances – it is symptomatic of the social focus of Hartmann's adaptation of Chrétien that whilst he plays down in this opening episode those elements which suggest a limited, baronial view of kingship,[64] he elaborates the moral dimension of knightly combat.

It would, however, be quite misleading to see Erec's initial combat as merely a moral exemplum. Rather the combat is still a dangerous passage of arms involving courage, strength and skill; and the expertise of the two combatants (Er 918: 'kunst'; 919: 'meisterschaft') and their manly fierceness (Er 760: 'zorn'; 845: 'ir vehten was manlîch') convey admiration for an assertive, competitive warrior instinct which counterpoints the view of combat as a moral instance. This interplay of admiration for warrior skill and courage, and a desire to see the outcome of combat as a moral, even a divine judgement which is determined by factors other than the purely military, informs the detail of Hartmann's combat descriptions and is central to the ideology of chivalry in the key period of the late twelfth century.

## The tournament and honour

Amongst the recurrent military situations in Arthurian romance around 1200, it was probably the tournaments that most closely resembled practices of real life, though even in this case the extent of literary stylization in the poetic accounts should not be underestimated. After occasional earlier indications, references to tournaments on German soil and especially in the borderlands connecting Germany and France increase markedly from the last third of the twelfth century onwards, as the vogue for tourneying spread from northern France.[65] The tournament episode in Hartmann's *Erec* is probably the earliest description of such an event in German literature. Indeed since twelfth-century historical sources in the narrower sense merely refer to tournaments without any substantial description, the poetic romances bring the earliest detailed accounts of tournaments at all; and the tournament in

---

[63] On vengeance as a legal right, even an ethical duty in the Middle Ages see Brunner, *Land und Herrschaft*, pp. 22–24.
[64] See above, p. 23.
[65] See Fleckenstein, 'Das Turnier als höfisches Fest', pp. 231f.

Hartmann's *Erec* is of all the more interest for the history of chivalry because, whilst it is admittedly a fictional one, it is seen through the eyes of a knightly author.[66]

There is much literary stylization in the tournament episode in *Erec*. For instance Hartmann draws on the story type of the three-day tournament.[67] But he also adds many realistic details in adapting and expanding Chrétien's account: the description of Erec's equipment (Er 2285–343), the squires who accompany Erec (Er 2344–50), the junketing of the knights in their brightly lit lodgings (Er 2372–77), the cleaning and adjusting of armour (Er 2407–10), and the informal jousting before the tournament proper (Er 2413–39; 2503–15) are all realistic tournament details not found in Chrétien's *Erec*.

However, Hartmann also alters Chrétien's tournament description to transform it, characteristically, into a learning and testing situation for the young hero. As we have seen, Hartmann presents Erec differently from Chrétien in the opening stage of the romance, for whereas Chrétien's Erec is a proven knight of great fame from the outset, Hartmann changes him into an inexperienced youth, and Hartmann departs from Chrétien to describe Erec's combat with Iders, and the tournament, as the first such enterprises he has ever undertaken.[68] Hartmann identifies more closely with the young protagonist than Chrétien does,[69] and his portrayal of Erec's passage from youth to manhood is a dynamic presentation of knighthood from the inside perspective of an author who seems to be projecting his own concerns, anxieties, and fantasies of success through the literary youth and knight Erec. The tournament plays an important part in Erec's passage from youth to warrior manhood, for the adjective *junc*, which characterizes Erec's inexperience in the opening of the romance, is applied to him for the last time during his preparation for the event (Er 2285, 2324, 2331). The tournament thus marks the precise point of Erec's transition from youth to adult knighthood. Here too is an echo of real life, for military exercises played an important part in the upbringing of noble youths in the twelfth century.[70] Hartmann elaborates on this real function to present the tournament as a learning experience for Erec. Indeed Hartmann's Erec seems to grow in stature in the course of the tournament, behaving modestly as befits a novice in the Saturday

---

[66] For a fuller account of the tournament in *Erec* see W.H. Jackson, 'The Tournament', pp. 238–48.

[67] Pérennec, *Recherches*, II, pp. 249–54.

[68] See above, pp. 25f.

[69] On this important shift of perspective between Chrétien and Hartmann see also Bertau, *Deutsche Literatur*, I, pp. 565f.

[70] E.g. Frederick Barbarossa himself is described as having been trained, 'as was customary', in military sports as a youth (Otto von Freising and Rahewin, *Gesta Frederici*, I, 27, p. 180).

evening revelries (Er 2378–403), showing courage and skill in combat by rushing to the aid of a beleaguered comrade without pausing to put on his helm (Er 2638–719), demonstrating the characteristic tournament virtue of generosity by not seeking profit for himself (Er 2617–22), and finally showing a confidence based on achievement when he issues a challenge to any of the opposition to joust in honour of his lady (Er 2764–807). The tournament, which in reality was often fought out with a pragmatic eye to the main chance and attended by much disorder in the twelfth century,[71] thus demonstrates in Hartmann's selective account a whole range of ethical virtues.

The account of the tournament in Hartmann's *Erec* matches the historical record in demonstrating the importance to the chivalric mentality of the acquisition of renown, public recognition (Er 2473, 2486, 2622: 'prîs'; 2535, 2713, 2806: 'êre') by the display of martial skill. For the knightly world the honour won in tournaments was a mark of skill, courage and team spirit – values which were positive qualities in the actual life of the military aristocracy and which could further the career even of lesser knights.[72] However, nowhere was there a sharper contrast between knightly ways of thinking and the official voice of the Church in the twelfth century than on this subject of the knight's pursuit of honour in tournaments. For whereas the knighthood saw this pursuit as a positive value (Erec himself ponders on the need to 'act well' in the tournament, 2258–61), clerical voices from within the Church saw it as sinful vainglory.[73] The official voice of the Church remained hostile to tournaments as a useless threat to body and soul throughout the twelfth century. Pope Innocent II banned tournaments as early as 1130, refusing Christian burial to any who were killed in them, and this prohibition was repeated at church councils in 1131, 1139, 1148 and at the influential third Lateran Council in 1179.[74] The prohibitions made their mark in Germany, as is witnessed by Archbishop Wichmann of Magdeburg's refusal of Christian burial to a noble killed in a tournament in 1175.[75] It is inconceivable that Hartmann, whose education gave him fuller access to canon law than most knights had, should have been ignorant of these prohibitions. Despite the Church's views, tournaments were increasingly practised in the second half of the twelfth century, and the growing popularity of the tournament in the face of the Church's censure is 'a measure of the degree to which the development of

---

71  See Barber and Barker, *Tournaments*, pp. 22–24.
72  Barker and Keen, 'The Medieval English Kings and the Tournament', pp. 219–23.
73  Good documentation in Harvey, *Moriz von Craûn*, pp. 113–26; Krüger, 'Das kirchliche Turnierverbot', pp. 407–09.
74  Hefele / Leclercq, *Histoire des Conciles*, V, part 1, pp. 688, 729, 825; part 2, pp. 1102f.
75  MGH Scriptores, 23, pp. 155f.; see Krüger, 'Das kirchliche Turnierverbot', p. 417.

chivalrous attitudes and values progressed independent of the official climate of ecclesiastical opinion'.[76]

Hartmann too, by his eulogizing expansion of the tournament episode, shows considerable independence of ecclesiastical opinion in his account of Erec's initiation into knightly manhood. But he also gives the tournament a more Christian coloration than Chrétien does by introducing the knights' attendance at mass. Already Chrétien tells of Erec's hearing a mass before his combat with Iders (EeE 700–06). In adapting this passage Hartmann adds that it is the custom of those who love tourneying to attend a mass (Er 662–67). In the tournament episode he again departs from Chrétien to add Erec's visit to church before his jousting (Er 2487–500) and the attendance of the participants collectively at mass before the main mêlée (Er 2539–43). Hartmann is thus more intent than Chrétien on linking the tourney with a religious observance. The celebration of mass before an important combat seems to have been a new practice in Germany in Hartmann's day, taken over from French custom.[77] If this was the case, then Hartmann's insistence on this point may have sprung from his desire, as a knightly author, to use the new genre of Arthurian romance as a means of influencing the development of knightly customs in real life – here in order to give Christian sanction to a collective knightly practice that was condemned by the official Church. References to knights attending mass before tournaments in other sources indicate that this custom did indeed take hold in real life from the late twelfth century onwards.[78]

Hartmann's treatment of the tournament reveals a concept of chivalry which is neither an archaic, un-Christian warrior heroism nor an ecclesiastical view of military office, but which joins warrior assertiveness and Christian observance in a new amalgam. However, the harmonization of chivalry and God's will, to which Erec gives voice when he trusts in God to protect his knightly honour in the tournament (Er 2498–500: 'Êrec trûwete im [= God] vil sêre / umb sîn ritterlîche êre / daz er der geruochte phlegen'), is not yet as firmly established in the tournament episode as it will be later in the romance. Erec's achievement in the tournament is valid in Hartmann's view, but it falls short of the qualities he will demonstrate in the later stages of the narrative, when his chivalry will be placed more emphatically in a metaphysical framework.[79]

---

[76] Keen, *Chivalry*, p. 83. However, even amongst clerics there were some voices that were not so hostile to tournaments as the official prohibitions would suggest (see Krüger, 'Das kirchliche Turnierverbot', p. 417).

[77] Schönbach, *Über Hartmann von Aue*, p. 21.

[78] Caesarius von Heisterbach, *Dialogus Miraculorum*, pp. 50f.; Niedner, *Das deutsche Turnier*, p. 81.

[79] See below, pp. 115f.

Indeed there is perhaps already in the tournament episode an intimation that Erec's success is not yet on a solid foundation, when the onlookers compare him in his achievement to Solomon, Absolom, Samson and Alexander (Er 2813–21). This lavish praise acquires an ironic tinge when one remembers that all four of these great figures of antiquity also fell victim to love's power – and only a hundred lines later Hartmann will tell how Erec too neglects his newly-won knightly honour for slothful love.[80] Seen in this light, the apparently exuberant praise of Erec after the tournament suggests a greater complexity in Hartmann's narrative perspective than we have encountered up to now, for at one level this praise continues the author/narrator's inside perspective, his identification with the young knightly hero (here in a fantasy of success), whilst in the larger framework of the text as a whole it expresses the more detached view of a learned author who knows of the crisis and ultimately of the even greater success that await the hero. With regard to the reception of the text by contemporaries, those (probably an educated minority) with the necessary background knowledge may have picked up the ironic signal, whilst others may have taken the praise straight. Precisely in the culturally heterogeneous period around 1200 we should beware of postulating a unified audience response to the literary structures of Arthurian romance.

## *Erec's* verligen *and the world of adventure*

The importance of honour and military prowess in the value system of knighthood in *Erec* is indicated by the fact that the hero's crisis, which motivates the main body of the narrative, lies in his neglect of military chivalry and honour for the ease of the marital bed (Er 2924–73). Further, just as Hartmann endows combat with a wealth of social and moral meaning, so he endows Erec's withdrawal from combat with a deeper and broader (or a more explicitly deep and broad) personal and ethical significance than it has in Chrétien's romance. Whilst Chrétien depicts the crisis in terms of love and chivalry, Hartmann widens it to involve Erec's whole being as knight, ruler and Christian as well as husband.[81] Hartmann also accentuates the social dimension of Erec's lapse from chivalry, stating that it robbed his court of joy and prestige (Er 2989–92). The personal and the social are thus linked in Erec's crisis in a way that is typical of Hartmann's portrayal of knighthood.

This deepening and widening of the crisis is important for an understanding of the rest of the romance. A major function of the

---

[80]  Green, 'Hartmann's Ironic Praise', passim.
[81]  See Ranawake, 'Erec's *verligen*', pp. 98f.

adventures which Erec undergoes after his lapse is to restore his honour by proofs of valour. Indeed in *Iwein*, Gawein interprets Erec's path as one of endangering, then securing his 'êre' (Iw 2791–98). But this is only part of the matter, for, in a mirror image of Hartmann's broadening of Erec's crisis beyond the neglect of honour, the remainder of the narrative, as well as restoring Erec's honour, also explores a wider range of personal and social values. With regard to the military ethic of knighthood, Erec's rehabilitation as a knight does not imply an unquestioning affirmation of the pursuit of glory by deeds of arms, rather the theme of honour is developed in such a way as to advocate restraint in the use of force and to cast a critical light on destructive violence.

Here a reflection is called for on the relation of the world of adventure into which the knightly hero of romance rides in order to prove himself, and the contemporary reality of Hartmann's day. Helmut de Boor, in a standard literary history, summed up the work of generations of scholars who had studied the fantastic components of the literary realm of knightly questing when he described this realm in terms of a turning away from the real world towards a free, unchecked ideality: 'Das Geschehen und Handeln wird aus allen Schranken irdisch zufälliger Gebundenheit gelöst, um sich in einem idealen Raum in freier Idealität entfalten zu können'.[82] Certainly, the German Arthurian romances are less closely bound in their persons and their geography to the known world of their audiences than is the heroic tradition (for instance the *Nibelungenlied*), and they are in many other ways stylized literary products. But recent work has shown that Hartmann's romances also relate more closely to the social concerns of the actual world around them than de Boor's generalization suggests.[83] Indeed the world of adventure in Hartmann's romances is more a selective processing of reality than a matter of unchecked fantasy, and the knight's self-proving in this world has more social ideology than 'free ideality' about it. More precisely, just as the scenes of feasting at Arthur's court reflect, in a stylized way, the festive life of real courts of the day,[84] so the realm of adventure which is set off against the civilized sphere of Arthur's court reflects, in a stylized way, the violence that was still endemic in the historical reality of the late twelfth century.

The opponents whom Erec meets in the main sequence of adventures form two co-ordinated lines of ascending social dignity.[85] They also form

---

[82] De Boor, *Geschichte der deutschen Literatur*, p. 65.
[83] See e.g. Kaiser, *Textauslegung*; Mertens, *Laudine*; Thum, 'Politische Probleme'; Pérennec, *Recherches*; Fischer, *Ehre*.
[84] On the feast as a meeting point of literature and life in aristocratic culture see Bumke, *Höfische Kultur*, I, pp. 12–14.
[85] See above, p. 97.

two co-ordinated lines of ascending sophistication in the ethical questions posed by the use of force; and the related topics of destructive violence and exemplary knighthood can usefully be approached by considering Erec's encounters along this ascending line in his three socially and ethically related pairs of encounters with, first, the two parties of robbers and the two giants, second, the counts Galoain and Oringles, and third, King Guivreiz.

## The robbers and the giants: robbery, captivity and ethical progress

Erec's entry into the world of violence is aptly marked by the fall of night (Er 3109) and his passage, with Enite, into a deep forest (Er 3114). The world of violence into which Erec rides 'nâch âventiure wâne' (Er 3111) is also the world that was addressed by the peace laws of the twelfth century, and Hartmann's account of Erec's journey of self-proving has strong affinities with these laws.

A major aim of the peace laws was to increase the safety of travellers and mitigate the damage of feuding by working against robbery and the holding of captives for ransom. The Rhenish Franconian peace of 1179 sought to counter the practice of ransom and to reinforce the concept of military activity as a legal process by decreeing that captives should be brought without delay before the competent judge.[86] On robbery, the same peace has a wide-ranging clause in which the emperor orders princes, nobles, freemen and *ministeriales*, that is to say the whole sword-bearing hierarchy, to pursue robbers, thieves and counterfeitors and those who harbour them.[87] How much impact such provisions had on the use of force in real life is open to conjecture.[88] However, they surely contributed to a new image of the warrior as knight in literature, for unlike the ancient heroic tradition, in which warrior activity was largely a matter of vengeance which often led to mass slaughter, the new genre of Arthurian romance presents the knightly hero in a fresh light precisely as the defender of justice against malefactors. Thus it is of programmatic importance that Erec's first encounters in the two phases of his quest (II A 1, II B 1) involve the crimes of robbery and unjust captivity which figured in the contemporary peace laws, and that, by killing the robbers (Er 3221–25, 3386–99), and the giants who hold the knight Cadoc captive (Er 5498–569), Erec carries out in the fictive world

---

[86] MGH Const., I, no. 277, c. 2 (p. 381): 'statim iudici ipsum representans iudicandum'.
[87] Ibid., c. 16 (p. 382): 'Statuimus etiam et imperiali auctoritate precipimus principibus, nobilibus, liberis et ministerialibus, ut persequantur predones, fures, latrones, falsarios monetarum et qui eos hospitantur, qui dicuntur cern'.
[88] For a sceptical view of the success of peace legislation in reducing actual violence see Arnold, *German Knighthood*, p. 16; Mortimer, 'Knights and Knighthood', p. 98.

of the romance the task assigned by the emperor in these laws to the real German knighthood of his day.

Hartmann also makes alterations to Chrétien's version of Erec's encounters with the robbers and the giants so as to show knighthood in a morally more favourable light. Chrétien describes the robbers, in the narrator's voice, as knights (EeE 2796, 2827, 2883, 2927: 'chevalier'). He also speaks of these knights as living by robbery in such a way as to indicate a familiar connection between the concepts 'chevalier' and 'roberie' (EeE 2796f., 2927–2931). Robbery and pillaging are recorded as activities of knights from the formative period of chivalry onwards. The pursuit of booty was a major means of livelihood for so many knights in eleventh-century France that the very origins of military chivalry have been said to lie close to professional robbery;[89] in Germany chroniclers from the late eleventh century onwards castigate knights for indulging in robbery and plunder;[90] and the peace laws of the twelfth century were directed largely against 'räuberische Ritter'.[91] But although Hartmann must have been aware of a possible connection of knighthood and robbery from his own, German context, the robbers are referred to as 'ritter' only once in his adaptation (Er 3186). The reference is in Enite's voice and is strongly motivated by the word 'chevalier' in Chrétien (EeE 2847). For the rest, whilst Hartmann refers to the robbers frequently in the narrator's voice as 'roubære' (Er 3116, 3128, 3190, 3229, 3298), he does not, despite the strong lead from Chrétien, apply the term *ritter* to them. Rather, what was in Chrétien's text a close association of the concepts 'knighthood' and 'robbery' becomes in Hartmann's adaptation more of an opposition between the two. This shift of emphasis in the terminology of knighthood is typical of Hartmann's adaptation, for Hartmann tends to withhold the term *ritter* from truly unsavoury characters or actions – a stylistic feature which characterizes the German author's projection of knighthood as a selectively flattering one.[92]

Hartmann further departs from Chrétien to have the robbers differently equipped. There is no suggestion in Chrétien's text that the robbers' equipment is different from that of other knights. Hartmann by

---

[89] Johrendt, *'Milites' und 'militia'*, p. 98.
[90] Lampert of Hersfeld, *Annales*, pp. 126f., 354; Ekkehard of Aura speaks of robbers plundering 'under the name of knights' (*Chronica*, p. 362: 'predones . . . sub nomine equitum'); Helmold of Bosau comments on the Saxon noble Wedekind of Dasenburg who 'perverted chivalry into robbery' (*Chronica Slavorum*, p. 370: 'semper militiae usum in rapinas detorserat').
[91] Fehr, 'Waffenrecht', p. 181; compare Gernhuber, *Landfriedensbewegung*, p. 146.
[92] Pérennec aptly discusses the 'fétichisme verbal' which causes Hartmann to avoid using the term *ritter* when the actions involved are most susceptible to criticism (*Recherches*, I, pp. 57–62). It is true that Iders and Mabonagrin, who show arrogant and homicidal traits, are referred to as *ritter* (Er 778: 'der ritter Îdêrs'; Er 9636: 'der ritter Mâbonagrîn'), but both these knights gain in ethical substance after their defeat at Erec's hands and thus they too ultimately illustrate a morally positive ideology of chivalry.

contrast describes them as being poorly armed, with unprotected arms and legs (Er 3226), and wearing not the normal body armour of the knight, but 'îsenhuot' and 'panzier' (Er 3231f.), that is to say sub-knightly gear such as Hartmann mentions elsewhere, also in an independent addition, as the equipment of the squires who accompany Erec to the tournament (Er 2349).[93] In this way Hartmann banishes the robbers to the fringe of the knightly world. It is as if, in adapting Chrétien, he were putting into practice the historically recorded custom of 'unknighting', of ousting from knighthood men guilty of serious crimes.[94] In doing so he conveys the impression of knighthood as a moral as well as a military and social order, and he keeps the glory of full knightly equipment out of the murky realm of highway robbery.

The encounters with the robbers and the giants show another feature of Hartmann's adaptation which steers the audience towards a selectively favourable view of chivalry, namely that Hartmann tones down the bloodiness and the brute violence of Chrétien's accounts of the knight's use of force. When Hartmann describes the wounds inflicted on the knight Cadoc by the scourges of the giants he dwells with even greater insistence than Chrétien does on the flow of blood, following the French text to describe the streams of blood which flow from the knight's wounds (EeE 4397–400; Er 5417–23), and adding a new passage which tells how Erec follows the bloodstained tracks of the captive knight (Er 5579, 5587) before reuniting him, covered in blood (Er 5605), with his lady. However, whereas Hartmann surpasses Chrétien in his evocation of bloodshed here, where the wounds are inflicted by non-knightly figures using sub-knightly weapons, he adopts the opposite procedure of reducing the violent detail, and especially references to bloodshed, in his descriptions of knights' combats and the use of knightly weapons. This procedure is evident in all the combat descriptions in *Erec*, irrespective of the status of the knight's opponents and irrespective of whether Hartmann expands or abbreviates the description in adapting Chrétien, and it is important enough to merit illustration.

The tendency is established already in the opening combat, between Erec and Iders. This combat follows the classic pattern of such knightly duels in literature from the late twelfth century onwards, with an opening lance charge followed by foot combat using swords.[95] Chrétien records the physical damage caused by the knights' weapons in detail, telling how Erec cuts Yder to the bone with a body blow (EeE 958) and cuts through his skull (EeE 980), and how both knights lose blood

---

[93]  See above, p. 45.
[94]  See below, pp. 229–32.
[95]  On the stylized ritual of knightly single combat in romances see Bumke, *Höfische Kultur*, I, pp. 227–36.

copiously (EeE 960, 970), so that their swords are red with blood (EeE 886). Hartmann's account of this prestigious combat is longer than Chrétien's (Er 755–950, EeE 863–992). But whilst Hartmann praises the strength and skill of both combatants (Er 833ff., 918ff.) and Erec's fairness in not taking advantage of his opponent's fall (Er 824–32), he gives no detailed account of the wounds inflicted. Hartmann never uses the word 'blood' in this description. He refers only later, and for a good motivational reason, to Iders's armour as being 'bloodstained' (Er 1185). In the actual combat description he replaces Chrétien's sharply visualized, painful account of blade cutting through flesh and bone and blood flowing, with praise of the combatants' courage, and with a series of images based on commerce and dicing (Er 837–43, 864–86, 913–20, 940–49) which draw a metaphorical veil over the wounds inflicted on each other by the knights.

Hartmann adopts more of an abbreviating style in Erec's combats with the robbers and the giants. These are non-courtly opponents, from whom little glory is to be won. But the debrutalizing tendency of his adaptation remains palpable. For instance, in Erec's defeat of the robbers, Chrétien tells how Erec's lance pierces an opponent a foot and a half into his body (EeE 2870f.), and transfixes another opponent's neck, piercing bone and sinew so that the warm red blood spurts out of the wound on both sides (EeE 3022–28), how Erec unseats an opponent who is crushed and drowned in a ford by the weight of his horse (EeE 3035–38), and finally how he hacks an opponent in two, drenching his sword with his victim's blood (EeE 3056–59). Hartmann omits all these gory details, stating only in general terms that Erec defeated the robbers with lance and sword (Er 3216–34, 3386–99). Similarly, in Erec's encounter with the giants, Hartmann does not take over Chrétien's references to the spilling of the giants' blood, brains and intestines (EeE 4449, 4472). Indeed Hartmann, characteristically, does not mention blood in this episode, even though Erec kills both giants (Er 5506–17) and decapitates one of them (Er 5558–69).

These are not merely superficial shifts of stylistic detail, but symptoms of an important difference of perception between the two authors with regard to military chivalry. The violence of Chrétien's combat descriptions has affinities with an archaic heroic style which celebrates warrior assertiveness.[96] However, in the voice of an educated author who shows such a sophisticated sense of literary form as Chrétien does, such stylistic violence also suggests some detachment from the military world of knighthood, or at least a willingness to realize in language the life-destroying potential as well as the social panache of

---

[96] Detailed illustration of Chrétien's indebtedness to the conventions of epic combat descriptions in Jones, 'Chrétien, Hartmann and the Knight', pp. 92–95.

knightly arms. Chrétien's combat descriptions indeed reflect the complex sociological situation of the courtly romance as a genre in twelfth-century France. For the French romances of this time were produced for secular, aristocratic patrons and audiences who might wish to see the knightly arms which were a mark of their social status portrayed in a flattering light, but they were also the work of clerically trained poets who looked at knighthood from the outside and mingled glorification with a note of sceptical irony.[97] As a knightly poet, Hartmann presents in his depiction of chivalry a poetic stylization of the profession and values of his own social class from more of an inside and legitimatory perspective than that of Chrétien. Whilst this inside perspective leads him to show a greater interest than Chrétien does in details of knightly equipment, it also leads him to play down the blood-letting function of this equipment and to intensify the moral dimension in his combat descriptions.[98]

The rescue of the captive knight Cadoc (II B 1) is the first combat that Erec undertakes for a purely altruistic reason. The episode is also a crucial turning point in Hartmann's presentation of the hero, and this indicates the central importance of the rendering of aid in Hartmann's conception of ideal chivalry. The Cadoc episode marks, first, a psychological change. During the sequence of episodes from his leaving Karnant after the shame of his *verligen* to his leaving Arthur's hunting party (Er 3093–5287) Hartmann presents Erec as being predominantly turned in upon himself, uncommunicative, restless, and brusque in the company of others, searching without clear purpose. His manner then changes from the captive knight episode onwards, and for the remainder of the romance he is more communicative, he acts more purposefully, takes fresh delight in the company of others and seems more at one with himself and the world around him. Seen in this light, Erec's suddenly hearing a woman's cry for help and his turning away from his path to bring help (Er 5296ff.) has a symbolic dimension marking the hero's turning outward, which ultimately brings an enhanced inner clarity and new social integration.[99]

The turning point has strong ethical connotations, for in each of the three pairs of related encounters which make up the main sequence of adventures (the robbers and the giants, the two counts who covet Enite, the two meetings with Guivreiz), the second encounter shows some

97  Bertau, *Deutsche Literatur*, I, p. 436.
98  For a keen understanding of the profession of arms and the projection of a positive image of knighthood as central factors in Hartmann's chivalric remodelling of Chrétien's narrative see also Jones, 'Chrétien, Hartmann and the Knight', passim.
99  On the symbolism of perception in Hartmann's presentation of Erec, and on the importance of the captive knight episode as a turning point in Erec's journeying see Ohly, *Die heilsgeschichtliche Struktur*, pp. 74f.; Fisher, 'Räuber, Riesen und die Stimme der Vernunft', passim.

ethical advance over the first, and communicates an exemplary aspect of chivalry. In the case of Erec's encounter with the giants, this episode, in comparison with his meetings with the robbers, delineates a more nuanced, restrained use of force, a model of behaviour which again shows a parallel between Hartmann's concept of military chivalry and the peace movements. A main aim of these movements was to replace the armed feuds of the warrior class with peaceful means of settling disputes. An important step in this direction was taken for the whole of Germany in the royal peace declared at Frankfurt in February 1234 and in the great imperial peace of Mainz, August 1235, both of which decreed that the use of force was legitimate only if the aggrieved party had first tried to reach a settlement by a peaceful judicial process.[100] Thus the armed feud was no longer to be recognized as an equal, alternative means of pursuing justice beside a judicial complaint, and was given only qualified recognition as a subsidiary means of last resort. An ethic of peaceful settlement had, however, been promulgated long before Hartmann's day, indeed from the beginnings of the peace movements, in writings which emanated from the Church, and which took their lead more or less explicitly from the New Testament ethos of turning the other cheek and repaying evil with good – a message which had special force when addressed to a warrior society whose feuds were more often fought out along the line of quick retribution.

The reforming message of peace and conciliation is central to the eleventh-century verse romance *Ruodlieb*, in which the unnamed Great King (*rex maior*) undertakes war only against aggressors, and pursues peace and conciliation in a spirit of Christian humility and charity, advocating the moral superiority of mercy over vengeance (IV, 141; compare V, 42), and warning Ruodlieb against seeking speedy retribution in a spirit of anger (V, 497–501).[101] The presentation of the hero in *Ruodlieb* as a young *miles* who leaves his homeland and undergoes various learning experiences foreshadows the theme of questing in the chivalric romances of the twelfth and thirteenth centuries. The advocacy of mercy and restraint in the use of arms in *Ruodlieb* provides a connecting link between the peace movements and the rise of knighthood as a literary theme. Moreover, the constellation of the Great King instructing the young *miles* Ruodlieb in the virtues of mercy and restraint typifies the importance of a royal model in the emergence of chivalry as an ethical code. *Ruodlieb* is indeed a revealing document in the early history of knighthood, indicating again the important role of the interface between clerical learning and lay nobility,

[100] MGH Const., II, no. 319, c. 4 (p. 429); no. 196, c. 5 (Latin text p. 243; German text p. 253); Gernhuber, *Landfriedensbewegung*, pp. 188f.
[101] On the ideal of Christian chivalry in *Ruodlieb* see Braun, *Studien zum Ruodlieb*, pp. 28–77.

and the early and original contributions of the German empire to the debate about the ideal function of the *militia*. No direct connection is suggested between *Ruodlieb* and Hartmann's adaptation of *Erec*. But the affinities between the two indicate again that some of the major concerns of chivalry were not merely imports from France, but also had roots in German soil.

Erec's encounter with the giants brings an attempt at peaceful settlement before the use of force as a mark of exemplary knightly restraint, and with characteristic modifications in Hartmann's adaptation. Already Chrétien's hero asks the giants to release their captive for ethical reasons, not at first with a threat of force (EeE 4416–18: 'Randez le moi, jel vos demant / Par franchise et par corteisie; / Par force nel vos quier je mie'). Erec's conciliatoriness is shortlived in Chrétien's work, and when the giants refuse to accede to his one peaceful request he immediately proceeds to use force (EeE 4423ff.). Characteristically, Hartmann's Erec shows more physical restraint than Chrétien's hero, and Hartmann brings a more sustained attempt at a peaceful settlement, expanding Chrétien's account so as to have Erec not merely once ask in peace for the captive's release, but three times address the giants in a conciliatory tone (Er 5435ff., 5457ff., 5487ff.), twice turning the cheek to provocative insults (Er 5448ff, 5477ff.) before using force (Er 5498ff.); and even now it is not an insult to himself that provokes his attack, but the sight of the knight being scourged all the more cruelly because of his (Erec's) intervention (Er 5492–97). It is as if Hartmann were taking every possible step to protect his hero against a charge of unthinking militarism.

Chrétien's and Hartmann's narratives both show a chivalric group consciousness in this episode, as the illtreatment of the captive is seen as an offence against knightly honour (EeE 4413–15; Er 5412, 5468–72). But Hartmann also brings broader ethical and even religious considerations to the fore. Erec's attempt to rescue the captive knight by peaceful means (Er 5490: 'mit güete'), despite the provocation of the giants, follows the spirit of the Great King's advice to Ruodlieb to return evil with good and to be slow to anger and retribution; and whereas Chrétien's Erec appeals to secular, aristocratic values of 'franchise' and 'corteisie' in trying to move the giants (EeE 4417), Hartmann's Erec puts his questions in God's name (Er 5438, 5475: 'durch got'). These alterations show Hartmann reshaping the mentality of Chrétien's knightly hero so as to feed into it important elements of the Christian view of knighthood propagated in the Church's peace initiatives. Hartmann also adds a new religious note in the narrator's voice in this key episode by speaking of God's aiding Erec in combat and by likening his victory to that of David over Goliath (5561–69). This is only one of a series of comments which convey a sense of divine guidance, or trust in

God's will, in Erec's actions and thoughts in the later stages of the narrative (Er 5516f., 7070–78, 8147–53, 8527–38, 8636–44, 9587, 9669–78, 10054, 10098, 10125–29).[102]

Hartmann's references to God's involvement in Erec's actions from the captive knight episode onwards are far more decisive, they carry far more authorial conviction than the (already significant) addition of Christian motifs in his account of the tournament. It is only after the knight has freely and actively placed his arms in the service of justice and an innocent sufferer that Hartmann gives chivalry emphatic Christian sanction. Together with Hartmann's presentation of the hero's use of force in terms of greater restraint, this new metaphysical line of motivation suggests a dual thrust in the German author's treatment of Chrétien's Erec et Enide: on the one hand a critical desire to provide corrective patterns of behaviour for the knighthood of his day to emulate, and on the other an encomiastic, collectively legitimatory view of knighthood as being not only a military and social order but also, when properly directed (the moral symbolism of Erec's riding through unpathed forest to follow a woman's cry for help, Er 5312ff.), one pleasing to God.

## Galoain and Oringles: lordship and violence

The second episodes in the two related lines of action in the Erec romances – Erec's and Enite's encounters with Galoain and Oringles (II A 2, II B 2) – present two important forms of violence in feudal society: violence against women, and the violent exercise of lordship.

Women were at risk in Germany in the twelfth century in a society in which violence was prevalent, and in which women were prized, and vulnerable, as objects in the formation of alliances and the transmission of lands. Acts of violence against women, especially rape and abduction, were criminal offences long before the twelfth century. A royal capitulary of Otto I in 951 drew on earlier, Carolingian legislation to punish those guilty of rape and abduction by excommunication and exclusion from marriage.[103] The Landfrieden of 1094 and 1104 punish rape with loss of a hand.[104] The peaces of Barbarossa's reign do not mention rape and abduction, which were simply subsumed under the more general immunity granted to women, for example in the Rhenish Franconian peace of 1179.[105] The specific crimes of rape and abduction

---

[102] See also Sieverding, Der ritterliche Kampf, pp. 59–65, especially p. 62: 'Das "Zufällige" der Chrestienschen "avanture" wird bei Hartmann ersetzt durch Gottes Willen'.
[103] MGH Const., I, no. 8 (p. 17).
[104] MGH Const., I, no. 427, cc. 3f. (p. 610); no. 430, c. 1 (p. 614).
[105] MGH Const., I, no. 277, c. 1 (p. 381); see Gernhuber, Landfriedensbewegung, pp. 235f.

figure again in the Saxon peace of 1221 and the royal peace of 1224, in both cases attracting the sterner punishment of death by decapitation.[106] The period from the tenth to the early thirteenth century thus shows a continuous legislative concern with crimes of violence against women, and a sharpening of the penalties for these crimes.

This constellation throws some light on Hartmann's addition of Enite's fabricated story of being abducted by Erec (Er 3865–84). Abduction was closely associated with the dishonourable crime of theft in German legal norms of the twelfth and thirteenth centuries.[107] This association is explicit when Galoain addresses Erec as a common thief (Er 4172: 'ir arger diep'). Indeed, whilst Hartmann projects a predominantly favourable image of knighthood in *Erec*, the knight appears in Enite's story in an unflattering light as a raptor of dubious origins. Criticism of the rapacity of knights is frequent in twelfth-century sources.[108] This was still a period of opportunity when many lesser knights were striving to improve their positions by the acquisition of land and by shrewd marriages. Georges Duby has pointed to the large number of abductions carried out by young knights in this period, and the measures taken in the interest of dynastic stability against abduction, as expressing deep tensions within the family structure of feudal society.[109]

Enite's presentation of herself as a young woman of noble birth who has been abducted by a social inferior[110] suggests for a moment the perspective of an established nobility fearful of its ranks being penetrated by upstarts. However, Enite's story remains a minor fiction within the larger romance, and it is rather the figures of established lordship, Galoain and Oringles, who appear as wielders of unjust violence. Galoain and Oringles are both counts (Er 3480, 6119), both men of substance (Er 3480, 6121: 'rîch'), each lord of a territory (Er 3479, 3786: 'des landes herre'; Er 6265: 'herre über ein rîchez lant'), each has a retinue of knights,[111] and each occupies a castle (Er 3606, 6708). Such lords in their castles were important wielders of power and key figures in the administration of justice in Germany.[112] The machinery of royal government was less stable and effective in Germany in the twelfth

---

[106]  MGH Const., II, no. 280, c. 7 (p. 395; on the dating of this peace see Gernhuber, *Landfriedensbewegung*, p. 88, n. 87); no. 284, c. 7 (p. 399).

[107]  Schnelbögl, *Bayerische Landfrieden*, p. 140.

[108]  E.g. Ortlieb's and Berthold's chronicles of the Swabian monastery of Zwiefalten present a grim picture of the *milites* as violent and persistent peace-breakers (*Zwiefalter Chroniken*, pp. 154f.; see also Fleckenstein, 'Vom Rittertum der Stauferzeit am Oberrhein', pp. 30–32); for further critical voices in chronicles see above, p. 110.

[109]  Duby, *Le chevalier, la femme et le prêtre*, p. 44.

[110]  See above, p. 57.

[111]  See above, p. 49.

[112]  On the castle as the nucleus of lordship see Brunner, *Land und Herrschaft*, p. 254; Arnold, *Princes and Territories*, pp. 180–83, 217–19 and often.

century than it was in England, more power lay in the hands of practically autonomous local lords, with their armed retinues, and the success or failure of peace legislation depended on their commitment.[113] Hartmann's portrayal of Galoain and Oringles takes up the theme of love's destructive power. But here, as often in the literature of the twelfth and thirteenth centuries, the erotic is closely related to the political in the sense of the exercise of lordship, for Galaoin and Oringles are also shown in a political light as breaching the very provisions concerning peace, justice and the protection of the innocent which were central to the peace laws, and which it should be their duty to defend.[114]

Both Galoain and Oringles at first approach Enite courteously and seemingly with sympathy for her plight (Er 3753ff., 6160ff.), but both then try to force a marriage against the woman's will (Er 3832, 6348). Forced marriages attracted the disapproval of the Church, which precisely in the twelfth century increasingly emphasized the mutual, freely given consent of both parties as a condition of Christian marriage.[115] And by expanding Chrétien's reference to the attendance of Oringles's chaplain at the forced marriage ceremony (EeE 4762–71) to include more clerics, even bishops and abbots (Er 6342f.: 'bischove und ebbete kâmen dar / und diu phafheit vil gar'),[116] Hartmann is not so much heightening a Christian sanction of Oringles's action as throwing a critical light on the power of the secular lord over the clergy in his lands. Hartmann makes the discrepancy between Galoain's attempt to steal Erec's wife and the lawful duty of a lord to keep the peace in his lands and protect travellers from violence explicit with a generalizing comment which focuses on the key concepts in the German *Landfrieden*: justice, peace and protection within a territory (Er 3678–84: 'daz was doch wider dem rehte / daz er dem guoten knehte / sîn wîp wolde hân genomen, / dô er in sîn lant was komen, / dâ ern bevriden solde / ob im iemen schaden wolde'). Finally, Galoain and Oringles show a classic trait of the tyrant by using physical violence against the unprotected in a spirit of vindictive anger, as Galoain kicks down the door of Erec's hostelry in an act of breaking and entering (Er 4046–48 – here Chrétien speaks only of Galoain 'entering' the building, EeE 3522), and Oringles strikes the defenceless Enite (Er 6515–23).

The initial courtly sympathy of Galoain and Oringles thus appears as an insubstantial cover for the often violent self-assertiveness which surfaces time and again in the history of medieval lordship. Moreover, it is indicative of Hartmann's hierarchical sympathies that, whereas he

[113] See Mitteis, *Staat*, pp. 331–33; Gernhuber, *Landfriedensbewegung*, pp. 90–92.
[114] See also Thum, 'Politische Probleme', pp. 62f. On the role of counts in jurisdiction stemming from *Landfrieden* in the twelfth century see Arnold, *Princes and Territories*, p. 187.
[115] Duby, *Medieval Marriage*, p. 17.
[116] See also Schönbach, *Über Hartmann von Aue*, p. 18.

portrays kings in a favourable light when adapting Chrétien, he sharpens the negative portrayal of the counts Galoain and Oringles. In general, Hartmann tends to sympathize with the lower levels of the aristocratic hierarchy, and to show respect for the topmost level, particularly for the king, but he does not identify so closely with the middle level of dynasts, which in Germany included particularly counts.[117] This tendency appears again in Hartmann's attitude towards Oringles's household, for he presents the count in a strongly negative light as a tyrant who loses self-control (Er 6515–24), but he shows Oringles's retinue in a morally favourable light as being critical of the count's forcing a marriage (Er 6331f.) and of his striking Enite (Er 6525–38). The retinue, which explictly includes ministerial knights (Er 6302: 'ritter'; Er 6332: 'dienestman'), here appears in a suggestive harmony with the (knightly) author as the defender of moral values against the abuse of power by a lord.

Chivalry further appears as a force for the good in that the knight Erec (Er 3634, 6135: 'der ritter Êrec') again restores moral order and protects a woman in distress by wounding Galoain and killing Oringles. It also indicates a personal, metaphorical dimension in Erec's combats that these two counts, like the first robber to speak in each of the two robber bands (Er 3194–214, 3318–35), lustfully covet Enite; for this egotistical passion links them with Erec's own transgression of neglecting chivalry for the marital bed. The identification of Erec's opponents with an aspect of his own erring self is intensified by the fact that Erec himself, like Galoain and Oringles, has treated Enite cruelly, using her as if she were his *kneht* (Er 3275). The objective symbolism of the romance indeed gives Erec's combats a moral and psychological dimension as projections of an inner process whereby Erec overcomes aspects of his own, erring self.[118] With this function, we can see the *militia* debate in the emerging romance drawing on the learned, Christian tradition of the battle of the virtues against the vices,[119] and again it is typical of Hartmann's presentation of knighthood as a moral phenomenon that he delineates this process more explicitly than Chrétien does within Erec's own subjectivity.

In Chrétien's and in Hartmann's versions Erec's killing of Oringles is followed by his reconciliation with Enite. But whereas the reconciliation takes the form in Chrétien's text of Erec forgiving Enide for her earlier words of criticism (EeE 4920–31), Hartmann also has Erec beg Enite's

---

117 See also Thum, 'Politische Probleme', pp. 61–66.
118 On the pervasiveness of the hero's encounters with aspects of his own self in *Erec* see Brall, 'Imaginationen des Fremden', p. 140.
119 Illuminating parallels between Hartmann's portrayal of Erec's ethical behaviour and the Christian tradition of conflict between *superbia* and *humilitas* in Fisher, 'Räuber, Riesen und die Stimme der Vernunft', pp. 371f.

forgiveness for his harshness towards her, and promise betterment in the future (Er 6792–803). The objective symbolism of Erec's killing an opponent, who is in part a projection of his own transgression of selfish love, is thus matched in Hartmann's adaptation by a confession of the hero which intensifies the sense of a subjective progression, an increasing moral awareness in him. This progression clearly has exemplary value. It marks a shift from male violence to a more tender and respectful treatment of women, a shift which is analogous in the ethical and emotional world of the romance to the protection of women urged in the legal language of the twelfth-century peace ordinances. Exemplary knighthood is, in Hartmann's works, intimately connected with moral awareness. It has an inner, self-correcting dynamic.

Further, the close interaction of the ideals of knighthood and kingship in *Erec* is again evident in the way that Erec is referred to as king, 'künec' in the closing stages of the narrative. In Hartmann's adaptation Erec is made regent by his father already on his first return to Karnant (Er 2917–23). However, from the shame of his *verligen* through the sequence of his penitential adventures until his reconciliation with Enite, he is never actually referred to as 'king'. Then at the moment of this reconciliation, Erec is described as 'der künec Êrec' (Er 6763), and from this point through to the climactic adventure of 'Joie de la curt' this royal terminology runs side by side with knightly designations for Erec.[120] The changing terminology of 'youth', 'knight' and 'king' for the hero ('jungelinc' – 'ritter' – 'künec') in the German *Erec* testifies to the importance of a biographical pattern of progress in Hartmann's adaptation of Chrétien's romance. The emergence of the charismatic nomenclature of kingship after Erec's first truly altruistic deed of arms, after his killing an aspect of his own erring self, and at the moment of reconciliation with Enite (a pattern of moral integrity) again indicates the key role of moral awareness and the defence of justice and the weak in the chivalric ideology which informs this pattern of progress, while in a broader historical context the interweaving of knighthood and kingship in Hartmann's first romance further marks the indebtedness of the chivalric ethic of the late twelfth century to older concepts of the ruler.

*Guivreiz:* âventiure, triuwe *and proper grounds for combat*

The ascending line of social dignity in Erec's opponents is matched by an ethical progression, for the last opponent in each of the parallel sequences II A and II B (Guivreiz), is a king, and Erec's two encounters

---

[120] See Green, 'The King and the Knight', pp. 178–82; Pérennec, *Recherches*, I, pp. 104–07.

with Guivreiz are concerned with matters of challenge and the proper grounds for combat which are ethically far more sophisticated than Erec's earlier encounters with manifest brutality. The Guivreiz encounters contribute further to the interweaving of knighthood and kingship, for Guivreiz himself combines royal and knightly qualities: he is a king (Er 4513, 4580) who seizes every opportunity of knightly combat (Er 4314: 'dehein ritterschaft er versaz'). Erec's two combats with this chivalric king lead not to death as a punishment for crime, but to a new chivalric friendship, and ultimately to Erec's integration into the community of the court. Further, Hartmann considerably alters and expands Chrétien's text so as to turn these two episodes into a veritable dialogue of the military aristocracy with itself on matters of social and military etiquette.[121]

In Erec's first encounter with Guivret, Chrétien tells in a mere four lines (EeE 3770–73) how the pair see each other, challenge and immediately join combat. Such spontaneity of battle is typical of Chrétien's knights, who are presented by the author, with a mixture of admiration and cool detachment, almost like fighting cocks. Hartmann identifies more with his knightly protagonists, thinks more from inside their situation, tones down their aggressiveness and seeks to justify the profession of arms by binding combats into a broader system of values. In the case of the first Guivreiz combat, Hartmann adds to Chrétien's version over fifty lines of dialogue in which the two knights debate the propriety of the challenge (Er 4326–77) before they give battle – Chrétien's chivalric fighting cocks become in Hartmann's adaptation self-conscious beings who debate an issue of military ethics before the implied tribunal of the work's audience. The very form of the exchange between Guivreiz and Erec is symptomatic of Hartmann's tendency to supply legitimizing explanations for the knight's use of force, and to introduce tempering delays between the initial urge to use force and its actual implementation. The substance of the argument also confronts two different conceptions of the proper grounds for combat. Although Guivreiz is a king into whose realm Erec has ridden uninvited and fully armed, it is not some reason of state that underlies Guivreiz's challenge, but rather the honour of victory (Er 4345: 'prîs'). It is significant in this connection that Guivreiz's challenge is based on the concept of 'âventiure' (Er 4340).

The word *âventiure* is one of the culturally most important of the flood of borrowings into German from the courtly and chivalric vocabulary of France in the last third of the twelfth century.[122] Probably the earliest

---

[121] On the relation of knighthood, nobility and status of birth in the exchange between Erec and Guivreiz after their first combat (Er 4442ff.) see above, pp. 79–81.
[122] On the early history of *âventiure* in German works see Oettli, *The Concept of 'âventiure'*, passim.

attestation of *âventiure* in connection with combat is in the Tristan romance adapted into German from French by Eilhart von Oberg about 1170–1190. The concept was evidently so unfamiliar to Eilhart's German audience that he provided an authorial explanation, stating that *âventiure* (*Tristrant* 5047) was a custom whereby young knights at Arthur's court rode out fully armed for two or three days, and whoever met another knight must give him combat 'whether or not it pleased him' (*Tristrant* 5052). This custom brought great renown to the knights (*Tristrant* 5056–58). The forest seems to be the normal setting for 'adventure' in Eilhart's work (*Tristrant* 5074f.). The motif of adventure as the knight's riding out from the court into the forest in pursuit of combat and honour appears only in one episode, on the fringe of the main action, in Eilhart's work. But it quickly became one of the main features of chivalric romance, developing into quests with at times complex moral, even religious dimensions. Here it is important to note that *âventiure* entered German literature, and acquired an important place in the developing ideology of chivalry, in a specific sense as a form of combat in which the only reason for battle was personal glory. This makes for a close link between *âventiure* and the tournament, and it is no coincidence that the rise of 'adventure' as a literary theme has close regional and chronological parallels with the vogue for tourneying which, in historical reality, also spread out from northern France particularly in the late twelfth century.[123]

Hartmann's *Erec* is the first German work in which the concept of *âventiure* plays an important part. Erec's opening combat, against Iders, his journey of rehabilitation after his *verligen*, and the climactic combat of 'Joie de la curt' are all described in terms of 'âventiure' (Er 221, 492, 1528, 3111, 7962, 7975, 7999, 8398, 8414, 8481, 9898). The new, chivalric concept of 'adventure' thus provides an integrative focus for the portrayal of the hero's progress in this pioneering romance. Guivreiz himself is closely associated with this concept, for it is his custom to ride into the forest in search of *âventiure* (Er 7398f.: 'dô er nâch sîner gewonheit / ze walde nâch âventiure reit'). His challenge to Erec also follows the convention of *âventiure* as defined by Eilhart, whereby only glory is at stake (Er 4345: 'prîs'), and the knight has to accept the challenge for better or for worse. Against this approach Erec's response rests on the view that a challenge is not appropriate against an unwilling opponent if this opponent has done no harm (Er 4359–61: 'ir sult ez durch got tuon / und mich mit gemache lân, / wan ich habe iu niht getân'). In other words, combat should be grounded in some reason, some cause beyond the fact of carrying arms and beyond the pursuit of glory. The exchange between these two knights thus again points to a

[123] See above, pp. 17, 103.

tension that runs through the ideology of chivalry, a tension between the pursuit of personal glory and the insistence on wider ethical considerations as sufficient legitimation for the knight's use of force.

This tension surfaces in modern scholarship in the way that critics vary in their assessments of Guivreiz's position, as his role in this episode is seen at times as conveying a trace of doubt about the legitimacy of his *âventiure*-based approach, at times in thoroughly exemplary terms as a demonstration of the proper mental attitude' which effective combat called for in a knight, and which Erec is only just beginning to show after the lapse of his *verligen*.[124] Erec and Guivreiz are both ethically far superior to the robbers, the giants, and the counts Galoain and Oringles in their use of force, and their exchange reflects a historical stage when the proper grounds for combat were still a matter of debate even within the knightly class. Again, military chivalry emerges as a living and developing complex at the end of the twelfth century rather than a fixed and codified set of rules.

Erec and Guivreiz emphatically agree, however, that a knight should, in his conduct of hostilities, act according to his 'triuwe' (Er 4352, 4374), and that a breach of *triuwe* would be incompatible with honour (Er 4358: 'âne ruom') and a cause of shame (Er 4355: 'laster'). With this linkage of *triuwe*, proper challenge and honour, Hartmann's version of the first combat between Erec and Guivreiz has affinities with one of the most important German peace ordinances of the twelfth century: the constitution against arsonists promulgated in Nürnberg in December 1186. We have seen that Frederick I, having tried to ban private warfare entirely at the outset of his reign in 1152, adjusted this policy later to accommodate the interests of the military aristocracy by recognizing the knighthood's right to use armed force in pursuance of quarrels, but at the same time regulating this right by formulating objective distinctions between legitimate feuding and mere untrammeled violence[125] This modified policy led to the introduction, in the ordinance of 1186, of two features that were new to the peace laws: first, this law for the first time in the written history of peace legislation decreed an advance declaration of hostilities, a *diffidatio*, three days ahead of military action, as a condition of a just feud;[126] and second, this constitution is the first peace law to use the expression 'violation of faith' (*fides*), which is how the law describes breaches of truce and failure to observe proper forms of challenge.[127]

[124] Elements of doubt in e.g. Meng, *Vom Sinn des ritterlichen Abenteuers*, p. 34; Green, *Irony*, p. 70. Exemplary readings in e.g. Scheunemann, *Artushof und Abenteuer*, pp. 42f.; Jones, 'Chrétien, Hartmann and the Knight', pp. 107f.

[125] See above, pp. 90f.

[126] MGH Const., I, no. 318, c. 17 (p. 451).

[127] Ibid., c. 17: 'de fide violata'; c.18: 'violator fidei'; c. 19: 'fidem suam violavit' (p. 451).

The word *fides* is here the Latin equivalent of the vernacular word *triuwe*, which term did indeed take the place of *fides* in these clauses when vernacular texts of the peace laws emerged in the thirteenth century.[128] And in the peace laws, as in Hartmann's poetic text, a breach of *triuwe* brings with it loss of honour.[129] We thus have a remarkable alignment of developments in peace legislation and in the courtly romance in that, in 1186, a German peace law promulgated in south Germany by the emperor in consultation with his nobles and *ministeriales*[130] departs from a century of previous ordinances to introduce the declaration of feud and the concept of violation of *fides* / *triuwe*, whilst within at most a few years of that date the knightly author Hartmann, also working in south Germany, departs from his French source to show an independent concern with the ethics of challenge and to place the spotlight on *triuwe* / *fides* as the touchstone of knightly integrity and the precondition of honour. These parallels do not necessarily imply that Hartmann's adaptation of Chrétien's *Erec et Enide* shows the influence specifically of the constitution of 1186 and must therefore be placed after that date.[131] For the provisions concerning proper feuding in this law, whilst new in the texts of peace legislation, were taken over from existing good practice in the customary law of feuding.[132] Hartmann too, as a young knightly author with a keen interest in the practice and ethics of combat, may also have drawn on this customary strand. What these parallels do show is an intensified concern of the German military aristocracy in the 1180s to preserve, and ethically regulate and legitimize, its right of carrying arms, a concern of social history which informs Hartmann's chivalric poetry and the imperial legislation of the day on specific common points of substance and terminology.

Again in Erec's second encounter with Guivreiz (II B 3) Hartmann departs from Chrétien to problematize the initiation of combat more fully, and to bring the question of the proper subjective attitude to combat more explicitly to the fore. Chrétien and Hartmann both tell how Erec and Guivreiz meet by darkness, fail to recognize each other, and join combat without a clarifying challenge or exchange of identities. In the passage of arms Erec, weakened by his earlier wounds, suffers his first defeat. Both versions thus show how a combat undertaken without a clarifying challenge almost leads to disaster. Indeed Chrétien

[128] E.g. a Bavarian peace of 1256 has the terms 'triulos' and 'so hat er sin triwe niht behalten' (MGH Const., II, no. 438, cc. 6f., p. 597).
[129] MGH Const., I, no. 318, c. 19 (p. 451): 'fidem suam violavit et de cetero omni honore suo carebit'.
[130] The preamble to the constitution against arsonists refers explicitly to the approval of *principes* and other *fideles*, both *liberi* and *ministeriales* (MGH Const., I, no. 318, p. 449).
[131] Haase, *Die germanistische Forschung*, p. 249 considers this complex as a possible dating criterion for Hartmann's work on *Erec*.
[132] See above, p. 91.

comments in the narrator's voice on Erec's folly in not revealing his identity (EeE 5006f.: 'Or fera Erec trop que fos, / Se tost conoistre ne se fet'). Whereas Erec himself shows no awareness in Chrétien's text of having acted recklessly, Hartmann typically presents this critical point differently, having Erec, in a passage without precedent in Chrétien, turn inward to blame himself for his defeat and accept it as a just punishment for his folly (Er 7010–23: 'swelh man tœrlîche tuot, / wirts im gelônet, daz ist guot. / sît daz ich tumber man / ie von tumpheit muot gewan / sô grôzer unmâze / daz ich vremder strâze / eine wolde walten / unde vor behalten / sô manegem guoten knehte, / dô tâtet ir mir rehte. / mîn buoze wart ze kleine, / dô ich alters eine / iuwer aller êre wolde hân: / ich solde baz ze buoze stân'). This self-indictment is a parallel in the martial sphere to Erec's begging Enite's forgiveness for his harsh treatment of her as his wife (Er 6792–801); and both these passages show Chrétien's more detached authorial attitude giving place to a closer identification of author and protagonist in Hartmann's presentation of Erec's chivalry as a subjective process of learning and self-correction.

That Erec has reached an important stage in his journeying after his second encounter with Guivreiz is indicated by Hartmann's referring, again independently of Chrétien, to God's guiding Erec through stormy seas to a safe shore (Er 7067–76). However, against some of the more extreme interpretations of Hartmann's *Erec* in terms of religious symbolism,[133] it should be emphasized that this reference to providential guidance, and Erec's self-criticism, imply more of a sanctioning than a rejection of secular chivalry. Erec's condemnation of the 'tumpheit' (Er 7013) which led him into this particular combat against Guivreiz does not involve a general condemnation of the dynamic pursuit of combat, for he later continues to seek out 'ritterschaft' (Er 7254), clearly with the author's approval. Nor does his condemnation of his own desire to win glory (Er 7022: 'êre') against Guivreiz and his knights imply a total rejection of renown as a motivation for chivalry, for he will still seek *êre* in his final combat (Er 8540–75).[134] It is not that Erec, as he gains in insight, rejects secular chivalry as was often done by voices within the Church.[135] Rather he expresses views which had exemplary value, as practical wisdom, in the secular, warrior mentality of knighthood: that a knight should know how to accept defeat gracefully, that courage should not be taken to the point of foolhardiness, and that it is a mistaken concept of honour that leads a knight to take on a massively superior force, as Erec does, for no other reason than a desire not to

---

133 E.g. Willson, 'Sin and Redemption'; Tax, 'Erecs ritterliche Erhöhung'; Bayer, *'bî den liuten ist sô guot'*.

134 The continuing importance of *êre* as a motive for Erec's actions in the later stages of the narrative is emphasized especially by Voß, *Artusepik*, pp. 104–06.

135 For the association of secular chivalry with sin see below, p. 151.

appear cowardly (Er 6879-88; compare Er 7010-23). Erec's proving of himself as a knight on his journey of rehabilitation thus involves his recognition of the value of prudence as well as his demonstrations of bravery and battle-skill.[136]

In short, the qualities that Erec's chivalry exhibits under divine guidance are still geared to social and military life in the world of the secular aristocracy. His learning process leads to integration in this world, and it is a prime function of his encounters with Guivreiz to articulate this pattern. Guivreiz embodies the community spirit of chivalry as well as its warrior energy. As king and knight he is an ambassador of the court, who seeks to draw Erec back into society: after each of his encounters with Erec he invites Erec and Enite to stay as guests in one of his castles (Er 4562-67, 7115-20). As such he is a morally positive opponent whose attributes Erec has to assimilate rather than to overcome. He is a projection of Erec's finer kingly and knightly self, that aspect which affirms friendship and community. Erec's acceptance of defeat at the hands of this integrative figure brings the period of his self-distancing from his fellow knights to an end, and is part of a chain of integrative symbolism which heralds Erec's return to court, a theme which dominates the closing stages of the romance.

## Mabonagrin: knighthood and the joy of the court

The linguistic evidence shows close parallels between the developing ideology of knighthood and that of courtliness in the twelfth century.[137] As knighthood acquired more of the characteristics of an aristocracy, it became more closely adjusted to the concept and the institution of the court. This interplay of chivalry and the court continued throughout the Middle Ages.[138] Hartmann's works yet again mark a key stage in this important aspect of the history of chivalry, and they show a development from the early Erec to the later Iwein in the vocabulary of courtliness.

The central terms in the socio-ethical vocabulary of courtliness – the adjective hövesch and the noun hövescheit – appear far less often in Hartmann's Erec than in his Iwein.[139] But the court plays an essential part in the composition and in the social and mental world already of Hartmann's first romance. The court is an important element in the composition of the romance, as Erec's journeying involves experience of

136 On the motif of bravery tempered with prudence in early writings on chivalry see Johrendt, 'Milites' und 'militia', p. 194.
137 See above, pp. 92f.
138 See Fleckenstein (ed.), Curialitas, passim.
139 Schrader, Studien, pp. 33-38; more detail below, p. 273.

various courts ranging from the utopian image of aristocratic harmony at Arthur's court, and the exemplary hospitality at Guivreiz's court, to the lordly brutality shown at the courts of Galoain and Oringles (one notes again the favourable view of royal courts). Hartmann's first romance thus shows not only the personal progress of the hero, but also various types of functioning of the court as a social institution.[140] The court is the main focus of aristocratic sociability in *Erec*. It is a public tribunal, rewarding martial achievement with praise (Er 1288–93, 2811–25, 9888–98), and censuring ethical lapses, for example when all at the court of Karnant regret Erec's neglect of chivalry (Er 2984–92) and when Oringles's retinue criticizes his brutal treatment of Enite (Er 6331f., 6526–37). Hartmann clearly conceives of the court as a normal place of social education, for instance when he adds, independently of Chrétien, Erec's reproof that Galoain has been 'brought up at a poor court' (Er 4202: 'ir sît an swachem hove erzogen').

This quite new exchange between Erec and Galoain makes explicit a convergence of the value systems of knighthood and courtliness in *Erec*, as Erec's charge that Galoain acts in an 'uncourtly' way (Er 4197: 'ir enthöveschet iuch') is matched by the narrator's comment that Galoain speaks 'vil unritterlîch' (Er 4169). We have seen how, from the middle of the twelfth century the word *ritter* reached out beyond the military sense of 'mounted warrior' to indicate a more general social status that commanded respect.[141] In the same period, and as an evaluative expression of the same social development, the epithet *ritterlîch* ('knightly', 'chivalric', 'chivalrous') also underwent a semantic expansion, reaching out beyond its original military and equestrian sense to include broader aristocratic qualities of sociability, politeness, generosity. This extension of the term *ritterlîch* is well under way in Hartmann's *Erec* and in other works of the late twelfth century;[142] and the close linking of knighthood and the court in *Erec* provides early evidence that socialization at courts played an important part in this extension of the concept of knightliness, taking it already a step along the road that led from the early medieval warrior to the gentleman of a much later age.

The theme of joy throws further light on the relation of knighthood and the court, for Hartmann presents the maintenance of communal joy as a task of exemplary chivalry. A concern with joy runs through much

[140]  See Giloy-Hirtz, 'Der imaginierte Hof', pp. 255–57. For Bertau, *Deutsche Literatur*, I, p. 566, Hartmann's *Erec* focuses on the psychology and the morality of the hero rather than on the court; for Ehrismann, 'Höfisches Leben', p. 99, it is courtly life rather than any unfolding of the hero's inner life that constitutes the main theme of the work. Such oppositions of interpretation in leading scholars suggest the need for further work on the relation of personal and social values in the courtly romance.
[141]  See above, pp. 54f.
[142]  See Pérennec, *Recherches*, I, pp. 75–79.

of the secular literature produced for the courts in the decades around 1200, giving this literature a tendency toward social utopia and establishing a connection between poetry and feasting in the rhythm of aristocratic life.[143] Joy is a leitmotif in *Erec*, and its loss and restoration is a central theme which Hartmann takes over from Chrétien and also develops independently.[144] Already Chrétien presents Erec's neglect of military chivalry as a lapse which saddens his companions (EeE 2443: 'Si conpeignon duel an avoient'), and Hartmann intensifies this motif by having Erec's sloth rob his entire court of joy (Er 2989: 'sîn hof wart aller vreuden bar'), so that knights, instead of flocking to his court as knights are drawn to the entourage of exemplary rulers in twelfth-century literature, leave the place to seek joy and sociability elsewhere (Er 2974–92). Joy is here not merely a subjective, private experience, but a cohesive force which binds individuals together to form a community, and Hartmann's adaptation intensifies the damaging consequences of Erec's lapse from *ritterschaft* for the community of the court. Consequently the restoration of joy to the court is firmly planted in the reader's mind as a goal of Erec's journeying from the outset.

The importance of joy as an integrative, communal value is again expressed by Hartmann independently of Chrétien when Erec, having been tricked by Gawein into visiting Arthur's court, complains that he lacks the joy that would enable him to contribute to the court (Er 5056–61: 'swer ze hove wesen sol, / dem gezimet vreude wol / und daz er im sîn reht tuo: / dâ enkan ich nû niht zuo / und muoz mich sûmen dar an / als ein unvarnder man'). Erec's refusal to spend any length of time at a court, even at that of King Arthur, at this stage of the narrative, sheds light on the emotional and ethical dynamic of his journey. Since the journey is, in part at least, a search for joy and fulfilment, one asks, in view of Erec's dissatisfaction on his unwilling visit to Arthur's court: what constitutes 'fulfilment' for Erec? Hartmann's *Erec* has often been interpreted as the story of Erec's losing and regaining his honour, his *êre*.[145] Indeed, the pursuit and winning of *êre* is a keynote of Erec's climactic adventure.[146] However, if the sole purpose of Erec's journey were to restore the warrior reputation that his *verligen* jeopardized, then the journey could end with his visit to Arthur's court after his victory over Guivreiz. For his victory over such a distinguished opponent has demonstrated his military prowess, and the acclaim bestowed on him by Arthur's company indicates that, in the eyes of aristocratic society, his knightly reputation is restored (Er 5085–88: 'ez enwart ouch grœzer

---

143   See Bumke, *Höfische Kultur*, I, pp. 12–14.
144   See Scheunemann, *Artushof und Abenteuer*, pp. 71f., 100–06; Eroms, *Vreude*, pp. 53–81.
145   Emmel, *Formprobleme*, p. 30; Maurer, *Leid*, pp. 49f.
146   See below, pp. 131f.

werdekeit / noch volleclîcher êre / nie manne erboten mêre / dan im dâ ze hove geschach'). Despite this acclaim by the highest chivalric instance in the romance, Erec yet insists on staying only one night with Arthur's company before riding off in search of further encounters (Er 5288ff.), evidently still experiencing a sense of unfulfilment. The three encounters which follow Erec's departure from Arthur's company then, as we have seen, demonstrate new ethical qualities in Erec: his altruistic aid for the captive knight, his reconciliation with Enite, his acceptance of defeat at Guivreiz's hands. Only after these encounters does Erec show renewed sociability by staying for two weeks as Guivreiz's guest (Er 7115ff.) and showing a positive desire to visit Arthur's court (Er 7798ff.), at which he had previously felt unfit to stay. This large-scale sequence of events again points to the central insight, which also informs much of the detail of Hartmann's project of knighthood, that the pursuit of honour, in the sense of social acclaim, whilst for the most part a laudable activity, is not of itself a sufficient condition of exemplary chivalry. Only the broader, more altruistic range of qualities shown in the adventures after the Arthurian interlude in the forest guarantees full exemplariness for Erec's knighthood, and with it a personal sense of joy and fulfilment.

Erec's progress merges programmatically with the theme of joy in the closing stages of the romance, which form a triple crescendo as Erec brings joy to the court of Brandigan by defeating Mabonagrin in the adventure of 'Joie de la curt' (Er 8002), to Arthur's court by bringing the widows of Mabonagrin's defeated opponents (Er 9944–50), and finally to his own kingdom when he inherits his father's crown (Er 10054–82). The 'Joie de la curt' adventure was often dismissed in early Hartmann criticism as redundant padding,[147] but is now recognized as a functional and well integrated summation of the main themes and values of the work.[148] As a combat between creative and destructive forms of love and warriordom, this climactic combat between Erec and Mabonagrin integrates the main thematic lines of the narrative, and is also a powerful and timely cultural statement when viewed in terms of the history of chivalry.

The adventure of 'Joie de la curt' has striking parallels with Erec's first combat. Unlike his other encounters, but like the combat against Iders, the combat with Mabonagrin is a publicly prepared encounter which follows a customary pattern; like Iders, but unlike any of Erec's other opponents, Mabonagrin champions a lady; in both combats, but in none of his others, Erec is explicitly fortified by thoughts of Enite (Er 935–39,

---

[147] E.g. by Sparnaay, *Hartmann von Aue*, I, pp. 98f: 'Man könnte überall den Abschnitt ausscheiden, ohne daß die Idee oder der Gehalt des Romans dadurch die geringste Änderung erführe'.
[148] Kuhn, 'Erec', pp. 144f.; Wünsch, 'Allegorie', p. 516; Cormeau, 'Joie de la curt', passim.

9181–87); and just as the encounter with Iders was the first serious combat Erec had ever undertaken (Er 1266: 'sîn erstiu ritterschaft'), so he describes himself before the 'Joie de la curt' encounter as still lacking in knightly reputation (Er 8547–54). The combat against Mabonagrin is thus, like that against Iders, something of an initiatory encounter, one in which Erec is tested as a knight, and in which the values of chivalry are articulated. This last adventure also takes up the theme of Erec's and Enite's *verligen*, the nature and consequences of which are restated in an intensified form in the life led by Mabonagrin and his partner. Like Erec and Enite in Karnant, Mabonagrin and his partner have withdrawn from the court because of their love, the unsocially self-centred nature of which is expressed in its very location, a garden magically closed off from the court of Brandigan by a wall of mist (Er 8698–753). Just as Erec's and Enite's *verligen* drove joy away from the court of Karnant (Er 2989–92), so Mabonagrin and his partner have robbed the court of Brandigan of joy (Er 9590–95), with the difference that Mabonagrin takes joy away from the court not merely by a passive withdrawal from communal life, but by an actively destructive cultivation of combat which has led to the death of 80 knights and the misery of their widows (Er 8324–58). Two of the central components in the developing ideology of chivalry – the ancient quality of warrior competence, and the newer quality of love – are thus subject in this pioneering romance to ethical criticism, as destructive egotism, when they are turned away from the community of the court. More fully than Erec's earlier opponents Mabonagrin has a symbolic value as a projection of Erec's erring self, and an embodiment of ethical dangers within the values of knighthood collectively. Further, Erec's victory over Mabonagrin, which is followed by his leading the couple out of their garden of private, asocial pleasure and his restoration of communal joy to the court of Brandigan (Er 9590–765), is richly expressive of release, reconciliation and integration, marking in personal terms Erec's and Enite's victory over their own earlier lapse, and in a broader historical perspective an optimistic programme which harmonizes the martial self-assertiveness and the emotional individualism of chivalry with the communal well-being of the court.

This optimistic programme has an ethical underpinning, for Hartmann presents Erec as an exemplary knight in the 'Joie de la curt' episode. Various aspects of exemplary knighthood have been brought to the fore in Erec's earlier combats, and now these are orchestrated to produce, in Hartmann's account of 'der ritter Êrec' (Er 8590) in his last combat a more broad-ranging and complex view of chivalry in ethical and behavioural terms than had ever appeared before in German literature: the 'Joie de la curt' adventure confirms the emergence in German literature of a model of chivalry which joins the military, the emotional, the social and the religious in a new amalgam, and which, after its crystallization at the end of the twelfth century, remained one of the most potent cultural icons of aristocratic society throughout the Middle Ages. Nor did Hartmann merely take this model over from Chrétien. Rather he shows a greater concern than Chrétien to formulate its components explicitly, and in doing so he introduces new elements into the portrayal of Erec as a knight in the 'Joie de la curt' episode which are in line with the tendency of his adaptation earlier in the romance.

The continuing martial basis of knighthood is evident in the praise of Erec's warrior courage (Er 8119–46, 8424–41). But Hartmann again, as he did in Erec's second encounter with Guivreiz, carefully draws a line between exemplary courage and reckless warriordom by adding that only a fool is totally without fear, whilst Erec did experience sensible, prudent, manly fear (Er 8619–31). This detailed touch is characteristic of the care with which Hartmann presents Erec in this episode as a model of feeling and behaviour, and characteristic too of his concern to set exemplary chivalry off sharply from unthinking battle-lust. The combat itself demonstrates Erec's great skill as well as his fierce strength and courage. And where Chrétien has the combat end in an exhausted brawl, with the two men blinded by blood and sweat (EeE 5979–6007), Hartmann presents Erec's victory in terms of martial expertise, as Erec uses wrestling techniques learned in his early years in England to throw his larger opponent and force a surrender (Er 9281–315).[149] Again, Chrétien's violent and detached view of combat gives place to the German knightly author's presentation of military chivalry, even in the form of wrestling, more affirmatively, as an expression of positive values, here as the fruit of training and acquired skill.

It is in keeping with the self-assertive warrior thrust in chivalry that the 'Joie de la curt' adventure is a means of winning honour for Erec. And when Erec himself, in a striking speech, welcomes the combat as the goal of his journeying and the means of enhancing his reputation (Er 8521–75), his enthusiastically existential tone (the theme of searching, Er 8521–26), his reference to divine guidance (8527f.: 'got hât wol ze mir getân / daz er mich hât gewîset her'), and the imagery he uses are reminiscent of the Church's crusading propaganda. Erec's view of the combat as a wager, in which he has little to lose and much to gain (Er 8530–75), invites comparison with the crusading metaphor of the battle

---

[149] England was well known for the cultivation of wrestling in the Middle Ages (Jusserand, *Sports*, pp. 172f.; Rickard, *Britain in Medieval French Literature*, p. 163); it is not clear whether Hartmann is linking up to this reputation, or simply thinking within the action in his reference to Erec's expertise. Wrestling was, in general, part of chivalric combat, especially 'in a judicial combat or in a combat *à outrance* where, repeatedly, an encounter which opened with lance and sword or axe would end in a hand-to-hand struggle' (Anglo, 'How to Win', p. 251).

against the heathens as an easy purchase of salvation, which any 'prudent merchant' (i.e. any wise knight) should grasp;[150] and the line in which Erec thanks God for guiding him to this encounter (Er 8257: 'got hât wol ze mir getân') is echoed precisely in a crusading song of Hartmann's own (MF 211,12: 'got hât vil wol ze mir getân'). However, it is crucial for an understanding of the ideal function of chivalry in the romance that, just as a metaphysical support is invoked for Erec's combat in this climactic encounter, it is not the hero's personal glory alone that is at stake, but also the ending of a destructive custom and the restoration of communal joy. Moreover, Hartmann intensifies the socially constructive dimension of this adventure and has Erec show a greater sense of compassion and piety than he does in Chrétien's version. Thus Hartmann intensifies the theme of rescue and release by adding to Chrétien's version the eighty widows of Mabonagrin's victims, whose release from suffering (Er 9953–62) is made possible by Erec's victory. Hartmann also adds Erec's feelings of pity at the plight of the widows (Er 8334–58, 9782–825), and he adds an explicitly religious dimension to Erec's chivalry when he has Erec express a humble trust in God and an acceptance of God's will (Er 8147–53, 8855–59). Again at the end of the work Erec's piety qualifies the status of honour, when Hartmann as narrator (and again without prompting from Chrétien's *Erec et Enide*) tells how Erec was wise and humble enough to attribute his *êre* to God's aid (Er 10085–106).

Hartmann may have been drawing, at least in part, on Chrétien's own later romance *Yvain* for his enhancement of a religious coloration in Erec's knighthood. There are indications that Hartmann may have known *Yvain* already when he was working on *Erec*.[151] The motif of the eighty sorrowing women whom Erec releases in the 'Joie de la curt' adventure could have been prompted by the 'Pesme Avanture' episode of Chrétien's *Yvain*, where Yvain releases 300 captive maidens (Yv 5185ff., 5771–809). More generally, Chrétien goes further in *Yvain* than he does in *Erec et Enide* in attributing Christian qualities to the hero, especially developing the ethical and emotional virtue of compassion, pity at the sight of human suffering.[152] Hartmann may have been prompted by this quality of Yvain's pity in portraying Erec's *erbarmen* (Er 9787, 9791, 9794, 9798). With *Yvain*, Chrétien was moving towards the religious ethos of his Grail romance, *Perceval*, and Hartmann's knowledge of *Yvain* may have encouraged the German author in moving

---

[150] On the motif of the *prudens mercator* see Bernard of Clairvaux's letter of 1146 urging participation in the crusade (MPL, 182, col. 566); Flori, *L'essor*, p. 212; Wentzlaff-Eggebert, *Kreuzzugsdichtung*, p. 19; Hölzle, *Die Kreuzzüge*, I, pp. 537ff.).
[151] Scheunemann, *Artushof und Abenteuer*, p. 103; Green, *Irony*, pp. 317f.; Pérennec, *Recherches*, I, p. 203.
[152] Pérennec, *Recherches*, I, pp. 187, 195ff.

in this direction himself already when he adapted Chrétien's first Arthurian romance.

Since the protection of widows was a duty laid on the ruler, and later the knight, in the Church's blessings of the sword,[153] Hartmann's introduction of the eighty sorrowing widows (whatever his immediate source) brings his portrayal of knighthood into closer affinity with these blessings than is the case in Chrétien's *Erec et Enide*. However, Hartmann is quite independent of the Church's views on the ideal function of the *militia* in the importance he attaches to human love as a component of exemplary chivalry, for instance when he has Erec draw strength and courage in combat from thoughts of Enite (Er 8860–73, 9181–87, 9230f.). Similarly, Hartmann attaches great importance to courteous social forms, especially in the conduct of men towards women. A typical instance of this is when Hartmann, independently of Chrétien, describes how Erec approaches Mabonagrin's lady, dismounting, tethering his horse, resting shield and lance against a tree, hanging his helm on the shield and pulling his coif back, all 'because he had excellent manners' (Er 8967: 'wan sîn zuht was vil grôz'). Such decorum is a reminder that knighthood was becoming increasingly associated with politeness of manners in Hartmann's day. Indeed the dimension of mannerly behaviour probably linked literary portrayals of chivalry more immediately to the daily business of life than did some of the profounder moral issues of the poetry, and in this way the courtly romance helped shape the behavioural values of the aristocracy.[154]

The themes of knighthood, kingship, honour and joy merge in a twofold climax to Hartmann's romance, as Erec brings joy to Brandigan and to Arthur's court by his achievement as a knight, thus winning the metaphorical crown of honour (Er 9891: 'der êren krône'), and then brings joy to his homeland when he receives the real crown of kingship (Er 10065: 'die krône von dem rîche'). The imagery of knighthood is indeed interwoven with that of kingship in the closing stages of *Erec*. The presentation of the hero as a bringer of joy gives unprecedented poetic prestige to the figure of the knight, as Erec now appears as a 'worker of wonders' (Er 9308, 10045: 'Êrec der wunderære'), and a saviour sent by God to release the court from suffering (Er 9587–609). The people of Brandigan themselves welcome Erec as a saviour knight in terms which combine secular euphoria with a sense of providential aid (Er 9669–78: 'ritter, gêret sî dîn lîp! / mit sælden müezest immer leben! / got hât dich uns ze trôste gegeben / und in daz lant gewîset. / wîs gevreuwet und geprîset, / aller ritter êre! / jâ hât dich immer mêre / got

---

153 Erdmann, *Entstehung*, pp. 74–77; Flori, *L'idéologie*, pp. 92f, 99.
154 For a thirteenth-century view of romances as books of manners which had a place in the social education of young nobles see below, p. 136.

und dîn ellenthaftiu hant / gekrœnet über elliu lant. / mit heile müezest werden alt!').

This is a novel tone in which to greet a *ritter* in German literature, and the metaphysical note in this greeting calls for comment. It may be doubted whether, as has been suggested, Hartmann here portrays Erec, in his knightly perfection, as an analogy to Christ the saviour.[155] Rather the knight Erec is here acclaimed in language such as had earlier been applied to kings in German literature.[156] In other words the greeting of the people of Brandigan derives not (or not directly) from the concept of Christ the redeemer, but from the concept of the king as a protector sent by God, and its stylistic prototype is laudation of the ruler. Here again we see the importance of a royal genealogy in the development of chivalric thinking, and it is a mark of the elevated position that knighthood had achieved by the last decade of the twelfth century that the term *ritter* could attract a degree of politico-religious acclaim that had been reserved in Carolingian times for the king.

### Chivalric values, aesthetic form and the historical situation of Hartmann's Erec

What light does the theme of knighthood throw on the controversial questions of the internal dynamics of Hartmann's *Erec*, and its position in the historical context of south-west Germany in the 1180s?

The dual structure of the narrative, comprising an initial cycle of success leading to marriage and social acclaim, which is followed by a crisis, then a second, longer, more arduous cycle of encounters which echoes the first cycle on a heightened level and leads to the reintegration of the hero, was established by Chrétien de Troyes in his *Erec et Enide* and his *Yvain*, and adapted into German with Hartmann's treatment of these two romances. In terms of the typology of narrative structure, this dual composition allowed for an increased complexity in the presentation of character and action, and in the relation of narrator, material and audience, as Chrétien, in these two romances, 'subordinates the "wish-fulfilment romance" to the weightier "formation romance", the forerunner of the novel of formation, or *Bildungsroman*'.[157] Hartmann creatively exploited the possibilities opened up by Chrétien in this dual structure, and it is particularly important for the ideological history of chivalry that this compositional innovation, with its gain in narrative

---

155   Willson, 'Sin and Redemption', p. 8.
156   See also Green, 'The King and the Knight', p. 181, referring to the praise of Louis III (of France) in the ninth-century *Ludwigslied*; the dedicatory praise of Louis the German in the *Evangelienbuch* of the monk Otfrid of Weißenburg (completed ca. 870) is another parallel.
157   Evans, 'Wishfulfilment', p. 133.

complexity, emerged in the same works which also brought knighthood from a more peripheral position to the centre in their respective literatures. Indeed, the new narrative structure embodied in Chrétien's and Hartmann's *Erec* and *Yvain / Iwein* is not only one of the major aesthetic achievements of medieval literature, but also a creative contribution to the twelfth-century debate on the nature and the ideal function of the *militia*, an expression of the rising prestige of knighthood, and, especially in view of Hartmann's knightly status, a mark of the knighthood's desire for cultural self-interpretation.[158]

However, on the ethical and social function of this literary project of knighthood, controversy currently reigns in Hartmann studies. For many years it was almost universally accepted that the pattern of crisis and reintegration in Hartmann's romances involved some inner progress in the hero, whether this dynamic was interpreted more along psychological, moral, sociological or even religious lines, and that an intended function of the works was moral improvement.[159] This consensus was broken by the appearance in 1983 of Rudolf Voß's study of Hartmann's two Arthurian romances and Hubertus Fischer's study of *Iwein*. These scholars differ widely in approach, Voß seeing the motivation of the action in objective, transcendent terms, whilst Fischer pursues a socio-historical line of interpretation. But both reject interpretations which see a psychological or ethical development within the hero; both argue strongly for a static conception of the hero, whom both see as being devoted to a self-oriented, aristocratic acquisition of honour at the end as at the beginning of the work; and both reject the dominant moralizing tendency in interpretations of Hartmann's romances, Voß interpreting the dual structure of *Erec* and *Iwein* not as a critical exploration of some moral failing within the hero (and in the society which he represents), but as a 'charismatic celebration of courtly-feudal culture', and Fischer seeing the concept of honour and the knight's journeying as a self-assertive individualism which lacks true ethical value.[160] Chrétien studies saw a similar development, also in 1983, with the appearance of Stephen Knight's sociologically oriented study of Arthurian literature, for Knight too sees no true moral process in Chrétien's presentation of chivalry, but the celebration of a warrior aggressiveness which is only superficially masked by a show of courtliness.[161] Recent work on Chrétien's and Hartmann's Arthurian romances thus shows fundamental clashes of view between interpre-

---

[158] See also Fromm, 'Doppelweg', p. 71.
[159] See the list of studies of Hartmann's romances along these lines in Voß, *Artusepik*, pp. 214–18 (n. 102).
[160] Voß, *Artusepik*, p. 161: 'die charismatische Auszeichnung der höfisch-feudalen Kultur'; Fischer, *Ehre*, p. 32 and passim.
[161] Knight, *Arthurian Literature*, esp. pp. 93–102.

tations in terms of self-centred warrior assertiveness, •and readings which continue to see in them a greater moral, civilizing function.[162]

Far from being purely a product of modern academic research, this critical controversy refreshingly echoes the medieval reception of Hartmann's works, for already medieval utterances on the social function of Arthurian romances anticipate the main poles of the current debate. Thus on the one hand the cleric Thomasin von Zerklaere, writing for a German audience a few years after Hartmann, advocates romances as useful educational reading for the young (*Der wälsche Gast* 1026: 'kint') because they offer examples of good behaviour which, claims Thomasin, have a beneficial effect on the audience (ibid. 1138: 'guot âventiure zuht mêrt'); and Thomasin urges young aristocrats to follow the example of the knights of the Round Table by pursuing honour (ibid. 1041–58). On the other hand the Franconian schoolmaster Hugo von Trimberg, writing almost a century later, roundly condemns stories of Arthurian knights as dangerous examples of foolhardy heroism which, so he claims, tempted the youth of his own day to risk body and soul in the pursuit of glory in jousting (*Der Renner* 21637ff.). What is for Thomasin an ethically positive quality of honour in the literary portrayal of knighthood (*Der wälsche Gast* 1058: 'êre') is for Hugo pernicious vainglory (*Der Renner* 21667f.: 'Werltlich lop, wîn und wîp / Verderbent manigen jungen lîp'). Thomasin and Hugo each mention Erec and Iwein amongst the literary knights whom they cite as examples to the contemporary youth, so we can take it that they were referring, amongst others, to Hartmann's romances. And while Thomasin anticipates the modern scholars who ascribe a moral, educative function to the theme of chivalry in Arthurian romance, Hugo's critical reading matches those who see it as a celebration of glory-seeking violence.

In this clash of views no one camp has a monopoly of the truth. Rather the coexistence of moralizing and amoral interpretations reflects a basic tension which is actually present in the romances of Chrétien and Hartmann, and which was present in the society for which these works were produced: a tension between a deep-rooted, self-assertive violence in the warrior aristocracy, and the development, both by the 'outside' influence of the Church and by measures 'internal' to the secular aristocracy, of moral and social controls, limitations, channelling mechanisms which sought to steer or harness this violence and to legitimize it as an instrument of social protection. This interplay of violence and control, self-assertion and morality is central to the ideology of chivalry, and is evident in the historical situation and the cultural documents of the German aristocracy at the time of Hartmann's literary activity. Voß and Fischer have made important contributions to

---

162 For this latter interpretation see e.g. Jaeger, *The Origins of Courtliness*, pp. 242–47.

an understanding of Hartmann's romances, and to our topic of knighthood, by standing out against a too vaguely idealizing, at times unhistorical and schematically moralizing tendency in Hartmann scholarship. However, they in turn court the opposite danger of underplaying the ethical dynamism and the emotional finesse of Hartmann's treatment of knighthood in the figure of the main protagonist.[163] We shall look at controversial aspects of *Iwein* later.[164] As regards *Erec*, Hartmann, as we have seen, develops the potentiality of what was a 'formation romance'[165] already in Chrétien's version explicitly in a dynamic direction by structuring the narrative around Erec's progression from untried youth through knighthood to kingship. This large progressive structure of the romance contains learning experiences and moments of insight and reorientation, in the treatment of which Hartmann intensifies the subjective dimension and also invites the audience to reflect on the patterns of behaviour exposed in this process. In terms of social function this suggests that Hartmann's poetic practice does indeed, in its intention, match Thomasin von Zerklaere's interpretation, that is to say that Hartmann conceives of his literary portrayal of knighthood, at least in part, as offering models of conduct and attitude by which an audience can take example.[166] This is not to suggest that Hartmann's romances are, after all, merely verse tracts spelling out banal rules of conduct. The central theme of the hero's finding himself as knight, husband and ruler has too vibrant a social, emotional and aesthetic resonance to justify such a reductivist interpretation, indeed the divergences of view in recent work are welcome because they convey a degree of cultural tension in Hartmann's romances, and in the ideology of chivalry, which has not always been adequately recognized. Nevertheless, the ethical dimension remains an essential component of Hartmann's aesthetic and of his concept of chivalry, even within the greater complexity which is emerging in recent studies.

Specifically the theme of the knight's use of force shows a progressive pattern in *Erec*. Erec's first combat brings retribution for insult and injury done to himself and his kinswoman Guinevere, and the first encounters in his longer sequence of journeying are acts of self-defence, whilst later encounters involve aid freely given to someone in distress (the captive knight episode) and finally the restoration of joy to an entire community (the 'Joie de la curt' adventure).[167] The work as a whole thus

---

[163] The limitations of the static models of interpretation adopted by Voß and Fischer are perceptively shown by McFarland, 'Narrative Structure', passim.
[164] See below, Chapter 8.
[165] Evans, 'Wishfulfilment', p. 133.
[166] See also Borck, 'Über Ehre', p. 2.
[167] On the progression from self-defence to combats for others in the second cycle of *Erec* see also Wünsch, 'Allegorie', pp. 516f.

shows a progression from vengeance, in the sense of retribution for harm done to self or kin, to the proferring of aid and the increase of communal wellbeing in the motivation of Erec's combats. The concept of vengeance as a form of justice was central to the aristocratic ethos in Hartmann's day.[168] This ethos of retribution is an important factor in Erec's first combat. But the ethical dynamic of later combat episodes also suggests that this retributive function within the kinship group is not the highest ethical goal of knighthood, is indeed no longer sufficient in itself to justify knighthood in moral terms in *Erec*. Rather, broader justification is needed by reference to aid, protection, the righting of wrongs, in short the exercise of arms in defence of justice beyond self and kin. These broader values are explored in the second, longer cycle of combats in *Erec*, and they will be even more pervasive in the second cycle of Hartmann's *Iwein*.

In that Erec's opening combat demonstrates his command of the ancient aristocratic nexus of retributive justice, whilst the second cycle of adventures shows the impact of newer ethical values of chivalry and gives the hero's combats the metaphysical sanction of divine guidance, the dual structure of *Erec* shows some affinity with the polemical contrast between the old and the new *militia* in crusading propaganda. Indeed, the concept of military chivalry as a moral process which could enjoy metaphysical sanction surely shows, in however indirect a way, some reception of crusading thought in the courtly romance. However, in the fictional world of Hartmann's *Erec*, which is seen through the eyes of a knightly author/narrator, the metaphysical dimension of combat has been removed from the domain of the Church as an institution, and it now serves more to legitimize knighthood as a lay, social order.

The theme of honour in *Erec* points in the same direction as that of the use of force as a class characteristic of knighthood in *Erec*: in the direction of qualified affirmation, and a position at the interface of secular warriordom and religious values. The pursuit of honour in the sense of social reputation sets Erec's knighthood off from the ascetic *nova militia* of Bernard of Clairvaux.[169] However, whilst Fischer is surely right to see honour as an essential feature of secular knighthood, and thus to dissociate the chivalric mentality from absolute, self-denying altruism, he goes too far in denying any true moral dimension to knightly values and seeing honour in Hartmann's romances solely as an expression of amoral self-assertion, 'Selbstverherrlichung'.[170] For one

---

[168]   The concept of vengeance as a duty owed to kin was even exploited by the Church in summoning knights to help 'their oppressed "brothers", the eastern Christians [. . .], and their "father" and "lord", Jesus Christ' by going on crusade (Riley-Smith, *The Crusades*, p. 16). This widening of the concept of aid rendered to kin is a suggestive antecedent in the crusading sphere to the ethical treatment of combat in Arthurian romance.

[169]   *De laude novae militiae*, cols 921–927; see Flori, *L'essor*, pp. 209–14.

[170]   Fischer, *Ehre*, p. 10.

thing, honour in itself involves not only the individual who receives it, but also the society which bestows it. Transactions of honour 'provide, on the psychological side, a nexus between the ideals of society and their reproduction in the actions of individuals – honour commits men to act as they should (even if opinions differ [from society to society] as to how they should act)'.[171] An action based on honour thus presupposes some gearing of the individual into a set of values affirmed by the community, and thus cannot properly be described as totally self-oriented. Further, and decisively for an understanding of his ideal concept of knighthood, Hartmann modulates and qualifies the pursuit of *êre* in various ways in *Erec*, buttressing its ethical quality. For Hartmann, as he states in a passage that is quite independent of Chrétien's text, the honour (*êre*) which lasts until death is connected precisely with humility towards God (Er 10085–106). This religious modulation of the concept of honour links the value-system of Hartmann's knightly romance to that of his religious legends as surely as the praise of courage and prowess connects it with that of secular heroic poetry.

Hartmann's works occupy a central position in the history of chivalric ideology. Already his first romance shows the impact of all the main strands that informed the development of knightly ethics in the key decades at the end of the twelfth century: the warrior heritage tempered by modulating influences from religion, from secular law and from the social world of the courts. As regards the position of Hartmann's *Erec* in the cultural context of his own day, the parallels between the image of chivalry elaborated in this pioneering romance and the German peace legislation, the *Landfrieden*, are particularly revealing.

The German peace laws of the last third of the twelfth century recognized the aristocracy's right to carry arms and to settle their quarrels by force, but they also sought, in a more detailed way than earlier legislation, to steer and limit warfare, to regulate the opening and the conduct of hostilities, and to further the idea that the use of arms should be part of a legal framework, and should have a protective function. Moreover, the mental world of *Erec*, in Hartmann's adaptation even more than in Chrétien's version, shows a notable degree of alignment with the tendency of these peace laws. R. Howard Bloch has drawn attention, in his study of medieval French literature and law, to the important parallels between the peace movements and chivalry – chivalry here seen both as a literary and a historical phenomenon. Against the view that chivalry is at bottom a glorification of warrior violence, Bloch emphasizes its inherent control mechanisms, arguing that chivalry, as a historical phenomenon, 'seems less an ideal

---

171  Pitt-Rivers, 'Honour and Social Status', p. 38 (quoted by Keen, *Chivalry*, p. 249).

appropriate to the flowering of a warrior caste than a formula for its decline' and 'can be situated alongside – and not in opposition to – contemporaneous ecclesiastical, municipal, royal and some seigneurial efforts to regulate private war'.[172] For Bloch, French courtly literature, as the chief cultural vehicle of chivalry, rather than legitimizing and stabilizing the clannish interests of the feudal nobility 'is perfectly consistent with the political strategy of monarchy – the creation of a nation of self-governing individuals responsible for themselves to the state as opposed to a federation of clans accountable to each other'. [173] Consequently courtly literature too 'can most appropriately be situated alongside the peace movements of the tenth through thirteenth centuries',[174] and the courtly text 'is seen less as a mechanism by which aristocracy affirmed its own solidarity and resisted change than as a forum for adaptation to the political realities of the postfeudal world'.[175]

Where Fischer and Knight underplay the ethical dimension of knighthood, Bloch perhaps underplays the degree of continuing warrior self-assertiveness in the ideology of chivalry, which he pushes rather too close to a bourgeois concept of citizenship than is apt for the political climate around 1200. Nevertheless, his alignment of chivalry with the peace movements is a valid and important insight which highlights the self-restraining, modulating strand in the development of knightly ethics. And this aligment is even more marked in Hartmann's *Erec* than in Chrétien's work, as the subjective ethical coloration in Hartmann's presentation of knighthood, and the parallels between Hartmann's romance and the German peace laws show. Like Hartmann's *Erec*, these peace laws show the consolidation of knighthood as a mark of social class.[176] They also define the proper use of arms in terms of *fides* ( = *triuwe*) and the defence of justice, and they pay particular attention to the ordered initiation of hostilities.[177] Furthermore, just as Hartmann draws on religious as well as secular energies in presenting knighthood, so the constitution against arsonists of 1186 involves the Church in the battle against the excesses of feuding by decreeing that arsonists should suffer excommunication as well as secular outlawry.[178] The amalgamation of the military, the aristocratic, the ethical and the religious in Hartmann's literary presentation of chivalry thus has close affinities with the German legal enactments of his day. Involvement in legal affairs, especially in processes of customary law, was a normal part of

---

[172]   R.H. Bloch, *Medieval French Literature and Law*, p. 197.
[173]   Ibid., pp. 237f.
[174]   Ibid., p. 256.
[175]   Ibid., p. 258.
[176]   See above, pp. 68f.
[177]   See above, pp. 123f; and R.H. Bloch, p. 113: 'The rules pertaining to initiation and cessation of hostilities were a crucial factor in the limitation of vendetta'.
[178]   MGH Const., I, no. 318, c. 7 (p. 450); see Otto, 'Abschließung', pp. 37f.

life for the secular aristocracy to which Hartmann belonged.[179] It is inconceivable that Hartmann, as an educated knight with a manifest interest in norms of behaviour, should have been ignorant of the contemporary peace laws. Indeed his treatment of Chrétien suggests that his *Erec* arose in the same social and political circumstances as the German peace laws of the last decades of the twelfth century. One senses that Hartmann knew the main thrust of this legislation and approved of it, already when he was working on his first Arthurian romance.

The peace ordinances throw light on the historical situation and the social function of Hartmann's presentation of knighthood in *Erec* in a number of ways.

First, the parallels between the literary portrayal of knighthood and the peace movements indicate that the concern with knighthood was not merely an internal literary matter in the late twelfth century. The elaboration of the figure of the knight as a new model of social identity in the literature of this period was indeed a major achievement of poets, who were not simply imitating contemporary social reality, but were also constructing and shaping emotional and ethical patterns in the texts. However, it does not detract from the creative poetic achievement of Chrétien and Hartmann if we remember that the literary constructions of chivalry in their works, as well as constituting a major aesthetic statement, were also part of a broader historical process which included the sober prose of the peace laws. The view that 'romance does not mirror the chivalric values of the feudal nobility; it creates them'[180] makes too generalized a distinction and sets the romance off too sharply from the mentality of knighthood as a historical phenomenon. The relation of romance to contemporary society is more complex than this, and should be seen as a dialectic, whereby the romances of Chrétien and Hartmann (in different ways as between the two authors) at once reflect *and* seek to shape the values of the secular aristocracy. In this dialectic they have a functional affinity with the German peace laws of the late twelfth century, which also reflect the values of a military aristocracy by recognizing the right of knights to settle disputes by military force (a far cry from modern political constitutions, which recognize such a right for the state, but not for the individual), but also seek to shape these values

---

[179] Schönbach, *Über Hartmann von Aue*, pp. 286–89; on the importance of legal considerations in *Iwein* see below, Chapters 7 and 8.

[180] Jaeger, *The Origins of Courtliness*, p. 209. If Jaeger, with this comment, underplays the extent to which romance draws on social reality, Haferland goes too far in the opposite direction and underplays the degree of aesthetic and ethical stylization in courtly literature with his thesis that these texts contain nothing which did not pre-exist in society (Haferland, *Höfische Interaktion*, p. 10: 'Nichts ist in den Texten – hier der hochhöfischen Epik und Didaktik –, was nicht zuerst in der Gesellschaft ist').

by locating them in a legal framework and by structuring the legitimate deployment of force.

With regard to social stratification within the *militia*, the ethics of the knight's use of force in *Erec* do not suggest an exclusive commitment to any one layer of aristocracy and rather confirm the findings reached in our earlier discussion of knighthood and nobility – that chivalry was more of an integrative ideology linking *ministeriales* and free nobles in the late twelfth century. As the son of a king, Erec has the social status of the great princely *milites* of royal blood in the actual royal households of Hartmann's day.[181] But for much of the narrative he is presented as a solitary, wandering knight who, in his existential modesty, shares features with real knights of relatively humble condition.[182] Hartmann's protagonist could thus invite identification across the hierarchy, from poor knights up to the sons of the emperor. At a higher ethical level, the theme of Erec's bringing help to those in need by the use of arms has been interpreted as a poetic legitimation specifically of the military service of the *ministeriales*.[183] This may be how some *ministeriales* reacted to the text; and indeed there is much in Hartmann's presentation of Erec, as in his other works, that suggests an authorial perspective at the lower end of the aristocratic hierarchy. However, the knight's aid is presented in *Erec* not only as a form of service, but largely in terms of protection, defence of justice and the defeat of criminals, and these were marks and duties precisely of lordship in the twelfth century. Seen in this light the romance assumes the quality of a *miroir de princes*, and the ethics of the knight's use of force are at least as much a preparation for and a legitimation of lordship as they are a literary processing of ministerial service. This poetic joining together of various levels of the aristocracy in a common task also has its parallel in the peace laws of Hartmann's day, for instance when the duty to pursue criminals is explicitly enjoined on the entire sword-bearing hierarchy, from princes through *nobiles* down to *ministeriales* in the Rhenish Franconian peace of 1179.[184]

Finally, the social and ethical values of knighthood add to the affinities linking Hartmann's literary world with contemporaneous tendencies in Hohenstaufen ruling circles, affinities which emerged already in Hartmann's treatment of the figure of Arthur in his adaptation of Chrétien's romances. The rise of the term *ritter* in Hartmann's works parallels the rise of the term *miles* in Hohenstaufen circles.[185] Hohen-

---

[181]   On the spread of knightly terminology at this level of the hierarchy in Germany in the second half of the twelfth century see above, pp. 69–71.
[182]   See also Thum, 'Politische Probleme', p. 61.
[183]   Kaiser, *Textauslegung*, pp. 114–26.
[184]   See above, p. 109.
[185]   See above, pp. 69–72.

staufen legislation encouraged the social differentiation of knights from other groups, and the imperial court acted as a focus for some integration of *ministeriales* and free nobles.[186] Hartmann's *Erec* provides literary analogues to all these developments, and these broad social trends are also matched by the parallels between Hartmann's ethical elaboration of chivalry and the peace ordinances issued by Frederick Barbarossa, as a further indication of some alignment of Hartmann's first romance with Hohenstaufen interests.

Indeed there are hints in Hartmann's presentation of Erec's kingship that he may have had the situation of the Hohenstaufen court in mind when he was adapting Chrétien's work. Pérennec has shown that Hartmann elevates Erec explicitly to the status of king earlier in the narrative than Chrétien does.[187] When Chrétien's Erec is welcomed by the people of Carnant on his first return with his new bride he is referred to as 'lor novel seignor' (EeE 2371), and the narrator comments: 'Onques nus rois an son reaume / ne fu plus lieemant veüz' (EeE 2398f.). But Chrétien does not directly credit Erec with the title 'king' until after the death of his father, when he is described, on the occasion of his coronation, as 'le novel roi' (EeE 6859; compare EeE 6867). Hartmann alters Chrétien's account by having Erec designated king by his father when he first returns to Karnant with Enite (Er 2921: 'daz er ze künege wære gezalt'), and Hartmann frequently applies the term *künec* to Erec from the moment of his reconciliation with Enite onwards, that is to say well before as well as after the death of his father (before his father's death: Er 6763, 7233, 7911, 8028, 8057, 8520, 8896, 9130, 9405; after his father's death: Er 10097, 10119). Thus for much of the narrative the son is in Hartmann's text, unlike in Chrétien's, explicitly and frequently styled as 'king' during the lifetime of his father. However, this is similar to the situation in Germany in the 1180s, where Frederick Barbarossa's son Henry was made king of the Romans in his infancy and became a real co-regent from the date of his knighting in 1184, six years before the death of his father.[188] Hartmann's modification of Chrétien's text thus matches the dynastic constellation of the German royal household, since in each case the royal son is both knight and king during the lifetime and rule of his father.

Hartmann's reshaping of the end of the romance points in a similar direction. Whereas Chrétien has Erec crowned at Arthur's court, Hartmann has him return to his homeland to receive the crown after his father's death.[189] With this new ending the German author turns away from the fictional world of adventure and transposes the work onto the

---

[186]  See above, pp. 60, 72.
[187]  Pérennec, *Recherches*, I, pp. 100–06.
[188]  Munz, *Frederick Barbarossa*, p. 360; Opll, *Friedrich Barbarossa*, pp. 105, 140.
[189]  See above, p. 29.

level of political and religious reality in his portrayal of Erec's kingship.[190] Moreover, precisely when Hartmann presents Erec, as king, in terms of a political reality which would be familiar to his German audience, he adumbrates, quite independently of Chrétien, a view of the king which would be pleasing to the actual Hohenstaufen rulers on three politically sensitive issues: hereditary succession, the loyalty of magnates to the king, and the securing of peace as a royal duty.

First, at the moment of Erec's receiving the crown, Hartmann comments approvingly on his hereditary succession to the kingship (Er 10064-73: 'hie emphienc er lobelîche / die krône von dem rîche / der sîn vater, der künec Lac, / unz an in mit êren phlac, / wan er vil manege tugent begie. / ouchn wart dehein vrumer vater nie / mit sînem sune baz ersat. / wer zæme baz an sîner stat? / got segene im sîn rîche: / er hât ez billîche'). The rhetorical question: 'Who could be better suited to follow him?' seems almost calculated to elicit the response that of course a king should be succeeded by his son. However, such a response would have been controversial in the last decades of the twelfth century, and pleasing to Hohenstaufen ears, for the Hohenstaufen family was at this time trying to replace the traditional German elective kingship with a hereditary monarchy such as was already more firmly established in France and England.[191] In this connection it is also interesting that when Hartmann tells of the ageing King Lac conferring the status of king on his son (Er 2917-23) he makes no reference to an elective element or to any consultation with the magnates. It is as if the transmission of royal power were entirely within the control of the ruling family.

Second, when Erec returns home after his father's death, Hartmann spells out at length the warm greeting accorded to him by the magnates of his kingdom (Er 10002-36), who are impelled by their due loyalty towards their royal lord (Er 10017: 'ir schuldic triuwe'). Having earlier omitted from his portrayal of Arthur's court the signs of baronial unrest that were present in Chrétien's work,[192] Hartmann here independently brings an account of baronial affection for and loyalty to the king. Hartmann tends to show less interest than Chrétien does in the relation of king and magnates; and when he now does give this relation a prominent place, he presents the magnates as a king would wish to see them, as loyally and willingly accepting his rule.

Third, apart from Erec's holding a great feast when he receives the crown (Er 10054-82), the only exercise of his kingship that Hartmann mentions is that the new young ruler secures peace in his kingdom (Er 10083f.: 'hie sazte er sô sîn lant / daz ez vridelîchen stuont'). This action

---

[190] See also Scheunemann, *Artushof und Abenteuer*, pp. 109f.; Kuhn, 'Erec', p. 146; Green, *Irony*, pp. 72, 316.
[191] Munz, *Frederick Barbarossa*, pp. 324, 397f.
[192] See above, pp. 22f.

carries over into the realm of kingship what has been a major theme of Erec's journeying as a knight: the protection of peace and justice, not least against such figures of lordly brutality as the counts Galaoin and Oringles, who precisely disturbed the peace of their own territories. This resolution of the narrative theme of protection also matches the actual political situation in Germany, where, from the early twelfth century onwards, it was customary for each new king to declare a peace at the opening of his reign as a declaration of authority.[193]

That Hartmann was indeed touching politically sensitive issues in his presentation of Erec's kingship is further indicated by the contrasting treatment these issues receive in contemporary (or near contemporary) poetic works which contain stronger oppositional strands. For example Ulrich von Zatzikhoven's *Lanzelet* opens with a justified baronial revolt against a tyrant king, and the barons later accept the young Lanzelet as successor to his father only on condition that he treats them better than his father did (*Lanzelet* 8210f.: 'ob er uns baz triutet / dan sîn vater der künic Pant'). Here the legitimacy of baronial opposition receives as much weight as praise of loyalty to the king.[194] Further, in *Reinhart Fuchs*, which has cogently been identified as a work of satire against the Hohenstaufen dynasty,[195] the declaration of a peace (*Reinhart Fuchs* 1239: 'lantvride') is not a mark of exemplary Christian kingship as in Hartmann's *Erec*, but an expression of the king's violent despotism.

The climax of the theme of kingship, in Erec's crowning, has a different political focus in Hartmann's and Chrétien's romances. The end of Chrétien's *Erec et Enide* contains a bow to Plantagenet/Angevin rule, for the Arthurian empire echoes that of Henry II of England, and Erec's kingdom is integrated into this empire, as the new young king receives his lands from the hand of Arthur (EeE 6544f.) and is crowned in Arthur's city of Nantes (EeE 6553). Hartmann severs this feudal bond and makes Erec's rule quite independent of Arthur. It may be doubted whether Hartmann, with this encomium of the ruler's autonomy, was seeking to sanction the independence of some German territorial magnate from the king.[196] For Erec himself is, at the end of the romance, very much a king, who has received the visible symbol of royal office, the crown (Er 10065), and who enjoys the loyal support of his magnates. Hartmann indeed endows Erec with features of the German kingship (which would have been a problematical matter had he kept Erec's feudal allegiance to Arthur), and he does so in a way that suggests sympathy for the contemporary Hohenstaufen rule.

---

[193] See above, p. 88.
[194] See also above, p. 24.
[195] Kühnel, 'Zum *Reinhart Fuchs*', passim.
[196] As suggested by Schulze, '*âmis unde man*', p. 45.

As with the portrayal of Arthur, Hartmann's affirmative presentation of Erec's kingship does not necessarily indicate royal patronage. His attitude would be compatible with his working with an eye on the Zähringen or the Altdorf Welf ducal households, both of which had sufficiently close relations with the crown in the 1180s for Hartmann to acquire news and perhaps even direct experience of affairs in the Hohenstaufen imperial and royal sphere through one or other of these channels.[197] What does emerge from the historical situation in the last decades of the twelfth century is some affinity of tendency between Hartmann's romance and the Hohenstaufen court with regard to the social, ethical, and legal strands of knighthood. Whether or not Hartmann had specific and detailed knowledge of developments in Hohenstaufen court circles, the evidence of this major social institution shows that the promotion of knighthood, which has emerged as a subjective characteristic of Hartmann's literary adaptation, also had an objective correlative in the social world of German aristocratic life in Hartmann's day. This objective correlative goes some way towards explaining the remarkable vitality and freshness of the theme of knighthood in Hartmann's *Erec*. The question now poses itself of what happens to this theme in Hartmann's other works.

[197]  See above, pp. 31f; below, pp. 279f.

# 4

# *Gregorius:* Knighthood in Perspective

Gregorius *and the three estates*

Hartmann's *Erec* broadened the canon of German literature by establishing Arthurian romance as a new genre. However, the social range of this work remains narrow in that it treats only lay society, and within lay society only the upper levels, the knightly world, so that, in enquiring after the social and cultural resonance of knighthood and knightly values in *Erec*, we were limited almost entirely to voices from within this world. Indeed it is an important feature of the courtly romance as a genre that, whilst it shows an enhanced complexity in stylistic values and in the exploration of the inner life, it also tends to social exclusiveness along aristocratic lines.

Hartmann's two shorter narrative works, *Gregorius* and *Der arme Heinrich*, differ from *Erec* in that their central themes are overtly religious, directly concerning the relation of the protagonist to God as well as to fellow humans – though the prominence given to the secular world in each of these works produces a sense of compositional experimentation and cultural heterogeneity which is characteristic of the developing literary scene in Germany at the end of the twelfth century. *Gregorius* and *Der arme Heinrich* throw particular light on the topic of chivalry in that both works open up the literary world of the secular aristocracy to include other areas of society. Each shows the noble protagonist interacting with non-courtly figures, so that we now have standpoints outside the secular aristocracy which place knighthood in a broader social and moral perspective than was the case in *Erec*.

Hartmann's two religious narratives have so much in common that they could aptly be treated together. However, chronologically and stylistically *Gregorius* is still closer to the early romance *Erec*, whilst *Der arme Heinrich* has affinities with the later *Iwein*.[1] The following chapters will reflect this distribution by treating *Gregorius* and *Der arme Heinrich* separately, with a chapter interposed on the chronologically problematical matter of Hartmann's poetry of love-service and of the crusade. This arrangement does not claim to solve the problem of the relative chronology of Hartmann's works. But it will illuminate the cultural complexity of Hartmann's concern with knighthood even (in some ways precisely) outside the genre of Arthurian romance.

Of all Hartmann's works it is *Gregorius*, a story of great sin (a double incest) and the power of repentance and divine grace, that has the broadest social canvas. From about the end of the tenth century increasingly frequent references appear in western Europe to a tripartite interpretation of human society in functional terms as comprising *laboratores, bellatores* and *oratores* – those who labour, those who fight and those who pray.[2] This schematic division, though of course a drastic simplification of social reality, was not a purely theoretical construct, but rather a reaction to social change, particularly to the emergence in the secular world of a specialized category of heavily armed, mounted warriors whose lifestyle set them apart from the labouring mass of the population. Thus the division of society into three orders, or estates, is another expression of the gradual emergence of knighthood as a distinct social order, which is seized in this functional categorization at an early stage in its development, when the military function was still dominant. The functional division of lay society into 'labourers' and 'fighters' then merged with the aristocratic developments which have been discussed in an earlier chapter, as the two lay categories were increasingly referred to with the socially hierarchical terms *miles* and *rusticus*, 'knight' and 'peasant'.[3]

It is a mark of the social breadth of *Gregorius* that the eponymous hero experiences the lifestyle of each of these three estates. As the outcast fruit of incest between his noble (ducal) parents, Gregorius is raised by a poor fisher family in the belief that he is of their kin, i.e. of rustic stock (Gr 1112: 'nâch gebiurlîchem site'; 1125: 'ze disem gebiurischen man'). From the age of six he is educated in a monastery under the protection of his spiritual father, the abbot, who sees in him a future monk; on discovering that he is not of rustic stock Gregorius insists on becoming a knight, then he unwittingly marries his own mother and becomes ruler

---

[1]    These stylistic groupings are supported by the way Hartmann figures as narrator in the various works (see Arndt, *Der Erzähler*, pp. 185f.; Cormeau / Störmer, *Hartmann von Aue*, p. 26).
[2]    Oexle, 'Tria genera hominum', pp. 494–500; id., 'Deutungsschemata', pp. 89–105. Leyser, 'Early Medieval Canon Law', p. 554 and Oexle, 'Deutungsschemata', pp. 91–95, also point to earlier occurrences of the concept of the three orders, which is a further instance of the historical antiquity of important aspects of medieval chivalry.
[3]    See also Oexle, 'Tria genera hominum', pp. 497–99.

over Aquitaine; and finally, after doing monumental penance for his sin, he becomes pope in Rome. Gregorius's life thus spans an early upbringing by a peasant family, followed by experience of the main branches of the two higher estates, active knighthood and lordship in the lay world, and monastic education and headship of the church in the clerical world. This social breadth is also expressed in the remaining personnel of the work, which is drawn from the realm of poor fisherfolk, the monastery, the ducal court of Aquitaine, and the leading families of Rome.

## The view of knighthood in the debate between the abbot and Gregorius

All the occurrences of the chivalric terms *ritter*, *ritterschaft* and *ritterlîch* in *Gregorius* figure in the two consecutive and integrally connected episodes of the debate between Gregorius and the abbot, which leads to Gregorius's becoming a knight, and Gregorius's victory over the aggressor duke, which leads to his unwittingly marrying his own mother.[4] Within the larger spiritual and social perspective of the work the narrative takes on a distinctly chivalric tone in this section as knighthood is presented first in a theoretical discussion, then in actual practice.

The interview between Gregorius and the abbot is particularly revealing in our context. Knighthood appears here in a socially contrastive light, as the youth who had believed himself to be of rustic parentage, and destined for a monastic career, suddenly sees the quite different and glamorous prospect of knighthood opening up before him. We thus have a rare confluence and contrast of the spheres of peasant, cleric and knight at a crucial point of decision as Gregorius debates his future with the abbot. The debate is all the more important for an understanding of Hartmann's conception of knighthood because the German author here adapts his French source, the *Vie du Pape Saint Grégoire*, with considerable freedom.[5] In the *Vie du Pape Saint Grégoire*, the dispute about Grégoire's becoming a knight, his knighting and his rejection of the abbot's offer of a rich marriage occupy little more than forty lines (A1 1112-56, B1 878-918), whilst Hartmann expands this section sixfold to take up over 250 lines (Gr 1479-731). Hartmann transforms the meagre exchange of words of the French work into a full-

---

[4] The 800 lines of these two episodes (1385-2184) contain 14 occurrences of the term *ritter*, 12 of *ritterschaft*, 5 of the adjective / adverb *ritterlîch*; the remaining 3206 lines of the narrative contain no occurrences of *ritter* or its derivatives.

[5] See Schottmann, 'Gregorius und Grégoire', pp. 87-91; McCann, 'Gregorius's Interview', passim; Herlem-Prey, *Le Gregorius*, pp. 142-49. Line references to the French work in this chapter are to Sol's critical texts of the manuscripts A1 and B1.

scale disputation, with the abbot bringing forward, in sequence, three objections to Gregorius's wish to become a knight and leave the monastery, the first a moral consideration (Gr 1515–29), the second based on Gregorius's lack of training (Gr 1536–70), the third on his lack of wealth (Gr 1659–74). The abbot's arguments thus beat a retreat from the moral to the pragmatic, and at each stage Gregorius produces counter-arguments, finally winning the abbot's (albeit reluctant) blessing on his project (Gr 1635–40, 1806–08).

The choice which faces the young Gregorius, between a monastic and a knightly future, must have made the narrative particularly relevant to an aristocratic audience, since the real aristocratic society of Hartmann's day offered the two career paths for men – knighthood, leading to secular lordship, and the Church. Gregorius's situation, for all its fictionality, thus held much with which a German aristocratic audience, most immediately its younger members, might identify. Indeed, one senses some self-projection of the clerically schooled, but knightly author Hartmann in his independent elaboration of the young Gregorius's arguments, as in his portrayal of the young Erec on the occasion of his first tournament. The formal symmetry and the dialectical argumentation of the exchange between Gregorius and the abbot probably reflect Hartmann's own school training,[6] and Hartmann's expansion of this exchange is as strong an indication of his knightly interests as was his expansion of the tournament episode in *Erec*.[7] Moreover, in the interplay of argument and counterargument between the two disputants Hartmann introduces, quite independently of his French source, a wealth of material about the pragmatics and the ethos of knighthood.

What view of knighthood emerges in Hartmann's additions and alterations to his source in this section of the work?

First, there is no precedent in the *Vie du Pape Saint Grégoire* for Gregorius's statement that a certain social status, a certain degree of birth and wealth is a normal prerequisite for becoming a knight (Gr 1494–503: 'ich weiz nû daz ich niene bin / disses vischæres kint. / nû waz ob mîne vordern sint / von selhem geslähte / daz ich wol werden mähte / ritter, ob ich hæte / den willen und daz geræte? / weizgot nû was ie mîn muot, / hæte ich geburt und daz guot, / ich würde gerne ritter'). Hartmann's independent addition here reflects the exclusive, aristocratic tendencies in the development of knighthood which are expressed also in other German sources of the late twelfth century, for instance in the legal provision of 1186 which forbade the granting of the

---

6  See also Schönbach, *Über Hartmann von Aue*, p. 432.
7  On Hartmann's treatment of the tournament in *Erec* see above, pp. 103–07; W.H. Jackson, 'The Tournament', pp. 240–48.

belt of knighthood to sons of *rustici*.[8] Gregorius's references to parentage and status of birth ('mîne vordern', 'geslähte', 'geburt') show that in his mind knighthood is normally accessible only to those who qualilfy by birth, and that he had assumed himself to be excluded by being the son of a *rusticus*.

Further, in linking *geburt* and *guot* as prerequisites of knighthood, Gregorius talks of knighthood in exactly the same terms as Enite talks of becoming a countess, when she says that she lacks the birth and wealth necessary for this noble status (Er 3809f.: 'ich entouc ze grævinne niht: / ich enhân geburt noch daz guot'). This similarity of expression does not, of course, mean that the terms *grâve* ('count') and *ritter* ('knight') are of equal status in Hartmann's world. But it does indicate that both terms are connected with an exclusive status of birth, and this again testifies to the increasingly prestigious social connotations of knighthood. Indeed Gregorius's words express, without any motivation from Hartmann's French source, the closing off of knighthood as a social order from which the vast majority of the population were normally excluded, and the gradual transformation of even the lesser knighthood into a (petty) aristocracy which was under way in Hartmann's day.

Second, Hartmann also provides a more nuanced view of the moral contrast between monastic and chivalric life than his source. The elaboration of a set of ideal ethical duties for the *militia* often went hand in hand in ecclesiastical circles with indictments of the actual behaviour and attitudes of those who wielded the sword, so that it is religious sources that provide the most trenchant criticisms of secular knighthood in the twelfth century. Moreover these clerical voices, whilst repeating the old indictments of violence against the *milites*, also criticized with increasing frequency during the twelfth century aristocratic social traits in knights (their pride, their pursuit of luxury, ostentation and glory), and this new emphasis provides further evidence, this time from outside the chivalric world, of the rising social prestige of knighthood and its gradual assimilation to the nobility.[9] Whatever the particular emphasis of criticism, secular knighthood was often associated in ecclesiastical sources with sin, an association expressed in the recurrent play on words, found in the twelfth century throughout the areas that experienced the rise of knighthood, that linked *militia* with *malitia*.[10]

No author treating secular knighthood in a work with a religious framework could escape the pull of the Church's critical tradition. Hartmann and the author of his French source both reflect this pull, but with a significant difference of emphasis. In the French work, the abbot

[8]  MGH Const., I, no. 318, c. 20 (p.451); see above, pp. 68f.
[9]  Flori, *L'essor*, pp. 331f.
[10]  On the *militia* / *malitia* play in Gerhoh of Reichersberg (Germany), Bernard of Clairvaux (France) and John of Salisbury (England) see Flori, *L'essor*, p. 207.

takes up the equation of *militia* and *malitia* to condemn the knights' way of life unreservedly as wicked (A1 1128: 'Que molt est mauvaise lor vie'; compare the link with malfeasance in B1 890: 'malfesant'). Nor does Grégoire attempt any moral counter to this condemnation, but merely asserts his wish to become a knight (A1 1129–34; B1 892–96). Criticism of knights is also well documented in German religious poetry before Hartmann. For instance Heinrich von Melk castigates knights for boastfulness, manslaughter and whoring (*Erinnerung an den Tod* 354–72) – the cardinal features of chivalric ideology, which appear in idealized form in knightly poetry as honour, combat and love, are here reduced to aggressive and lustful forms of sin in a way which is typical of the Church's critical strand of comment. Similarly, in Heinrich von Veldeke's *Servatius* (like *Gregorius* the legend of a holy man, and Veldeke's *œuvre*, like Hartmann's, spans secular and religious modes) knights appear as figures of sin, with one 'ridder' dying unshriven after a life of violence which involved the very opposite of the duties prescribed in the Church's reform movement: oppression rather than protection of the poor, widows, orphans and the Church (*Servatius* 5580–602); and another, 'einen riddere, einen ovelen man' (*Servatius* 5877) also dying an unrepentant sinner. Both knights go to hell, but are saved by the intercession of Saint Servatius. Thus the tales have the double purpose of demonstrating the saint's metaphysical influence and warning knights against the typical sins of their class.

Hartmann's French source and precedents in German poetry thus gave him grounds to follow a religious tradition of criticism of knighthood. Consequently it is all the more remarkable that in the exchange between Gregorius and the abbot he precisely strengthens the moral case for knighthood. The abbot still, in Hartmann's text, begins by linking knighthood with malfeasance (Gr 1520: 'missetât'). But this is no longer a total condemnation of the knightly life as in the French work, because Hartmann's abbot speaks only of the particular case of one who turns away from God and leaves the clergy to become a knight (Gr 1517–21).[11] More importantly Hartmann radically alters the French version by introducing a counter-argument to the abbot's condemnation of chivalry and having Gregorius defend chivalry, when properly undertaken, as a way of life pleasing to God (Gr 1530–35: 'Grêgôrius antwurte im dô: / "ritterschaft daz ist ein leben, / der im die mâze kan gegeben, / sô enmac nieman baz genesen. / er mac gotes ritter gerner wesen / danne ein betrogen klôsterman" '). The categorical indictment of knightly life by a representative of the Church in the French work has here provoked a moral, even religious justification of knighthood in the adaptation of the

---

[11] See also Schottmann, 'Gregorius und Grégoire', pp. 88f.; McCann, 'Gregorius's Interview', pp. 90f.

German knightly author.[12] Gregorius speaks here 'in the optimistic belief that properly conducted chivalry may be of itself a divinely ordained *officium*'.[13] Something of this belief underlies Hartmann's authorial attitude in adding a metaphysical, even biblical dimension to the protagonist's knighthood in the later parts of *Erec*.[14]

Moreover, this positive view of chivalry also has precedents within the Church, for precisely in the twelfth century there were clerical voices which praised the *militia*, even outside the crusading context, as an honourable profession pleasing to God.[15] An interesting parallel to Gregorius's giving moral precedence to knighthood in the service of God over a monastic life without vocation (Gr 1535: 'ein betrogen klôsterman') is provided by the German clerical author Gerhoh of Reichersberg, who as early as the 1120s asserted that the *milites* could find salvation within their military calling so long as they served the commonwealth rather than personal profit. Gerhoh also describes properly ordered service in the retinue of an honourable lord as a surer way to salvation for knights than a disordered conversion of the knight to a life as monk or hermit.[16] The Church too needed retinues of knights to protect its massive holdings and consequently had a pragmatic interest in not pressing calls for a withdrawal from the world too far. This clerical advocacy of secular chivalry shows that Gregorius is not, in his arguments, adopting a purely oppositional stance, but drawing in part on a strand of thought within the Church, and one with which Hartmann himself might have come into contact in his own schooling.

Third, and finally, the entire argument about the practical difficulties of Gregorius's becoming a knight is Hartmann's independent addition (Gr 1536–620, 1665–727).[17] This argument has two parts, each with a similar structure (again one notes the rather schoolmasterly composition), as the abbot briefly points out practical difficulties in Gregorius's plans (Gr 1536–42, 1547–57; and 1665–74), to which Gregorius responds with longer counter-arguments (Gr 1543–46, 1558–620; and 1675–727). In the debate as a whole Gregorius has more lines than the abbot, as befits his position as the formal victor.[18] However, Hartmann has neither protagonist to the debate categorically denigrate the way of life advocated by the other.[19] Rather the young Gregorius expresses more respect and sympathy for the monastic life (which he praises warmly, Gr 1507–10) and the abbot more understanding of knighthood (though

---

12  See also Herlem-Prey, *Le Gregorius*, p. 143.
13  Ashcroft, *'Miles dei – gotes ritter'*, p. 67.
14  See above, pp. 115f.
15  See also below, pp. 256–58, on John of Salisbury.
16  Gerhoh of Reichersberg, *De aedificio Dei*, cols 1301f.; see Flori, *L'essor*, pp. 262f.
17  See also McCann, 'Gregorius's Interview', p. 85.
18  Schönbach, *Über Hartmann von Aue*, pp. 430f.
19  See also McCann, 'Gregorius's Interview', p. 90.

he disclaims technical expertise, Gr 1625–33) in Hartmann's version than in his source. The abbot takes a sceptical, 'realistic' line on the difficulties facing Gregorius. He looks at knighthood from the outside, albeit with the perspective of one who has observed the aristocratic world and discussed the practicalities of military life with experts (Gr 1547f.: 'sun, mir saget vil maneges munt / dem ze ritterschaft ist kunt'). Gregorius replies in a spirit of optimistic enthusiasm. He speaks from inside a knightly ethos which combines fascination for the glamour of jousting and an idealistic ethic of effort. Hartmann's creative expansion thus makes the exchange between Gregorius and the abbot into a morally and emotionally far richer and more subtle expression of contact and exchange between the knightly and the monastic worlds than the abrupt confrontation in his source.

The abbot's first practical objection is that an upbringing in school without training in horsemanship makes a youth unfit for the profession of arms (Gr 1536–42, 1547–57). This is a further reminder that knighthood was still at this time integrally connected with mounted warfare and was still a skill that had to be acquired: one was born noble, but one had to train to become a knight. The prediction that Gregorius will be laughed at for his clumsiness in riding (Gr 1538–41) is echoed in other literary presentations of heroes who lacked a knightly upbringing, and doubtless this motif had some grounding in reality.[20] Indeed the need for training, involving as it did regular access to expensive equipment, was a potent material factor barring access to knighthood for those not born into or enjoying the patronage of a family of substance, quite apart from any legal constraints. Gregorius's reply that he is young enough to learn shows a typically Hartmannesque concern with self-improvement through effort (Gr 1543f.: 'herre, ich bin ein junger man / und lerne des ich niht enkan'). Gregorius's long account of his daydreams of chivalric success (Gr 1582–620) shows a theoretical mastery of techniques of riding in the joust, down to the detail of exactly where to place the spur, and this technical vocabulary of jousting indicates again that Hartmann was up to the moment in developments emanating from France in this important practical area of knightly life.[21]

Gregorius's view of chivalry acquires specific regional connotations when he comments that he is not in spirit from Bavaria or Franconia,

---

[20] See Ulrich von Zatzikhoven, *Lanzelet*, 296–99, 402–12, 486–97, 561–76; Wolfram von Eschenbach, *Parzival*, 173,11–174,6.

[21] E.g. the word *puneiz* (lance charge), which rapidly gained popularity in descriptions of modern chivalric combat, is first attested in *Gregorius* (1614, 2118; see note to line 1614 in Wachinger's revision of Paul's edition). The abbot's bemused response that Gregorius's knightly jargon is 'all Greek to me' (Gr 1630: 'ich vernæme kriechisch als wol') produces a humorous note from the cultural clash between a new world of modish chivalric jousting and an older world of monastic learning.

and that in thought he can ride even better than the knights of Hainault, Brabant and Hesbaye (Gr 1573–78: 'ich enwart nie mit gedanke / ein Beier noch ein Vranke: / swelh ritter ze Henegouwe, / ze Brâbant und ze Haspengouwe / ze orse ie aller beste gesaz, / sô kan ichz mit gedanken baz'). Gregorius's laudatory reference to the knights of the Low Countries, which formed the north-western border areas linking the German empire to France, has been adduced to support the view that Hartmann was writing with the support of the Zähringen court, for the Zähringen family was connected by marriage with the comital family of Hainault, whose affairs must have been much discussed at the Zähringen court, especially in the years 1184 to 1188 in connection with controversy about the succession to the county of Namur.[22] This possibility cannot be excluded. However, there is more direct evidence of knightly concerns of this border area being received in Germany through the Hohenstaufen court than through the Zähringen connection, for Count Baldwin V of Hainault cultivated close relations with the imperial court from 1184 onwards. His son Baldwin [VI] was sent to the imperial court to learn the language and the ways of the court, and was actually knighted in the city of Speier at Whitsun 1189 by Barbarossa's son Henry, king of the Romans.[23] The fame of the knighthood of these border areas could thus have been transmitted to a German knightly author at least as plausibly through a Hohenstaufen as through a Zähringen channel.

There is also a pointer linking *Gregorius* with the Welfs, for between 1210 and 1213 the north German cleric Arnold of Lübeck produced a Latin version of Hartmann's work at the behest of the Welf magnate, Duke William of Brunswick.[24] None of this evidence is firm enough to give favour to any one of the three main hypotheses about the court with which Hartmann may have been associated in his literary activity. What is clear is that Gregorius's reference to the fame of the knights of the Low Countries agrees with the historical record, which shows frequent tourneying in northern France and the Low Countries in the 1170s and 1180s.[25] By linking jousting skill with these areas, Hartmann again emerges as a reliable observer of the contemporary scene in his independent addition to his source. And the way in which Hartmann has his protagonist distance himself from Bavaria and Franconia (which appear implicitly as backward areas) and take the chivalry of Hainault

---

22 Bertau, *Deutsche Literatur*, I, pp. 566, 621f.; Mertens, *Gregorius Eremita*, p. 29.
23 *La Chronique de Gislebert de Mons*, pp. 234, 237; see above, pp. 70f.
24 See Ganz, 'Dienstmann und Abt'; Mertens, *Gregorius Eremita*, pp. 105–08.
25 See the tournaments visited by Baldwin V of Hainault from 1168 to 1183, in *La Chronique de Gislebert de Mons*, pp. 95, 97, 101, 108, 116f., 123f., 127, 133, 144; Gislebert comments with pride on the 'flowering' of knighthood in Hainault at this time (ibid., p. 95: 'cum multis militibus quibus tunc temporis Hanonia florebat').

and Brabant as the model to surpass, suggests the humorous perspective of Hartmann associating himself, as a Swabian knight, with the
modish north-western marches rather than the inner German areas.

The last practical objection raised by the abbot in face of Gregorius's
determination to leave the monastery bears on the material base
necessary for knighthood. Neither the *Vie du Pape Saint Grégoire* nor
Hartmann gives a detailed account of the forms whereby Gregorius
becomes a knight. Hartmann merely tells us that the abbot had fresh
(secular) clothes cut for Gregorius and then 'made him a knight in the
appropriate manner' (Gr 1646f.). Later we hear that Gregorius has
warhorses, arms and squires (Gr 1722-25) – again this is a realistic touch,
for the knight as a military figure was, from the late eleventh century
onwards, normally accompanied by one or more squires, who were
needed to tend horses and equipment.[26] There is no indication in
*Gregorius* of a ceremonial *Schwertleite* such as obtained in the princely
knightings at this time. Rather the accent is on the practical matter of
arming, and the implied social tone is that of the lower end of the
knightly world, where the assumption of arms was of existential
importance in its own right, not only as an apanage of lordship.

After Gregorius's assumption of arms, Hartmann follows his French
source to have the abbot offer Gregorius a rich marriage as an
inducement to stay (Gr 1659-64), and Hartmann characteristically
develops the offer by adding a new exchange on the need for material
wealth to support the lifestyle of the knight (Gr 1665-727). The abbot's
comment that Gregorius will be embarrassed by his lack of material
wealth now that he is a knight (Gr 1665f.: 'dû hâst gewunnen ritters
namen: / nû muostu dich dîner armuot schamen') is a further indication
that the term *ritters name* referred in Germany around 1200 not only to
chivalry as an ethical duty, but also to knighthood as an elevated social
status.[27] The abbot clearly regards material wealth and good connections
(Gr 1671: 'vorder habe' and 'vriunt') as essential to the knight. This too
matches the historical record, which shows that the cost of maintaining
the knightly lifestyle was rising markedly in the late twelfth century.[28] It
is as if the abbot sensed this rising cost, and its consequence that less
wealthy knights had to struggle to maintain their positions, when he
warns that Gregorius's (believed) lack of means will be his undoing: (Gr
1672: 'sich, dâ verdirbestû abe'). Yet again Hartmann's addition to his
source touches a matter of practical concern to the contemporary
knighthood, particularly those of lesser means; and the abbot's
reference to wealth and social connections as normal conditions of

26   Fleckenstein, 'Das Rittertum der Stauferzeit', p. 103.
27   See above, pp. 55-61.
28   See above, p. 46.

knightly life again throws light on the aristocratic tendencies in the development of knighthood.

Gregorius's counter to this argument by reference to his 'poverty' (Gr 1666: 'armuot') combines material and ideal considerations in a way that is typical of an important strand in the mentality of secular knighthood. On the material side, Gregorius proposes to earn the means to support his new life by fighting to acquire wealth (Gr 1686, 1717, 1726: 'guot'); and after leaving the monastery he plans to fight in the hire of the beleaguered duchess as her 'soldenære' (Gr 1876).[29] The romantic notion that knights were a category quite separate from mercenaries has long since been dispelled, and it is clear that, especially with the acceleration of a monetary economy in the twelfth century, knights were glad to fight for pay.[30] Indeed, throughout the history of medieval chivalry 'we are told, and repeatedly, that it is one of the virtues of the military profession that it is an avenue to riches'.[31] However, the acquisition of material wealth was never, of itself, sufficient to provide an ideological legitimation of knighthood, and it is not merely materialistic considerations that move Gregorius to become a knight and leave the monastery (indeed the abbot's offer of a rich marriage and a suitable endowment would have provided him with ample material inducement to stay), but a powerful emotive impulse and an ethos of arms and honour which emerge in his two long, self-expressive speeches (Gr 1558–624, 1675–731).

These speeches also echo in subject and manner key aspects of Hartmann's presentation of chivalry in *Erec*. Put in another way, the young Gregorius, at the point of his transition from the bookish monastic life to the active life of knighthood, speaks of chivalry in the terms used by the narrator Hartmann and the protagonist Erec in Hartmann's first romance, so that Gregorius's utterances seem to convey fantasies and enthusiasms of the author himself from an inside perspective. Gregorius's fantasy of tourneying (Gr 1582–620) echoes the tone and technical detail of the narrator's account of the formal jousts in *Erec*, for instance the challenge joust between Erec and Roiderodes (Er 2764–807). Indeed this youthful dream of the splendour of arms again expresses, in the thoughts of the fictional character Gregorius, that selectively flattering perception of chivalric weapons which also underlay the procedures of the author Hartmann in adapting Chrétien's *Erec*.[32] In the speech in which he rejects the abbot's offer of a good

[29] Compare the *soldier* who receives Erec's mount as a gift in the tournament (Er 2635).
[30] See Painter, *French Chivalry*, pp. 15f.
[31] Keen, *Chivalry*, p. 154; on the moral discussions prompted by the coexistence in chivalry of the mercenary element and the ideal duties of protection see Krüger, 'Das Rittertum', pp. 313–20.
[32] See above, pp. 110–13.

marriage and insists on seeking his own way (Gr 1675–731) Gregorius takes up, again without any motivation from the *Vie*, a central ethical theme of Hartmann's *Erec*: chivalry as the pursuit of honour (Gr 1677, 1714, 1717: 'êre') and the avoidance of ease (Gr 1677, 1680, 1683: 'gemach').[33] In Gregorius this idealistic theme acquires a specific social note as Gregorius praises the 'poor' knight (Gr 1684, 1693: 'arm') who pursues wealth with honour (Gr 1717: 'guot und êre') as being superior to the great lord whose inherited wealth tempts him into a life of ease (Gr 1681–87).[34] Here again Hartmann views knighthood with particular sympathy for the lower end of the hierarchy, in this case the 'arm man' (Gr 1693) who seeks for honourable advancement through the application of effort.

### The moral evaluation of chivalry in Gregorius

Despite Hartmann's dramatic expansion of the interview between Gregorius and the abbot, it remains an episode within the larger scope of a narrative which has the complex of sin, repentance and divine grace as its central focus. And since the knightly career which Gregorius takes up after this exchange leads to the sin of incest, the question poses itself as to the moral place of chivalry in the work as a whole. Hartmann himself points to an element of paradox in Gregorius's story by referring to him at key points as a 'good sinner' (Gr 176, 2606, 4001). The interpretation of Gregorius's sin has then exercised scholars ever since Anton Schönbach's influential study a century ago.[35] Recent work still shows wide differences of view,[36] and this is a controversy we must discuss in so far as it bears on the moral evaluation of knighthood in *Gregorius*.

There are two basically opposed lines in this controversy. According to the first line, Gregorius follows a legitimate sense of vocation in becoming a knight, and the sin he becomes involved in by unwittingly committing incest with his own mother is an 'objective' one, it does not spring from a personal, inner defect in Gregorius; rather he remains free of personal guilt.[37] This view involves no moral criticism of the knightly

---

[33] For the antithesis of *êre* and *gemach* see *Erec* 2966–73; Gregorius's use of the verb *verligen* (Gr 1683) echoes *Erec* 2971, 10123.
[34] See also Henne, *Herrschaftsstruktur*, p. 17.
[35] Schönbach, *Über Hartmann von Aue*, pp. 100–02.
[36] Useful recent discussions of the conflicting views in Duckworth, *Gregorius*, pp. 1–63; Herlem-Prey, 'Schuld oder Nichtschuld', pp. 3–5.
[37] See e.g. Herlem-Prey, 'Schuld oder Nichtschuld', passim. The view that Gregorius incurs guilt in becoming a knight (see e.g. Sparnaay, *Hartmann von Aue*, II, pp. 74–76) was questioned already in important studies by Dittmann, *Hartmanns Gregorius*, pp. 226f. and Cormeau, *Hartmanns von Aue 'Armer Heinrich' und 'Gregorius'*, pp. 55–64.

phase of Gregorius's existence. According to the second line, Gregorius's becoming a knight and leaving the monastery, and then his activity as a knight, are already signs of an inner, moral defectiveness, which is then confirmed by the incestuous marriage.[38] With regard to the moral status of knighthood it is important to note two different tendencies within this second line of interpretation: a more gradualist view maintaining that, although knighthood is connected with moral defectiveness in the specific case of Gregorius himself, this does not involve a categorical condemnation of chivalry as such;[39] and a more dualist view that sees *Gregorius* as a radically anti-chivalric poem of world denial which shows the disintegration of courtly concepts of value, and in which the idealized model of knighthood presented in Arthurian romance is 'toppled from its pedestal' and the socially privileged knightly aristocracy powerfully criticized, not least on the grounds of its militaristic violence.[40]

Not only does Hartmann strengthen the moral case for chivalry in his treatment of the debate between Gregorius and the abbot, but by having the abbot dwell on practical hindrances rather than on detailed moral objections to knighthood, Hartmann also allows Gregorius to demonstrate an insight into the ethos and the practice of chivalry which suggests an inner fitness for knighthood, and which convinces the abbot that he is not after all, a monk at heart (Gr 1635f.: 'dû bist, daz merke ich wol dar an,/ des muotes niht ein klôsterman'). The one episode which shows knighthood in action in Gregorius (Gregorius's defeat of the duke who is assailing his mother) also endows *ritterschaft* with positive value.

This account of the hero's freeing a noble lady whose castle is under siege is quite untypical of the saint's life as a religious genre. Rather it was taken into the story by a French author from the emerging genre of chivalric romance, which was developing the image of the knight as a rescuer figure.[41] Gregorius's release of an innocent woman from a lordly aggressor echoes Hartmann's portrayal of Erec as a rescuer knight and foreshadows elements in Iwein's career.[42] Nor is it merely a case of Hartmann's taking over motifs from the French *Grégoire*. Rather he makes systematic alterations to the French account of Grégoire's combat which parallel his treatment of knighthood in adapting Chrétien's *Erec*. Thus in the French work, Grégoire appears from the outset as an accomplished warrior, whilst Hartmann proceeds differently to show him acquiring military experience and growing in skill before the single

38 See e.g. Duckworth, *Gregorius*, pp. 139–224.
39 Willson, '*Amor inordinata*', p. 101; Duckworth, *Gregorius*, pp. 175f.
40 Ernst, 'Der Antagonismus', II, p. 100.
41 Sparnaay, *Hartmann von Aue*, II, pp. 172–79.
42 See above, p. 132; below, pp. 245–48.

combat (Gr 1972–98). This modification again shows Hartmann's concern to present military chivalry in a positive light, as a matter of training and skill (Gr 1994: 'kunst ze ritterschaft'), not merely brute force, and it is also reminiscent of Hartmann's modifying the opening section of Chrétien's *Erec* to show the young Erec in transition from youth to chivalric manhood. Gregorius's almost touchingly earnest welcome of battle as a means of ensuring that his 'young days' will not be spent in idleness (Gr 1868–76) has no precedent in Hartmann's French source,[43] but it echoes Erec's pondering before the tournament on how important it is for a young man to do well in his early years (Er 2254–58). Like Erec, Gregorius tries more self-consciously and reflectively than his French counterpart to do what is proper in a knight – which is to say that the knightly author Hartmann identifies more closely with his protagonist than did the authors of his French sources, and is more concerned to articulate chivalric values in the very detail of the narrative and in the workings of the protagonist's mind.

Hartmann also strengthens the concept of Gregorius as a saviour knight.[44] For example in a passage of his own creation, he again takes us inside Gregorius's mind and brings a classic early formulation of a triad of ideal knightly motives when he refers to the service of God, the pursuit of honour, and aid for an innocent woman as Gregorius's grounds for combat (Gr 2070–74: 'durch got und durch êre / wolde er verliesen sînen lîp / oder daz unschuldige wîp / lœsen von des herren hant / der ir genomen hâte ir lant'). It is in keeping with Hartmann's intensification of the theme of release that his account of Gregorius's combat has echoes of the climactic 'Erlösungsabenteuer' in *Erec*: the combat between Erec and Mabonagrin.[45] Here Gregorius's description of the combat in gambling terms (Gr 2028–66) echoes the tone, imagery and argument of Erec's joyful acceptance of the adventure of 'Joie de la curt' (Er 8521–75); Hartmann's Gregorius, like his Erec, attends mass before the combat (Gr 2080–83; Er 8635–40); and after the combat the narrator's praise of Gregorius's winning honour and liberating his mother's lands is almost a direct quotation of Mabonagrin's praise of Erec (Gr 2165–70; Er 9605–09).

The description of the actual combat in *Gregorius* also shows the same selective features as Hartmann's combat descriptions in *Erec*. In the *Vie du Pape Saint Grégoire*, Grégoire sorely wounds the duke, who falls to the ground, and Grégoire then carries him back into the city (A1 1425–1500; B1 1185–1202). Most of the manuscripts of the *Vie* tell of the duke being 'covered in blood' and having 'fainted from loss of blood' (e.g. A1 1479,

---

43 See also Herlem-Prey, *Le Gregorius*, p. 81.
44 Ibid., pp. 263–65.
45 Ibid., p. 263, n. 113.

1493–1496). In Hartmann's adaptation the combat follows a carefully considered plan, which Gregorius carries out intelligently (Gr 2104: 'sinneclichen'). The combatants are closely matched, but Gregorius gets the upper hand and pulls his still mounted opponent captive into the city (Gr 2139–61). This method of capture by leading an opponent still mounted from the field (Gr 2143: 'zoumen') was a mark of particular skill and courage in contemporary tournament tactics.[46] Also Hartmann omits all reference to bloodshed. Such highlighting of the skill of combat and playing down of its brutality was a characteristic tendency in Hartmann's adaptation of Chrétien's *Erec*. And it is in keeping with this flattering stylization of battle that Hartmann departs from the French *Grégoire* to introduce ladies and knights as spectators of Gregorius's combat (Gr 2112–15), almost as if it were a public tournament.

The echoes of Erec in Gregorius continue into Hartmann's account of Gregorius's rule after his marriage to his mother, for just as Hartmann altered the close of Chrétien's romance to show Erec as a model king bringing peace to his kingdom, so he adds a passage in praise of Gregorius's qualities as a ruler which has no precedent in the *Vie*,[47] and in which Gregorius (like Erec) appears as a strong enforcer of peace in his lands (Gr 2263f.: 'Sîn lant und sîne marke / die bevridete er alsô starke'; compare Er 10083f.: 'hie sazte er sô sîn lant / daz ez vridelîchen stuont'). Just as Hartmann gave more prominence than Chrétien to religious considerations in his portrayal of the protagonist in *Erec*, so he now adds to the *Vie* passages which show Gregorius as being mindful of God in his actions as knight (Gr 2070–74), and as ruler, when Gregorius refrains from territorial aggrandizement 'for God's sake' (Gr 2269: 'durch got'; 2273: 'durch die gotes êre'). Again one notes Hartmann's independent interest in the peace-keeping function of the ruler and in its metaphysical dimension.

In short, when Hartmann portrays knighthood in action in *Gregorius*, his procedures and his implicit evaluation of knighthood remain close to those of his first romance. Gregorius's progression from untried youth through knighthood to the status of ruler echoes, precisely in Hartmann's independent additions, the overall pattern of Erec's progress. And knighthood and secular rule are associated in *Gregorius*, as in *Erec*, with positive qualities of skill, courage, a desire for self-improvement, aid for the innocent, awareness of God's will as well as with the pursuit of honour.

This value-loaded presentation of the secular world is difficult to reconcile with the view that Hartmann's *Gregorius* offers a total rejection

---

[46] See Bumke, *Höfische Kultur*, I, p. 354.
[47] See also Herlem-Prey, *Le Gregorius*, p. 103.

of secular values and specifically the values of knighthood.[48] However, the position with regard to the portrayal of Gregorius's own personal status is also perhaps morally more complex than a harmoniously positive reading of his knighthood might suggest. Gregorius is indeed the formal victor in the debate with the abbot.[49] But W. J. McCann is probably right to detect 'a double motion' in this debate, with the articulate young scholar presenting on the surface a reasoned apologia for knighthood, and a logical justification of his own wishes, whilst beneath the surface Gregorius's own use of the terms 'tumpheit' (Gr 1484) and 'gir' (Gr 1622, 1800) hints at an emotive, irrational drive which is less than morally ideal.[50] The possibility is raised by this emotive, impetuous note that Gregorius's thirst for honour (Gr 1714: 'waz solde ich âne êre?') is capable of an ethically less admirable interpretation than that implied by his own rejection of a life of ease, and indeed Gregorius has been viewed by a critical line of scholarship as being sinfully self-deceiving in his pursuit of chivalry.[51] This line of interpretation seems no less partial than a reading of Gregorius's chivalry in terms of unproblematical exemplariness. And yet the text gives purchase to both approaches in such a way that even the experienced reader is at times unsure how to receive it, unsure how to place the protagonist's intentions in a moral framework. One senses a degree of complexity in the text which allows, indeed seems almost to invite, different reader responses to Gregorius's inner life.

The complexity is due not least to the operation of the different moral perspectives of monastic or clerical spirituality and secular, aristocratic culture in *Gregorius*. What in the one perspective is a legitimate, even exemplary aspiration to honour can appear in the other as a morally questionable assertion of self – and both these perspectives are in play in *Gregorius*. Seen in this light, Hartmann's own mediating position as an educated knight with a sympathetic understanding of clerical and of secular ways of thinking again emerges as an important factor in his poetic achievement, a factor conducive to moral complexity in the

[48] See also Wells, 'Gesture', p. 186: 'If Hartmann rejects the values of knighthood as a satisfactory final goal for his hero, his rejection is perhaps less total than has sometimes been suggested to the extent that he draws on the established canon of gestures found in other classical courtly MHG works and his use of this canon indicates a bond between the courtly figures and the clerics [. . .]'. The finding in this chapter, that Hartmann's treatment of the French *Vie du Pape Saint Grégoire* matches his treatment of Chrétien's romances in showing knightly combat in a more favourable, less violent light than his French sources, further supports Wells's view that knightly forms are not fundamentally rejected in *Gregorius*, and Wells's analysis of gestures in *Gregorius* highlights from a different angle the close association of secular aristocratic and clerical ways of thinking that emerges in so many ways in Hartmann's treatment of chivalry.
[49] Schönbach, *Über Hartmann von Aue*, pp. 430f.
[50] McCann, 'Gregorius's Interview', pp. 92–94.
[51] See especially Duckworth, *Gregorius*, pp. 140–64 and often.

presentation of personality, and, in the case of the good sinner Gregorius, even paradox and enigma.[52]

Nor does the narrator's laudatory portrayal of Gregorius's actions as knight and ruler mean that life in the secular world appears, after all, as morally unproblematical in *Gregorius*. The aristocratic concern with *êre*, that is social position, reputation and acclaim, figures in a double light in the work, in connection with morally good and with morally reprehensible actions. Thus 'êre' is linked with God's will and the defence of innocence when Gregorius liberates his mother (Gr 2070–74), but with the devil's work when the sister is held back from resisting her brother's incestuous attention by the fear of public shame (Gr 385–90), and with greed and envy in the unseemly struggle for the office of pope amongst the citizens of Rome (Gr 3145–54). This critical strand of thinking again places at least a hint of a question mark behind Gregorius's own enthusiastic and emotive advocacy of the pursuit of 'êre' in his exchange with the abbot. The reader wonders after all about his motives, and looks for other evidence in Gregorius's words and actions to help clarify the position.

Gregorius leaves the monastery with two stated aims: to win honour as a knight (Gr 1675–731), and to travel until God's grace reveals to him who he is (Gr 1802–05: 'ich engeruowe niemer mê / und wil iemer varnde sîn, / mir entuo noch gotes gnâde schîn / von wanne ich sî oder wer'). Events seem to justify Gregorius's leaving the monastery, for storms carry him precisely to his place of origin, where he also wins great honour (Gr 2167: 'michel êre'). But now, when Gregorius could find out who he is by telling his story, he remains silent. Moreover, instead of travelling until he finds out who he is, he settles into the life of husband and ruler. The sequence of events could allow the interpretation that Gregorius's becoming a knight and leaving the monastery was not a moral lapse, for these actions were essential to his discovery of his own identity, but that he does lapse when he allows himself to be sidetracked from the noble search for self-discovery (a task he himself had formulated in lines 1802–05) by the acquisition of prestige, a wife, and lordship over lands.[53] In moral terms, Gregorius's personal failing would be an excessive sense of shame which prevents him from revealing even to his own wife what he knows about his origins. Seen in

---

[52] This reading in terms of cultural complexity, even tension, matches the view of Hartmann's narrative commentary as being more multi-layered than is often supposed (see Ranawake, 'Mehrschichtigkeit des Erzählens', passim); precisely Gregorius's interview with the abbot, which is essentially Hartmann's independent creation, expresses cultural tension between the spheres of monastic spirituality and knighthood, using the clerical, scholarly form of the debate.

[53] W. Ohly, *Die heilsgeschichtliche Struktur*, p. 31 illuminatingly describes Gregorius's settling into marriage and lordship without having completed his task of discovering his parents, and therefore his own identity, as 'eine Art von geistlichem *verligen*'.

this light, Gregorius's concern with *êre*, which was juxtaposed with his desire for self-knowledge when he left the monastery, turns out to be, in his case, also a hindrance to self-discovery. However, Hartmann as narrator makes no mention of guilt or sin in his presentation of Gregorius's actions as knight and ruler. It is not until Gregorius unwittingly commits incest with his mother that the narrator speaks of his sin, or guilt (Gr 2277–94). The narrator does not provide any comment to the effect that this incest is the result of a previous inner failing on Gregorius's part, and he refers to Gregorius as 'the good sinner' (Gr 2552, 2606) at the very moment when he discovers his wife's identity and therefore his own position. With this attitude of the narrator, Hartmann seems to be steering the reader towards viewing Gregorius less as a man with a specific personal, moral defect than as a well-intentioned person who becomes involved in a fateful process which is ultimately beyond human (or at any rate beyond the narrator's) understanding.[54]

Whatever view one takes of the question of Gregorius's sin, it is clear that, in the work as a whole, one of the central values of knighthood – the aristocratic concern with honour – is subject to critical scrutiny. However, with regard to the moral evaluation of knighthood it should also be pointed out that ethical criticism is not restricted to the lay aristocracy in this work but extends to all areas of society, to all three estates, for the derision with which the monks receive the poor fisherman's speech (Gr 1123: 'Diu bete was der münche spot') and the greed revealed in the competition for the office of pope (Gr 3145–54) show less than ideal attitudes in various sections of the Church, whilst the harshness and greed of the fisherman who takes Gregorius to the rock shows that low birth (Gr 2949: 'von alsô swacher geburt') is no guarantee of ethical excellence in the world of Hartmann's *Gregorius*. This breadth of criticism (which is also balanced by morally positive features in all areas of society), together with the socially unspecific discussion of sin in prologue and epilogue (Gr 6–170, 3959–88) suggests that, in his development of the religious theme, Hartmann was not concerned to reveal the shortcomings of a particular sector of society, but to treat questions of sin, repentance and grace in general. Further, the pursuit of *êre* was qualified already in Hartmann's presentation of knighthood in *Erec*, so that even on this point the difference between Hartmann's first knightly romance and his first religious legend is less extreme than has at times been suggested. Particularly Hartmann's independent addition of Erec's Christian humility in thanking God for the honour he has won (Er 10085–106) foreshadows at the end of *Erec* the religious framework of reference which will dominate in *Gregorius*.

[54] See also Cormeau / Störmer, *Hartmann von Aue*, p. 114.

*Penance, contrition and the inner life*

Finally, whilst Hartmann shows much interest in the motivation of sin, for instance in his account of the causes of incest between Gregorius's parents (Gr 323–420), he shows a greater preoccupation, both in the authorial comments of prologue and epilogue (Gr 1–170, 3959–88), and in the presentation of the action, with the proper reaction of the individual to his sin, that is to say with the question of penance and contrition. With this question Hartmann links up to an important and symptomatic trend in twelfth-century religious thought.

The twelfth century was a period of increased concern with individual experience, with introspection and the pursuit of self-knowledge in various branches of religious and intellectual life.[55] The emergence of a mystical theology devoted to studying the possibility of the soul's union in love with God is one of the best documented manifestations of this introspection. But this trend also found expression, at a more practical level of the Church's teaching, in an intensified concern with the sacrament of penance, a matter which gained in importance as the Church sought to increase its influence on lay society (including the knighthood) in the course of the movements of reform and peace. Thus ecclesiastical voices laid a new stress on the individual's self-examination, emphasizing that external penance was not the same as inner repentance, and that effective amendment called for inner change and purity of intention in the sinner.[56] David Duckworth aptly places Hartmann's *Gregorius* in the framework of these new tendencies in moral and spiritual psychology in his interpretation of the work as a journey of self-discovery.[57] Nor is it a case of Hartmann taking over this modern concern with the inner life, with sincerity of individual feeling as opposed to the objective ritual of imposed penance, from his French source. Rather in adapting the *Vie du Pape Saint Grégoire*, Hartmann himself draws independently on the modern theological trend to intensify the theme of sincere penitence, that is to say the subjectively validating correlative of formal penance, as is most strikingly clear in the independent attention he pays to the spiritual value of contrition (*riuwe*) in prologue, narrative action and epilogue (Gr 162–65, 2699–706, 3983–88).[58] Thus Hartmann not only expands and develops the chivalric and courtly dimension of the narrative, he also includes new tendencies of

---

[55] Southern, *The Making of the Middle Ages*, pp. 215ff.; Morris, *The Discovery of the Individual*, passim; for further recent work on inwardness, self-knowledge and the searching of conscience in the twelfth century see Schnell, 'Abaelards Gesinnungsethik', pp. 15–24.

[56] Morris, *The Discovery of the Individual*, pp. 71ff.

[57] Duckworth, *Gregorius*, pp. 71–85 and often.

[58] See also Herlem-Prey, 'Schuld oder Nichtschuld', pp. 19, 22.

twelfth-century religious thought and practice in his adaptation. This is another mark of the central importance for Hartmann's *œuvre* of his intermediate position as an author speaking from within the knightly class, but showing intimate contact with clerical and pastoral ways of thinking.

Indeed *Gregorius* is a fascinating document of the interaction of the world of the secular aristocracy with that of clerical learning and pastoral spirituality in the twelfth century. The chivalric rescue episode, which is so unfamiliar to the religious legend as a genre, and Hartmann's own elaboration of the exchange between Gregorius and the abbot, reflect the rising importance of knighthood as a social category, and of chivalry as a legitimatory ideology, in the very composition of the narrative, whilst the overarching religious theme of sin, repentance and divine grace also relativizes this knightly thrust and suggests its limitation in the perspective of ultimate existential and metaphysical questions of sin and redemption. With regard to the controversy in Hartmann studies about the evaluation of the secular world in *Gregorius*, and the place of the work in Hartmann's *œuvre* as a whole, the discussion of Hartmann's treatment of knighthood in this chapter suggests weaknesses in the view that Hartmann, having been a programmatic advocate of courtly, chivalric culture in *Erec*, radically rejects it in *Gregorius* in favour of a general ideal of withdrawal from the world. Rather Hartmann's treatment of his source in *Gregorius*, and the place of knighthood within the work as a whole support the model of interpretation formulated by Christoph Cormeau as a 'kritisch-optimistische Relativierung laikaler Kultur'.[59] That is to say that the work links up to the aesthetic discussion of patterns of aristocratic behaviour in the courtly romance (thus implying a mainly lay target audience), and brings a critical scrutiny, but not a fundamental rejection, of secular values. In terms of genre *Gregorius* is something of an experiment, a mixture of religious legend and courtly romance both in structure and social function.

With regard to Hartmann's status as author, *Gregorius* confirms the importance of his position at a juncture of clerical learning and secular aristocracy. Further, Hartmann's treatment of the theme of penitence adds to the importance of the inner life, the realm of subjective experience and moral self-examination which he enlarged already in his adaptation of Chrétien's *Erec*, and which is a key feature in religious sources and in the secular literature of aristocratic self-understanding in the twelfth century. In the next chapter we shall see this authorial attitude acquire new traits in Hartmann's literary projection of himself as lover.

[59]  Cormeau / Störmer, *Hartmann von Aue*, pp. 140f.

# 5

# Knighthood, Love Service and the Crusade in Hartmann's *Klage* and his Lyrics

*The figure of the knight in twelfth-century* Minnesang

The decades from about the middle of the twelfth century witnessed one of the most important developments in the history of German literature – the emergence of the vernacular love lyric in the shape of the courtly lyric, or *Minnesang*. An early group of lyric poets can be discerned in the period from the 1150s to the 1170s, with a regional focus in the area of the Danube, and apparently little influenced by the modern Romance lyric, the strophic forms of these early German *Minnesänger* often remaining close to epic poetry, and love appearing usually as a reciprocal emotion or one which brings unfulfilled yearning for the woman. From about 1180 a great increase in the output of lyric poetry is recorded, for a decade or so the regional focus of *Minnesang* shifts westward to the Rhine, and the songs of these Rhenish *Minnesänger* show the reception of the Romance lyric in form and theme. Formally the songs of the Rhenish poets are longer and more complex than their German predecessors, and the impact of the Romance lyric is clear in that the German *Minnesänger* now take over strophic forms, and presumably with them melodies, from Provençal and northern French colleagues.[1] Thematically the main concern of the lyric is now with *hohe Minne*, 'high love' or 'courtly love', a pattern in which the male lover woos a lady of high social status, the lady mindful of the constraints of her reputation, which usually precludes any intimacy with the man,

---

[1] Frank, *Trouvères et Minnesänger*, passim; Aarburg, 'Melodien', pp. 384–421; Schweikle, *Mhd. Minnelyrik*, I, pp. 85–91.

whilst the man, as poet/singer/lover, thrust into a position of constant service with little hope of reward, expresses his wooing and its emotional, ethical and at times overtly social tensions in lyrics which, although they profess a subjective, personal emotion were intended entirely for public performance.

Who were these poets who played the role of suffering and rarely rewarded lovers in singing love songs in German courts from Hartmann's youth onwards? Commenting on the cultural manifestations of German knighthood, Benjamin Arnold remarks: 'The fantastical representations of knighthood displayed in the vernacular poetry of the Hohenstaufen epoch were almost wholly the work of clerics and professionals at a small number of princely courts, clerical households, and urban milieux, to which the *ministeriales'* knightly sense of identity or *esprit de corps* owed next to nothing'.[2] This comment is a timely warning against exaggerating the number of knights who were active as poets, and an apt reminder of the important role of clerics in the rise of vernacular poetry. As we shall see, the courtly romance was, in its early stages, the work of clerical authors.[3] Nevertheless, in the generality of his formulation, Arnold in turn risks giving a misleading impression of the sociology of vernacular poetry in the German courts at this time by underplaying the knightly contribution. Hartmann von Aue was, himself, one of the most productive and influential poets of the Hohenstaufen epoch, and it is a key contention of this study that his works show precisely a strong sense of knightly identity. Furthermore, with regard to the practice and the social connotations of *Minnesang*, evidence suggests that, in its decisive formative period of the late twelfth century, the art of the love song was regarded in Germany as predominantly an affair of the secular aristocracy, a point on which even scholars as far apart as Hans Naumann and Joachim Bumke agree.[4]

Literary references in various genres indicate that the singing of love songs was a respected accomplishment in the German aristocracy in the late twelfth century: an early lyric strophe tells of a knight singing 'in Kürenberg's fashion' (MF 8,2f.), Heinrich von Melk presents the singing of love songs ('troutliet') as a characteristic activity of an elegant lord in courtly dalliance with ladies (*Erinnerung an den Tod* 610–13) and Hartmann himself lists such singing as one of the qualities of an ideal young knight (AH 70f.). Particularly the critical voice of Heinrich von Melk in a rhymed sermon carries much weight, since there would seem little point in a moralist taking as a sign of the transience of worldly pleasures a practice that was not widespread. Evidence of the

---

[2] Arnold, *German Knighthood*, p. 99.
[3] See below, p. 210.
[4] Naumann, 'Die Hohenstaufen als Lyriker', pp. 23, 29; Bumke, *Mäzene*, p. 124; id., *Höfische Kultur*, II, pp. 685f.

historically real poets points in the same direction. The social status of the *Minnesänger* of the twelfth and thirteenth centuries has recently been subjected to critical scrutiny by Joachim Bumke, who maintains that they can be divided sociologically into the two classes of noble lords and professional poets.[5] None of the nineteen or so *Minnesänger* of the twelfth century up to and including Hartmann is known as a professional poet, the earliest attested professional *Minnesänger* being Walther von der Vogelweide, who was working from the 1190s through to about 1230.[6] As to clerical status, whilst some of these early *Minnesänger*, for instance Hartmann himself, clearly had some school education, the evidence we have nevertheless places them in a secular way of life. Bumke's conclusion is that, according to the present state of knowledge, *Minnesang* was, at least in its early decades, a product of one social category: the nobility.[7] However, the German nobility, as we have seen, had many gradations at this time, and the question of the relative contributions to *Minnesang* of the old free nobility and the *ministeriales*, who by the late twelfth century were increasingly acquiring aristocratic status, is currently a matter of controversy after Bumke has shown that the precise social status of many lyric poets of the twelfth and thirteenth centuries is less certain than had earlier been thought. For Bumke the distinction between free nobles and *ministeriales* is of no consequence already for the first generation of *Minnesänger*, whilst Bernd Thum and Gert Kaiser in different ways see this distinction and the position of the *ministeriales* as having an important bearing on literary developments in lyric and narrative poetry in the late twelfth century.[8] We shall return to this question.

What is clear is that, in so far as we have evidence about the social status of the poets of *Minnesangs Frühling* up to and including Hartmann

---

5  Bumke, *Ministerialität*, p. 67: 'adlige Herren und Berufsdichter'.
6  Bumke describes Walther rather guardedly as 'der erste "sichere" Berufsdichter' amongst the lyric poets (*Ministerialität*, p. 68). The problem of Walther's social origins remains unsolved. He is never described as a *ritter*, though he may have stemmed from a knightly family (Heger, *Das Lebenszeugnis*, p. 220 regarded it as almost beyond doubt that Walther was of knightly stock, 'ritterbürtig'; recent scholarship is more sceptical, see Edwards, ' "Nur ein fahrender"?', pp. 108f.). If Walther was indeed a poet of knightly family who for some reason did not take up arms, he would form an interesting parallel to the Archpoet, one of the foremost Latin lyric poets, who had connections with the imperial court in the early years of Barbarossa's rule through his patron, the chancellor Rainald of Dassel, for the Archpoet describes himself as being 'of knightly stock' (*Die Gedichte des Archipoeta*, IV,18,2: 'ortus ex militibus'); he claims that he chose to study letters so as to avoid the physical rigours of military life (ibid., IV,18,3; on the Archpoet's origins and life see also the introduction to Watenphul's and Krefeld's edition, pp. 19–30).
7  *Ministerialität*, p. 67: 'Die Sache nur eines Standes: der Herren oder des Adels'; see also Bumke, *Höfische Kultur*, II, p. 685: 'Den Adligen gehörte der Minnesang, den Fahrenden die Spruchdichtung'.
8  Bumke, *Ministerialität*, p. 67; Thum, *Aufbruch und Verweigerung*, pp. 157f., 359, 405–15; Kaiser, 'Minnesang – Ritterideal – Ministerialität', passim.

himself, they belong somewhere within the hierarchy stretching from the highest free nobles such as Emperor Henry VI (if he is indeed the Kaiser Heinrich of *Minnesang*) and Count Rudolf von Fenis-Neuenburg, through the fascinating and symptomatic transitional figure of Friedrich von Hausen, who was of a free noble family but is also recorded as an imperial *ministerialis*,[9] down to Hartmann von Aue, who describes himself as a 'dienstman' (AH 5), a ministerial, but who probably had a socially less prestigious position than Friedrich von Hausen, since no non-literary attestation of him has been found. However, this hierarchy is also that upper section of the German population whose members were qualified by birth to become knights, indeed some *Minnesänger* are also recorded as knights: Henry, later emperor, was knighted at the great Mainz court of 1184,[10] Friedrich von Hausen is praised by Gislebert of Mons as a 'probissimus miles',[11] and Hartmann von Aue describes himself as a *ritter* (Iw 21, AH 1). In sum, the love lyric in Germany in Hartmann's day and in the preceding decades appears as the self-presentation of the mixed aristocracy of free nobles and *ministeriales*, who also shared the social distinction of knighthood. At the same time, some of these early lyric poets, not least Hartmann himself, show clear signs of access to clerical learning, so that it would be quite misleading to separate the aristocracy's poetic self-presentation off too sharply from clerical influences. Indeed, time and again, the vernacular poetry of Hohenstaufen Germany presents itself as a complex cultural product at the interface of clerical learning and a knightly sense of identity, or in other words, as a product of social contact and mixing between *milites* and *clerici* at lordly courts.[12]

Moreover, throughout twelfth-century *Minnesang*, when the male lover is socially characterized within the songs, it is as a knight. This is true even for the earliest lyric poets, indeed early *Minnesang* is characterized by a frequent use of the term *ritter*. In Kürenberg's strophes the knight appears as an object of the lady's desire, a *ritter* singing from the crowd (MF 8,3), a 'courtly' knight (MF 7,20: 'eines hübschen ritters gewan ich künde'), a 'noble' knight (MF 8,20: 'ritter edele'), a 'handsome' knight (MF 10,21: 'ein schoene ritter') wooing a lady like a falconer entices his bird (MF 10,17–24). Meinloh von

---

[9]  On Hausen's social status see Rieckenberg, 'Leben und Stand'.

[10]  See above, p. 70.

[11]  *La chronique de Gislebert de Mons*, p. 230.

[12]  On the importance of contact between knights and clerics for the formation of courtly culture in the twelfth century see Fleckenstein, 'Miles und clericus', pp. 321–25. Court chaplains who were versed in worldly and aesthetic matters were particularly important figures in this contact-zone of clerical and aristocratic worlds; see the sympathetic literary portrayal of such a figure in the *Tristan* of Gottfried von Straßburg, in the shape of a cleric who is skilled in music, languages and other courtly accomplishments, and who acts as tutor to Queen Isolde and her daughter (7696–727).

Sevelingen tells of a 'ritter' (MF 14,4) sending a secret message asking to lie in his lady's arms, and the lady expresses her love for a 'young man' (MF 13,27: 'einen kindeschen man') – again one notes the association of knighthood with early manhood. The Burggraf von Regensburg has a woman express her subjection to a 'good' knight (MF 16,2) and think with longing of lying in his arms (MF 16,23ff.). In Dietmar von Aist's songs a lady sends a message of hope to a 'noble' knight (MF 32,21), a 'ritter' sends a message of love to a lady (MF 38,14ff.), a lady thinks of a 'good' knight (MF 39,4: 'eime ritter guot') and a lady remembers the long winter nights she spent in joy with a 'handsome' knight (MF 40,5: 'ein ritter wol geslaht'). A poetic world of some consistency emerges in these early lyrics, in which love is mutual, or it is the woman who yearns and the man who leaves, whilst the communication by means of polite messengers, and the references to battlements, falconry, horse and armour conjure up the social world of the secular aristocracy as the stage for these vignettes. It is important for an understanding of the chronology and the cultural forces at work in the rise in prestige of knighthood in twelfth-century German literature to remark how firmly the self-confident lover is presented as a knight in these early songs, and how socially prestigious the term *ritter* is, connected as it is with the laudatory adjectives *hübsch, edel, guot, wol geslaht* and with the freedom of riding away and leaving a yearning lady. Moreover the prestigious image of knighthood appears here in lyrics composed already in the generation from about 1150 and seemingly little touched by French influence; this poetic evidence matches the testimony of the *Kaiserchronik*, another Bavarian work of this early period, which also presents a socially elevated concept of knighthood, linking the knights with the ancient royal duty of protection and distinguishing them in status from peasants and merchants.[13]

Ursula Peters has suggested that the shift of the word *ritter* from a term of service ('Dienstwort') to being the central concept of noble life should be seen in connection with the reception of French lyric poetry in the western reaches of the German empire by Friedrich von Hausen and other noble Rhenish *Minnesänger* who were in the immediate or broader ambience of Emperor Frederick I, and who were composing after the early Danubian lyric.[14] Further, for Peters the concept of knighthood expressed in these lyrics is not so much the reflection of an actually existing knightly class in Germany, but rather an ideological import from France, by means of which the great nobles in the Hohenstaufen sphere of influence sought to make the idea of faithful service attractive as a disciplinary model.[15] Peters's emphasis on the important contribu-

[13] See above, pp. 58–60.
[14] Peters, 'Niederes Rittertum oder hoher Adel?', pp. 255f.
[15] Ibid., p. 256.

tion of the imperial court to the development and propagation of chivalric ideas and practices is welcome,[16] but her ideological interpretation of the German nobility's acceptance of knighthood is perhaps too narrow. For one thing it is of doubtful value to see the rise of knighthood so exclusively in terms of 'service', for knighthood was from the outset a matter of military power as well as service. And second, the high prestige of the term *ritter* in early *Minnesang* and in the *Kaiserchronik* in the inner German area before the large-scale reception of French lyric poetry by the Rhenish *Minnesänger* indicates again that the rise in prestige of knighthood in twelfth-century Germany was not merely an ideological import from France but had roots in the social culture of the German aristocracy. Indeed the literary evidence of an early social and cultural enhancement of the term *ritter* in vernacular German works that were independent of French sources matches the findings of Jean Flori who, in his study of the term *miles* in historical sources, comments with surprise on the application of the old royal ideology of protection to the knighthood in the German empire as early as ca. 1100, and on the German ordinances of 1152 and 1186 which marked certain legal privileges of knighthood by law a century before such enactments are recorded in France.[17] All these factors warn against seeing the German empire globally as always lagging behind France in the rise of knighthood, and they suggest that, whilst the French influence was undeniably very important in the fields of social and literary culture,[18] essential aspects of the ideological and social enhancement of knighthood in the twelfth century also show a greater independence in the German developments than is often thought to be the case – on this point the evidence of clerical authors, imperial ordinances and vernacular poetry points in the same direction.

From the Rhenish *Minnesänger* onwards, i.e. in the last two decades of the century, the word *ritter* occurs far less often in lyrics than it did earlier: the 28 pages of *Minnesangs Frühling* devoted to the early poets Kürenberg, Meinloh von Sevelingen, the Burggraf von Regensburg, the Burggraf von Rietenburg and Dietmar von Aist have eleven occurrences of *ritter*, whilst the 360 pages of lyrics from Kaiser Heinrich to Hartmann von Aue have only nine occurrences. This dramatic drop in frequency of the term 'knight' does not, however, indicate a change in the implied social status of the lover but is due to a stylistic shift, for the early *Minnesang* is characterized by an extensive use of objective forms in which the poet speaks not in his own person but in the voice of, or about, another, and all the eleven occurrences of *ritter* in *Minnesang* from

---

[16] On *Minnesang* in Hohenstaufen circles see below, pp. 186f.
[17] Flori, *L'essor*, pp. 265–67, 246f.
[18] On the reception of French aristocratic culture in Germany in the twelfth century see Bumke, *Höfische Kultur*, especially I, pp. 83–136.

Kürenberg to Dietmar von Aist are in such contexts: eight in womens' strophes, two in messengers' strophes, one in a narrative strophe. The word *ritter* is thus closely connected with objective forms in the courtly lyric, especially with womens' strophes.

However, precisely these forms are used far less often after ca. 1180 than they were in earlier *Minnesang*, and this accounts for the drop in occurrence of the term *ritter*. When the later poets do use such forms, the lover still appears as a *ritter*: of the nine occurrences of *ritter* from Kaiser Heinrich to Hartmann, six are in womens' strophes and one in a messenger's strophe. But these have now become little used forms, and from the Rhenish poets onwards the courtly lyric is dominated for the rest of the century by the first-person singing of the male lover, i.e. the lover is still, in so far as he is identified socially, a knight, but instead of third-person references to him by the persona of a lady, or a messenger, we now have predominantly a subjective, inside perspective of the poet/lover/knight expressing his own (stylized, role-bound) feelings. The outside world now plays less of a part than it did in early *Minnesang*, but what little we hear of the activities of the singer/lover still places him firmly in the knightly world, for instance when his love conflicts with his military obligations – a conflict which Hartwig von Rute expresses with the wry humour of one who has had enough of knight service on distant imperial campaigns when he comments that, since a man clearly cannot serve the emperor and women too, he will quit the service of the emperor, who has kept him away from women for too long.[19] However, in *Minnesang* from Friedrich von Hausen onwards, such references to a concrete outside world are fragmentary and usually subservient to the presentation of a rich inner life of the lover's emotional suffering, self-questioning, hope and disappointment.

In terms of the social status of the poets and the figure of the lover in the songs, this new poetic genre of *Minnesang* is thus, in the twelfth century, neither a socially undetermined exploration of subjective emotional values, nor a comment on knighthood and knightly values from outside the group, but rather a socially restricted performance art, a self-presentation of the social category 'knighthood'. Paradoxically, precisely this apparently subjective and personal poetry has a certain sociologically cohesive tendency as, in the act of composing for and singing to an audience, men from various levels of the aristocratic hierarchy, from high nobles down to lesser *ministeriales*, stylized themselves as knightly lovers, thus projecting in this new cultural model

---

[19] MF 116,22–25. The theme of conflict between knightly duty and love is frequent in the Rhenish *Minnesang* of the last decades of the twelfth century (see Schweikle, *Mhd. Minnelyrik*, I, p. 539); considerable reluctance of knights to take part in long campaigns is documented historically in the recurrent difficulties encountered by Frederick Barbarossa in raising armies for his expeditions to Italy (see Munz, *Frederick Barbarossa*, pp. 298f.).

that which was common to the various hierarchical levels and thereby reinforcing a group ethos of knighthood which cut across these levels and set knights off from the masses, no longer only by their military function but now – in poetry at least – by a sophisticated capacity for feeling and love service.[20] Nor should the idealization of women in the courtly lyric blind us to the main social orientation of the genre in Hartmann's day, which was concerned more with a cultural legitimation of knighthood than with promoting the self-realization of women, for the ideal of womanhood in the courtly lyric remains chiefly instrumental to the man's love service, which in turn is a means of projecting an ideology of exemplary – and male – knightliness.[21]

*Lessons in love: the* Klage

The increased importance of love in the mental world of the German aristocracy from the late twelfth century onwards is reflected in the emergence of a new type of literary work for which the designation 'Büchlein' has been proposed.[22] These are didactic texts often using dialogue, letter form or the situation of an advisor figure to instruct young ladies and knights, or knightly youths, in questions of love and broader behaviour, often behaviour at court. Thus in the *Winsbecke*, written between ca. 1210 and ca. 1220, a father instructs his son in marriage (8,1ff.) and the love service of ladies (9,1ff.), then in jousting and the ethics of military chivalry (17,1ff.), in behaviour at court and in other social situations (22,1ff.) and finally in the avoidance of sin and crime (53,1ff.). Whether the *Winsbecke* reflects the autobiographical reality of an ageing East Franconian noble addressing his son who, as a young knight, was perhaps about to visit some great court we cannot know, but this is the situation presented in the poem. The situation must have been a familiar one in knightly families, and the attention paid by the father to instruction in love service and polite behaviour at court suggests that these matters had come to occupy an important place in the socialization of knightly youths, at least at an ideological level.

---

[20] On this integrative function of *Minnesang* see also Haubrichs, 'Deutsche Lyrik', p. 88.
[21] See also Bumke, *Höfische Kultur*, II, p. 503: 'Das poetische Idealbild der Frau [in der höfischen Dichtung] zielte nicht auf Möglichkeiten der Selbstverwirklichung, sondern es stand ganz im Dienst des neuen Gesellschaftsentwurfs, der auf die höfische Vorbildlichkeit des adligen Ritters ausgerichtet war.' The continuing legal disadvantagement of women, and the double standard of morality which took a far graver view of extra-marital sex in the case of women than of men warn against exaggerating the inroads that the courtly idealization of women made into the deeply rooted patriarchalism of medieval society; on the patriarchal conditioning of Hartmann's portrayal of Enite see Pratt, 'Adapting Enide', pp. 80–84.
[22] Huschenbett, 'Minne als Lehre', p. 51.

Hartmann was writing at a time of transition, when some elements of the aristocratic ideology which is presented in the *Winsbecke* as an integrated and received programme, were still only just emerging, and when the various components were only beginning to interlock to form the new chivalric model. All the main points in the father's advice in the *Winsbecke* are present in Hartmann's treatment of knightly youth. However they are not yet all brought together in a received scheme, but presented partially, in different works, in a process of aesthetic and cultural exploration, analysis and adjustment. Marriage and the ethics and practice of military chivalry are central in *Erec* and figure again in *Gregorius*, the duties of landed lordship will be directly addressed in *Iwein*,[23] whilst the ethics of love service are treated in Hartmann's lyrics and his *Klage*. The *Klage* is one of the earliest examples of the 'Büchlein' type of text, and it indicates Hartmann's delight in breaking new formal, thematic and ethical ground in German literature – an innovative and exploratory thrust in his work which has not always received the attention it deserves. Moreover, the combination of learned rhetoric and the vernacular theme of love in the *Klage* again expresses Hartmann's historically significant position as an educated knight, an author who had enjoyed a clerkly education but who was a knight by his function in society, and who could thus mediate between the cultural spheres of learning and chivalry.[24]

The situation expressed in the *Klage* is that a youth has for the first time been struck by love – for a lady who is unwilling to accept him. Most of the text is devoted to a debate between the youth's body and his heart. The body first complains of the pain of unrequited love, to which the heart, as the higher moral principle, responds by urging the body to increased effort, and finally the body accepts the heart's advice, promises assiduous service and addresses a closing plea for favour to the lady. The figure of the 'jungelinc' (Kl 7) again, as in Hartmann's alterations to his French sources in *Erec* and *Gregorius*, shows the German author's preoccupation, especially in his early work, with learning and initiation processes in the transition from youth to early manhood. The youth of the *Klage* is never referred to as a *ritter*, but his leisure activities are those of the secular aristocracy: listening to poetry and song, pursuing the hunt and falconry as well as dancing and other sports (Kl 679–85); and his heart uses a metaphor from the sphere of riding skills to convey the concept of steadfast service (Kl 1551–66).[25] There is no doubt that a contemporary hearer or reader would recognize

---

23  See below, pp. 217–26.
24  See Mertens, ' "Factus est per clericum miles cythereus" ', passim.
25  On these knightly skills and pastimes in the *Klage* see also Schönbach, *Über Hartmann von Aue*, pp. 315f.

in this 'jungelinc' not merely a youth of unspecified social status, but a knightly youth.

The youth of the *Klage* also shows personality traits similar to those added independently by Hartmann in describing the passage of Erec and of Gregorius to knightly manhood; for instance his recognition of his inexperience, combined with an eager willingness to learn and a desire to win approval (Kl 1470-84) match the inner disposition of the young Erec as he prepares for his first tournament (Er 2248-61) and of the young Gregorius when he tells the abbot of his willingness to learn chivalry (Gr 1543-46). Hartmann shows much affinity as author/narrator with his young hero in *Erec* and in *Gregorius*[26] and the affinity is even greater in the *Klage*, for the youth is himself named Hartmann: 'von Owe Hartman' (Kl 29). The *Klage* is thus a fictive inner autobiography, and the debate between the young Hartmann's heart and his body (i.e. the rest of his physical person) clearly expresses a tendency to self-presentation which runs through Hartmann's *œuvre*, and which seems particularly strong in his treatment of knightly youth in his early works. If, as is likely, the *Klage* was written before or alongside *Erec*, and surely before *Gregorius*, then the experience gained by Hartmann in projecting himself imaginatively in the *Klage* may well have conditioned his approach to the young knightly protagonists in these two narrative works.

As regards the mentality of the knightly youth 'Hartman', three factors merit special attention in the heart's advice in the *Klage*. First, in warning that love is incompatible with ease, 'gemach' (Kl 617, 860), and advocating the energetic pursuit of 'sælde' and 'heil' (Kl 742-54), the heart unfolds an ethically dynamic and optimistic plan of action and speaks of love in the same terms as Hartmann the narrator and his young protagonists speak of chivalry in *Erec* and *Gregorius*.[27] Second, the virtues required of the lover in the *Klage* have a broad aristocratic and even Christian character: liberality, good bearing, humility, loyalty, constancy, purity of heart, modesty, courage (Kl 1301-17: 'milte', 'zuht', 'diemuot', 'triuwe', 'stæte', 'kiuscheit', 'schame', 'manheit'). And third, by demonstrating such qualities the lover will not only deserve the lady's reward, he will win the respect and affection of God and the world (Kl 1346: 'got und diu werlt minnet in'); indeed, at one point the youth goes so far as to say that even if he receives no reward

---

[26]   See above, pp. 104, 157.
[27]   The young Gregorius's enthusiastic programme of knightly activity in Gr 1675-720 corresponds so closely in ideas, imagery, and vocabulary to the heart's urgings in Kl 742-90 that Hartmann must surely have been consciously drawing on the heart's idealistic advice in composing Gregorius's speech (see especially the imagery of hunting in Kl 742-54, 781-84 and in Gr 1697-706 and the common line Kl 754, Gr 1706: 'mit kumber sælde koufen' - on both occasions rhyming with 'erloufen'). For the pursuit of 'gemach' as a negative quality compare Kl 613-17, 859-68; Er 2931-33; Gr 1677-83.

from the lady his efforts will be worthwhile because 'people' (Kl 1101: 'diu werlt') will value him all the more highly. All these factors suggest that the programme of love in the *Klage* is not at all an art of seduction in an Ovidian sense, it has no erotic instruction as such, it is rather an optimistic plan of broad ethical and social education;[28] and the experience of love is not an end in itself, but a means towards the end of making the knightly youth fit for his place in society. This functionalizing of love service is reminiscent of Hartmann's exploration of the metaphorical dimension of knightly combat as a means of discussing broader ethical questions in poetic form; and the reason why Hartmann can speak of military knighthood and love in the *Klage*, *Erec* and *Gregorius* in such similar terms is because both are in Hartmann's mental world geared into a common process of aristocratic socialization with Christian overtones.

A social historical consideration of the ethics of love in the *Klage* also suggests a particular relevance to the lesser knighthood. The debate amongst historians about whether the honour of arms should be seen as spreading upwards from lesser men or descending from the great nobles in the military formation of knighthood[29] has its counterpart in the cultural history of chivalry in the controversy amongst literary scholars as to whether the courtly lyric and its ideology of love service originally sprang from the social perspective of the lesser knighthood, as a legitimation of their social rise, and then spread upwards to form a class ideology for the entire aristocracy,[30] or whether this new development percolated downwards from the high nobility.[31] Whatever the question of origins (which in any case may be too sharply posed in terms of an either / or choice between higher and lower levels of aristocracy as the progenitors of courtly love) there were strong integrative tendencies linking the old free nobility and the *ministeriales* in Hartmann's day, for both shared the honour of arms and the cultural and leisure activities of the knightly aristocracy. Hartmann's presentation of military chivalry and of love primarily serves these integrative tendencies, reaching out to all levels of the aristocratic hierarchy. Nevertheless there are moments in the *Klage* as in Hartmann's other works which suggest that the ideology of chivalry is also being developed particularly from the perspective of the serving knight, and Bernd Thum is surely right to see in Hartmann's

---

[28] See also Gross, *Hartmanns Büchlein*, pp. 35–37; Wisniewski, 'Hartmanns *Klage-Büchlein*', pp. 362–69; Gewehr, *Hartmanns 'Klage-Büchlein'*, pp. 217–30; Mertens, ' "Factus est per clericum miles cythereus" ', pp. 9–14.
[29] See e.g. Leyser, 'Early Medieval Canon Law', p. 566.
[30] Köhler, 'Die Rolle des niederen Rittertums'; id., 'Vergleichende soziologische Betrachtungen'.
[31] Peters, 'Niederes Rittertum oder hoher Adel?', pp. 257–60; see also Mertens, 'Kaiser und Spielmann', pp. 465f.

literary projection of love service some reflection of the social mentality of the *ministeriales*, a mentality based on prestigious service in pursuit of reward and social recognition.[32] Just as Hartmann became in real life a 'dienstman' (AH 5) in the service of some lord, so the youth in the *Klage* seeks acceptance as a lady's 'dienstman' (Kl 1568), 'triuwe' and 'stæte' are qualities of the good vassal and also of the lover (Kl 1311), and the lady is seen in the same terms as a feudal lord, as someone who will reward faithful service 'if she is a good woman' (Kl 1631: 'ist si denne ein guot wip').

Indeed the ideology of love service in the *Klage* is a transference into the amatory sphere of the feudal relationship of service and lordship as it may have been seen from the lower end of the feudal hierarchy by a young serving knight optimistically hoping that merit would find reward. This pattern is reminiscent of Gregorius's hopes of social advancement through knightly effort, and just as Gregorius's advocacy of a knightly pursuit of fortune is accompanied by a criticism of great lords whose inherited wealth tempts them into sloth,[33] so in the *Klage* the heart scorns those who benefit from wealth and good social connections (Kl 771: 'friundes hilfe und sin guot'), and maintains that true honour and love must be won by moral qualities (Kl 779: 'tugende unde sinne'). In the spheres of love and of military knighthood Hartmann thus seems to identify particularly with the socially (relatively) less privileged figure who has to make his way by effort and merit, and this again suggests the importance of a standpoint at the lower end of the aristocratic hierarchy, a standpoint which is at times asserted so vigorously in Hartmann's works as to push the socially integrative function of the chivalric ideology into the background.

### The ethics of service and reward in Hartmann's lyrics

The lover is explicitly referred to as a *ritter* only once in the eighteen lyrics which appear in current editions under Hartmann's name, and this is in a song of doubtful authenticity (XII = MF 214,34ff.). However, the reasons for doubting Hartmann's authorship of this lyric[34] have nothing to do with its categorization of the lover, who appears in the songs confidently attributed to Hartmann clearly as a knightly figure, casting his love in terms of experiences central to the social reality and

---

[32]  Thum, *Aufbruch und Verweigerung*, p. 408.
[33]  See Gr 1681-92 and above, pp. 157f.
[34]  These are discussed by Salmon, 'The Underrated Lyrics', pp. 812f. and Reusner, 'Anhang', pp. 133-36. The song is now commonly attributed to Walther von der Vogelweide, and the third person reference to the lover as 'ein ritter' (MF 214,36) is reminiscent of the style of the early Danubian *Minnesang*.

the ideology of knighthood: warfare and vassalic service. His song of pain bears the blazon of winter (I,1,3 = MF 205,3), the lover is his own enemy (I,2,2 = MF 205,11), striking himself with his own sword (I,5,9 = MF 206,9), obliged to take vengeance for the emotional injury done to him by his lady (III,4,6 = MF 207,28); he could more easily tolerate being in feud with the emperor than being rejected by his lady, for at least a man can flee from the imperial troops, but love's suffering accompanies him everywhere (IV,2,5–10 = MF 209,19–24) – a comparison which has a remarkable combination of specificity and breadth of horizon in its implicit social placing of the lover; and finally, as a crusader, he draws on the language of knightly captivity in tournament or warfare to describe himself as a prisoner set free on parole (XVII,1,5 = MF 218,9).[35] The recourse to chivalric metaphors in Hartmann's lyrics is all the more noteworthy because metaphors drawn from military life are not common in twelfth-century *Minnesang*[36] and because Hartmann's own use of figurative language is 'very limited'.[37]

Whilst the military aspect of knighthood provides metaphors for individual moments in the lover's own emotional experience, the pattern of service and lordship, which informed the ministerial knight's social existence, also conditions the structure of his amatory experience in Hartmann's lyrics as in his *Klage*. The *Klage* presents Hartmann as a youth at the beginning of love service, optimistically hoping for reward but promising constant service come what may, and his lyrics take up and vary this theme of service. We do not know what the chronological sequence of Hartmann's lyric production was, or whether he intended his songs to form a particular aesthetic sequence, even perhaps a cycle portraying the emotional development of the lover through various stages of a relationship.[38] However, although it is not clear just what degree of continuity of (imagined) experience links the songs, there are certainly echoes, cross-references and thematic variations from song to song which permit a discussion of the lyrics in the three categories of songs of hope and reciprocal love, complaints at unrewarded service, and rejection of love service. Moreover, it is in keeping with the interests of his social group that in his lyric exploration of love service the ministerial poet Hartmann pays particular attention to the concept of reward.[39]

---

[35]   See W.H. Jackson, *'prison et croisié'*, p. 117.
[36]   See Edwards, 'Erotisierung des Handwerks', p. 127. Heinrich von Morungen is the only twelfth-century German lyric poet to draw more heavily than Hartmann on military chivalry for the metaphorical presentation of love (on Morungen see Kohler, *Liebeskrieg*, pp. 58–67).
[37]   Salmon, 'The Underrated Lyrics', p. 813.
[38]   Reusner, 'Anhang', pp. 178f. lists twelve different sequences proposed by scholars for Hartmann's songs.
[39]   See also Thum, *Aufbruch und Verweigerung*, p. 406.

The most joyful and hopeful of Hartmann's songs of secular love is 'Ich muoz von rehte den tac iemer minnen' (XIII = MF 215,14). This is also the only one of his songs in the dactylic rhythm which was taken over from the Romance lyric by Hausen and his followers, and Hartmann may have chosen this rhythm deliberately to express a mood of joy. The situation of the song is that the lover has met the lady alone, without surveillance (not a self-evident undertaking in the real public life of the courts) and she has given him some (unspecified) grounds for hope. However, even this song of joy, like the *Klage*, presents love service as a broad ethical and social education, for the lover maintains that he turns his mind towards God and the world all the better because of his lady (MF 215,19f.). The woman's song 'Swes vröide hin ze den bluomen stât' (XIV = MF 216,1) is unique in Hartmann's lyrics in that the lady proposes to give herself physically to the lover, although this decision runs against the advice of those close to her and puts her honour at risk (MF 216,20: 'êre'). Typically, this promise of physical love is also ethically motivated by reference to the pattern of service and reward. The situation of the woman caught between the rival claims of social reputation and love in this song is reminiscent of the position of Isolde in the Tristan tradition, with the important difference that Tristan and Isolde are driven by a force (expressed in the love potion) which brooks no resistance, whilst Hartmann's lady seems moved more by the ethical duty of rewarding faithful service, reflecting that her 'triuwe' (MF 216,23) calls for her to respond because the man merits reward (MF 216,17: 'sît erz wol gedienet hât'). The Tristan theme is thus informed by a certain deterministic concept of love, whilst love in Hartmann's songs, as often in the courtly lyric, is constructed more by analogy with the feudal relationship of lord and vassal which presupposes a greater moral freedom.[40]

The lady's willingness to bestow physical favours is, however, an exceptional moment, a piece of wishful thinking on the man's part, for most of Hartmann's lyrics follow the dominant pattern of *Minnesang* in the last two decades of the twelfth century in that they are complaints at the absence of reward from the lady. Within this pattern it is characteristic of Hartmann that in several songs he looks for an ethical reason for the lack of reward and has the lover turn inward to blame himself, his own 'wandel', 'unstaetekeit' or 'schult' for this lack (I,2,5ff. = MF 205,14ff.; I,4,6 = MF 205,24; III,2,10–12 = MF 208,5–7; VII,2,3f. =

---

[40] The difference between the mainstream of the courtly lyric and the Tristan tradition on this point is reflected in the fact that precisely in the lyric Heinrich von Veldeke and Bernger von Horheim distance themselves from the love inflicted on Tristan by the magic potion (MF 58,35ff.; 112,1ff.). Bernger's song is based on a lyric by Chrétien de Troyes (see Frank, *Trouvères et Minnesänger*, pp. 24f.).

MF 211,37f.).[41] The precise nature of this putative lapse or flaw is nowhere stated; indeed it seems to be the paradigm of acceptance of personal responsibility rather than any specific fault that concerns Hartmann in his lyrics. This pattern of introspection and its civilizing connotations (civilizing because the search for an inner enemy or cause for disaster is a step along the road to self-control, self-improvement) is reminiscent of the tendency of knights in Hartmann's romances to accept defeat or some other calamity as a punishment for a personal lapse.[42] Indeed, it is a sign of the mental affinities that link Hartmann's various works, even when of different genres, that he uses the same chivalric metaphor of the man's own sword striking him to express this central pattern of acceptance of responsibility both in a lyric (I,5,9 = MF 206,9) and in the romance *Iwein* (Iw 3224).

The exceptional image of the lady who is willing to reward the lover's service, and the recurrent image of the lover blaming himself for the absence of reward, both postulate a meaningful causal connection between service and reward, merit and favour in Hartmann's songs, and consequently each of these images implicitly affirms love service as an ethically rational system. However, some of the songs in which the lover states his intention to serve constantly also contain 'latent criticism of the conventional subservience of the poet to his lady',[43] and this criticism is openly expressed in one of Hartmann's most vigorous and original songs: 'Maniger grüezet mich alsô' (XV = MF 216,29). Here the singer declines an invitation to go and pay court to knightly ladies, expresses a preference for 'poor' women, amongst whom he might find one who returns his affection, and thinks back to having offered his love to a lady who merely looked at him disdainfully – an experience he intends not to repeat. The main polemical thrust of this song is a rejection of one-sided love service in favour of reciprocal love, but this rejection also has interesting social overtones. The personal and social placing of the song is made specific by Hartmann's naming himself as the singer whose experience is being related (MF 216,31f: 'Hartman, gên wir schouwen / ritterlîche vrouwen'). Such an authorial signature is frequent in narrative literature of the twelfth century, but extremely unusual in the courtly lyric.[44] The utterance is thus not that of a nameless singer, but specifically that of the one known to his audience as the ministerial knight Hartmann von Aue. This placing at the lower end of the aristocratic hierarchy by biographical information (and by the personal knowledge a primary audience had of the author) is accompa-

---

[41] See also Seiffert, 'Hartmann von Aue and his Lyric Poetry', pp. 19–21; Cormeau / Störmer, *Hartmann von Aue*, pp. 83–86.

[42] See above, p. 102.

[43] Salmon, 'The Underrated Lyrics', p. 825.

[44] Reusner, 'Hartmanns Lyrik', p. 11.

nied inside the song by a perspective from below, which conveys social distance between Hartmann and high ladies, as he stands tired before them (MF 216,35f.)[45] and then rejects them as 'too high a goal' (MF 217,5). Hartmann's advocacy of reciprocal affection also involves a social shift in the object of love, as he threatens to turn down from the high lady to occupy himself 'mit armen wîben' (MF 217,1), in order to find reciprocity. Much has been written on just who Hartmann meant by 'poor women',[46] and it may be that he did not have a specific category in mind other than that they were not the great ladies at court. But however loosely one interprets *armiu wîp*, their condition must surely be seen as socially more modest than that of the ladies who kept the poet standing, and this is significant.

There is surely a note of humour in 'Maniger grüezet mich alsô'. But however one reads the tone of the song, it remains a revealing document of a knightly mentality in that it expresses a serving knight's irritation with a poetic manner based on unrewarded service. Hartmann's threat to turn his attention socially downwards from the great lady was a dramatic new step in the development of the courtly lyric, in that it opened the way for a non-aristocratic woman to figure as a worthy object of love, and it is perhaps no coincidence that this step should have been taken by a poet who, as a *ritter* and a *dienestman*, was low enough in the aristocratic hierarchy to recognize the notion of unrewarded service as being against the interests of himself and his class, and high enough to voice his irritation.[47]

### Knighthood and conversion: Hartmann's crusading songs

The contribution of the crusades to the rise of chivalric terminology in Germany is less clear than might be thought. The crusade was preached in Christendom from the end of the eleventh century as a supreme military-cum-religious duty of the warrior class, whilst the term *ritter* is first documented ca. 1060/1065 and appears ever more frequently during the twelfth century. It would seem plausible to see a causal connection between the Church's formulation of a new Christian ideal of the warrior in its reforming and crusading propaganda and the rise of a new chivalric terminology, and indeed Bumke sees the spread of this terminology from the end of the eleventh century largely as a reflex of

[45] Schönbach, *Über Hartmann von Aue*, pp. 293f. sees in this gesture of standing a transference of vassalic custom into the sphere of love service.
[46] See Seiffert, 'Hartmann and Walther', pp. 95f.; Reusner, 'Anhang', p. 145.
[47] See also Peters, 'Niederes Rittertum oder hoher Adel?', p. 260; Thum, *Aufbruch und Verweigerung*, pp. 412ff.

the Church's propaganda.[48] However, recent work suggests that the German vernacular terminology based on the word *ritter* was, in its early stages, more secular and less religious in its connotations than this interpretation implies, for the rise in prestige of the term *ritter*, which is particularly marked in German sources from about the middle of the twelfth century, seems to have come about mainly in feudal military and courtly social contexts, whilst 'evidence that *ritter* terminology came to be viable in the context of the *militia Dei* before the end of the twelfth century is hard to find'.[49]

It is interesting in this connection to compare the first phase of *Minnesang* (ca. 1150 to ca. 1180), where we have seen the word *ritter* firmly established in a decidedly secular meaning to indicate the male lover, with the first German epic on a crusading theme, the *Rolandslied*, written probably in the 1170s, in which the term *ritter* is sparingly used and the notion of religious warriordom is conveyed by such old heroic terms as *helt, degen, recke, wigant* – it is one of the paradoxes of the early history of knighthood in Germany that the *nova militia* preached by Bernard of Clairvaux[50] found expression in this ancient heroic vocabulary. The strong secular connotations of *ritter* terminology are shown by the fact that, in the *Rolandslied*, three of the four occurrences of *ritter* (4490, 4776, 4964) and three of the five occurrences of *ritterlich* (4898, 4996, 8006) relate to, or are used by pagans, whilst of the two occurrences of *ritterschaft* one is explicitly connected with music and dance as an expression of vain arrogance (287f.: 'tanz unde riter scaft / unt ander manige hoch uart').[51] Nor is the rise of the word *ritter* in the secular sphere merely an oddity of the German vernacular, rather it has its parallel in the Latin terminology of knighthood, for in the late twelfth century the word *miles* was associated at least as strongly with secular glory, military power and an elevated social status as with service and Christian humility.[52]

All this is not to argue that the Church's propaganda after all made no significant contribution to the development of a knightly ideology, but it does seem timely to warn against exaggerating this specifically religious contribution, and to note how the semantic history of knightly

---

[48] Bumke, *Ritterbegriff*, p. 113: 'wenn ein adliger Herr seit dem Ende des 11. Jahrhunderts *miles* 'Ritter' genannt wird, so steht dahinter bewußt oder unbewußt das christliche Ritterbild der Reform- und Kreuzzugsbewegung'.

[49] Ashcroft, '*Miles Dei – gotes ritter*', p. 67.

[50] On the concept of Christian chivalry in Bernard's *De laude novae militiae* see Flori, *L'essor*, pp. 210–14.

[51] See Ashcroft, '*Miles Dei – gotes ritter*', p. 66.

[52] W.H. Jackson, 'Knighthood and Nobility', p. 808; the knighting ceremonies too were essentially secular in origin, and maintained strong worldly connotations beside the religious associations which they exhibited especially from the second half of the twelfth century onwards (Flori, 'Les origines de l'adoubement chevaleresque', p. 247).

vocabulary again indicates a powerful secular thrust in the rise of chivalry in the key period of the twelfth century – a thrust to the strength of which the Church testified precisely by its continuing criticism of secular chivalry. To many observers from within the Church, knightly life in the last generation of the twelfth century indeed seemed spiritually perilous in the ostentatious violence of feud and tournament, the frequent licentiousness of its sexual mores and the more sublimated but still extremely worldly entertainment and social intercourse at court.[53] Moreover, the sense of a need for reorientation within knighthood was urgently brought to the fore during the period of Hartmann's poetic activity by a major crisis in the crusading sphere.

The First Crusade (1096–1099) had been chiefly a French and Norman affair and had led to the taking of Jerusalem and the foundation of the four crusader states of Antioch, Edessa, Tripoli and Jerusalem. The reconquest of Edessa by the Muslims in 1144 had stimulated the Second Crusade (1147–1149), this time with a large German contingent, but the enterprise was a military failure. Sultan Saladin's reconquest of Jerusalem in 1187 was a further disaster, which led to the Third Crusade (1189–1192) with German, French and English participation under the respective rulers Frederick I, Philip Augustus and Richard I. This venture too brought setbacks for the Germans as Barbarossa was drowned on 10 June 1190 while bathing in the river Saleph; then his son, Duke Frederick of Swabia, died of a disease on 20 January 1191 whilst laying siege to Acre. Barbarossa's son and successor, Emperor Henry VI, planned a crusade and sent an expedition to Syria in 1197, but the emperor died before he could join the army, the crusaders returned home, and again the German experience of crusading was linked with failure.[54]

What is important for our topic is that the shock of the loss of Jerusalem confronted the knighthood of Christendom with a religious duty at a time when the various strands of influence that made up the ideological and social model of chivalry were coming together in poetry and in the forms of socialization at the great courts and the tournament venues of western Europe. The confrontation is documented historically in the two great imperial courts held at Mainz in 1184 and 1188. These courts were high points in the rule of Frederick Barbarossa and in the history of knighthood in twelfth-century Germany, for they show the crystallization of knighthood as a social community which embraced the legally distinct layers of *ministeriales* and free nobles, and they demonstrate a fundamental tension in chivalric culture, as the court of

---

[53]  On clerical criticisms of the *militia* see above, p. 151; on clerical criticisms of the court see also Schreiner, ' "Hof" (*curia*)', pp. 90–115 and Bumke, *Höfische Kultur*, II, pp. 583–94.
[54]  Runciman, *History of the Crusades*, III, p. 97: 'The whole Crusade had been a fiasco and had done nothing to restore German prestige'.

1184, with the knighting of two of the emperor's sons and the attendant
military display and lavish feasting, marks the secular glory of chivalry,
whilst the court of 1188, at which the emperor and his son Frederick
took the cross, was called in order to gather a crusading army, and was
dominated by crusading sermons and appeals for a turning of
knighthood towards the service of God.[55] Hartmann himself lived
through these crucial years of crystallization and tension in German
chivalry, and the appeal for a new direction of knighthood is expressed
programmatically in his treatment of the crusade in his lyrics.

News of the fall of Jerusalem and preparations for a military campaign
to restore the Holy City to Christian rule led to a spate of propaganda for
the crusade in writings and sermons from Church sources and in
Romance and German vernacular songs, which were delivered by
troubadours and *Minnesänger* at the courts of Christendom.[56] As we
have seen, members of the knightly class to which the Church
addressed its propaganda were also active as *Minnesänger*, and their
songs provide fascinating comment on the crusade from within this
class, for the impact of the crusading campaign led to an important new
thematic development in the vernacular lyric in the late 1180s, as the
newly established poetic theme of love service was suddenly confronted
with the religious and military reality of the knights' crusading
obligations. Interestingly, the German knightly poets make fewer
references to the concrete political, military and geographical realities of
the crusade than the Romance troubadours, and they concentrate more
exclusively on the personal, religious and moral dimensions of the
undertaking.[57] The dominant theme of German crusading lyrics of the
late twelfth century is that of parting from the beloved, a theme explored
by Friedrich von Hausen (MF 45,37; 47,9), Albrecht von Johansdorf (MF
86,1; 87,5; 87,29; 94,15; compare also 89,21) and Heinrich von Rugge
(MF 102,1) in connection with the crusade of 1189/1192 (on which
Hausen lost his life). These poets bring variations on the theme of
conflict between the ties of love and the crusade, always urging
participation in the crusade. However, the very insistence with which
they dwell on the pain of parting from the beloved perhaps also conveys
some coded doubts about the value of the crusade and suggests a less
than wholehearted response of German knighthood to the venture.[58]
Hausen's famous song 'Mîn herze und mîn lîp, diu wellent scheiden'
(MF 47,9) has a paradigmatic value in this connection, for the inner
division of the knight who goes on crusade whilst his heart stays with
his lady expresses the tension within the knightly class between the

55   Fleckenstein, 'Friedrich Barbarossa und das Rittertum', passim.
56   For the corpus of lyrics see Hölzle, *Die Kreuzzüge*, passim.
57   Ibid., I, p. 621.
58   See also Müller, 'Tendenzen und Formen', p. 261.

religious duty of the crusade and the pull of a secular, aristocratic world that was acquiring its own cultural value. Here, as often in the courtly lyric, the apparently private, emotional theme (in this case the experience of a divided self) is also a means of giving aesthetic form to group concerns of the knighthood as a whole, and the lover's attitude towards his lady is also a vehicle whereby the poet explores his place in society.

The crusade is of central importance in three of Hartmann's songs (V = MF 209,25; VI = MF 211,20; XVII = MF 218,5). It is a matter of dispute whether Hartmann's crusading songs arose in connection with the crusade of 1189 or that of 1197, or indeed whether they spread over both ventures, the decisive crux throughout the debate being whether MF 218,19 refers to the death of Sultan Saladin (3 March 1193), which would place this song at least after that date, or to the death of Hartmann's own lord, which may have been earlier.[59] It is, however, clear that the songs express a knightly point of view after the shock of the loss of Jerusalem. They also provide further evidence of a Hohenstaufen imperial connection in Hartmann's poetry. Wolfgang Haubrichs places one of Hartmann's crusading songs (V = MF 209,25) in the context of the Hohenstaufen imperial court in 1188 and relates another (XVII = MF 218,5) to the preparations for Henry VI's crusade.[60] Günther Schweikle connects all Hartmann's crusading songs with the Hohenstaufen court, going so far as to suggest that the lord whose death Hartmann mourns may have been Frederick Barbarossa himself,[61] whilst Peter Hölzle surmises that Hartmann may have taken the cross at an imperial court held by Henry VI in 1195.[62] None of these specific attributions can claim to be proven. Nevertheless, it remains true that at least in a broad sense Hartmann's crusading songs belong within a Hohenstaufen sphere of influence, for the crusades of 1189 and 1197 were planned by the successive Hohenstaufen emperors Frederick I and Henry VI, and by seeking to win knights for the crusade Hartmann was lending his voice, at whichever court he was singing, to a knightly venture under imperial leadership.

Indeed the Hohenstaufen court seems to have been a major focus for the courtly lyric at a decisive stage of its development in Germany, in the last two decades of the twelfth century, that is to say in the last decade of Barbarossa's rule and under his son Henry VI, and during (also probably preceding) Hartmann's poetic activity, for a number of *Minnesänger* of these decades share features of style and also have

59   For the views on this crux see Reusner, 'Anhang', pp. 151f., 157f.
60   Haubrichs, *'Reiner muot* und *kiusche site'*, passim.
61   Schweikle, 'Der Stauferhof', pp. 255–59.
62   Hölzle, *Die Kreuzzüge*, I, p. 593.

Hohenstaufen connections: Friedrich von Hausen, Bligger von Steinach, Ulrich von Gutenburg, Bernger von Horheim, Henry VI himself (if indeed he is the 'Emperor Henry' of the manuscripts) and perhaps Heinrich von Rugge.[63] It was largely these poets who were instrumental in adapting into German the latest style of Romance lyric with its complex strophic forms and its characteristic theme of the male lover's service of his lady – the theme which is also central to Hartmann's *Klage* and his love songs. The most productive of these poets in the Hohenstaufen ambience and the most interesting for the history of chivalry is Friedrich von Hausen, whose work is so dominant as to give rise to the view that there was something of a school of Hohenstaufen lyric poets grouped around Hausen. Hausen was, like Hartmann, both knight (in Hausen's case an imperial *ministerialis*) and *Minnesänger*, and his work, like Hartmann's, includes lyrics of love service and crusading songs. Of all the earlier lyric poets, Hausen seems to have had most influence on Hartmann, and chronological and regional evidence makes Hartmann's knowledge of Hausen's songs, even a personal meeting of the two poets, easily possible.[64] Hausen had close Hohenstaufen connections, for he is recorded already in 1171 in the service of Archbishop Christian of Mainz, who was a trusted ambassador for the emperor in high-level affairs, and from 1186 until his death on crusade in May 1190, Hausen appears in the entourage of the young King Henry VI and of Barbarossa himself.[65] Consequently a link between Hartmann and Hausen would imply at least some channel of communication between Hartmann and the Hohenstaufen court. The history of the courtly love lyric thus matches the political circumstances of the crusades in the last two decades of the twelfth century to suggest that developments at the Hohenstaufen court were of some importance (though it remains uncertain how directly) in conditioning Hartmann's lyric poetry, just as Hartmann departs from Chrétien's narrative to show an alignment with Hohenstaufen interests in adapting *Erec*.

Hartmann's crusading songs are characterized by a concern with the interplay of service, reward and reciprocity, an affirmation of knightly honour within a broader ethical framework, and an insistence on inner, moral renewal.[66] These themes run through the various genres in which

---

[63] See Naumann, 'Die Hohenstaufen als Lyriker', pp. 22–26; Schweikle, 'Der Stauferhof', p. 248; McDonald / Goebel, *German Medieval Literary Patronage*, pp. 73–75; Bumke, *Mäzene*, pp. 126–30.

[64] Reusner, 'Anhang', p. 171; Seiffert writes firmly of 'Hausen's influence on Hartmann' ('Hartmann von Aue and his Lyric Poetry', p. 21).

[65] Rieckenberg, 'Leben und Stand', pp. 166–68. The reliable and informed chronicler Gislebert of Mons describes Hausen as one of the *familiares* and *secretarii* of the emperor (*La Chronique de Gislebert de Mons*, p. 272). On Archbishop Christian's trusted service of Barbarossa see Opll, *Friedrich Barbarossa*, pp. 91f., 107, 109 and often.

[66] See also Wentzlaff-Eggebert, *Kreuzzugsdichtung*, p. 197.

Hartmann worked to form a characteristically Hartmannesque set of concerns, and all come together in the crusading song 'Dem kriuze zimet wol reiner muot' (V = MF 209,25). The song is a call to participation in the crusade, but it goes further to correct the view, which was probably widespread in knightly circles, that mere physical participation could secure heavenly reward, and to assert the need for spiritual purity in the crusader. No other German crusading song of the twelfth century calls so emphatically for inner conversion, for purity of mind and deed in the crusader. This emphasis may reflect specifically the crusading propaganda of Pope Celestine III in 1195,[67] or the religious mood of the *curia Jesu Christi* in Mainz in 1188,[68] when the German knights were summoned to follow Barbarossa's example and join the *militia Christi* of the crusading army,[69] but whatever the immediate social context of Hartmann's song, such a linking of military knighthood with spiritual purity is particularly appropriate in an author who, even in his first Arthurian romance, presents the practice of arms in a strongly ethical light. Put in another way, Hartmann's tendency to endow combat with a metaphorical, ethical dimension may already in *Erec* be seen as a transference of crusading patterns of thought into the sphere of secular chivalry.

In 'Dem kriuze zimet wol reiner muot' Hartmann connects his commitment to the crusade with the death of his earthly lord, and this loss gives his crusading vow an added dimension, as he proposes to share the spiritual reward for his venture with his deceased lord (MF 210,31–34: 'Mac ich ime ze helfe komen, / mîn vart, die ich hân genomen, / ich wil ime ir halber jehen. / vor gote müeze ich in gesehen'). This intention is in keeping with the Church's teaching,[70] and the motif of the shared reward figures elsewhere in crusading songs with the knight's beloved as the beneficiary.[71] Hartmann also refers to the death of his lord in a love song (MF 206,14) and (perhaps) again in a crusading song in the famous crux: 'und lebte mîn her Salatîn und al sîn her / dien bræhten mich von Vranken niemer einen vuoz' (MF 218,19f.). It may be that Hartmann's lord was a figure of much importance for his death to be mentioned in so public a genre as the courtly lyric, and scholars have recently looked to Emperor Frederick I[72] (d. 1190), Duke Berthold IV of Zähringen[73] (d. 1186) and Welf VI, duke of Spoleto, who

---

Hölzle, *Die Kreuzzüge*, I, pp. 565ff.
Haubrichs, *'Reiner muot* und *kiusche site'*, pp. 303f., 319–24.
Fleckenstein, 'Friedrich Barbarossa und das Rittertum', pp. 1033f.
See Schönbach, *Über Hartmann von Aue*, pp. 161f.
For example Albrecht von Johansdorf and Hartmann himself both speak of the beloved receiving 'half the reward' for the crusader's journey ('halben lôn', MF 94,34; 211,22).
Schweikle, 'Der Stauferhof', pp. 257–59.
Bertau, *Deutsche Literatur*, I, pp. 621f., 676; Mertens, *Gregorius Eremita*, pp. 81f.; id., 'Das literarische Mäzenatentum der Zähringer', pp. 127f.

held prestigious court in Ravensburg[74] (d. 1191). In the absence of more direct evidence the identity of this lord remains uncertain. However, Hartmann's reference to the death of his lord as an event that has had a deep impact on him remains an unusually personal, autobiographical note in the predominantly role-bound world of contemporary *Minnesang*, a note which again indicates a strong tendency to self-expression in Hartmann's works, here more precisely a vassalic element, as the ministerial knight Hartmann presents himself to his audience as a loyal vassal even after his lord's death. It is also a feudal concept of the crusade as a form of vassalic knightly obligation owed to God as the supreme lord that underlies Hartmann's appeal, in 'Dem kriuze zimet wol reiner muot', to the knights to risk their lives in return for the benefits God has given them (stanza 2 = MF 209,37ff.). The interpretation of the crusade as a feudal obligation was widespread in crusading propaganda from lay and even church sources in the twelfth century;[75] for instance in Bishop Godfrey of Würzburg's address at the *curia Jesu Christi* in 1188 'it was [the] appeal to knighthood and to the feudal concept of service which carried the day'.[76] Thus in Hartmann's songs and in a strand of contemporary religious preaching, the appeal to service of God in the crusade builds upon and stabilizes social values of the feudal knighthood.

Indeed in general, although the crusade involves some turning away from the world for the 'I' of 'Dem kriuze zimet wol reiner muot' (in stanzas 3, 4 and 6), secular values are by no means rejected wholesale in the song. When, in stanza 2, Hartmann addresses knights who have sought glory ('hôhen prîs', MF 210,4) in worldly deeds of arms the reference surely includes participation in the tournament, for this was the military activity most directly concerned with the accretion of honour; and whilst the poet appeals to such knights now to devote their arms to God (MF 210,5 ff.) this does not imply a fundamental rejection of secular knighthood and the pursuit of glory, for he goes on to promise that the crusade will bring both worldly praise and the soul's salvation (MF 210,10: 'der welte lop, der sêle heil'). Just as Hartmann's addition of religious observances to Chrétien's account of the tournament in *Erec* showed the German author's desire to endow a secular practice of chivalry with an ethical, even religious significance,[77] so his promise of secular glory to the crusader is, especially in a song which has an almost penitential insistence on inner, moral purity, a powerful affirmation of a central secular norm of chivalry even in a religious context. Seen in this light the crusade acquires an ideologically utopian dimension in

---

[74]  Thum, 'Politische Probleme', pp. 67–70.
[75]  See Hölzle, *Die Kreuzzüge*, I, p. 575.
[76]  Munz, *Frederick Barbarossa*, p. 386.
[77]  See above, p. 106.

Hartmann's knightly thinking, offering to the knight who takes the cross with pure intention the prospect of reconciling the salvation of his soul with the enhancement of secular, military glory – two values which, outside of crusading propaganda, were often seen by the Church as conflicting with each other. Moreover it is important to note that Hartmann's stance has its historical parallel, for whilst the *curia Jesu Christi* transformed the German imperial knighthood into a *militia Christi*, this did not involve a total abandonment of the knighthood's secular ideals, rather Barbarossa himself undertook the crusade 'for the sake of God and worldly honour'[78] and whilst actually on crusade held chivalric combat games as the guest of the King of Hungary in May 1189.[79] On this issue of the affirmation of secular honour within a religious framework Hartmann's poetic utterances again emerge as neither idiosyncratic nor fantastical, but as an expression of a knightly mentality which is also documented in historical sources.

The readiness of knights actually to participate in the lengthy and dangerous undertaking of a crusade should not, however, be exaggerated. The very urgency of crusading propaganda suggests that there was much resistance to be overcome by the late twelfth century; for instance, despite the religious enthusiasm of the Mainz court of 1188, the actual turnout of knights for the departure of Barbarossa's crusade from Regensburg in May 1189 fell below expectations,[80] although the army remained the largest single force yet to leave on a crusade.[81] Criticism of knights who fail to go on crusade is a recurrent theme in crusading songs,[82] surfacing in 'Dem kriuze zimet wol reiner muot' when Hartmann speaks of the folly of those who withhold their military service from God (MF 210,3–6). In the single stanza 'Swelch vrouwe sendet ir lieben man' (VI = MF 211,20) Hartmann addresses two further problems of crusading morale – hostility to the venture amongst women, and anxiety amongst crusaders about the behaviour of their women at home – by calling on women to encourage their partner's departure on crusade and to match the crusader's valour with a virtuous life at home. Here again Hartmann's poetry is attentive to the actual circumstances of knightly life.

Hartmann's third crusading song, 'Ich var mit iuweren hulden, herren unde mâge' (XVII = MF 218,5), has been seen as the expression

---

[78] Arnold of Lübeck, *Chronica Slavorum*, IV,7, p. 128: 'tam pro Deo quam pro honore temporali'; this and the passage in n. 79 from Arnold of Lübeck are quoted by Fleckenstein, 'Friedrich Barbarossa und das Rittertum', p. 1034. It is interesting to note that this same Arnold translated Hartmann's *Gregorius* into Latin hexameters under the patronage of Duke William of Brunswick-Lüneburg (see above, p. 155).
[79] Arnold of Lübeck, *Chronica Slavorum*, IV,8, p. 131.
[80] Jungbluth, 'Das dritte Kreuzlied Hartmanns', pp. 152f.
[81] Runciman, *History of the Crusades*, III, p. 11.
[82] See Hölzle, *Die Kreuzzüge*, I, pp. 502–08.

of an inner crisis in the poet which followed the death of his lord and led to his religious commitment to the crusade,[83] as a polemical contribution to the discussion in *Minnesang* about the nature and value of love,[84] and as a response to the political situation of the crusade of 1189,[85] or that of 1197.[86] The sheer variety of these interpretations indicates the cultural breadth of a work which is a peak of achievement in twelfth-century lyric and which, as the farewell utterance of a crusader preparing to leave lords, kin and lands, documents an important knightly experience.

Although Hartmann's crusading propaganda affirms the pursuit of secular glory within a religious framework it brings a radical rejection of the one-sided love which was the central theme of contemporary court singing. In 'Ich var mit iuweren hulden' Hartmann takes the feudal pattern of service (MF 218,16: 'diente' and 'dienen') and reward to the point of complete reciprocity in the crusader knight's love of God (stanza 3), and he plays this reciprocal love off against the one-sided love of the *Minnesänger*, which he rejects as a mere empty hope, 'wân' (MF 218,22; 218,26). With this polemic, Hartmann is also turning away from his own *Klage* and his earlier songs in which he had presented his own love as a 'wân'.[87] Indeed, despite the difference in tone between the joyful religious confidence of 'Ich var mit iuweren hulden' and the irritated secular humour of 'Maniger grüezet mich alsô', both songs are connected in that they show Hartmann stepping outside the main lyric convention of his day to distance himself in public song from the literary theme of unrequited love service; and the advocacy of mutual love in these two songs, be it secular love for a 'poor woman' or the crusader knight's love for God, involving as it does a break with an established socio-poetic convention, testifies to the central importance of reciprocity in Hartmann's view of human relations.

Moreover, just as the conflict between body and heart has a wider resonance in Hausen's crusading song, so Hartmann's rejection of unrequited love also articulates a broader cultural criticism which is expressed in his dismissal of the mere 'words' of the *Minnesänger* in favour of the 'deeds' of the crusader (MF 218,13f.: 'Sich rüemet maniger, waz er dur die minne tæte. / wâ sint diu werc? die rede hœre ich wol'). The opposition of words and deeds touches on an important ambivalence in the preoccupation with love service as a legitimatory

---

83 Wentzlaff-Eggebert, *Kreuzzugsdichtung*, pp. 201–03; Blattmann, *Die Lieder Hartmanns von Aue*, pp. 276ff.
84 Kuhn, 'Minnesang als Aufführungsform'; Reusner, 'Kreuzzugslieder', pp. 346f.
85 Jungbluth, 'Das dritte Kreuzlied Hartmanns'.
86 Mertens 'Kritik am Kreuzzug Kaiser Heinrichs?'.
87 Relevant occurrences of *wân* in Kl 1077: 'ein vil ungewisser wan' and in Hartmann's songs I (MF 205,7: 'den langen wân'), III (MF 208,23: 'ein lieber wân'), IV (MF 209,6: 'bî ungewisseme wâne'), VII (MF 212,1: 'lieben wân').

model in the literature of the knightly class, for precisely the aesthetic
and emotional finesse of the courtly lyric, whilst marking the claim of
knighthood to cultural refinement, could also appear as self-indulgent
introspection at odds with the knight's public duty in the *vita activa*,
especially the military obligations which were sanctioned by religion in
the context of the crusade. In this sense, Hartmann's appeal to knights
to turn away from the mere words of *Minnesang* and embrace the action
of the crusade anticipates, at one level, Wolfram von Eschenbach's
assertion that songs without the backing of warrior deeds should not
win the love of a discerning woman (*Parzival* 115,11–14: 'schildes ambet
ist mîn art: / swâ mîn ellen sî gespart, / swelhiu mich minnet umbe sanc,
/ sô dunket mich ir witze kranc'). In their different ways the knightly
poets Hartmann and Wolfram were both reminding their audiences of
the continuing military function of chivalry. At a time when knighthood
was acquiring more aristocratic connotations and becoming a broader
social distinction as well as a matter of military function such reminders
were particularly timely.

A final point concerns the tone of 'Ich var mit iuweren hulden'. The
song has a remarkably self-confident, forceful ring. It opens and closes
on the first person singular 'ich', and this self remains vividly and
assertively present throughout the song, commanding a wide religious,
political and cultural horizon, with the singer taking an almost stately
leave from lords and kin (stanza 1), seeing himself in relation to Sultan
Saladin and all his army (stanza 2) and launching a scathing attack on
the *Minnesänger* as self-deluding purveyors of one-sided love (stanza 3).
This strength of tone and breadth of vision have led one scholar to
suggest that we have here the voice of a ruler rather than that of a lesser
knight, and to interpret the song as a piece of role-play in which
Hartmann speaks not in his own voice, but in the *persona* of Emperor
Frederick Barbarossa himself.[88] 'Ich var mit iuweren hulden' may well
have been an appeal to the knighthood to take part in the crusade of
1189, and the singer's attack on the lyrics of unrequited love would have
been particularly appropriate in a Hohenstaufen context, for such lyrics
were favoured precisely by the *Minnesänger* who were connected with
the Hohenstaufen dynasty at this time. However, the forcefulness and
the broad sweep of the song do not suggest that Hartmann is here
speaking in anyone's *persona* other than his own, rather they testify to
the maturity of voice in Hartmann's crusading songs, and to the social
pride that was an important element in the group mentality of German
knighthood by the end of the twelfth century. More precisely, the song
illustrates how the Church's propaganda for the crusade was accepted
by the knightly class in such a way as to enhance the prestige of even the

---

[88] Jungbluth, 'Das dritte Kreuzlied Hartmanns', pp. 152–56.

lesser ministerial knights, such as Hartmann himself, by providing a metaphysical legitimation of the profession of arms and by linking the various levels of the secular aristocracy in a common ideology of ethical obligation (MF 218,12: 'wie kûme ich bræche mîne triuwe und mînen eit!') in which the condition of being a *miles Christi* was shared by the least knight and the emperor himself.[89]

Indeed of all Hartmann's songs, it is perhaps the two in which he rejects the one-sided love of the lyric tradition that show the social mentality of knighthood in sharpest relief, the irritated sense of rejection in 'Maniger grüezet mich alsô' marking the social distance between the lesser knights and the upper reaches of the aristocratic hierarchy, whilst 'Ich var mit iuweren hulden' projects an integrative crusading ideology which allows even a lesser *ministerialis* to show a lordly self-confidence. In this way Hartmann's discussion of the ethics of love in his songs echoes his treatment of chivalric combat in his romance *Erec*, in that both express an interplay of hierarchical divergence and convergence which is central to the self-understanding of the German knighthood at the end of the twelfth century.

[89]  On the ideological attractiveness of the Church's ideal of chivalry for the social self-interpretation of the German *ministeriales* around 1200 see also Kaiser, 'Minnesang – Ritterideal – Ministerialität', especially p. 191.

# 6

# *Der Arme Heinrich:*
# Lord, Peasant and Lay Literacy

### Hartmann and lay literacy

Of Hartmann's four narrative works *Der arme Heinrich* is the only one in which military activity plays no part, and the one in which least reference is made to the court. It is an indication of the importance of these two spheres of the court and military activity for the concept of knighthood around 1200 that, with only three occurrences in its 1520 lines (AH 1, 34, 1340) the term *ritter* appears less frequently in this than in any other of Hartmann's narrative works.[1] However, despite, and in some ways because of, the paucity of strictly knightly terminology *Der arme Heinrich* remains a revealing work for our study.

The opening of the work marks an important stage in German literary history, for when Hartmann introduces himself as a *ritter* (AH 1), this is (depending on the chronological priority of *Der arme Heinrich* and *Iwein*, where Hartmann also presents himself as a *ritter*, Iw 21) the first recorded instance of a German narrative author explicitly describing himself as a 'knight'. The introduction also provides further information about the author-knight Hartmann: that he was sufficiently well educated (AH 1: 'gelêret') to read books, and that he was a ministerial knight (AH 5: 'dienstman was er zOuwe'). The role of the *ministeriales* has been discussed earlier.[2] Here comment is called for on knighthood and literacy.

Literacy was not the norm for German knights in Hartmann's day. The questions of why, where and in what form Hartmann received the

---

[1] Occurrences of *ritter* and total line numbers in the other three narratives: Er 134/10135; Gr 14/4006 ; Iw 83/8166.
[2] See above, pp. 64–69, 74–83.

literate education to which he refers with some pride in *Der arme Heinrich* and again in *Iwein* (21) permit only speculative answers within the framework of the possibilities that existed at the time.[3] Perhaps (as a younger son?) Hartmann was originally destined for a career in the Church, educated accordingly, and then returned to secular life due to a change in family circumstances (perhaps the death of an elder brother) which called for the line to be secured. Two greater and better-documented German nobles whose careers took this course in Hartmann's day were Count Bernard II of Lippe (ca. 1140–1224) and Philip of Swabia (1177–1208), the youngest son of Frederick Barbarossa.[4] Or he may have been schooled at the wish of his feudal lord, who perhaps planned from the outset to have him as an educated knight to co-operate with clerics in the administration of the lord's affairs. As early as the eleventh century, Ekkehard of St Gall speaks of day pupils receiving an education in the monastic school to help them handle their property, without any intention of becoming clerics.[5] The consolidation of larger lordships and the growing complexity of estate management can only have increased the need for such men qualified in administration in subsequent generations. With regard to the place of Hartmann's education it is extremely unlikely that, as the son of a ministerial family, he had the 'private' house tutoring available to, for instance, Barbarossa's children; rather he probably attended a monastic or cathedral school. Hartmann's account of Gregorius's education in the monastery (Gr 1159–1200) goes well beyond what was in his French source, and the German author may here have been drawing on his own autobiographical experience of school.[6] Hartmann's works in general suggest that he had some training in the liberal arts and some acquaintance with the literature of Latin antiquity and with theological issues. Gregorius's subjects of study – divinity and law as well as grammar (Gr 1181–97) – go well beyond a rudimentary education and may reflect Hartmann's own course of study.

Hartmann's schooling and his literacy are reflected in the style of his poetry in various ways. He tends to parade his schooling particularly in his early works, especially in *Erec*. For instance he has far more

---

[3] The fullest account of Hartmann's 'Bildung' is still Schönbach, *Über Hartmann von Aue*, pp. 179–339; see also Mertens, *Gregorius Eremita*, pp. 163–65.
[4] On Bernard of Lippe see Goez, *Gestalten des Hochmittelalters*, pp. 273–89; on Philip of Swabia see Csendes, *Heinrich VI*, pp. 213f.
[5] *Casus S. Galli*, c. 135 (MGH Scriptores, 2, p. 142), quoted by Thompson, *Literacy*, p. 87.
[6] See also Schönbach, *Über Hartmann von Aue*, pp. 220–24. *Gregorius* should not, however, be pushed too hard for autobiographical clues; particularly the older view that the island monastery in *Gregorius* suggests Reichenau on Lake Constance as the place of Hartmann's education is now considered unlikely because of the high noble exclusivity of this monastery; for a *ministerialis* like Hartmann a reform monastery or a cathedral school would be more likely institutions (see Mertens, *Gregorius Eremita*, pp. 163f.; Cormeau / Störmer, *Hartmann von Aue*, p. 37).

reminiscences of Latin school authors in *Erec* than in later works,[7] and his style shows a more frequent and obtrusive, self-conscious use of rhetorical ornament in *Erec*, especially in the long descriptive passages which characterize this work, than is the case in his later works.[8] The form of the disputation between body and heart in the *Klage* also reflects Hartmann's schooling,[9] and this work often gives the impression of being an exercise in style and dialectic (though this is not to trivialize the treatment of love and ethical disposition in the *Klage*). In his later works Hartmann achieves a narrative voice in which the rhetorical figures are less obtrusive and 'blend more discreetly into the narrative surroundings'.[10] The difference is particularly detectable in the stylistic shift from *Erec* to *Iwein*. However, Hartmann never denies his book-learning, he only deploys it with increasing grace in his later works, and the habit of reading and interpreting texts, which he acquired in his schooling, continued to leave its mark on his poetic practice.[11]

The prologue to *Der arme Heinrich* also gives important information about Hartmann's understanding of his poetic task, especially when viewed together with the prologues to his other works. The *Klage* is introduced as an expression of the amorous pain of the young 'von Owe Hartman' (Kl 29). The prologue to Hartmann's *Erec* has not survived, so we do not know how the German author reacted to Chrétien's self-confident praise of his own 'mout bele conjointure' (EeE 14). The prologue to *Gregorius* presents the work as an act of penance by which the author seeks to atone for the worldliness of his earlier, youthful utterances (Gr 1–5, 35–42). In *Iwein*, Hartmann describes poetry as something to which he turns his hand when he has 'nothing better to do' (Iw 23f.: 'swenner sîne stunde / niht baz bewenden kunde'), adding that he has devoted himself to 'things people like to hear about' (Iw 26f.); beside this giving of pleasure, Hartmann also ascribes a moral function to his poetry in the prologue to *Iwein* by presenting Arthur as a model to be imitated in the pursuit of 'rehte güete' (Iw 1–20). In the prologue to *Der arme Heinrich*, Hartmann states that he has consulted various written sources to find material for his work (AH 6–11), and as regards the aim of his poetry he speaks of easing stressful times, promoting the glory of God and increasing his own favour amongst people (AH 10–15). The reward (AH 21: 'lôn') which Hartmann seeks for his work is of a spiritual kind, as he requests that anyone who hears

---

[7]   Schönbach, *Über Hartmann von Aue*, pp. 178–91.
[8]   See Salmon, *The Works of Hartmann von Aue*, pp. 120, 182f., 197f., 210f.; on rhetorical devices of Latin literature in Hartmann see also Fechter, *Lateinische Dichtkunst*, pp. 37–61.
[9]   See Mertens, ' "Factus est per clericum miles cythereus" ', pp. 2–5.
[10]   Salmon, *The Works of Hartmann von Aue*, p. 247.
[11]   On the impact of the commentary tradition of the schools on Hartmann's literary technique in *Iwein* see Hunt, '*Iwein* and *Yvain*', p. 163; W. Freytag, 'Topische Argumente', passim.

or reads the work may intercede with prayer on his, Hartmann's, behalf (AH 22–28). This request for intercession and the author's dual aim of pleasing God and his human audience both figure already in the epilogue to *Gregorius* in formulations very close to those of *Der arme Heinrich* (compare Gr 3989–99 and AH 18–25).

Nowhere in his prologues or elsewhere in his works does Hartmann refer to a commission by a patron or to any material reward for his efforts. The prologues show a strong sense of communication with an audience, the two religious works also explicitly seek God's favour, and thus Hartmann's poetry appears as a self-motivated activity, the function of which can range from giving pleasure to an audience to the imparting of moral truths and the processing of matters of spiritual importance within the poet. Of course Hartmann is drawing on rhetorical traditions in his prologues, and this warns against taking every utterance here as a statement of autobiographical truth.[12] But neither should we dismiss the prologues as empty convention unless there is positive evidence to undermine them. The tenor of the rest of Hartmann's works tends to support the prologues in presenting an image of Hartmann not as a 'professional' minstrel or cleric poet dependent upon his art for material reward, but as a culturally more complex figure who could exercise some choice in his literary activity, and for whom poetry had more than an element of self-expression and self-interpretation. Further, the keen sense of audience in Hartmann's works also indicates the importance of group values as well as the individual psyche, so that the self-presentation of the knightly author Hartmann also has a certain paradigmatic value as the self-interpretation of knighthood as a social category.

It has often been pointed out that the degree of book-learning to which Hartmann draws attention in *Der arme Heinrich* and in *Iwein* was rare in a knight at this time.[13] This is doubtless true, but as J.W. Thompson has shown, while the expansion of learning should not be exaggerated in the Hohenstaufen age, instruction in reading and in writing 'began to occupy the attention of laymen more and more' in Germany in this period.[14] R.W. Turner usefully distinguishes between three levels of literacy in the twelfth and thirteenth centuries: '(1) the professional men of letters; (2) the cultivated amateur; and (3) the pragmatic reader'.[15] He goes on to point to an increase of lay involvement in royal government

---

[12] The relation of rhetorical and personal authorial situation has been the subject of controversy especially with reference to the prologue to Hartmann's *Gregorius*: see Schwietering, *Demutsformel*, pp. 77–79; Brinkmann, 'Der Prolog', p. 20; Mertens, *Gregorius Eremita*, pp. 76–83; Haug, *Literaturtheorie*, pp. 132–34.
[13] Wapnewski, *Hartmann von Aue*, p. 12; Cormeau / Störmer, *Hartmann von Aue*, p. 36.
[14] Thompson, *Literacy*, p. 97.
[15] Turner, 'The *miles literatus*', p. 931.

in England after the mid-twelfth century, and claims that here 'most knights were at least pragmatic readers, functional literates in today's terms, capable of handling simple Latin as a tool in their many tasks of government'.[16] Evidence on this point is thinner and less well researched for Germany, but there is some indication that here lay literacy was at a lower level than that postulated by Turner for England.[17] Nevertheless, even though probably few German knights were even pragmatic readers, and fewer still *literati* of Hartmann's level, Hartmann's works do mark a trend towards increased lay literacy. The duality of clerical literacy and lay illiteracy was beginning to become eroded in the twelfth century, a period which is characterized by increasingly complex interactions between the worlds of clerical learning and lay nobility, with the Church seeking to influence lay life in the Christian reform movement, clerical authors producing poetic and historiographical works for secular patrons, and now with Hartmann, an author related to clerical learning by his education, and belonging to the lay aristocracy by his status as a knight, working at the interface of these two worlds and using the tools of clerical learning in the task of lay self-interpretation from a new perspective, but one which was of immense importance for the future – that of lay literacy.[18] Seen in this broad context, Hartmann's status as an educated, literate knight places him amongst a minority in his social class, but in the vanguard of a major development in European intellectual and literary history.

## Knighthood and moral insight

While the first occurrence of *ritter* in *Der arme Heinrich* indicates that the entire narrative is filtered through the mind of a literate knight, the two remaining occurrences of the word relate to the protagonist and flank the central theme of the work, Heinrich's conversion to 'eine niuwe güete' (AH 1240).

Heinrich is introduced as a lord of 'Ouwe' (AH 49) in Swabia (AH 31), who has all the qualities a *ritter* should have in his youth to win admiration (AH 34f.). The local reference suggests that the encomium of Heinrich, which prefaces the main action (AH 36–74), can be taken to express the social ideal of knighthood as it was actually perceived in

[16] Ibid., p. 931.
[17] See Bumke, *Höfische Kultur*, II, pp. 601–06.
[18] D.H. Green places Hartmann's works in a transitional mode linking oral and literate cultures by showing how Hartmann conceived of a possible dual reception of his work, by private reading and by public recital ('The Reception of Hartmann's Works', pp. 361–68); importantly, Green draws attention to the novelty of Hartmann, as a vernacular poet, reckoning with incipient lay literacy in his audience, which again suggests a watershed situation (ibid., p. 368).

Hartmann's own surroundings. The encomium begins with a statement of Heinrich's high birth and material wealth, the pairing of 'geburt' with 'rîcheit' and with 'guot' (AH 39, 45) echoing Gregorius's dream of becoming a knight if only he had 'geburt und daz guot' (Gr 1502). Then Heinrich's character is sketched by reference to qualities of a more personal, ethical and cultural nature (AH 50–74). Heinrich is free of falseness and boorishness (AH 51: 'dörperheit'), enjoys social prestige, is a 'flower of youth' and a 'mirror of worldly joy', he is loyal, a model of decorum, eager to protect those in need and his own family, generous, a fine singer of love-songs. In this presentation of the (in worldly, social terms) complete young lord, the term *ritter* has stretched far beyond its purely military sense to become a broad socio-cultural concept which embraces all the secular qualities associated with high birth in Hartmann's day. Knighthood has become a cultural model which could act as a rallying point for the various levels of the lay aristocracy.

In its listing of qualities that build up an exemplary model of chivalry, the encomium of Heinrich has a close affinity with Hartmann's orchestration of ethical and social qualities in the 'Joie de la curt' episode at the close of *Erec*, and it is a further mark of the importance of the court for the rise in prestige of knighthood that, just as Erec's supreme knightly deed restored joy to a court, so the only occurrence of the adjective *hövesch*, 'courtly', in the critical text of *Der arme Heinrich* is in Hartmann's praise of the young knightly lord Heinrich (AH 74: 'er was hövesch unde wîs'). However, there is a crucial difference between Erec's knighthood in the later part of Hartmann's first romance and that of the protagonist at the beginning of *Der arme Heinrich*, for whereas Hartmann departed from his source in order to add a religious dimension to Erec's chivalry,[19] he makes no reference to Heinrich's relation to God in his opening encomium, which remains pointedly within a purely worldly domain.[20] This deficit is elaborated and made good in the main body of the narrative. Heinrich is struck by leprosy, and having heard that he can only be healed by the heart's blood of a maiden, he withdraws from the aristocratic world in despair to live with the family of a tenant-farmer, whose daughter becomes attached to him and offers her life in sacrifice. At the last moment, Heinrich prevents the girl's death and accepts his leprosy as God's just punishment, whereupon God miraculously heals him. Finally the girl and Heinrich marry.

[19] See above, p. 132.
[20] In view of this contrast with *Erec* and the insistence with which Hartmann uses the terms 'werltlîch', 'werltvreude', 'werlt' (AH 57, 61, 73) in the opening encomium of Heinrich it is difficult to agree with Cormeau's implication that the narrator does not distance himself at all from the 'Leitbild' presented in this encomium (Cormeau / Störmer, *Hartmann von Aue*, pp. 150f.).

Such a summary of the external action does little justice to the
emotional and moral subtlety of the work, which emerges not least in
Hartmann's treatment of the shifts of attitude in Heinrich. When
Heinrich withdraws from aristocratic society he distributes his wealth to
needy folk and to the church (AH 251–56) – a gesture which shows
concern for the fate of his soul, but remains at a material level. Three
years later (a symbolic number) he shows a typically Hartmannesque
acceptance of responsibility and recognition of suffering as a punishment for moral failure when he describes his leprosy as a merited
affliction which he has earned by his earlier neglect of God (AH 383–
411). However, this theoretical insight is not yet backed up by action, for
Heinrich goes on to accept the girl's offer of self-sacrifice, thus slipping
back into a superstitious, magical, or medical rather than a moral or
religious interpretation of his affliction. The existential breakthrough
comes when Heinrich, seeing the girl bound and naked, and about to be
killed, suddenly grasps the moral reality of his situation and refuses to
allow her to die. Hartmann conveys this breakthrough in a powerful
imagery of moral insight with a gesture of seeing, as Heinrich looks at
the girl and at himself (AH 1234), and a radical inner change as
Heinrich's old self (AH 1239: 'sîn altez gemüete') gives way to a new
spirit (AH 1235: 'einen niuwen muot'; 1240: 'eine niuwe güete'). There
are clearly religious overtones in this imagery of conversion from old to
new.[21] This new moral insight is also developed in an inner monologue
which leads to Heinrich's crucial decision to accept God's will (AH
1241–56).

A process of insight and change in the protagonist, an 'Erkenntnis-
und Wandlungsprozeß des Helden' is common to all Hartmann's four
narratives.[22] The structuring of this process differs from work to work,
and its precise dynamic is the subject of critical controversy, especially
as to whether any gradual process of development should be postulated
as underlying the dramatic moments of insight and reorientation.[23] But
however we judge this controversy, these moments of insight are
important acts of interpretation on the part of the author and invitations
to reflection in the audience. Moreover, Heinrich's process is a purely
inward one, purely moral in quality, without the exercise of military
force which forms an objective correlative to moral action in Hartmann's

---

[21] See H. Freytag, 'Zu Hartmanns Konzeption des *Armen Heinrich'*, pp. 254f.
[22] Cormeau / Störmer, *Hartmann von Aue*, p. 158; this observation holds good for the
*Klage* too, in which the poet's *lîp* also undergoes a process of change and gains in moral
insight.
[23] See the discussion of this point in Buck, 'Heinrichs Metanoia'. Later scholars have
tended to share the scepticism shown by Buck towards the idea of a gradual development
in Hartmann's characters; for an extreme criticism of all developmental interpretations of
Hartmann's *Erec* and *Iwein* see Voß, *Artusepik*, passim.

Arthurian romances. Rather in *Der arme Heinrich* we see the knightly author Hartmann exploring an inner, moral world which had previously been the province of the Church.

In the hands of clerical authors the theme of conversion often led to the sinner's leaving the secular world, and indeed the manuscript B strand of the *Armer Heinrich* transmission alters Hartmann's ending in this direction by having Heinrich and the maiden not consummate the marriage but withdraw to a monastic life.[24] However, for all the religious thrust in *Der arme Heinrich*, it is important that in Hartmann's text Heinrich's reorientation leads to a return to the world of secular lordship and social ties, a renewal of wealth and social prestige, and to marriage. Heinrich also resumes his knightly identity when he treats the maiden's anger courteously, 'als ein vrumer ritter sol / dem schœner zühte niht gebrast' (AH 1340f.).[25] This return to the secular world and this evocation of knightly courtesy after Heinrich's *metanoia* suggest that the theme of moral reorientation in *Der arme Heinrich* does not involve a total rejection of the cultural model of chivalry which was elaborated in the opening encomium of Heinrich, but rather its purification and completion, or underpinning, by the addition of the religious dimension of humility, self-knowledge and attention to God.

The process of underpinning can be observed specifically in Hartmann's treatment of *êre* in *Der arme Heinrich*. The honour and praise which Heinrich enjoys at the beginning of the work (AH 35, 46, 55, 57, 69, 73) proves to be transient because it is not grounded in the service of God. Heinrich himself recognizes that he was a worldly fool to believe that he could enjoy honour and wealth without God (AH 399: 'âne got'). Later he shows his new spiritual integrity by setting considerations of social reputation aside when he accepts the possibility of shame and mockery (AH 1351: 'laster unde spot') rather than see the maiden die.[26] Then, when he finally achieves greater wealth and prestige than ever before, the narrator emphasizes that he humbly attributes this to God, and consequently his honour is now on a firm and lasting footing (AH 1430–36). Heinrich's attitude here corrects his earlier, morally incomplete concept of honour and echoes the attitude of Erec who, in an independent addition of Hartmann's at the end of his first romance, is careful not to act like a fool and attribute his honour solely to his own worth, but rather thanks God for his success, which, as in Heinrich's

---

[24] Text of the B addition in the editions of *Der arme Heinrich* by Haupt, p. 62; and Gierach, p. 82.

[25] The B manuscript tradition has *hvbsch* instead of *vrum* as the adjective qualifying *ritter* in line 1340 – another sign of the increasingly close association of knighthood and courtliness.

[26] On *êre* and *spot* in *Der arme Heinrich* see the comments in Buck, 'Heinrichs Metanoia', pp. 392–94.

case, ensures that his honour will stand the test of time (Er 10085-106; compare AH 1430-36).

It is a basic pattern in Hartmann's works that the pursuit of secular prestige, of all that is conveyed in the concept of *êre*, which was a central value of contemporary aristocratic society, is neither unreservedly advocated nor unreservedly condemned, rather it is affirmed, but only in so far as it is compatible with a larger ethical or religious framework. Put in broader terms, in *Der arme Heinrich*, as in *Gregorius* and in *Erec*, a religious dimension relativizes but does not reject outright the values of secular, knightly culture. On this crucial point the difference between the various genres of Hartmann's poetry is a matter of degree rather than an absolute one, and the reader detects an authorial voice that runs through the various genres to give Hartmann's works a certain coherence – though not uniformity – of attitude as an *œuvre*.

## Aristocracy and peasantry

The main piece of information which Hartmann provides about Heinrich's social status is that his birth is 'unwandelbære / und wol den fürsten gelîch' (AH 42f.). The 'wol' here is open to the different interpretations that Heinrich's lineage is 'the equal of', or less specifically 'comparable to' that of princes – an ambiguity which has led scholars to place Heinrich at various levels of the *Heerschildordnung* which defined the feudal hierarchy in Hartmann's day.[27] It may be that Hartmann was being deliberately imprecise here, and that it was sufficient for his purpose that Heinrich should be seen to be at least of free noble stock. The maiden by contrast is the daughter of a free peasant (AH 269: 'ein vrîer bûman'), and her marriage to a free noble raises the question of the relation of peasantry and aristocracy with a directness which is hardly paralleled in the literature of the period.

As we have seen, the second half of the twelfth century was a period of increasingly pronounced social differentiation in Germany. This was a time when the peasantry and the knighthood were acquiring sharper class contours in contra-distinction to each other, with even the lesser *milites* acquiring increasingly aristocratic connotations and the *rustici* suffering greater social limitations.[28] A literary consequence of this class distinctiveness was that the thirteenth century saw a marked growth of satire and criticism in the treatment of the peasantry, directed in Neidhart's songs, and in the *Helmbrecht* of Wernher der Gartenaere, against the figure of the upstart young peasant who apes knightly and

[27] Various views on this point in Henne, *Herrschaftsstruktur*, pp. 232-34.
[28] See above, pp. 55-61, 63-69.

courtly ways, and in *Seifried Helbling* against the peasant family which finds a way into the lesser aristocracy by marriage.[29] This strand of criticism reflects the social reality of some social mobility at the juncture of peasantry and knighthood as, despite legislative attempts to keep the two classes distinct, families at the upper level of the peasantry tried to establish positions in the lesser aristocracy, whilst some knightly families facing economic difficulties failed to keep up with the rising cost of the noble lifestyle and slipped down into the peasantry.[30] A historically interesting grey area thus existed in the relations between peasantry and aristocracy, in which there was some mingling of the classes, producing such transitional figures as the 'half-knights' scorned at the end of the thirteenth century by the schoolmaster and moralist Hugo von Trimberg as being 'neither peasant nor knight' (*Der Renner* 1467: 'halpritter'; 1064: 'weder gebûre noch ritter'). This grey area was a focus for tension and for a socially motivated negative view of the peasantry among knightly families who feared an erosion of their privileges.

It would, however, be quite misleading to take the note of social tension and the derogatory literary portrayal of the upstart peasant as a complete and reliable picture of the actual relations between aristocracy and peasantry in Germany in the central Middle Ages. For one thing the negative strand in the literary treatment of the *rustici* was also motivated by internal literary factors, which sets limits on its value as evidence for the historical reality of social relations.[31] Further, the Christian view that physical labour had a place in the divine plan provided a metaphysical basis for a more respectful view of the peasantry. More pragmatically the secular aristocracy were a landowning as well as a military class, and this dimension of landowning involved much practical contact of nobles with the *rustici*, especially with the upper level of peasants: those who exercised delegated managerial functions over labourers, or who themselves held farms in rent from a lord. Such higher and wealthier *rustici* at times appear as *meier* in vernacular sources. In historical reality precisely these *meier* had the best chances of rising into the lesser aristocracy, though such ascent was probably more controversial after the legislation of the late twelfth century which sought to exclude sons of *rustici* from knighthood.[32]

---

[29] On the theme of the upstart peasant in thirteenth-century German literature see Schindele, '*Helmbrecht*', especially pp. 163–68, 175–79; Liebertz-Grün, *Das andere Mittelalter*, pp. 31ff.

[30] On this social mobility in the thirteenth century see Feldbauer, *Herren und Ritter*, p. 59; Dopsch, 'Probleme ständischer Wandlung', pp. 235, 243, 249; Rösener, 'Bauer und Ritter', pp. 686–90; W.H. Jackson, 'Zum Verhältnis von *ritter* und *kneht*', pp. 28–35.

[31] Liebertz-Grün, *Das andere Mittelalter*, p. 32.

[32] Schulze, 'Meier', cols 439f.

It is this relation of higher peasant, or tenant farmer, *meier* (AH 295, 354, 876, 1396, 1437) to noble lord, and the rise of the farmer's daughter by marriage to a free noble that forms the social class framework of *Der arme Heinrich*. In this work Hartmann devotes more space to the non-aristocratic world than any other narrative poet of the period, and he presents an unusually sympathetic view of peasant figures and of their relation to the aristocratic world. The opening encomium of Heinrich contains a linguistic reflex of prejudice against the peasantry when Heinrich is described as being free of all 'dörperheit' (AH 51). But this term is not exploited in the work to show a problematical relationship between aristocracy and peasantry and to express disdain of the latter, as it will be some years later in Neidhart's songs.[33] Rather Hartmann presents the farmer in a positive light, taking up the Christian view of the dignity of labour when he describes the farmer's life as a gift from God (AH 295f.). Heinrich himself is a kind lord who, unlike other, harsher masters, has not overburdened the *meier* with exactions (AH 267–82). Here Hartmann sketches an ideal of generous lordship which involves not only the knightly world but also the relation of aristocracy to peasantry, a relation which must have assumed a greater importance in the actual life of aristocratic families, perhaps especially lesser knightly families, than the selective social projections of courtly literature suggest. Hartmann also endows the peasant sphere with moral value, for the farmer's treatment of Heinrich is seen as a mark of his *triuwe* (AH 290), so that the reciprocal pattern of loyalty, service and reward (AH 285–89) applies to the relation of aristocracy and peasantry as well as within the knightly world; and the maiden's self-sacrificing *güete* (AH 522) and *triuwe* (AH 1001) also show that Hartmann's highest moral values are not restricted to the aristocratic world.

Heinrich's marriage to the maiden forms a morally satisfying conclusion to the narrative, but it is highly problematical in terms of the social hierarchy of Hartmann's own day, for there is no instance of such a marriage between a free noble and a daughter of a free peasant family in the German historical record throughout the twelfth and thirteenth centuries.[34] The main interpretative crux lies in Heinrich's invoking not only a moral ground for the marriage (that he owes his health to the maiden, AH 1493–96), but also some justification in terms of social status with his claim that the girl is 'as free as I am' (AH 1497: 'nû ist si vrî als ich dâ bin'). In an important study which appeared almost a century ago Aloys Schulte claimed that Hartmann's *Armer Heinrich* is based on an acute observation of social gradations, and that, although the marriage

---

33   On Neidhart's usage see Beyschlag, *Die Lieder Neidharts*, pp. 681f. s.v. *dörpel, dörper*.
34   Beyerle, 'Der *Arme Heinrich*', pp. 33f. On the substantial number of free peasants in twelfth-century Germany see Arnold, *Princes and Territories*, p. 155.

was against the custom of Hartmann's day, it did not directly offend against the laws governing social status, but was rather a 'quasi-mésalliance'.[35] Schulte's case rests on the premise that, although the girl is of peasant stock, the fact that she is of a 'free' peasant family would have sufficed to ensure that Heinrich's noble line was not damaged by the marriage. However, it is difficult to reconcile Schulte's view of a theoretically possible parity of peasant freedom and noble freedom with the increasingly sharp legal distinction that was being made between peasant and knight in Barbarossa's reign. Franz Beyerle took up this point to argue that the equation of noble freedom and peasant freedom which Heinrich makes in line 1497 ran directly against the legal mentality of the German nobility around 1200, according to which the marriage of a free noble and a free peasant could only have been seen as a *mésalliance* that would have resulted in any offspring not being able to sustain the father's free noble status.[36] Beyerle interprets the marriage as an expression of the religious ideas of the poem, he sees in Heinrich's claim to an equality of freedom beween the maiden and himself a criticism of the contemporary German nobility's exclusive, hereditary class consciousness, and he sees Hartmann here drawing on a Christian concept of spiritual humility rather than on contemporary social reality.[37] Recent critics have further developed the religious aspects of Beyerle's reading, which is now the dominant line of interpretation in work on *Der arme Heinrich*.[38]

However, Beyerle's view that Hartmann by-passes social reality when he has Heinrich place himself and the maiden in the same category of freedom calls for further comment. It is striking with just what an air of realism Hartmann develops the action of *Der arme Heinrich*, how close he seeks to bring it to a contemporary audience. Author and protagonist are associated with each other, both linked to 'Ouwe', Hartmann as 'dienstman' (AH 5), Heinrich as 'herre'(AH 48), and both are brought close to the audience because of the local setting of the action in Swabia (AH 31), which contrasts with the remoter settings of Aquitaine in *Gregorius* and Britain in the Arthurian romances. The association of author and protagonist has led to hypotheses that the story was based on the family history of Hartmann's feudal lord,[39] or of Hartmann himself.[40] Each of these lines of interpretation on *Der arme Heinrich* has

---

35  Schulte, 'Eine neue Hypothese', p. 268: 'eine halbe Mißheirat'.
36  Beyerle, 'Der Arme Heinrich', esp. p. 33.
37  Ibid., pp. 42–45.
38  See Borck, ' "Nû ist si vrî" '; H. Freytag, 'Zu Hartmanns Konzeption des Armen Heinrich'.
39  This view was widely held in earlier scholarship, e.g. by Schulte, 'Eine neue Hypothese', pp. 262f.
40  See Beyerle, 'Der Arme Heinrich', p. 42 for the view that, in portraying a *mésalliance* that sprang from the highest moral causes, Hartmann may have been trying to give a poetic

recently been invoked to lend support to the view of a Zähringen or a Welf connection in Hartmann's work.[41] In the absence of further evidence such hypotheses remain tantalizingly speculative. But the internal evidence of Hartmann's works in general shows a recurrent tendency for Hartmann to relate his literary material to the world around him, and this tendency produces a particularly strong sense of authenticity in *Der arme Heinrich*. This is a work of great spiritual and emotional subtlety, which yet gives the impression of being grounded in a socially real world. Even the marriage is socially as well as spiritually motivated. Suggestively, the maiden's father is described from the moment of his introduction as a 'free' peasant (AH 269) and as the best endowed of his station in the land (AH 281f.). From the outset a contemporary audience would thus recognize the maiden's family as being at the top of the peasant class in terms of personal freedom and wealth. Heinrich improves their prestige and wealth (AH 1439: 'êre unde guot') even further after his healing by giving them in freehold (AH 1442: 'zeigen') the substantial farm (AH 1443: 'daz breite geriute') which they had held as tenants, and its complement of workers (AH 1444: 'die liute'), so that by the time Heinrich raises the question of marriage the maiden's father is an independent landowner.[42] Also Heinrich requests and obtains the approval of his *familia* (AH 1464: 'mâge unde man') for the marriage, which corresponds to contemporary practice and again adds to a sense of social as well spiritual propriety in the presentation of the marriage.

It should be emphasized that there is an explicit social gap between Heinrich and the maiden in the text, for he is at least of free noble status whilst she describes herself as being 'of low estate' (AH 1170: 'lîhtes künnes'). Nevertheless, the account of the marriage is so bedded into a sense of local history and so carefully motivated socially within the text that one wonders whether Hartmann wished to give the impression that, whilst such a marriage may have been a *mésalliance* with harmful

idealization of a postulated decline of his own ancestors from the free nobility to ministerial status.

[41] Mertens ('Das literarische Mäzenatentum der Zähringer', pp. 123f.) connects the story with a Zähringen *ministerialis* 'Henricus de Owen'; Bayer (*Hartmann von Aue*, pp. 95–99) maintains that Hartmann used the *Historia Welforum* in *Der arme Heinrich*, and he links Hartmann to Duke Welf VI, and the monastery of Weißenau. Neither argument amounts to proof; particularly the 'parallels' which Bayer adduces between *Der arme Heinrich* and the *Historia Welforum* are too unspecific to prove Hartmann's knowledge of the chronicle.

[42] Henne (*Herrschaftsstruktur*, pp. 238–41) takes this new material status of the maiden's family as sufficient, together with their personal freedom, to legitimize the marriage socially; Boon, 'Die Ehe', also argues that such a marriage may have been 'durchaus möglich' in Hartmann's day (p. 99). Neither of these scholars brings the specific evidence that would be needed to justify their harmonizing interpretations against Beyerle as regards the socio-legal thinking of the period around 1200, but in turn their readings are attentive to a note of realism in the text that Beyerle's interpretation does not fully account for.

consequences for the free noble's lineage in his, Hartmann's own day, it could have been more acceptable some generations earlier, before the legal hardening of class boundaries between peasantry and aristocracy, which is documented in the German peace laws of the second half of the twelfth century. Seen in this light, Hartmann's provocative equation of peasant freedom and noble freedom (placed in the voice of a lord of Ouwe whom Hartmann's contemporary audience must have taken as having lived some way back in the past) would appear to Hartmann's audience as both a moral challenge and the evocation of an archaic social mentality, according to which the crucial division of society was still that between free and unfree (*liber* and *servus*), not yet that between knight and peasant (*miles* and *rusticus*).[43] To gain a historical grounding for such a mentality one need go no further back than about three generations from the time of Hartmann's writing, and it may be that the story of Heinrich, which existed in some written form before Hartmann's version (Hartmann speaks of 'ein rede die er geschriben vant', AH 17), was originally a product of this earlier state of German society.[44]

Viewed in the context of Hartmann's other works, *Der arme Heinrich* is the culmination of that strand in Hartmann which ranks achievement and moral excellence above the privileges of birth and inheritance.[45] Indeed *Der arme Heinrich* is the only one of Hartmann's works to bring this ideal to the forefront in the narrative action, as the mutual, self-sacrificing *triuwe* of the maiden and Heinrich overcomes what was in Hartmann's day the social barrier separating aristocracy and peasantry. Hartmann's *œuvre* as a whole expresses a class-conscious aristocratic world in which status of birth is of leading importance. However, there is less aristocratic disdain of the lower orders of society in Hartmann's works than is often the case in the literature of this period. Georges Zink has pointed out that Chrétien de Troyes maintains a more consistently aristocratic standpoint in his works than Hartmann does.[46] There is little direct evidence of attitudes towards non-aristocratic areas of society in Hartmann's *Erec*, since the work focuses so narrowly on the knightly and courtly world; but nowhere in this or any other work of Hartmann's

---

43   On the gradual replacement of the older pairing *liber* / *servus* by the new pairing *miles* / *rusticus* from the eleventh century on see above, p. 59; Rösener, 'Bauer und Ritter', p. 667.

44   Karl Bertau may well be on the right track when he mentions *Der arme Heinrich* in connection with the rise of families from obscure and modest conditions under Emperor Henry IV in the late eleventh century: 'Andere stiegen aus völliger Anonymität, ja Unfreiheit auf, "servientes" und "clientes", die der Freilassung bedurften, Leute von der Art des Meiers im "Armen Heinrich", dessen wohl jetzt aktuelle Geschichte Hartmann von Aue 100 Jahre später erzählen wird' (*Deutsche Literatur*, I, p. 159); see also Mertens, *Gregorius Eremita*, p. 162.

45   On the 'nobility of virtue' in Hartmann see above pp. 79–81; Zink, '*Geburt*', pp. 29–31; Borck, ' "Nû ist si vrî" ', pp. 47–49.

46   Zink, '*Geburt*', p. 29.

is there a gesture of such lordly disdain towards commoners as when, in Chrétien's version, the count, Enide's uncle, menacingly wields a baton to force back the press of 'vilains' (EeE 801–04).[47] In *Gregorius* the monks' mockery of the humble fisherman's speech (Gr 1123–26) conveys Hartmann's criticism of the monks' lack of humility, not his authorial identification with their disdain. The praise of lesser women against the haughtiness of aristocratic ladies in Hartmann's song points in a similar direction.[48] In view of these hints, the portrayal of a non-aristocratic family in positive moral terms in *Der arme Heinrich* is less surprising than it might at first appear.

Hartmann, it should be stressed, is not, even in *Der arme Heinrich*, advocating a social programme of dismantling class barriers, or pleading for the rise of the peasantry. Rather, as a knightly poet he himself remains on the aristocratic side of the boundary. He is concerned primarily with ethical and social behaviour within the aristocracy, and his location of moral excellence in a peasant family aims at making a moral point to his aristocratic audience. Nevertheless, Hartmann's works suggest some limitation in the stereotype view that the knighthood was characterized by a contempt for the non-aristocratic classes which hampered its own faculty of self-criticism.[49] Rather it is precisely the knightly author Hartmann who shows in *Der arme Heinrich* respect for the *rustici* and considerable aristocratic self-criticism.

*Der arme Heinrich* thus emerges as a revealing work for the state of lay, aristocratic society and culture in south-west Germany around 1200. The claim of propriety for a marriage linking a free peasant woman to a free noble lord harks back to a time before the sharpening of class distinction between knighthood and peasantry in the twelfth century. Socially, the application of the term *ritter* to the *dienstman* Hartmann and to the young lord Heinrich shows the concept of knighthood at the end of the twelfth century stretching across the aristocratic hierarchy; and the opening encomium of Heinrich presents chivalry as a bundle of secular values which drew the various levels of this hierarchy together in a common ideology. Culturally, the filtering of a narrative of such literacy and such

---

[47] The terms *vilain* and *vilenie* (examples from EeE: *vilain* 1, 198, 241, 475, 798, 802, 804, 6912; *vilenie* 572, 998, 1794, 1838, 2422) are favourite contrasts to *cortois* and *corteisie* in Chrétien. Because of their social as well as ethical, aesthetic or emotional connotations they give the aristocratic prejudice against commoners a firm place in Chrétien's language, which on this point surely reflects a strand of mentality in the great courts of northern France. In German the terms *dörperlich* and *dörperheit* were coined on the model of French *vilain* and *vilenie* (see Bumke, *Höfische Kultur*, I, p. 79), but Hartmann never uses *dörperlich*, and he uses *dörperheit* only twice (AH 51, Iw 7121), so that on this point his language seems less conditioned by aristocratic prejudice than Chrétien's.

[48] See above, pp. 181f.

[49] See e.g. Gernhuber, *Landfriedensbewegung*, p. 147, n. 27: 'Die Verachtung, die der Ritter den bäuerlichen und bürgerlichen Kreisen entgegenbrachte, war sicherlich kein geeignetes Fundament kritischer Selbstbetrachtung'.

emotional and moral subtlety through the medium of a knightly author shows the high achievement that the lay aristocracy was now capable of at the interface with clerical learning.

Finally, *Der arme Heinrich* is revealing for the spiritual energies that inform Hartmann's works. Hartmann's *œuvre* is a complex self-interpretation of secular, aristocratic culture at a crucial stage in its development. In this self-interpretation public esteem, focused mainly on the court as the chief source of secular prestige, plays an important and at times problematical role. But a certain turning away from the court is also important in this process, a readiness at times to place other values above the claims of immediate prestige, a degree of turning inward which is connected with the experience of personal suffering and the awareness of suffering in others, and which leads to reflection, inner reorientation and greater self-knowledge.[50] This emotional and moral realm of personal, almost private experience, figures in Erec's journey of knightly rehabilitation, in Gregorius's solitary penance, and, perhaps most intimately, in the account of Heinrich's withdrawal from the court and aristocratic society. In *Iwein* the court will again assume a more important role, but beside the public voice of the court, some of the inwardness and reflectiveness of *Der arme Heinrich* will also be preserved as a major feature of Hartmann's portrayal of knighthood in his last Arthurian romance.

[50] On this 'readiness to turn away from the court' and this adumbration of an 'image of the individual as a private figure' in Hartmann's works see also Seiffert, 'Hartmann and Walther', pp. 100f.

# 7

# Knighthood in *Iwein*:
# Voices of the Characters

## Introduction: knighthood and narrative voice

The new mode of courtly narrative literature arose first in twelfth-century French and Anglo-Norman or Plantagenet courts, as a product of clerical authors. It was also clerics who made the earliest adaptations of French *romans* into German.[1] Hartmann von Aue's immediate predecessor or older contemporary, Heinrich von Veldeke, composed secular love lyrics, a saint's life and an adaptation of the French treatment of Virgil's *Aeneid*. Veldeke's works thus foreshadow the thematic range (without matching the authorial vigour and consistency of personal voice) of Hartmann's *œuvre* and suggest, in a way that points to the future, a poet who draws on the resources of clerical and lay worlds. However, whilst Veldeke's exact social status remains uncertain,[2] Hartmann, in the prologue to his *Iwein*, not only names himself (Iw 28: 'er was genant Hartmann / und was ein Ouwære') as the author, or adaptor of the story (Iw 30: 'der tihte diz mære'), but also describes himself as an educated knight (Iw 21: 'Ein rîter, der gelêret was') who spends his leisure hours in writing poetry. Together with Hartmann's self-introduction as a *ritter* in *Der arme Heinrich* (AH 1 ff.), this utterance marks an important development in the history of medieval German literature, for we have here the earliest recorded instance of a narrative poet who presents himself explicitly as a knight.

In terms of the sociology of production Hartmann's works thus mark a point where the courtly romance makes a transition of class from clerical

---

[1] Bumke, *Mäzene*, p. 71.
[2] Where earlier scholars often saw Veldeke as a knight, recent research tends more to see him as a 'courtier cleric' or a 'clerically trained courtier' (Bumke, *Mäzene*, p. 116).

to knightly authorship.[3] It should be remembered that the earlier works of the formative period of courtly literature, whilst clerical in authorship, yet responded to the needs of secular patrons and audiences, so that the continuing conditions of literary reception modify the sharpness of a shift of authorial category. Nevertheless the emergence of the poet/ narrator as an explicitly knightly figure brings about a new play of forces within the text, as the mediating voice now shares more features of self-understanding with his secular, knightly characters than is the case with a clerical narrator, and thus this development has a bearing on the internal narrative dynamics as well as the external sociology of courtly romance.

Neither Hartmann's statement of his narrative intentions in the prologue to *Iwein* nor Gottfried von Straßburg's praise of the clarity and purity of Hartmann's style (*Tristan* 4628-30: 'wie lûter und wie reine / sîniu cristallînen wortelîn / beidiu sint und iemer müezen sîn') have prevented precisely *Iwein*, which is, together with *Der arme Heinrich*, the most mature, supple and controlled of Hartmann's narrative poems, from becoming over the past thirty years subject to more critical contention than almost any other work of medieval German literature, with controversy ranging from the surface meaning of key textual detail through debates on continuity or discontinuity of characterization, on change or stasis in the ethical value system of the work, on the interplay of religious and secular elements, and on the social motivation of the work, up to a fundamental questioning of its inner coherence.[4] Indeed the particular phenomenon of a seeming transparency of narration yet filtered through two very different, but highly literate and reflective minds (Chrétien's and Hartmann's), which is characteristic of *Iwein*, gives purchase to readings in terms of both exemplary or classical simplicity and ironic complexity.

Two contentious strands call for particular mention at this point. First, an increased concern with narratology has led, in the case of Hartmann's *Iwein*, to widely diverging assessments of the author's voice, especially in the making or suggesting of ethical value judgements, with some scholars arguing for a note of sustained, albeit indirect, ironic criticism in the author's voice with regard to important aspects of knighthood, whilst others prefer a more affirmative reading. Second, scholars have shown, with various degrees of reflection, basic disagreement about what constituted acceptable conduct in a knight according to the ethical and/or legal horizon of Hartmann's contempor-

---

[3] See also Jaeger, *The Origins of Courtliness*, p. 243.
[4] Even the view that Iwein undergoes some kind of moral progress, which appeared as a near consensus view in a useful survey of *Iwein* research in 1982 (Wells, 'The Medieval Nebuchadnezzar', pp. 381-88), has been challenged, and the consensus broken, by the studies of Voß and Fischer.

ary audience, and this unsureness about what could be relied on as an instinctive audience reaction has contributed to the interpretative aporia in work on the author's voice in *Iwein*. Each of these two strands of controversy has a direct bearing on the topic of knighthood. This chapter and the next, while continuing a pluralist approach, will pay particular attention to the related questions of the horizon of expectation that can plausibly be postulated for Hartmann's audience with regard to the evaluation of knightly conduct, and the poet's sympathies on this issue, always bearing in mind that the poet's voice in *Iwein* is explicitly that of a knight, and that consequently a literary analysis of this voice yields historical insight into the mental world of German knighthood at an important stage in its development.

An enquiry into the voice and sympathies of the poet and *ritter* Hartmann cannot properly be limited to the utterances made in the narrator's commentary, to the exclusion of the speech and thought of the fictive characters. That the narrator's commentary does not always convey the whole truth of the poet's views, and that even in medieval literature some degree of discrepancy exists between poet and narrator is now widely recognized, especially for the genre of romance.[5] This does not, of course, mean that the narrator's commentary is necessarily and inherently unreliable, rather it may simply be narrower than the poet's whole truth, which is conveyed in the speech of characters as well as in the narrator's voice. Indeed authors often place their most important truths in the mouths of their fictive characters rather than in narrative commentary.[6] Direct speech and directly recorded inner monologues of the characters are a particularly important feature of Hartmann's *Iwein*, both in comparison with his own *Erec* and in his adaptation of Chrétien's *Yvain*, and this stylistic feature has a bearing on our topic of knighthood. Direct speech takes up a far higher proportion of Hartmann's *Iwein* than it does of his *Erec*.[7] Further, whereas Hartmann reduces the proportion of direct speech in adapting Chrétien's *Erec*, he increases it and consequently reduces the proportion of narratorial telling and commentary in adapting *Yvain*.[8] This increase in the incidence of direct speech gives Hartmann's *Iwein* a certain dramatic and scenic quality which accounts to some extent for the critical controversies about the author's voice. Moreover this stylistic shift is accompanied by an increase in complexity and a broadening of range in Hartmann's handling of the theme in comparison with his *Erec*.[9]

5  See Green, *Irony*, esp. pp. 218ff.
6  Friedemann, *Die Rolle des Erzählers*, p. 165; Wiehl, *Redeszene*, p. 22.
7  Wiehl, *Redeszene*, p. 11.
8  Ibid. p. 70.
9  See also Zutt, *König Artus*, p. 72.

This stylistic and thematic tendency can be observed specifically in Hartmann's treatment of knighthood. In *Erec*, Hartmann as author and narrator has a high degree of identification with the knightly hero, presenting the world largely in a narrow, knightly perspective, whilst his later works show some widening of the angle of vision and view knighthood in relation to other values and other areas of life to a greater extent than is the case in *Erec*. Some widening of social perspective, accompanied by a relativizing reflection on knighthood, figures already in *Gregorius*, especially in the debate between Gregorius and the abbot. In *Der arme Heinrich*, although the hero remains in the secular world to the end, specifically knightly concerns are treated only in relation to matters of more general, especially moral relevance. With *Iwein* Hartmann returns to Arthurian romance, the genre *par excellence* for the literary demonstration of chivalric values. However, whilst knighthood is again more consistently at the centre of the stage than it was in Hartmann's two religious narratives, Hartmann's tendency to place knighthood in relation to other, broader spheres and values is now, in *Iwein*, developed within the genre of Arthurian romance – not least in scenes of direct speech.

The close relation of knightly concerns and the use of direct speech is evident in Hartmann's treatment of Chrétien's *Yvain*. It has long been recognized that Hartmann remains closer to the French text in adapting Chrétien's *Yvain* than was his practice with *Erec*.[10] This does not, however, imply a generally reduced independence and thoughtfulness on Hartmann's part, for he makes many shifts of detail and emphasis, and some substantial changes in the way narrator and characters view the action, and this is nowhere more evident than in the two poets' treatments of chivalry. Hartmann shows a particularly marked independence of Chrétien in his account of Iwein's peripeteia, that is to say in the phase of narrative beginning with Gawein's advice and ending with Iwein's awakening from his madness (Iw 2770–3596, Yv 2484–3035). Iwein, having won a wife and lands by defeating and killing Askalon, here follows Gawein's advice to take a year's leave from his wife in pursuit of tournaments; he overstays his allotted leave, as a result of which he is condemned before Arthur's court as a traitor who has forfeited his honour and his rights of marriage, lordship and knighthood; this devastating blow causes Iwein to lose his reason and regress to an animal state of living in the wild, from which he is restored to health by the lavish application of a healing salve by a lady. This is the central crisis in the work, the collapse of Iwein's identity and social relations, after which he will painfully restore himself in the rest of the work.

---

[10] Useful discussion of Hartmann's treatment of Chrétien's texts in Cormeau / Störmer, *Hartmann von Aue*, pp. 169–74, 198–200.

In connection with this crisis Hartmann brings three of his longest and weightiest additions to Chrétien's *Yvain*, considerably lengthening and altering the substance of Gauvain's advice to Yvain (Yv 2484–538, Iw 2770–912) and the public denunciation of Yvain (Yv 2722–73, Iw 3111–96), and adding the new matter of the hero's monologue on his awakening from madness (Iw 3508–83). These passages are three of the most impressive instances of direct speech, or the direct recording of inner thought, in *Iwein*, and in each of these passages Hartmann dwells in a quite independent way on key issues of knighthood. The hero's crisis thus prompts the German, knightly poet to reflect, through the words or thoughts of the three most articulate characters in the romance, on knighthood independently of Chrétien's work, so that these passages, together with the conversation between the abbot and his pupil in Hartmann's *Gregorius*, form an eloquent document of a German knightly consciousness at the close of the twelfth century. These three passages will be considered in this chapter as expressions of the personal, social and ethico-legal structure of knighthood in Hartmann's world. The next chapter will then treat the ethics of combat situations and the role of chivalric values in the broader context of the work as a whole.

*Iwein's awakening: the basis of a chivalric identity*

The account of Iwein's flight into the forest, his madness and recovery, forms a crucial turning point in the romance and, with its archetypal pattern of collapse and restoration of personality, invites interpretation at a variety of levels, from psychoanalytical models of regression and individuation to specifically Christian or more broadly mythical patterns of death and rebirth or descent to the underworld.[11] For our purposes it is essential to note that Hartmann presents this archetypal experience of loss and renewal of identity in specifically knightly terms.

Iwein's alienation from self and society is indicated by the loss of his knightly qualities (Iw 3257: 'der ie ein rehter adamas / rîterlîcher tugende was, / der lief nû harte balde / ein tôre in dem walde') and by his becoming, like the wild herdsman earlier, 'gelîch einem môre' (Iw 3348; compare Iw 427), the very opposite in appearance and activities of a courtly knight (Iw 3350–57). Iwein's awakening (Iw 3505ff.) has been interpreted in broad cultural terms as expressing the awakening to self-awareness of a new human world in the twelfth century.[12] However it is also a specifically knightly model of identity that informs Iwein's self-

11    See Wells, 'The Medieval Nebuchadnezzar', pp. 392–97.
12    Wehrli, 'Iweins Erwachen', p. 185.

awareness on his awakening. There are close verbal parallels between Iwein's dream monologue and Gregorius's outpouring of his dreams of knighthood. Indeed it is a basically similar conception of chivalry that underlies both passages,[13] as the monastic pupil Gregorius and the *gebûre*, the 'peasant' Iwein each thinks that, given access to chivalric equipment, he could vie with the most experienced knights (Gr 1575–78, Iw 3556–62), each imagines himself tourneying (Gr 1584: 'so turnierte mîn gedanc'; Iw 3574: 'ez turnierte al mîn sin'), and each thinks of military chivalry in dynamic, thrusting terms as a means of hunting out honour and fortune (Gr 1701: 'erjagen', 1704: 'jagete', 1705: 'erloufen'; Iw 3523: 'bejaget', 3525: 'bejagete'). A self-assertive ideology of chivalry is expressed here which draws on the mentality particularly of those knights of twelfth-century reality described by Georges Duby as *iuvenes*, that is to say primarily young knights who were not yet established with landed responsibilities and who formed a particularly aggressive element in feudal society.[14]

*Iuvenes* (or *iuveneles*, *iuniores*) appear frequently as aggressive and ambitious military figures in German historical sources from the late eleventh century through to Hartmann's day.[15] We can therefore be sure that the figure of the self-assertive young knight seeking exercise of arms, prestige and often material gain in military undertakings was a familiar one to Hartmann and his German audience. The persistence of Hartmann's literary processing and stylization of this figure becomes all the more evident if, in addition to the links we have just noted between *Gregorius* and *Iwein* on this point, we remember those that connect *Gregorius* and *Erec* in the knight's pursuit of honour,[16] and Hartmann's massive expansion in *Erec* of the tournament episode – the military activity *par excellence* of the young knight and an institution which provides some of the closest connections between literature and life in the history of chivalry. Moreover, in terms of the internal dynamics of *Iwein*, the identity-model of chivalry that emerges in Iwein's dream monologue on his awakening is still that which guided his actions in the earlier stages of the work,[17] so that in discussing this model we are in a twofold sense looking at the foundation of his chivalric identity.

Iwein's monologue shares further ground with the debate between Gregorius and the abbot in that both reflect developments in twelfth-

---

13 See McFarland, 'Narrative Structure', pp. 138–42.
14 Duby, 'Les "jeunes" ', passim.
15 Lampert of Hersfeld, *Annales*, p. 228, 16–26; p. 356, 12–16; Otto of Freising and Rahewin, *Gesta Frederici*, II, 23, p. 322, 23ff.; Berthold of Zwiefalten, *Chronik*, pp. 240, 253; Helmold of Bosau, *Chronica Slavorum*, p. 324, 16–18; for young bloods of the type described by Duby in Cologne in the late twelfth century see Zotz, 'Städtisches Rittertum', p. 614.
16 See above, pp. 157f.
17 See McFarland, 'Narrative Structure', p. 142; on Iwein's actions as knight in the opening cycle see below, pp. 237–45.

century Germany in the social groupings of peasant/*rusticus* and knight/ *miles*. As long as the young Gregorius believed himself to be the son of fisherfolk he could legitimately hope for a monastic career, for the church provided some way forward for lowborn talent, but knighthood remained a fantasy for which he believed he lacked the prerequisites of birth and wealth (Gr 1494–503). We have seen that this passage in *Gregorius*, which has no equivalent in the *Vie du Pape Saint Grégoire*, reflects the social division between peasants and knights which became increasingly marked during the twelfth century and which received a legal expression in Hartmann's day, when the *Constitutio contra incendiarios* of 1186 forbade the granting of the belt of knighthood to the sons of peasants.[18] The relation of peasant and knightly condition does not figure in the consciousness of Chrétien's Yvain, who conceives of himself in completely knightly terms as soon as he awakes, experiencing only aristocratic shame at his nakedness (Yv 3020–23). Hartmann, however, adds a social dimension to Iwein's monologue by having Iwein, in his state of semi-consciousness, seemingly believe for a while that he actually is a *rusticus*, a 'gebûre' (Iw 3557, 3573) with the spirit of a knight (Iw 3581: 'rîterlîches muotes'), which corresponds to the young Gregorius's believing that, as a pupil in the monastery, he was the son of a *rusticus* despite his thoughts being turned to chivalry (Gr 1572: 'sô stuont ze ritterschaft mîn muot'). In adapting both the *Vie du Pape Saint Grégoire* and Chrétien's *Yvain*, Hartmann thus departs from his source to project into the hero's consciousness the distinction of status between peasant and knight which was a live issue in Germany in his day, and in doing so he gives a poetic expression, in the mental structure of his characters, to the consolidation of knighthood as a mark of aristocratic social class.

This view of the social contours of Iwein's monologue receives support from René Pérennec's illuminating observation that Iwein's conception of himself as a peasant who has the spirit of a knight is reminiscent of Guivreiz's declaration to Erec that his (Erec's) *tugent* is such as to merit nobility whatever his parentage (Er 4451–59), with the difference that in *Erec* it is 'la condition noble' and in *Iwein* 'la condition chevaleresque' that appears as 'une grandeur fixe', as the closed system into which entry is sought from below.[19] In other words, Hartmann talks about the knightly status in *Iwein* in terms similar to those he used in *Erec* for the condition of nobility, a comparison we have already made with regard to Hartmann's reference to some status of birth ('geburt') and wealth ('guot') as normal prerequisites for knighthood in *Gregorius*.[20]

18 See above, pp. 150f.
19 Pérennec, *Recherches*, I, pp.. 216f.
20 See above, p. 151.

It is tempting to speculate that this shift of emphasis from *Erec* to Hartmann's later works could reflect an important specific moment in the gradual crystallization of knighthood into a mark of aristocratic class in German society, with *Erec*, if written before the promulgation of the *Constitutio contra incendiarios* in 1186, representing a stage when knighthood was, in theory at least, more open of access, whilst *Gregorius*, which is usually placed after 1186, and *Iwein*, which Hartmann wrote by common consent after 1186, representing the more closed class defined in the law of 1186. However, knighthood is simply not presented in relation to other social categories in Hartmann's *Erec*.[21] Consequently, the impression of social distinction, even caste, that emerges more clearly in knighthood in *Gregorius* and *Iwein* may be the result of the widening of Hartmann's poetic angle of vision which, however briefly, does in the later works place knighthood in relation to peasantry and thus makes explicit a degree of exclusiveness which may have been taken for granted already by the poet and audience in *Erec*. What is clear is that Hartmann, in his adaptation of Chrétien's *Yvain*, as of the *Vie du Pape Saint Grégoire* and of Chrétien's *Erec*, draws independently on the social mentality of his own time and surroundings and that his adaptations in various ways reflect the growth of aristocratic tendencies in knighthood which are also evidenced in the historical sources.

At the moment of awakening, then, Iwein's thoughts draw on a deep, instinctive level of his being, at which 'rîterschaft' figures as self-assertion and as a mark of social class. Hartmann's location of this concept of chivalry at such a point in his protagonist's consciousness reflects its fundamental importance for the social mentality of the German aristocracy at this time. And it is indicative of an important difference of texture between the two works that whereas Hartmann actually portrayed the crossing of a class barrier in the marriage between Heinrich and the daughter of a tenant farmer in *Der arme Heinrich*, the possibility that a 'gebûre' might become a knight by virtue of his excellence of spirit alone is relegated to the realm of unreal dream in *Iwein*.

## Gawein's advice: knighthood, marriage and lordship over lands

The advice given by Gawein to his newly married friend has an important motivational function in Hartmann's as in Chrétien's romance, since it leads to Iwein's requesting permission to leave his wife and lands. However, the content and tenor of this speech are quite

---

[21] See above, pp. 61f.

different in the two works, for whereas Chrétien's Gauvain bases his speech on a concept of courtly love (the idea that a man should better himself for the sake of his mistress or wife, Yv 2489–92) and on a more Ovidian analysis of love's psychology (pleasures are all the more intense for being delayed, Yv 2515–26), Hartmann plays down the topic of love which dominates the passage in Chrétien and builds on the brief, two-line comment in *Yvain* about the danger of a man losing in valour when he becomes 'del reaume sire' (Yv 2498) to have the 'German' Gawein introduce a discussion, some seventy lines long, of the relation of knighthood to marriage and lordship over lands (Iw 2807–78). The *ritter* and poet Hartmann thus again thrusts the topic of knighthood to the fore, and this reflection on an important practical concern in the sociology of knighthood, projected through the voice of the leading Arthurian knight, throws a revealing light on the place of chivalry in aristocratic life.

Hartmann's Gawein expresses his views on the proper relation of knightly activity to landed responsibility by producing one of the most striking pieces of social caricature in the literature of the period, the negative image of the man who, on marrying and setting up household, gives up knightly ways to become a rural squireen, a *Krautjunker*, whose unkempt hair and dress (Iw 2819–21) take him close to the peasantry in appearance, and whose conversation is dominated by such material concerns as the cost of storm damage and the price of grain (Iw 2824–33). Hartmann here provides another contrastive perspective on knight-hood, this time setting the knightly lifestyle off against the claims of rural estate management, the 'hûs' (Iw 2808, 2825, 2834, 2839, 2844, 2851). In this perspective knighthood is associated with conspicuous material consumption, with travelling and the aristocratic virtue of *largesse* (Iw 2811: 'rîten' and 'geben'). And Gawein's reference to the squireen's giving up expensive pleasures and clothes cut in a knightly fashion (Iw 2813–18) should be seen in the context of the medieval tendency, which gained ground especially from the twelfth century onwards, to reflect social status in manner of dress.[22]

Already in the Carolingian period members of the German high nobility set themselves apart from lesser men by wearing magnificent long tunics, and the spread of courtly culture in the twelfth century brought a change in the style of dress, in that now the broader social level of the knightly order adopted long 'Prachtgewänder', while the short Frankish tunic remained characteristic of the peasantry.[23] Several decades before Hartmann, the author of the *Kaiserchronik*, in a passage which allegedly records legislation by Charlemagne, but which in fact

---

22   See Lehmann-Langholz, *Kleiderkritik*, pp. 19–23; Bumke, *Höfische Kultur*, I, pp. 172–74.
23   Lehmann-Langholz, *Kleiderkritik*, pp. 19–23.

reflects the social climate of the mid-twelfth century, speaks of peasants being allowed to wear only black or grey clothes (14788–802), hence by implication allowing knights to dress more brightly. Later sources often reiterate this view of appropriate peasant clothing, and especially from the thirteenth century onwards speak explicitly of knightly features of dress.[24] Hartmann reflects the general tendency to indicate social status by dress in details which he adds to Chrétien's *Yvain*. Thus Hartmann refers independently to 'junkherren' and 'knehte' who are clad according to their station (Iw 308: 'gecleidet nâch ir rehte'), and he describes Iwein as being restored to knightly appearance when he puts on fine clothes such as he had worn in his dream (Iw 3587–96). Hartmann links the concepts of knighthood and fine peacetime attire when he refers to 'cleider / die nâch rîterlîchen siten / sint gestalt und gesniten' (Iw 2814–16), and this independent comment indicates that knighthood is no longer solely a military function, but is linked in peaceful contexts with an expensive and stylish mode of dress. The history of costume thus points again to the growing social distinctiveness of knighthood in the late twelfth century.

Gawein's warning that a man's chivalry may fade (Iw 2806: 'zergân') on his marrying and becoming lord of a household opens up a further dimension of knighthood in the period around 1200 – its close association with youth and early manhood. We have seen that in *Erec* the word *ritter* was applied primarily to young men who were not seen in the exercise of lordship. The link between the concepts of knighthood and youth is typical of the German vernacular evidence of this period, as is indicated in Joachim Bumke's informative list of the adjectives applied to the noun *ritter* in the period up to ca. 1250, for against the 50 occurrences of the adjective *junc* in connection with *ritter*, distributed over 16 works, Bumke notes only six occurrences of *alt*, distributed over four works, with only one instance of *alt* (the grey-haired knight on a journey of penance in Wolfram's *Parzival*, 446,10) before about 1220.[25] This age distribution of *ritter* reflects the historical phase when

---

[24] A *Trutzstrophe* in Neidhart's songs defines silk and gold as appropriate for knights (Winterlied 34, IXa, 6: 'ritter solten tragen billîch sîden unde golt' – on the significance of clothes in Neidhart's presentation of the rivalry between peasant and knight see Lehmann-Langholz, *Kleiderkritik*, pp. 160–89). The notion of gold as a mark of knightly status seems to have gained firm hold in the later Middle Ages (*Seifried Helbling* VIII, 657ff.; Petersen, *Das Rittertum*, p. 125: 'Mit dem Ritterschlag erst erwirbt der Adlige das Recht, Gold zu tragen'); Johannes Rothe, *Ritterspiegel* 765–80, derives the association of knighthood and gold from practices of the ancient Greeks before Troy – the derivation is historically inaccurate, but a further sign of the importance of the classical past for medieval theorizing about chivalry. On the difference between knights' and squires' garb see Schultz, *Höfisches Leben*, I, p. 322.

[25] Bumke, *Ritterbegriff*, pp. 119, 122. The association of knighthood with 'youth' seems at times even more pronounced in Germany than in France around 1200 (see W.H. Jackson, 'The Concept of Knighthood', p. 46).

knighthood was still a warrior function, a *vita activa* calling for physical robustness – a point too easily lost sight of in scholarly debates about the ethical and the social class dimensions of chivalry in courtly literature.

However, it is the claim of the household, not the biological fact of ageing that prompts Gawein's warning about the danger of Iwein's 'rîterschaft' fading, and this sociological consideration reflects the importance in knightly ideology and in actual aristocratic life of the period between a youth's becoming a knight and his taking over (often on the death of his father or on receiving lands at marriage) lordship over landed possessions. Georges Duby has discussed the formative influence of this period of 'youth' on the self-understanding of the twelfth-century aristocracy, not least with regard to the themes of courtly literature.[26] The transition from knightly bachelordom to marriage and lordship is, after all, the main plot framework in chivalric romance around 1200, and at one level this plot framework is a poetic processing of the fantasies and hopes connected with the historically real period of 'youth'.[27] This period, conceived as a sociological rather than a biological quantity, probably loomed larger in the lifespan of the medieval aristocracy than might at first be thought, for, contrary to popular myth, marriages often took place relatively late even in aristocratic circles,[28] following an often long period of bachelor semi-dependence, much of which was spent away from immediate home and family.[29] For the knight this was an important period of socialization involving the acquisition of interpersonal and military skills in periods of residence in lordly households.[30] In terms of personal relationships this time of youth was conducive to the formation of fraternal relationships, i.e. a horizontal bonding which, together with the powerful forces of patriarchalism, helped to institutionalize the long periods of youth.[31] One thinks here of the stock motif of the hero's friendship with Gawein in Arthurian romance, and it is no coincidence that precisely Gawein, the foremost exemplar of bachelor knighthood, should be the one to

---

[26] Duby, 'Les "jeunes" ', *passim*; id., *Le chevalier, la femme et le prêtre*, pp. 223–39, 289–98.

[27] See also Evans, 'Wishfulfilment', *passim*.

[28] Delort, *Life in the Middle Ages*, p. 118. Borst, *Lebensformen*, p. 71 refers to research calculating the average age of marriage in a series of German high noble families as 30.5 years for men, 22.1 years for women – this is a high age for men, given the relatively short life-expectancy at the time; Freed, *The Counts of Falkenstein*, pp. 65–67 shows the combination of late marriages and a violent lifestyle as characteristic of leading noble families in south Germany in the twelfth century. This recent research on family structures in the German nobility suggests that some of the insights gained by Duby's work on northern France can fruitfully be applied to German literature (for a critical discussion of the application of Duby's work on the 'Jeunes' to courtly literature see now Peters, 'Von der Sozialgeschichte', *passim*).

[29] Gillies, *Youth*, pp. 8f.

[30] See above, pp. 27–29.

[31] Gillies, *Youth*, p. 22.

remind Iwein of the continuing claims of chivalric activity. Morever, the period of youth had a certain integrative function with regard to the different hierarchical levels of the *ordo militaris*, for it was at this stage, before the assumption of full lordship, that there was perhaps most in common in the lifestyle of young men of different material status, and there was close interaction between the sons of great lords and knights of lesser condition in residence at lordly households and in group military exercises.

It is a recurrent feature in Hartmann's adaptations of French source material that he shows a more intimate concern than Chrétien or the author of the *Vie du Pape Saint Grégoire* with material aspects of knighthood, and on this point again Hartmann's own social status, as a knight, has left its imprint on his work. In the case of Gawein's speech the material, practical concern is with the place of chivalry in the life of the married and settled lord of a household. A danger for the practice of chivalry was that established men, once having entered upon an inheritance and set themselves up as lords of households (Iw 2818, 2850: 'wirt'), might withdraw from the expensive display of chivalry at tournaments and great courts, thereby diminishing the prestige of knighthood and reducing the material benefits accruing to poorer knights from the public *largesse* of the wealthy. Gawein addresses this danger by warning Iwein not to neglect the duty of *largesse* (Iw 2811: 'geben') and by urging him to devote some of his newly-won wealth to the furtherance of his knightly honour in tourneying (Iw 2899–911), an activity in which, as is shown in Hartmann's *Erec*, material benefits could sink down from wealthy lords to poor knights by the practice of generosity.[32] The participation of great lords in tournaments also ensured a livelihood in a pragmatic way for the retinues they equipped and sustained, so that advocacy of the tournament in this period was in the material and ideological interests of the knights who were members of such retinues. Viewed in this light, Gawein's speech can indeed be seen as defending the interests of the lesser knights of his day.[33]

Important as these two aspects of youth and the group interests of the less wealthy knighthood are for an understanding of the relation of 'rîterschaft' and the 'hûs' in Gawein's speech, they do not exhaust the problematics of this relation. Rather, as has recently been argued in a major and controversial study of Hartmann's *Iwein*, we are dealing here with a fundamental tension between two important aspects of aristocratic life – the material base in the possession of lands, and the socially constitutive, ostentatious but expensive and often physically dangerous pursuit of honour – that runs through the history of the

[32] W.H. Jackson, 'The Tournament in the Works of Hartmann von Aue', p. 245.
[33] Hunt, 'Beginnings, Middles and Ends', p. 98.

medieval nobility.[34] The tournament acted as a focus for this tension from its beginnings through to the revivalist efforts of the tourneying societies in late fifteenth-century Germany, and it is important for an understanding of the historical resonance of Gawein's speech to note that a sense of conflict between these two aspects of the noble life surfaces in texts relating to the tournament in various parts of Europe. As early as the mid-twelfth century Ludwig II of Thuringia wrote to his brother Heinrich Raspe urging him to desist from useless military games in order better to attend to affairs of state,[35] and the same complaint appears in poetry, with Count Jofrois of Poitiers being urged to return from his errant chivalry in England to defend his assailed lands: 'Certes mult te fusse plus gent, / Que tu defendisses ta terre, / Que cha fusses folie querre' (*Joufroi de Poitiers* 3682–84). Similarly Gereint, in the *Mabinogion*, is told by his father 'that it would be better for him to spend the flower of his youth and his prime defending his own boundaries than in tournaments which bring no profit, though he win fame therein' (*Gereint, Son of Erbin*, p. 246), whilst the poet Reinmar von Zweter, in a strophe delivered perhaps at the court of Duke Frederick II of Austria, warns knights that excessive tourneying can lead to neglect of their household: 'Unt swer turnieren minnet also sêre, / daz er dâ bî vergizzet der hûsêre, / dern hât der mâze niht behalten' (121,7–9). Against these voices which remind tourneying knights of the claims of the household, we hear the opposite note of authors urging participation in tournaments as a touchstone of true chivalry in French and German works,[36] or commenting dismissively on men who stay at home when true knights should be travelling in pursuit of honour,[37] whilst the author of the satirical *Seifried Helbling* at the end of the thirteenth century pokes fun at the contemporary Austrian knights who prefer working their farms to fighting.[38]

Just as remarkable as the wide regional and chronological spread of these utterances on the problematical relationship of chivalry to the claims of the household is their broad hierarchical relevance, stretching as they do from princes down to the lowest level of the aristocratic hierarchy, where the lifestyle of the lesser knights was little different from that of the upper level of peasants. The aristocratic ethos called for some demonstrative exercise of arms at all levels of the noble hierarchy,

---

[34] Fischer, *Ehre*, pp. 73ff.
[35] F. Peeck (ed.), *Reinhardsbrunner Briefsammlung*, no. 63, pp. 57f., quoted by Mertens, *Laudine*, pp. 67f.
[36] E.g. *Histoire de Guillaume le Maréchal* 4288ff.; *Tirol und Fridebrant* 29,1–5.
[37] E.g. *Herzog Ernst* 8–30; *Histoire de Guillaume le Maréchal* 1530ff. (England as a poor place for errant chivalry), 1889ff. and often.
[38] *Seifried Helbling*, I, 820ff.; XV, 87ff.; compare the dismissive comment about nobles who prefer heaving sacks of corn to jousting in Hermann von Sachsenheim, *Die Mörin* (mid-fifteenth century) 4940–43.

and clearly at all these levels there was also some awareness of tension between the pursuit of chivalric glory, with its attendant material costs and physical risks, and the claims of landed lordship, what Hartmann and other German authors call the *hûs*, be it the affairs of state in a princely household or the price of grain for a petty Swabian noble.

To conclude this brief survey of the chivalric and the economic, or domestic aspects of aristocratic life, it is particularly from about the late twelfth century onwards that tension is expressed in the relation of these two spheres. The growing concern for the claims of the *hûs* in poetic utterances is matched by the emergence in the late Middle Ages of theoretical writings on the duties of the head of a household.[39] We are dealing here with a slow evolution. Nevertheless, it seems that already in Hartmann's day the economic aspects of life were beginning to assume greater weight in the aristocratic mentality and to enter into a problematical relationship with the developing values of chivalry. Put in another way, we glimpse here an early stage in a process of central importance in the social history of medieval Europe: the slow transformation of the upper level of secular society from a warrior aristocracy into a demilitarized landed gentry, a transformation that was not complete until the end of the Middle Ages or later. It is as if Hartmann dimly sensed the importance of this evolution, this retreat from active chivalry, and used Gawein's speech as a vehicle for commenting on it.

The intrusion of the unkempt knight-turned-farmer into the stylized world of courtly romance has provoked widely differing reactions from recent scholars, Hartmann's version of Gawein's speech being interpreted variously as an aesthetic lapse caused by the German's author's thinking too much in terms of his local audience,[40] as unsound advice, inappropriate to Iwein's new role in Laudine's world,[41] as a vehicle for ironic criticism of Gawein's concept of chivalric honour,[42] and conversely as sound advice which has the poet's backing and is intended as an exemplary statement of aristocratic values.[43] Such conflicting readings typify the current lack of consensus on the tone of voice of the knightly poet Hartmann and on the status and evaluation of central aspects of chivalry in a work which has the status of a classic of courtly literature.

---

[39]  Fischer, *Ehre*, p. 80.
[40]  Ruh, 'Zur Interpretation von Hartmanns *Iwein*', p. 49; Huby, 'L'interpretation des romans courtois de Hartmann', p. 33.
[41]  Wiegand, *Studien zur Minne und Ehe*, pp. 230f.; Selbmann, 'Strukturschema', p. 75.
[42]  Thum, 'Politische Probleme', pp. 55f.; Ranawake, 'Zur Form und Funktion der Ironie', pp. 100–02.
[43]  Homberger, *Gawein*, p. 25; Mertens, *Laudine*, pp. 37f.; Zutt, *König Artus*, pp. 39–44; Sinka, ' "Der höfschste man" ', p. 475; Fischer, *Ehre*, pp. 73ff.

With regard to the poet's voice, a number of factors suggest that, in Chrétien's *Yvain*, Gauvain's advice is not so much a serious statement of what the author considers to be exemplary conduct, but rather an exercise in persuasion, which is delivered with a note of humour and which does not invite the audience's full assent.[44] Thus Chrétien's Gauvain presents a manifestly one-sided, impetuous, exclamatory argument. The concept of courtly love and the amatory psychologizing that form the backbone of his case have a distinctly literary flavour; and the narrator's comment that Yvain decides to ask for permission to leave 'whether it were wise or foolish' (Yv 2544: 'Ou face folie ou savoir') suggests at least some reservation on the poet's part as to the wisdom of the action. However, none of this applies to the German work, where Gawein's advice is more serious and considered in tone.

In Chrétien, Gauvain's outburst is an extension of the Arthurian knights' collective pleas (Yv 2479ff.), and it appears as a temptation of the married hero by the group to which he formerly belonged; but Hartmann encourages us to trust Gawein's advice by introducing him with an epithet of maximum moral reliability as 'her Gâwein der getriuwe man' (Iw 2767), and he makes Gawein's advice more nuanced and personal by dropping Chrétien's reference to the collective urgings of Arthur's knights and having Gawein speak privately to his friend (Iw 2767–69). Whereas Chrétien's Gauvain opens his speech with a challenging rhetorical question which is calculated to move Iwein by provocation ('Are you one of those who lose in prowess because of their wives?', Yv 2484–86), Hartmann's Gawein opens quite differently with a reflection on the interplay of human effort, fortune ('sælde') and honour (Iw 2770–82) which gives his exhortation a more serious, even philosophical ring.[45] Moreover, at several points Gawein's speech takes up maxims, topics or motifs that figure elsewhere in Hartmann's own poetry, so that he speaks like a man who has digested Hartmann's teaching. Gawein's opening reflection is reminiscent of the heart's discussion of the relation of human effort, 'êre' and 'heil', in the *Klage* (Kl 755–68); his reference to Erec's *verligen* and subsequent knightly rehabilitation (Iw 2791–98) gives Hartmann's own earlier romance a positive place in his exhortation; his plea that even a head of household should still show 'rîters muot' (Iw 2855) echoes Hartmann's own introductory laudation of Arthur as a king 'der mit rîters muote / nâch lobe kunde strîten' (Iw 6f.);[46] his comment that it is better to be a man of

---

44 Hunt, 'Beginnings, Middles and Ends', pp. 92ff.
45 See also Hunt, 'Beginnings, Middles and Ends', p. 96.
46 The expression *ritters muot* is not attested before Hartmann (Bumke, *Ritterbegriff*, p. 149). It is fitting that this expression should first appear in and perhaps have been the creation of an author whose work shows an unprecedentedly intimate concern with the ethical and mental values (*muot*) as well as the social and material dimensions of chivalry.

spirit and honour without wealth than a wealthy but degenerate lord echoes the young Gregorius's views (Iw 2879–83; compare Gr 1681–87); and his play on the words *muot* and *guot* echoes passages in *Erec* and *Gregorius* (Iw 2905–08; compare Er 2262–65, Gr 606–23).

Gawein is still the leading bachelor knight in Hartmann's adaptation, urging the pursuit of chivalric *êre* (Iw 2774, 2777, 2797, 2801, 2852, 2863, 2901, 2903), but his advice carries a greater moral authority than that of Chrétien's Gauvain because it is less impetuous, more considered, and shows an understanding of the two sides to a case. Thus Gawein in his advocacy of 'rîterschaft' explicitly recognizes the validity of the established lord's duty towards his household (Iw 2850–58: 'der wirt hât wâr, und doch niht gar. / daz hûs muoz kosten harte vil: / swer êre ze rehte haben wil, / der muoz deste dicker heime sîn: / sô tuo ouch under wîlen schîn / ob er noch rîters muot habe, / unde entuo sich des niht abe / ern sî der rîterschefte bî / diu im ze suochenne sî'). This is the central, generalizing point of Gawein's advice, and it is an attempt to accommodate the rival claims of the chivalric and the economic aspects of aristocratic life without sacrificing one for the other. Honour, if it is to be well founded ('ze rehte'), calls for commitment in both directions – a typically Hartmannesque pattern of thought. Nor does Gawein show a disregard for Laudine's position, for whereas Chrétien's Gauvain urges Yvain to leave his wife without mentioning a time to return, Hartmann has Gawein advise Iwein to ask for an appropriate leave for a specific time that will have the queen's blessing (Iw 2886: 'und gewinnet mit minnen / der küneginne ein urloup abe / zeinem tage der vuoge habe'). Here again the one-sided impetuosity of Chrétien's Gauvain gives place in Hartmann's adaptation to a more balanced recognition of Iwein's responsibilities. This is typical of the entire episode, in which Chrétien's Gauvain appears as a tempter figure urging Yvain to break loose (Yv 2500: 'Ronpez le frain et le chevoistre') whatever the consequences (Yv 2506: 'Que que il vos doie coster'), whilst Hartmann's Gawein is a serious mentor figure recommending a course of action that will appropriately meet the various claims pressing on his friend. Whatever the degree of Chrétien's ironical detachment from Gauvain's advice, Hartmann thus seems not to criticize Gawein's counsel, rather his alterations enhance the seriousness and reliability of this counsel so that we may take Gawein as having the German poet's backing in his defence of the chivalric ethos.

It is likely that, in composing the figure of the 'Krautjunker' with his material concerns, Hartmann was indeed thinking of his local, southern German audience.[47] This is in keeping with his recurrent tendency to relate literary structures to the reality of the here and now, a tendency

---

[47] Rosenhagen, 'Zur Charakteristik Hartmanns von Aue', p. 99.

which is evident in the narrator's stance from the beginning of *Iwein*, when Hartmann distances himself from Chrétien's rejection of the present day and insists that he is happy to live precisely in this present time (Iw 48–58; contrast Yv 29–32). In the case of Gawein's advice this tendency leads Hartmann to transform Chrétien's rhetorically sophisticated deployment of the poetic game of courtly love into a pragmatic discussion of material relevance to the landed aristocracy in his own audience. Moreover it is not merely a local or trivial issue that Hartmann raises here but a matter of central importance in the self-understanding of the secular aristocracy in a time of social change, and the accommodation of lordship and chivalric participation in tournaments, which Gawein advocates as appropriate to Iwein's status, has its parallels in the historical reality of the late twelfth century. For example Count Baldwin V of Hainault, who was knighted in 1168, married in 1169 and succeeded his father as count in 1171, is recorded as visiting tournaments in France and the Low Countries from 1168 to 1183.[48] Thus Baldwin sought out tournaments as a fresh young knight and for over ten years as the married head of the comital household of Hainault. His patronage of the tournament brought material benefit to the knights maintained in his retinue and helped promote the chivalric fame of Hainault to which Hartmann himself refers (Gr 1575). The comital family of Hainault was connected by marriage with the dukes of Zähringen and had close political links from 1184 onwards with the imperial court.[49] Consequently news of the tourneying exploits of the knighthood of Hainault under Baldwin V could easily have reached Hartmann. However, this specific possibility is less important than the fact of the existence of leading figures who combined tourneying and lordship and could thus act as models in the real world for the advice given by Gawein to Iwein in Hartmann's romance. Seen in this light Gawein's advice, far from being the fantastical expression of a purely fictional, poetic world of chivalry, urges on Iwein, and on Hartmann's German audience, a pattern of aristocratic life that had some basis in reality.[50]

---

[48] See *La Chronique de Gislebert de Mons*, pp. 95, 97, 101, 108, 116f., 123f., 127, 133, 144; W.H. Jackson, 'Knighthood and Nobility', p. 804.

[49] See above, p. 155.

[50] An interesting echo of Gawein's advice is found in *Reinfried von Braunschweig* (12520–37), written ca. 1300. The author here praises Reinfried as an exemplary ruler who continues to cultivate jousts and tournaments after his marriage, unlike many contemporary lords who 'verligen sich' (12522) and no longer visit jousts and tournaments once they are married, preferring a life of ease to one of honour, and not trying to combine 'hûsêre' and 'ritterliche tât' (12536f.). This passage indicates a serious reception of Gawein's advice as providing guidance for the actual conduct of noble life in Germany.

*Lunete's accusation: knighthood and* triuwe

In the accusation scene at Arthur's court even more emphatically than in Gawein's advice Hartmann alters what was in Chrétien's *Yvain* a speech based on the rhetoric of courtly love to one based on broader concerns in the social life of the contemporary aristocracy, with the difference that whereas Gawein's advice focused on the relation of knighthood to the economic aspect of lordship, in the accusation scene Hartmann places knighthood in the context of central ethical and legal norms.

In Chrétien the unnamed 'dameisel' (Yv 2705) who charges Yvain couches her indictment in the imagery of love poetry, railing at Yvain as a thief who has stolen his lady's heart (Yv 2722–53) and presenting Laudine as the very exemplar of a sighing, yearning and sleepless lover counting the days of separation (Yv 2754–61). In an alteration that is characteristic of his tendency to place the protagonists' actions in a wider network of obligations, Hartmann has the indictment delivered by Lunete, who is linked to Iwein by a debt of gratitude that goes back to before the beginning of the action (Iw 1178–97), and whose furtherance of Iwein's cause with Laudine has made her an unwitting accomplice in Iwein's transgression (Iw 3137–59, 3184–86). Moreover, Lunete's indictment is quite different in tone from that of Chrétien's damsel. Lunete's opening charge that Iwein is a 'verrâtære' (Iw 3118) and guilty of 'untriuwe' (Iw 3122) echoes the damsel's opening description of Yvain as 'le desleal, le traïtor' (Yv 2719), but whereas the damsel backs up this charge by reference to the ethics and the language of courtly love, Lunete never mentions love, rather her speech remains in the world of social and legal obligations recognized in contemporary life and draws on forensic rhetoric and the vocabulary of contemporary law to express these obligations.[51]

Lunete first states the general grounds for the charge, namely that Iwein has offended against Laudine (Iw 3127–36) and herself (Iw 3137–51), then she adds the specific grounds that by his failure to return Iwein has abused his marital position, treating Laudine like a concubine (Iw 3171: 'kebsen') and failing to protect her person and lands (Iw 3158: 'ir lîp unde ir lant'). There is no trace in Lunete's speech of Laudine as a forlorn and yearning lover, rather she appears in a political and legal light as a noble and powerful ruler (Iw 3170: 'edel' and 'rîch') whose honour has been threatened (Iw 3136: 'êre') and who now seeks public retribution. Lunete draws her charges together in a formal accusation

---

[51] See also Hagenguth, *Hartmanns 'Iwein'*, pp. 81–87; Mertens, *Laudine*, p. 42. In assessing the literary texture of *Iwein* it should be remembered that at this time the language of legal proceedings was still far closer to everyday speech than is the case today, so that Hartmann's use of 'legal language' does not imply a recondite, specialist jargon.

that Iwein lacks *triuwe* (Iw 3174–83), and she derives from this charge the sentence that he should be rejected by all honourable folk (Iw 3175–80) and cast out from Arthur's retinue (Iw 3187–89), just as Laudine has already withdrawn the rights of marriage from him (Iw 3190–96). It is in keeping with the amatory rhetoric of Chrétien's version that the damsel speaks only of Laudine's withdrawing her favour (Yv 2767–73), and typical of Hartmann's adaptation that he broadens the sentence to involve Iwein's entire social being, for Lunete calls for nothing less than Iwein to be stripped of his social privileges and treated as an outcast. We are reminded of the way Hartmann, in adapting Chrétien's *Erec*, opened up the social dimension of the hero's knightly transgression by having his lapse from chivalry rob his court of joy as well as himself of honour (Er 2966–92).

Lunete's sentence that Iwein's breach of *triuwe* should lead to his exclusion from aristocratic society reflects a principle of contemporary German law which is expressed succinctly in the *Sachsenspiegel*: 'Wer so truwelos beredet wirt, adir vluchtig uz des riches dinste, deme verteilet man sine ere unde sin lenrecht, unde nicht sinen lip' (*Landrecht*, I,40). That is to say that the man guilty of a breach of *triuwe* loses his honour and the right of fief, which corresponds to the punishment decreed for breach of *fides* in the *Constitutio contra incendiarios*.[52] In other words he forfeits his rights in aristocratic society, he becomes 'rechtelos' (*Sachsenspiegel, Landrecht*, I,40). Lunete clearly speaks within this framework of reference when she calls on Arthur to treat Iwein as a man in breach of *triuwe*: 'Nû tuon ich disen herren kunt / daz sî iuch haben vür dise stunt / vür einen triuwelôsen man' (Iw 3181–83). Indeed *triuwe* was the central ethical and legal value of aristocratic society in Hartmann's day, ranging in meaning from a specific promise to the whole complex of obligations which linked the individual to others, whether through ties of clan, feudal obligation, friendship or hospitality. The principle underlying Lunete's accusation and the legal utterances of the time, that a man can only be considered to have honour (*êre*) if he also maintains loyalty, fidelity (*triuwe*) reflects the character of relations in a society that still depended heavily for its functioning on the integrity of the given word and on the reliability of individuals in holding to commitments that were often merely orally agreed.

Iwein's transgression is that, in overstaying his leave, he has broken a formal promise and thus become guilty of a breach of faith which, in the eyes of those affected, especially Laudine, casts doubt on his reliability in a more fundamental sense, hence the severity of Lunete's indict-ment.[53] However, whilst broadening the charge laid against Iwein,

---

[52] MGH Const., I, no. 318, c. 19 (p. 451).
[53] See also Zutt, *König Artus*, pp. 21–24.

Hartmann also adds a passage, independently of Chrétien, and before Lunete's arrival at Arthur's court, in which Iwein reflects with remorse (Iw 3090: 'riuwe') on his failure to return by the appointed day (Iw 3082–95), so that the objective charge of betrayal is preceded by a subjective feeling of guilt in the hero; and after the indictment, Hartmann comments in the narrator's voice that precisely Iwein's 'triuwe' (Iw 3210) causes him pain when he hears Lunete's accusation. Hartmann thus exploits the broad semantic range of the term *triuwe* by taking Iwein's failure to return to his wife and lands as the occasion for a broadside delivered by Lunete against breach of *triuwe* (a broadside whereby the poet emphatically reminds his audience of the importance of this value), whilst from the larger perspective of the narrator he reassures his audience that Iwein does indeed possess the essential moral quality of *triuwe* (which he will demonstrate in the later stages of the romance), even though he is guilty of the specific breach of promise that led to Lunete's charge.

What is particularly important for our purpose is that Hartmann gives the terminology of knighthood a prominent place in Lunete's accusation, when she speaks of Iwein offending against 'rîters triuwe' (Iw 3173), and in the sentence of loss of honourable status, when she calls for the forfeiture of Iwein's knightly position: 'Und mac sich der künec iemer schamen, / hât er iuch mêre in rîters namen, / sô liep im triuwe und êre ist' (Iw 3187–89). Neither of these formulations is based on Chrétien's text – indeed Chrétien never once uses the term *chevalier* or *chevalerie* in Gawein's advice or in the damsel's accusation – and each shows Hartmann independently of his French source associating the relatively new terminology of chivalry with social norms and rituals of great antiquity.

The central importance of *triuwe* as a social value reaches back to the Frankish and Germanic periods.[54] However, whilst *triuwe* appears as an essential quality of the knight in Hartmann's *Erec*,[55] his *Iwein* is the earliest text in which the phrase *ritters triuwe* appears.[56] Lunete's call that Iwein should be stripped of his knightly status also has considerable historical resonance. Throughout the prehistory and early history of knighthood there is not only evidence of rites of passage into the warrior status (the arming, later knighting ceremonies), but also testimony, though sparser and less frequently studied, of the loss of military status as a punishment for crime. Karl Leyser has shown, in an illuminating essay, that ecclesiastical and mixed legislation as early as the ninth century prescribed the loss of the *cingulum militare*, i.e. the loss of

---

[54] Mitteis-Lieberich, *Deutsche Rechtsgeschichte*, pp. 28, 52f.
[55] See above, pp. 123f.
[56] Bumke, *Ritterbegriff*, p. 150.

military status, either permanently or temporarily whilst doing penance, for certain grave crimes.[57] Interestingly for the judgement passed on Iwein, this loss of military standing was often combined with the forfeiture of marriage: 'These were evidently seen as the foremost amenities and attributes of secular life which the penitent must forfeit to earn forgiveness'.[58]

There are instances of such sanctions being imposed on noble offenders as early as the ninth century, with no less a person than Emperor Louis the Pious being subject to ecclesiastical law, laying aside the *cingulum militare* in 833 in order to do penance for his misdeeds and being reinvested with it in a solemn reconciliation with episcopal approval in the following year.[59] The charge laid against the German King Henry I ' by his Saxon enemies in 1073, that his crimes were so grave that, were he to be judged by ecclesiastical laws, he would forfeit his marriage and the *miliciae cingulum* and be excluded from all secular affairs, especially from the kingship,[60] indicate that the provisions of the Carolingian Church had by this time 'become part of a living body of law'.[61] This is indicated for the early twelfth century in the account of a council held at Beauvais in 1114 under the presidency of a papal legate, at which a certain Thomas de Marle, accused of numerous crimes, was (in his absence) deprived of the *cingulum militare* and 'deposed from every worldly honour as a criminal and infamous enemy of christianity'.[62] The withdrawal of the military belt as a punishment for transgression figures already in Roman law, and it is from this source that John of Salisbury draws the punishment in his *Policraticus* (VI,13) – again it seems that categories of military and social order inherited from Roman antiquity and reinterpreted to suit the contemporary reality had some influence in shaping the concept of knighthood in the twelfth century.[63] This view of military standing as a privilege which should be withdrawn from those unworthy of it receives an interesting expression in the *Livre des Manières* of Etienne de Fougères, bishop of Rennes and chaplain to Henry II of England, when Etienne comments that, just as knights should receive their sword at the altar in church in recognition of their Christian duty (617–20), so the knight who gives himself to crime (including *traïson*, 623) should be judged at the altar (629–32) and cast out of the knightly order (625: *desordener*) by having his sword taken away and his spurs struck off (626–28). Etienne probably wrote his

[57]  Leyser, 'Early Medieval Canon Law', p. 555.
[58]  Ibid., p. 556.
[59]  Ibid., p. 560.
[60]  Lampert of Hersfeld, *Annales*, p. 198, 18–20.
[61]  Leyser, 'Early Medieval Canon Law', p. 561.
[62]  Ibid., p. 562.
[63]  For other instances of this influence see Keen, *Chivalry*, pp.110–12; Bosl, *Die Grundlagen*, pp. 199–201.

treatise between 1174 and 1178,[64] and it presents a developed ideology of the military status in knightly terms, as a matter for *chevaliers* (537, 580, 590, 628, 650, 663, 674) and as an *ordre* (585) which combines the aristocratic and the moral, since knights should be of free birth (589) and should be expelled from the order for crimes (623–28).[65]

Beside these voices from the Church, military standing could also be forfeited by lay judgement. Thus William of Malmesbury tells that William the Conqueror expelled a knight from the *militia* because of his shamefully striking at Harold's dead body on the field of Hastings.[66] The custumal issued by Count Dietrich of Lahr in 1154 guaranteeing the rights of his *ministeriales* includes the provision that 'breach of the custumal itself entailed expulsion from the retinue, and fellow-knights were expected to become the enemies of such felons'.[67] An assize of King Roger II of Sicily, dated 1140, decreed that men who were not of knightly birth but had nevertheless taken up the knightly lifestyle should be stripped of the *militie nomen*, i.e. of their military, by now 'knightly', standing – a formulation that corresponds remarkably closely to Lunete's call for Arthur to deprive Iwein of *rîters name*.[68] In Barbarossa's constitution against arsonists of 1186 it was the regional judge who should deprive sons of priests, deacons and rustics of the belt of knighthood.[69] And a few years after Hartmann's *Iwein*, Wolfram von Eschenbach tells in *Parzival* how the high noble Urjans was condemned by a judgement at Arthur's court to forfeiture of his knighthood and social privileges for the crime of rape: 'von schildes ambet man dich schiet / und sagte dich gar rehtlôs, / durch daz ein magt von dir verlôs / ir reht, dar zuo des landes vride' (*Parzival* 524,24–27).[70] One notes the alignment of chivalry as a moral order with the concept of territorial peace ('des landes vride') in this incident. Urjans is at first condemned to death for his crime (*Parzival* 524,28–30; 527,15–22), and only after Gawein's intercession on his behalf is the sentence reduced to that of eating out of a trough with the dogs for four weeks (*Parzival* 528,25–30).

In the wider context of the history of knighthood this brief survey of the forfeiture of military standing again reminds us of the important continuity which links the chivalric world of the twelfth century back to the Carolingian period, here in a moral as well as a military sense, for it was clearly not the case that all the moral aspects of chivalry were

---

[64]  See Lodge's introduction to his edition of the *Livre des Manières*, p. 22.
[65]  On Etienne's concept of *chevalerie* see Flori, *L'essor*, pp. 315–19.
[66]  Leyser, 'Early Medieval Canon Law', p. 562.
[67]  Arnold, *German Knighthood*, p. 84.
[68]  See Otto, 'Abschließung', p. 27; Fischer, *Ehre*, p. 72.
[69]  MGH Const., I, no. 318, c. 20 (pp. 451f.); see Leyser, 'Early Medieval Canon Law', p. 562.
[70]  On Wolfram's treatment of this incident see Matthias, 'Ein Handhaftverfahren', pp. 34–40.

suddenly, from the late eleventh century onwards, grafted onto what had until then been a purely violent warrior mentality and ideology. The theory and practice of this forfeiture also throw further light on the interface of the church and secular warriordom which is essential for an understanding of the development of chivalric ideology. The evidence of forfeiture in the twelfth century also shows an important political tendency in the development of knighthood, namely the attempt of kings to exercise some control over entry into knighthood and some disciplinary power of expulsion; this tendency in turn is one aspect of the broader efforts of rulers to secure more stable and peaceful conditions of social life, efforts which were expressed in the German empire particularly clearly in the *Landfrieden*.

With regard to Hartmann's version of the indictment of Iwein and its likely impact on a German audience, it is striking how closely Lunete's speech corresponds to the historical evidence of the forfeiture of military standing, since the forfeiture of Iwein's marriage (Iw 3190–96) and the call that he should be stripped of 'rîters name' (Iw 3188) and ousted from the company of honourable men (Iw 3175–83) are all matched in the historical record. Further, the fact that Lunete calls on precisely the king, Arthur, to oust Iwein from his knightly status, is in keeping with the attempts of the Hohenstaufen ruling dynasty to enhance royal control over the *militia* in contemporary Germany.[71] What is important about these and the other legal elements in Lunete's speech as regards the reception of Hartmann's work is that, just as knights in Hartmann's audience must have recognized some of their own material concerns in Gawein's advice, so they must have felt the terms of Lunete's accusation to be relevant to their moral conduct; indeed Lunete's insistent reiteration of the concept *triuwe* (eight times in lines 3173–95) seems calculated to hammer home to the audience the message that there can be no honour or proper chivalry without *triuwe*. Throughout Hartmann's works knighthood is both a social status and a moral code, and Hartmann seems even more concerned in *Iwein* than he was in *Erec* to underline not only the panache and social privileges but also the moral duties attached to *ritters name*.

Finally, the broad resonance of Lunete's charge helps motivate the intensity of Iwein's reaction. Lunete delivers a sentence of proscription, *Acht*, on Iwein,[72] a sentence based on 'the idea that infamous conduct thrust a man out of the society of his princely, noble and knightly companions'.[73] The sentence seems unduly harsh in relation to Iwein's lapse. However, Hartmann is less concerned with a legalistic balance

---

71   See also Fischer, *Ehre*, pp. 72f.
72   Matthias, 'Yvains Rechtsbrüche', pp. 188–97.
73   Leyser, 'Early Medieval Canon Law', p. 562.

between lapse and punishment than with the general importance of *triuwe* in chivalric ethics, and with the protagonist's subjective reaction to the charge. Significantly, Iwein does not take issue with the judgement, rather in a typically Hartmannesque way he recognizes that he is at fault, blames himself for the disaster that has befallen him (Iw 3221: 'Er verlôs sîn selbes hulde: / wan ern mohte die schulde / ûf niemen anders gesagen: / in hete sîn selbes swert erslagen'),[74] and carries out the sentence of outcasting and unknighting upon himself, tearing off the fine clothes that indicate his knightly status (Iw 3234ff.), running off into the wild forest (Iw 3237ff.) and becoming reduced to the sub-knightly way of life from which we saw him awakening at the beginning of this chapter.

One dimension of the forest's symbolism in *Iwein* is that it forms a metaphorical expression of Iwein's estrangement from his own self, from marriage, lordship and knighthood, and here again the moral and psychological symbolism of the romance has a basis in social ritual, for the forest was closely associated with proscription and outlawry: 'Da der Friedlose die menschliche Gemeinschaft fliehen muß, wird er zum Waldgänger (*homo qui per silvas vadit*)'.[75] Without pushing the analogy of Iwein and the proscribed felon too far it is also worth noting that proscription (*Acht*) took many forms in the high Middle Ages, and that it was often not intended as a permanent sentence but as a disciplinary measure from which the offender could hope to redeem himself by compensation or atonement to the satisfaction of the offended party.[76] Seen in this light, the status of the proscribed felon has much in common with that of the penitent in the Christian system, and that of the lover whose lady has withdrawn her favour in the sphere of courtly love. At various stages in his narration of Iwein's fall, his estrangement and his ultimate reconciliation with Laudine, Hartmann draws on each of these three models to present an account of knightly crisis and rehabilitation in which legal, Christian and courtly patterns of thought and experience are blended into a new aesthetic and cultural whole.

In that the three passages of direct speech, or inner thoughts, that have been discussed in this chapter all give knighthood a greater prominence than the corresponding passages in Chrétien's *Yvain*, the voices of Hartmann's characters testify to the continuing importance of knighthood as a theme in Hartmann's last romance, just as the author's

---

[74] This metaphor also figures in Hartmann's lyric poetry (I,5,9 = MF 206,9; see above, p. 181). The metaphor links the chief knightly weapon with the idea of moral punishment, and its appearance in the poet's voice in Hartmann's song, and in Iwein's thoughts in the romance, suggests a close identification of author and protagonist at this moment of self-indictment.

[75] Kaufmann, 'Acht', col. 27.

[76] Ibid., cols 30–32.

introduction of himself as a 'rîter' (Iw 21) takes up the knightly perspective of narration that characterized Hartmann's *Erec*. However, the fact that these passages also place knighthood in relation to a range of other social and ethical values also perhaps suggests a less enthusiastically committed view of chivalry in *Iwein* than was the case in Hartmann's first romance, and an enhanced desire to place knighthood in a broader framework of reference. The narrative action of *Iwein*, which will be discussed in the next chapter, further develops this more nuanced, more reflective, view of knighthood in various ways.

# 8

# Knighthood in *Iwein*: Social, Legal and Ethical Dimensions of the Action

*Arthur's realm – Laudine's realm*

It has been a commonplace of Chrétien and Hartmann scholarship since Hildegard Emmel's compositional study that, whereas Arthur's court is the main point of orientation of the narrative in *Erec* (albeit with some qualification in Hartmann's treatment of the close of the work), the position changes in *Yvain* / *Iwein* as Laudine's realm emerges as a second, even rival instance beside Arthur's court in a structural development which points forward to the emergence of the Grail realm in Arthurian romance.[1] Nor is it merely a schematic rivalry between Arthur's court and Laudine's realm. Rather the two spheres each have a different focus of social meaning in their relation to the hero. Arthur's court is in *Yvain* / *Iwein*, as it was in *Erec*, primarily the place of bachelor knighthood, of the *iuvenes*, whilst Laudine's realm is the sphere of marriage and lordship. Hartmann sharpens this sociological contrast in adapting Chrétien's *Yvain* in his treatment of Laudine, whom the German author presents, by comparison with Chrétien, less as a courtly mistress in love, and more as a ruler moved by political considerations, foremost the need to defend her lands.[2] The two realms thus represent the two poles of the aristocratic ethos which were discussed in the previous chapter: the ostentatious pursuit of glory (the Arthurian world) and the obligations of settled lordship. Arthur's court and Laudine's realm in *Iwein*, like Arthur's court and the hero's own kingdom in *Erec*, each embodies an essential part of the larger whole of feudal, aristocratic ideology, and each is essential to the value system of Hartmann's romances.

[1] Emmel, *Formprobleme*, pp. 38f.
[2] See also Wiegand, *Studien zur Minne und Ehe*, pp. 55–89; Mertens, *Laudine*, pp. 14–21.

With its presentation of Iwein's transition from bachelor knighthood at Arthur's court to married lordship in Laudine's realm, *Iwein* processes a fundamental social tension in the aristocracy of his day. Further, even for an age when legal matters and legal language were less sharply distinct from the concerns of everyday life and the language of poetry than is the case in modern European societies, *Iwein* shows a remarkable concern with legal forms and legal consequences. Hardly an episode in the work is without legal interest, and legal considerations have played a major part in recent studies of *Iwein*.[3] The social resonance of the theme together with the network of legally relevant actions and utterances create a strong sense of social concreteness and objectivity in Hartmann's last romance. This relatively sharp delineation of the contours of external reality is also accompanied in *Iwein* by a strong concern with the inner life, with subjective thoughts and feelings, with personal moral reflections and with the individual, inner realm of intentions as well as the communal realm of legal obligation. More strongly in *Iwein* than in *Erec*, one senses a gap between the external world and the protagonist's inner life, which is becoming more autonomous.

Iwein is presented as a knight throughout the romance. His mental breakdown – itself a suggestive motif in a work which shows more awareness of distance between the inner life and external reality than Hartmann's first romance – is played out as a loss and recovery of knightly identity.[4] Iwein's chivalry is indispensable to the action; and this chivalry is meshed into and relativized by the broader social, legal and ethical dimensions of the work. In terms of the presentation of the hero, the work has a threefold dynamic: a sociological dynamic in the transition from bachelor knighthood to married lordship; a legal dynamic in the hero's relation to justice; and a personal, ethical dynamic in that the hero increases in moral awareness and in the sensitivity of his relation to others.

It is perhaps even more true of *Iwein* than of *Erec* that Hartmann is concerned with combat less as a purely military exercise than as an expression of social and ethical values. However, the very proposition of an ethical dynamic in the theme of chivalry in *Iwein* is questionable after recent studies which firmly argue that the work presents an ethical, or even basically amoral, stasis.[5] The discussion of the combat situations in

---

[3] E.g. the wide variety of approaches in Cramer, ' "Sælde und êre" '; Hagenguth, *Hartmanns 'Iwein'*; Thum, 'Politische Probleme'; Mertens, *Laudine*; Schnell, 'Abaelards Gesinnungsethik'.

[4] See above, pp. 214–17.

[5] See Voß, *Artusepik*, pp. 125ff. for the view that Iwein undergoes no ethical development in the romance, and Fischer, *Ehre*, pp. 29ff. for a challenging discussion of Iwein as 'der unmoralische Held'.

*Iwein* and their broader dimensions, which follows in the rest of this chapter, will have to take issue with a far more contentious body of research than was the case with Hartmann's first romance.

## The opening cycle: honour and self-assertion

*Iwein* shares a basic structural similarity with *Erec* in that both romances comprise an opening cycle in which the hero defeats a knightly opponent and wins a wife, then a crisis in the hero, and a second, longer cycle of encounters in which the hero is tested and proven anew. In *Iwein*, as in *Erec*, this dual structure includes an exploration of the nature and function of military chivalry. However, there is an important difference between the two romances in the opening cycle in that in *Iwein* the hero not only defeats but also kills an opponent.

In Hartmann's first romance the hero never killed a knightly opponent in single combat. Rather, after defeating Iders, Guivreiz and Mabona-grin he showed mercy in exchange for the defeated knight's surrender (*sicherheit*), whilst the opponents whom Erec killed were for the most part non-chivalric figures, and the killing took place in self-defence or following the hero's obligation to protect the weak.[6] The opening cycle of *Iwein* presents the new situation of the hero's killing a knight in a combat of his own choosing. This situation has provoked a flood of conflicting interpretations, with scholars using the evaluative termi-nology of knighthood to argue that Iwein is guilty of 'unchivalrous conduct',[7] or that he is still 'the perfect knight' in this episode.[8] The debate continues, with recent contributions adducing new evidence to support the view that Iwein's actions are ethically unquestioned,[9] or to indicate precisely a deficit in the hero at this stage.[10] The controversy has a double interest in our context in that it indicates a lack of agreement about the inner dynamics of one of Hartmann's maturest works, and in a broader sense unsureness about the practical morality of knighthood, as a concept of 'chivalrous' conduct is invoked both by those who see Iwein as an exemplary figure and by those who see him as subject to criticism.

Critics have levelled the legal charges of breach of *triuwe* and even

---

[6]  See also Green, 'Homicide', pp. 19–24.
[7]  Sparnaay, *Hartmann von Aue*, II, p. 48: 'Iwein verstößt [. . .] gegen den ritterlichen Anstand'; Wapnewski, *Hartmann von Aue*, p. 75 sees Iwein's action as being 'gegen alle Regeln ritterlichen Kampfes'; P. Kern, 'Interpretation der Erzählung', p. 342 also speaks of an 'unritterliche Handlungsweise'.
[8]  Le Sage, ' "Âne zuht" or "âne schulde?" ', p. 109.
[9]  Voß, ' "Sunder zuchte" ', passim.
[10]  Schnell, 'Abaelards Gesinnungsethik', pp. 33–39.

murder against Iwein in the opening cycle.[11] These are perhaps the two most serious charges of a secular nature that could be laid against a knight in Hartmann's day, as emerges from the body's comment in Hartmann's *Klage* that he will do anything for his lady's sake save for magic (*zouber*), murder (*mort*) or anything that offends against *triuwe* (Kl 1120f.). No voice inside the text charges Iwein with murder or breach of *triuwe* in this opening cycle. Rather this reading is based on the interpretation of gestures and verbal comments as conveying to the audience critical messages which are not made fully explicit. The legally weighty charges of breach of *triuwe* and murder are based on the manner of Iwein's riding out to the spring, and of his pursuit of his wounded opponent. However, these passages fail to support the critical weight placed on them by some readers.

First, Iwein's journey to the spring has to be seen in the light of the preceding combat between Iwein's cousin Kalogrenant and the lord of the spring, Askalon. Kalogrenant is riding in search of *âventiure*, which he defines solely as the pursuit of personal glory through combat (Iw 527–37). We shall consider Hartmann's attitude towards *âventiure* later.[12] It is sufficient here to say that Kalogrenant's pouring water on the magic stone conjures up a devastating storm – and the anger of the lord of the fountain. Legal concerns are even more evident in combat situations in *Iwein* than they were in *Erec*. This emerges already in the first words spoken by a combatant to his adversary in *Iwein*, as Askalon's reproof of Kalogrenant follows Chrétien's text quite closely (Iw 712–30; Yv 491–506), and also corresponds in its legal thinking and vocabulary exactly with the law of feuding as it was formulated in Germany in Hartmann's day in the constitution against arsonists of 1186.[13] Askalon appeals to the contemporary legal norms of proper feud when he accuses Kalogrenant of being faithless, 'triuwelôs' (Iw 712) for having done him damage without a previous declaration of intent (Iw 713: 'mirn wart von iu niht widerseit') and without grounds (Iw 728: 'âne schulde'). Askalon himself formally declares his intent to attack Kalogrenant by issuing the challenge, the *diffidatio*, which breaks peaceful relations (Iw 720: 'iu sî von mir widersaget'; 729: 'hien sol niht vrides mêre wesen'). So far Askalon appears as a responsible ruler defending the integrity of his lands against unprovoked devastation – the very embodiment of the legal ethic of the contemporary German peace laws. However two features in the ensuing combat detract from this exemplary image.

---

[11] Cramer, ' "Sælde und êre" ', p. 35; Willson, 'Kalogrenant's Curiosity', p. 293; Wapnewski, *Hartmann von Aue*, p. 75.
[12] See below, pp. 259–63.
[13] See Cramer, ' "Sælde und êre" ', p. 35; W.H. Jackson, 'Friedensgesetzgebung', p. 254.

Chrétien has the two knights join combat immediately after Askalon's defiance (Yv 517ff.). Hartmann independently has Kalogrenant first reply to the lord of the spring by averring his innocence (Iw 731: 'mîn unschulde') and trying to win Askalon's favour by peaceful means (Iw 731–33). But Askalon refuses to listen to the plea and promptly attacks (Iw 734ff.). It is as if Askalon were more intent on a passage of arms than on seeing justice done, as if he, like Guivreiz, only in a more aggressive way, were determined to fight even against an unwilling opponent.[14]

The close of the combat points in a similar direction. In the actual feuds of the military aristocracy it was of the utmost importance to secure firm agreements between the parties on the cessation of hostilities. In the more stylized literary world of romance too, a concept of combat emerges in which the victor proves his courtesy by making defeat as honourable as possible for the vanquished, thus integrating knightly combat into broader forms of social interaction.[15] Hartmann attaches great importance to these harmonizing tendencies, for the combats between knights in his works normally end with gestures of peace and reconciliation, which are not merely vague expressions of fraternity, but also have the purpose of preventing, by a formal restoration of peace, a chain of hostilities from developing. This purpose is met when the vanquished gives a promise of surrender and security (*sicherheit*: Er 1014ff., 4447ff., 9377ff; Gr 2181ff.; Iw 3776ff., 7563ff., 7577).[16] After a single combat the accent is on chivalric companionship and mutual honouring (Er 4478–569, 9387–97), after a feud it is on pragmatic considerations of reparation and guarantees of peace (Gr 2178ff.; Iw 3782–84). Askalon's behaviour at the close of the combat with Kalogrenant is neither that of a wise ruler nor that of a courteous knight, and it runs against the ethico-legal norms of Hartmann's combat situations, for he treats the vanquished Kalogrenant with insensitive harshness, does not even speak to his defeated opponent but simply takes his horse as booty (Iw 747–51). Instead of bringing the increase of honour and companionship which followed Erec's combats with Guivreiz and Mabonagrin, Askalon's contemptuous treatment brings Kalogrenant unmitigated shame (Iw 756: 'schame'; 757, 790, 796, 807: 'laster'). Further, and this point would be immediately clear to an audience for whom the rituals of conflict were of practical concern, by declaring an end to the peace between himself and Kalogrenant and then not troubling to effect a reconciliation after his victory, Askalon

---

14  On Guivreiz's attitude see above, pp. 121–23.
15  Haferland, *Höfische Interaktion*, pp. 28ff., 126ff.
16  Hartmann's concern with an ordered end to combats matches a general tendency of the peace mevements, for '[the] rules pertaining to initiation and cessation of hostilities were a crucial factor in the limitation of vendetta' (Bloch, *Medieval French Literature and Law*, p. 113); on *sicherheit* see also Green, 'Homicide', p. 21.

remains in a state of enmity towards Kalogrenant. Askalon has declared war, and instead of then making peace, he has humiliated an unwilling opponent.

The view that Iwein is guilty of a breach of *triuwe* in attacking Askalon rests on the premise that Iwein is legally in the same position as Kalogrenant when he rides to the spring.[17] However, the shame inflicted on Kalogrenant by Askalon means that Iwein is in a different position from Kalogrenant with regard to the contemporary norms of combat. Iwein, unlike Kalogrenant, has legitimate grounds for attacking Askalon. He is exercising his legal right, arguably his duty, to seek retribution for the humiliation of a relative.[18] Iwein himself claims this right publicly (Iw 805–07: 'er sprach "neve Kâlogrenant, / ez richet von rehte mîn hant / swaz dir lasters ist geschehen" '), and Hartmann as narrator comments approvingly that Iwein's reaction is a mark of 'vrümekheit' (Iw 813). Iwein's reaction is in tune with the sense of justice of the contemporary knightly aristocracy, for whom an offence against honour called for retribution (*râche*) and in which aid for a kinsman was a prime duty.[19] Further, Askalon has by his defiance of Kalogrenant broken off his relation of *triuwe* without restoring this relation after the combat.[20] And since Iwein legitimately takes up the (unsettled) cause of a kinsman, it is questionable whether there is need for him to issue a fresh *diffidatio*.[21] Iwein and Askalon are indeed in a position comparable to that of Parzival and Orilus who, in Wolfram's work, attack each other without a *diffidatio* 'because they were not bound by *triuwe*' (*Parzival* 262,16f: 'newederhalp wart widersagt; / si wârn doch ledec ir triuwe'). A major purpose of the three days' advance *diffidatio* in legislation on feuding was to prevent treacherous surprise attacks. But there is no question of Iwein's attempting a treacherous surprise attack on Askalon; rather he seeks open combat. Indeed there is too much that is positive or neutral in terms of contemporary aristocratic norms in Hartmann's account of the circumstances leading up to the combat to justify the grave charge of breach of *triuwe* laid against Iwein by some modern critics, but by no-one in the text, for his conduct at this stage.

The combat itself between Iwein and Askalon is described by the narrator (and knight) Hartmann in laudatory terms as one fit for the eyes of God himself (Iw 1020–22). Nevertheless a vigorous strand of

17   Cramer, ' "Sælde und êre" ', p. 35.
18   See also Wiehl, *Redeszene*, p. 254.
19   Brunner, *Land und Herrschaft*, pp. 23, 57.
20   As Brunner points out (*Land und Herrschaft*, pp. 73f.), the issuing of a *diffidatio* suspends relations of law and *triuwe/fides* between the two parties. Hence the importance of formal peace agreements after any passage of arms, in order to restore the framework of law and morality.
21   See also Mertens, *Laudine*, p. 48.

Hartmann scholarship sees criticism of Iwein in the manner of his pursuit of his wounded opponent. First, the narrator's comment that Iwein pursued Askalon 'âne zuht' (Iw 1056) has been taken to imply that the pursuit is a violation of 'knightly propriety'.[22] The expression 'âne zuht' does not occur elsewhere in Hartmann's works. However, comparative studies have shown that this phrase does not necessarily have a moral connotation, that it is applied by other authors to actions, including pursuits in combat situations, without moral condemnation, in the sense of 'at full pelt', 'without reserve'.[23] Second, Iwein is accused of a crime ('Rechtsbruch') in striking at his fleeing opponent from behind (Iw 1105f.). According to this view such a blow 'violates the rules of international knightly combat and is of course forbidden'.[24] This assessment springs from too rigid, undifferentiated and anachronistic a view of what constituted 'chivalrous' conduct around 1200. There was not, at this time, a fixed and codified set of international rules whereby knights fought out their combats. Rather there were different norms operating and developing in the various fields of tournaments, jousts and serious warfare. The only support that Matthias adduces for the view that Iwein's blow from behind is a 'Rechtsbruch' is Niedner's comment that such attacks from the rear were against tournament etiquette.[25] However, Iwein and Askalon are enemies engaged in serious combat (Iw 1003: 'vîent'; 1011: 'grôz ernest unde zorn'), and neither the knight Hartmann nor his implied audience would have judged the legitimacy of a blow in serious combat by reference to the norms of the tournament. Since Askalon is fleeing, Iwein has no choice but to strike from behind or to forgo the legitimate fruits of victory. In serious combat it is for the vanquished to offer surrender (which would have amply contented Iwein), not for the victor to hold back in pursuit. Thus illustrations of single knightly combat between figures of virtue and figures of vice in manuscripts of *Der wälsche Gast* show the virtuous knight clearly attacking his vicious, and fleeing, opponent from behind.[26] In short, neither the narrative action in *Iwein* nor the external evidence of contemporary combat norms justify the labelling of Iwein's final blow as a criminal act.

Nor is the manner of Iwein's killing Askalon such as to justify the charge of murder according to the legal norms of Hartmann's day. From

---

[22]  See Sparnaay, *Hartmann von Aue*, II, p. 48; Wapnewski, *Hartmann von Aue*, p. 75; compare Gottzmann, *Deutsche Artusdichtung*, p. 115.
[23]  Salmon, ' "Âne zuht" ', pp. 559f; Le Sage, ' "Ane zuht" or "âne schulde?" ', pp. 105–09; Voß, ' "Sunder zuchte" ', passim.
[24]  Matthias, 'Yvains Rechtsbrüche', p. 157.
[25]  Niedner, *Das deutsche Turnier*, p. 42: 'Vor allem durfte man natürlich nicht von hinten auf den gegner stechen'.
[26]  See the thirteenth-century illustrations reproduced in F.W. von Kries (ed.), *Thomasin von Zerclaere: Der welsche Gast*, IV, p. 12, nos 5, 6, 7, 8.

the Germanic period onwards, and throughout the Middle Ages, legal sources and the living sense of right of the military aristocracy continued to distinguish between honourable killing and murder.[27] Originally, secrecy was the essential characteristic of murder. Later, more general considerations of treacherous behaviour emerged as criteria. The ancient distinction between honourable and dishonourable killing was preserved in the peace laws of the twelfth and thirteenth centuries, and even the Latin text of peaces of 1221 and 1224 uses the German word 'mord' to designate secret and therefore particularly culpable homicide.[28] In the peace of 1224 any killing or wounding with a knife is treated as 'mord'.[29] Presumably the authorities were widening the concept of murder in an attempt to exercise tighter control. Murder, like breach of *triuwe*, brought forfeiture of honour and legal status – the murderer was 'erenlos' and 'rehtlos'.[30] Hartmann's use of the terms *mort* (Er 6109; Kl 1120; Iw 6686) and *mordære* (Er 5443; Gr 99) indicates that he was familiar with murder as a special category of homicide. But although narrator and characters within the action repeatedly refer to Iwein's 'slaying' Askalon, using the verb *erslagen* (Iw 1122, 1159, 1228, 1357, 1399, 2065, 2088, 2095, 2275, 2317, 2323), the term *mort* is never applied to his action, not even when Askalon's widow Laudine, and later Lunete, hurl abuse at Iwein (Iw 1389–402, 3111–96). There is no indication in the text that Iwein attacks Askalon in a dishonourable, treacherous, secret manner. Askalon himself issues a challenge by 'greeting' Iwein as one enemy should greet another (Iw 1003: 'als vîent sînen vîent sol'), thus confirming an open enmity between the two which clearly sets the combat, fought as it is with knightly arms between two willing parties, apart from the realm of murder.

However, if the charges of murder and breach of *triuwe* seem ill-founded, this is not to say that Iwein is presented in an unquestioningly idealizing light in the opening cycle. In order to understand Iwein's moral status better, we need to look more closely at the theme of insult and honour, and into the inner life of Iwein's thoughts and feelings.

A major concern of the opening cycle of *Iwein* is to show the danger of mockery and insult. This theme provides a sharp insight into the mentality and the practical morality of aristocratic society, as indeed the part bantering, part mocking exchanges at Arthur's court around Kalogrenant's story, for all their literary stylization, also reflect forms of social exchange and interpersonal tensions (the interplay of competitive-

[27] Schröder and Künßberg, *Lehrbuch der deutschen Rechtsgeschichte*, pp. 80, 384, 837; Grimm, *Deutsche Rechtsaltertümer*, II, pp. 179–84.
[28] MGH Const., II, no. 280, c. 9 (p. 395) and no. 284, c. 9 (p. 400): 'Qui alium clam occiderit, quod mord dicitur'.
[29] MGH Const., II, no. 284, c. 11 (p. 400).
[30] MGH Const., II, no. 196, c. 24 (p. 246).

ness and comradeship) in the actual lordly retinues of the day. Hartmann shows a strong interest in this matter of insult and mockery, criticizing it as an abuse to be avoided, particularly amongst knights, and this in passages independent of Chrétien. Thus Erec reproves Count Galoain: 'daz ir scheltet einen man, / der ie ritters namen gewan' (Er 4200f.), and Iwein asserts: 'ichn sol kein rîter schelten' (Iw 4969). Wolfram points in the same direction when he has Gawein assert that mockery, 'spot', is incompatible with true chivalry (*Parzival* 612,4–20). It is not merely a general conception of politeness that underlies this pattern, but particularly the threat of violence that could easily result from the trading of insults amongst men who were quick to the sword. Iwein's phrase 'ichn sol kein rîter schelten' corresponds closely to the code of military discipline issued for the imperial army on the Italian campaign of 1158, where it is a punishable offence 'if one knight has insulted another knight'.[31] No direct link between this code and *Iwein* is suggested; however, the similarity of wording indicates that some of the civilized forms of behaviour which characterize courtly literature may derive not only from the social discourse with women which is claimed to have had a refining effect on manners, but also from the need to maintain discipline amongst warriors.

The abuse of *schelten* and *spot* is thematized and subject to explicit criticism in the opening cycle of *Iwein* in the figure of Keii. Keii embodies the spirit of envy, mockery and insult in Hartmann's romances.[32] He habitually seeks to diminish rather than to increase the honour of others (Iw 108–12, 137–50, 231–41). His mockery of Iwein's intention to avenge his cousin's shame (Iw 810–36) rings on in Iwein's mind during his combat with Askalon (Iw 1062–71). And Iwein's victory over Keii in his first defence of the spring is presented as a fitting punishment for Keii's 'ungevüegez schelten' and his 'tägelichen spot' (Iw 2562f.). Iwein's treatment of his defeated opponent also contrasts favourably with that of his predecessor as lord of the spring with regard to the norms of combat, for whereas Askalon insultingly disdained to speak to the defeated Kalogrenant and took his horse as booty (Iw 747–51), Iwein pays Keii no shame (Iw 2588: 'dehein unêre') other than to tease him for his defeat (Iw 2589–600), and he immediately hands Keii's mount back to Arthur (Iw 2601–08). Iwein thus appears as a knight who inflicts neither more shame nor more material damage on a defeated opponent, even the rascally Keii, than is appropriate to the situation.

But if Iwein's actions seem beyond legitimate reproach in his combats with Askalon and Keii, a more differentiated view emerges in the

---

[31] Otto of Freising and Rahewin, *Gesta Frederici*, III, 31, p. 460: 'Si miles militi convitia dixerit'.
[32] On Hartmann's portrayal of Keii see Haupt, *Der Truchseß Keie*, pp. 33–46.

narrator's recording of Iwein's thoughts. Recent work has drawn
attention to the importance attached to subjective intentions in the
ethical evaluation of behaviour in *Iwein*.[33] This line of interpretation can
throw further light on the ethical dynamics of the opening cycle. We
have seen that Iwein's combat against Askalon is legitimate according to
the sense of justice of the contemporary secular aristocracy, as an act of
retribution for an injury done to the honour of a kinsman. Iwein himself
publicly states this legal ground when he announces his intention to
avenge his cousin's shame 'by right' (Iw 805–07). He also publicly states
that he is not moved by Keii's mockery (Iw 856–78). In his public
utterances Iwein thus appears as a man eager to defend the honour of
his kin, and not troubled by Keii's scorn. However, a different emphasis
emerges in Hartmann's rendering of Iwein's private thoughts. When
Iwein rides out he thinks only of securing the combat for himself, and
the narrator comments on his desire to acquire *êre* (Iw 911–49). Also, in
pursuing Askalon, Iwein thinks only of Keii's mockery and of the need
to win a visible proof of victory to secure his *êre* at court (Iw 1062–71). On
both these occasions Chrétien also refers to the desire to avenge his
cousin's shame as a factor in Yvain's motivation (Yv 747–49, 896f.). On
each occasion, Hartmann drops this concern for another person's
shame, which is an ethically legitimizing factor, from his account of
Iwein's thoughts and intensifies Iwein's concern with his own reputation and his own status in the Arthurian company.

It is Iwein's private thoughts rather than his public words or his
military actions which suggest after all some distance of the author/
narrator from his character in the opening cycle. Or at best these
thoughts show that Iwein's chivalry is here ethically narrower, more
proprietorial (Iw 913: 'mîn rîterschaft'), more self-concerned than it will
be later in the romance. Indeed, if the charges of breach of *triuwe*, and
murder, import far too heavy a censure on Iwein, the view that the rest
of the romance represents no ethical progress over the opening cycle[34]
underestimates the dynamism and the sensitivity of Hartmann's
romance. Iwein is something of a mixed character in this opening cycle.
He shows signs of an essential goodness, for instance when he alone
greets Lunete at Arthur's court (Iw 1194f.). Thus there is no reason to
question the reliability of the narrator's reference to his 'grôziu triuwe'
(Iw 3210) even after he has overstayed his leave from Laudine.
However, Iwein's chivalry in the opening cycle also shows a certain
impetuosity, and a degree of concern for his reputation, which are
psychologically authentic traits, but which leave some room for ethical
doubt. Iwein's experience of love exhibits a similar impetuosity and is

33   Borck, 'Über Ehre', p. 5; more fully Schnell, 'Abaelards Gesinnungsethik', passim.
34   See Voß, *Artusepik*, pp. 125–32; Fischer, *Ehre*, pp. 112–19.

recorded by the narrator with a similar note of detachment, as Hartmann tells how love 'turned Iwein's senses' (Iw 1336: 'verkêrten die sinne'; compare Iw 1519–21) and how he is so preoccupied with Laudine's beauty that he merely feigns concern for the grief of her retinue (Iw 1431–45).

Further, Iwein's concern with his own reputation in the opening cycle links up with his overstaying his leave from Laudine, for it is the acquisition of glory (Iw 3048: 'prîs') in tournaments that will keep him away from his duties as husband and ruler and precipitate Lunete's morally excessively ferocious but emotionally understandable questioning of his integrity (Iw 3111–96). With regard to Iwein's personality, this degree of self-concern can be seen as an accidental feature which has to be modified so that his essential goodness can emerge unmixed.[35] In terms of the social ideology of the romance, Iwein's thoughts and actions in the opening cycle show him embedded in the value-system of the Arthurian world, the value-system of bachelor knighthood. Indeed the note of detachment in the narrator's presentation of Iwein in this part of the romance suggests not so much Hartmann's reservations about Iwein as a person, but rather a certain distance of the author from this value-system, a topic we shall take up in discussing Hartmann's attitude towards *âventiure*. Seen from this point of view, the sociological theme of transition from bachelor knighthood to married lordship interacts closely with the ethical theme of progress from chivalry which is based more on self-assertion and the pursuit of *êre* to chivalry as defence of justice and aid for those in need.

*The main cycle: justice and moral reflection*

In *Iwein* as in *Erec* the hero's journey of rehabilitation is in part a mirror image of his lapse. Erec's lapse was to spend too long in bed with his wife. Consequently he met and defeated embodiments of false love in restoring himself. Iwein's failure to return to Laudine by the appointed day involves neglect of a woman, neglect of his duty as a ruler over lands, and neglect of a legally binding promise involving a deadline. Consequently on his journey of rehabilitation Iwein meets and defeats opponents who threaten the security of women and lands, he fights in defence of justice, and he demonstrates his awareness of the importance of keeping pledges. Every one of the six combats in which Iwein is involved after the restoration of his knightly identity (Iw 3596: 'dô wart er einem rîter glîch') is a rescue act of some kind. Further, the concerns

---

[35]  For a view of Hartmann's presentation of character in terms of 'essence' and 'accident' see T.R. Jackson, 'Paradoxes of Person', pp. 294–99.

of the peace laws are even more pervasive in Iwein's than in Erec's journey of rehabilitation.

From the opening cycle of *Iwein* onwards, Hartmann attaches even more (or even more explicit) importance to the theme of peace-keeping than Chrétien does. In a passage that is quite independent of Chrétien, Hartmann has the widowed Laudine reflect on the absolute need to find a suitable man to secure the peace of her kingdom (Iw 1899–916). Her concern is well founded in the narrative by the nuisance of the spring's devastating effects, which call for a valiant protector. Her thoughts also match the primacy placed on the establishment of peace by the ruler in Hohenstaufen sources, and they echo Hartmann's own accounts of the assumption of secular lordship in *Erec* and in *Gregorius* – just as it was customary for Hohenstaufen rulers to declare a peace at the beginning of their rule, so Erec, Gregorius and Laudine all immediately seek to secure *vride* when they assume the responsibility of rule.[36] The use of force to establish peace was the essential military adjunct to legislative acts of peace in the historical reality of the twelfth and thirteenth centuries. In the fictional world of *Iwein*, the spring has to be defended by force. Iwein's failure to return to Laudine's realm on time calls into question his reliability as protector. He then has to demonstrate this reliability during his journey of rehabilitation, which he does by defeating peace-breakers. Indeed this entire journey is geared towards the defence of peace (in the sense of order and security) and justice which were also the central concerns of the *Landfrieden* in the Germany of Hartmann's day.[37]

Already Iwein's first military encounter after his healing is with a peace-breaker, Count Aliers, who is oppressing the lady of Narison. It is typical of a broader touch of realism in the portrayal of military life in *Iwein* than in *Erec* that the Aliers episode is not a stylized, literary single combat, but echoes the feuding warfare that was endemic in Germany, for Aliers has devastated the lady's lands (Iw 3781: 'und ir verwüestet hete ir lant') with his army (Iw 3705: 'mit her'). Such warfare was a particular nuisance in Hartmann's familiar Swabia, which suffered perhaps the least peaceful conditions of any area of the German empire in the twelfth and thirteenth centuries, and where the Landfrieden had particularly sharp relevance.[38] In Hartmann's own time, perhaps whilst he was working on *Iwein*, Berthold V of Zähringen was in feud with the Hohenstaufen Duke Conrad, the feud ending with Conrad's violent

---

[36] Er 10083f.: 'hie sazte er sô sîn lant / daz ez vridelîchen stuont'; Gr 2263–67: 'Sîn lant und sîne marke / die bevridete er alsô starke, / swer si mit arge ruorte / daz er den zevuorte / der êren und des guotes'; compare Iw 1904–16, where Laudine expresses her desire to secure peace in her lands (1905, 1910: 'bevriden'; 1915: 'guoten vride'). In each of these three works Hartmann proceeds independently of his source to introduce the concept of the ruler's securing peace.

[37] See also Thum, 'Politische Probleme', pp. 56–59.

[38] Thum, 'Politische Probleme', p. 60.

death in August 1196.[39] Iwein's handing over the defeated Aliers into the captivity of the lady of Narison, to whom Aliers then gives hostages and securities in order to pledge reparation for the damage done to her and to restore peaceful relations (Iw 3776–84), is in line with contemporary practice in the settlement of feuds.

Iwein's next encounter, which involves a dragon and a lion, takes us into the realm of animal symbolism and will be considered later.[40] The theme of violation of the peace is developed in a clearly brutal direction in Iwein's third encounter, his defeat of the giant Harpin. Harpin has devastated and burned an unnamed lord's lands (Iw 5842: 'verwüestet und verbrant'), and taken the lord's six sons captive, hanging two of them before their father's eyes (Iw 4471–81), all for no good cause, but merely because the lord has refused the giant his daughter (Iw 4463–73). Harpin's actions violently breach the peace laws which sought to combat feuds that lacked good grounds, to limit the despoliation of lands and to prevent the holding of captives (let alone hanging them) as a means of forcing ransom.[41] Harpin is uneasily placed on the edge of the aristocratic world. His only weapon is a bar (Iw 5022: 'stange'), an unchivalric weapon which is characteristic of giants, but Iwein also addresses him as a 'rîter' (Iw 4969). A contemporary audience would doubtless see in this figure a criticism of the worst violence of the sword-bearing class, here discreetly attributed to a non-courtly figure, and Iwein's killing of Harpin is explicitly seen as an act of aid (Iw 4511: 'helfe unde rât') and deliverance (Iw 4519: 'belôste') and as a defence of justice (Iw 4963: 'iuwer reht') in which those involved call on God's aid (Iw 4853–68, 4889, 5014–16).

The fourth encounter in the series of combats develops the theme of justice, for it is a formal, public judicial combat in which Iwein champions Lunete and is confident that he will be aided by God and her innocence (Iw 5169: 'got und ir unschulde') in defeating her accusers. Iwein's victory rescues Lunete from death. This theme of deliverance is treated in hyperbolic fashion in Iwein's fifth encounter, a combat against two giants which brings about the release of 300 women from captivity and forced labour (Iw 6186–220, 6835–66). Finally, Iwein's last combat relates to justice, a woman and lands, as Iwein champions a younger sister who is threatened with the loss of her rightful inheritance. We shall return to this judicial combat later.[42]

The leitmotif of Iwein's combats in the opening cycle was honour, *êre*. Honour remains a valid concern in the main cycle. For instance Iwein

---

[39] Heyck, *Geschichte der Herzöge von Zähringen*, pp. 441f.; see also below, p. 280.
[40] See below, pp. 248f.
[41] See above, pp. 90f.
[42] See below, pp. 263–70.

sees his *êre* at risk when he faces a seemingly irreconcilable conflict of
obligations (Iw 4870–88), and the narrator comments approvingly on
Iwein's and Gawein's striving for *êre* in terms reminiscent of the
advocacy of chivalric effort in *Erec* and *Gregorius* (Iw 7171–83).[43] This
continuing affirmation of honour should warn us against interpreting
the ethical view of chivalry in the later parts of *Iwein* too simply as a
purely self-denying altruism. But it is even more misleading to go to the
opposite extreme by denying any ethical progression in Iwein's chivalry
and seeing his combats solely as forms of self-glorification throughout
the work.[44] For the self-assertive pursuit of *êre* is no longer anywhere
near as important a factor in the circumstances of the combats and in
Iwein's inner thoughts in the second cycle as it was in the first; rather
the leitmotifs of the combats in the second cycle are now concerned with
service (Iw 3856, 4868, 4910, 5104, 5121, 6002: *dienest/dienen*), aid (Iw
3418, 3847, 3849, 3864, 4313, 4798, 4904, 5091, 5919, 5985: *helfe/helfen*)
and rescue and release (Iw 4227, 5162, 5356, 5835, 6371, 6862: *lœsen/
erlœsen*), that is to say the accent shifts to the knight's helping others.

The shift in the objective framework of Iwein's combats has an inner
correlative in the presentation of the hero's inner life in the main cycle,
for Iwein now exhibits a wider and more nuanced range of moral and
emotional experience than he did in the opening cycle.

The second encounter of Iwein's journey of rehabilitation, his aid for a
lion struggling against a dragon, clearly signals a moral interpretation of
his chivalry. With this episode, and the ensuing friendship between
Iwein and the lion, the knightly romance absorbs features of animal
fable and the bestiary – both genres, incidentally, which were cultivated
in clerical literature, so that yet again Hartmann's work draws on and
intermingles the cultural worlds of secular aristocracy and clerical
learning. The educated members of Hartmann's audience would
recognize a morally symbolic potential in the very situation of a conflict
between lion and dragon, and Hartmann, perhaps with an eye to those
who might not grasp the objective symbolism of the conflict, makes its
morally symbolic quality evident. Iwein's following the sound of the
lion's roars of pain (Iw 3828–45) echoes Erec's following the cries of the
captive knight's companion (Er 5296–319) – a situation which, as we
have seen, marked an important reorientation in Erec's practice of
arms.[45] Hartmann also marks the moral importance of the situation in
*Iwein* by having the hero pause in indecision (Iw 3846: 'zwîvel') and

[43] E.g. the criticism of 'verlegeniu müezekheit' (Iw 7171) echoes the motif of *verligen* in
*Erec* (Er 2971, 10123) and *Gregorius* (Gr 1683), and the praise of effort expended in pursuit
of honour (Iw 7213: 'arbeit umb êre') echoes the young Gregorius's readiness to embrace
'arbeit' in order to win 'guot und êre' (Gr 1714–20).
[44] As does Fischer, *Ehre*, pp. 104–39.
[45] See above, p. 113.

reflect (Iw 3848: 'bedâhte sich') before deciding to aid the 'noble animal' (Iw 3849: 'dem edelen tiere'). A moral choice is being exercised here on the basis of reflection, and Iwein's aid for the 'noble animal' indicates a fundamentally ethical orientation in his use of arms.[46]

From now on Iwein's chivalry is associated with the qualities of his companion, the lion. The description of the lion as the 'noble' animal alerts the audience to the broad range of positive qualities traditionally attached to the lion, and which now become associated with Iwein. Iwein himself sees the lion as an exemplar of 'rehtiu triuwe' (Iw 4005). The legal dimension of Iwein's combats matches the lion's function as an emblem of justice.[47] Both dragon and lion were emblems of military power in aristocratic society, hence their popularity as heraldic devices. But the lion commonly combined power with precisely those 'chivalrous' qualities which Iwein demonstrates in the later part of the romance: 'It was credited not only with great courage, power and resolution, but with a slowness to anger and a noble compassion, killing only when hungry, sparing the prostrate and allowing any prisoners it encountered to go home unscathed'.[48] Seen in the light of these attributes, Iwein's rescuing the lion by killing the dragon encapsulates, in an emblematic situation, a central ethical dynamic of Hartmann's literary treatment of chivalry – rejection of the unchecked militarism which was symbolized in the dragon, and cultivation of the qualities which were traditionally associated with the lion. Furthermore, these qualities of justice, power, compassion, and merciful treatment of the vanquished, which were attributed to the lion, were also features of the ideal ruler, as expressed for instance in the figure of the Great King in *Ruodlieb*, so that the association of Iwein with the lion suggests again the indebtedness of chivalric ethics to ideals of kingship.

The ethical orientation of Iwein's chivalry merges with emotional experience in the theme of compassion, identification with the suffering of others. As has often been observed, Iwein shows more pity for the suffering of others in the later parts of the romance than in the opening cycle.[49] On this point too, Iwein exhibits a quality attributed to the lion in

---

[46]  See also Linke, *Epische Strukturen*, p. 150; P. Kern, 'Interpretation der Erzählung', p. 346. Fischer scornfully dismisses Linke's interpretation as misplaced moral Kantianism (*Ehre*, pp. 61–66). However, whilst some of Linke's formulations do shift Hartmann too close to the idealist thinking of the late eighteenth century, Fischer's attack on Linke, as Robertshaw observes ('Ambiguity and Morality', p. 124), 'is entertaining, but it serves mainly to camouflage the gap in his own argument', for Fischer himself declines to offer an interpretation of Iwein's fight with the dragon.

[47]  See Fr. Ohly, 'Vom geistigen Sinn des Wortes', pp. 18f.; for further interpretations of the lion in *Iwein* see Lewis, *Symbolism*, pp. 70–82.

[48]  Payne, *Medieval Beasts*, p. 19; on the dragon see ibid., p. 82.

[49]  See e.g. P. Kern, 'Interpretation der Erzählung', pp. 352–54; Selbmann, 'Struktur-schema', p. 67; Kraft, *Iweins Triuwe*, pp. 127ff.; Sieverding, *Der ritterliche Kampf*, p. 155.

the bestiary tradition. The sense of being moved by the suffering of others is a recurrent feature of Iwein's inner life and a spur to combat and aid after his rescue of the lion (Iw 4740f.: 'nû erbarmet diz sêre / den rîter der des lewen pflac'; compare 4507–09, 4853–60, 4932f., 5163–65, 6009–12, 6407–16), and this emotional and moral experience of suffering opens up another large-scale pattern in the text. In a narrator comment which Hartmann adds independently of Chrétien he states that a personal experience of suffering leads to a greater understanding of the suffering of others (Iw 4389–92). This concept of the experiential value of deep suffering underlies all Hartmann's narrative works. Indeed the basic pattern of initial success – crisis – rehabilitation, which is common to all these works, is not a merely abstract moral scheme, but a working out of this experiential insight. If Iwein shows more compassion in the second cycle of the romance, this is in part because he has been shocked by his own experience of crisis into a greater feeling for the suffering of others. Paradoxically the hero's lapse, by forcing him to experience the anguish of failure and rejection, also makes possible a greater moral and emotional insight.

The second cycle of the romance, after the catastrophe of Lunete's indictment and Iwein's breakdown, is further characterized by a heightened consciousness, a greater mental reflectiveness and self-awareness in the hero. In the opening cycle Iwein seemed to rush rather automatically into actions in order to secure his reputation amongst those immediately around him, whereas the combats he undertakes in the later part of the romance involve more conscious deliberation and mental discernment, 'eine neue Dimension von Bewußtsein'.[50] Already in Erec Hartmann enlarged the area of the hero's subjectivity in adapting Chrétien,[51] and he develops this tendency further in Iwein, expanding the dimension of subjective consciousness in his account of Iwein's rehabilitation. A compositional expression of this heightened consciousness is the use of monologue. Hartmann's expansion of monologue, including the direct recital of inner thoughts, is his most marked quantifiable departure from Chrétien in the handling of direct speech in Iwein.[52] This stylistic shift produces a greater sense of reflectiveness in Iwein, which in turn gives Hartmann's presentation of knighthood a more introspective quality than is the case in Chrétien's work. Moreover, just as Hartmann articulated the ethos on which Iwein's chivalry was based in the opening cycle in a newly composed monologue immediately after his awakening (Iw 3509–93),[53] so the more

[50] Hahn, 'güete und wizzen', p. 203; see also Kraft, Iweins Triuwe, pp. 175, 181; Schnell, 'Abaelards Gesinnungsethik', pp. 32–36.
[51] See above, pp. 119f., 124f.
[52] Wiehl, Redeszene, pp. 78, 208f.
[53] See above, pp. 214–17.

complex make-up of his chivalry in the later stages of the romance is expressed in another monologue which is entirely Hartmann's creation (Iw 4870–913).

These two monologues again encapsulate an ethical dynamic of chivalry, this time as direct expressions of the hero's own understanding of his practice of arms, the first monologue looking back to an unreflecting, self-assertive pursuit of success which, in the grey dawn of Iwein's awakening, has acquired the illusory quality of a dream (Iw 3513: 'troum'), and the second expressing the ethically and emotionally more complex, more discriminating qualities which Iwein's chivalry exhibits after his rescue of the lion. As in the meeting with the lion and the dragon, it is a question of choice as to which of two parties to help that prompts this second monologue; and because the two parties now have equal moral claims, Iwein is faced with a true dilemma which forces a broad-ranging reflection on his situation and his values. In this second inner monologue Iwein remains concerned with his own honour (Iw 4875: 'mîn êre'), concerned not to appear a coward (Iw 4911–13). This is not the voice of total self-denial. But he is also moved by pity for the suffering of others (Iw 4905f.), he is ethically aware, anxious not to break his 'triuwe' (Iw 4902), eager to help (Iw 4904: 'helfe') and to serve (Iw 4910: 'ze dienste'), anxious to do what is right (Iw 4892: 'so daz ich rehte gevâr'). Such ethical pondering, like Iwein's desire to help the lion, has a paradigmatic quality, suggesting again the need for thought, for deliberation in the knight's use of force.

There is a paradigmatic quality too in Iwein's turning to God for good counsel in his dilemma (Iw 4889). God did not figure at all in Iwein's first inner monologue after his awakening. When he looked back over his former success, his thoughts remained entirely in the secular sphere of honour and social status (Iw 3509–83). But during Iwein's later encounters of aid and compassion Hartmann modifies Chrétien to make more frequent reference to God, placing Iwein's chivalry, in his companionship with the lion, under God's protection.[54] The reference to a metaphysical dimension suggests a continuing view of knighthood in *Iwein* as being, if properly conducted, a way of life pleasing to God. This echoes Hartmann's tendency of adaptation in *Erec*, albeit with the difference of tone that the divine guidance of the knight is presented in *Erec* with a confident, biblical ring as the narrator refers to David and Goliath (Er 5558–68), whilst the piety of *Iwein* is more personal and

---

[54] See the detailed discussion of references to God in the later stages of *Iwein* in Sieverding, *Der ritterliche Kampf*, pp. 140–56. Sieverding concludes that God appears more clearly in Hartmann than in Chrétien as the hero-knight's protector, and that Iwein appears more often in Hartmann's than in Chrétien's romance as the implementer of God's will.

reflective, and the narrator seems more restrained, less euphoric in claiming a metaphysical sanction for knighthood.

With regard to the military encounters themselves, the motif of devastation of lands (Iw 716–19, 3781, 5842) and the conflict between two armies (Iw 3703–84) bring more of the real world of feud warfare into *Iwein* than was present in *Erec*. However, in his account of actual passages of arms, Hartmann goes even further in *Iwein* with the tendency of adaptation we saw in *Erec*, which is to reduce the violence and the gory detail of Chrétien's descriptions. Throughout *Iwein*, as in *Erec*, Hartmann shows a remarkable reluctance to refer to blood shed by knightly weapons and to evoke wounds in any anatomical detail. What Hartmann effects is a stylistic debrutalization of combat.

The tendency is evident as early as the combat between Iwein and Askalon. Chrétien tells us that both knights lose much blood (Yv 844), that Esclados's brain and blood pour out onto his hauberk (Yv 869), and that Yvain can hear the groans of his mortally wounded opponent (Yv 888f.). Hartmann has none of this painful detail, and never even refers to blood in his account of this combat.[55] The combats in the rest of the narrative show a similar pattern. In the battle against Aliers, Chrétien tells of an enemy's back being broken by the force of Yvain's charge (Yv 3161), of Yvain's lance and sword being covered with blood (Yv 3214f.) and of the horses of fleeing knights being disembowelled (Yv 3267). Similarly Harpin's blood wets Yvain's lance 'like sauce' (Yv 4202); the seneschal in his death throes writhes in the stream of 'warm, crimson blood' (Yv 4536f.); in the combat between Yvain and Gauvain 'boiling hot' blood flows (Yv 6210–12), and the sword which Yvain throws away on learning his opponent's identity is 'covered with blood' (Yv 6272). Hartmann does not take up any of these violent details or references to blood, nor does he compensate for this by adding new gory details. Rather Hartmann's combat descriptions remain more anodyne than Chrétien's in an almost literal sense. Hartmann shows a particular fastidiousness in relating – or not relating – the hero to bloodshed. The term 'blood', as noun or verb (*bluot, bluoten*) appears only six times in *Iwein*. Each of these six occurrences is based directly on Chrétien, none is an independent product of Hartmann's imagination, and most are functional to the action. The bleeding of Askalon's corpse (Yv 1177–98; Iw 1360–64) spurs Laudine's retinue to search for Yvain. When Chrétien and Hartmann tell of the lion drinking the blood of a deer (Yv 3448; Iw 3899) it is a beast that draws blood, and Hartmann interestingly adds the independent comment that to suck blood like this would have been no good thing for the lion's human master (Iw 3900) – even in contact with the animal world Hartmann is at pains to keep his hero's hands free of

55   See also Le Sage, ' "Âne zuht" or "âne schulde?" ', p. 107.

blood. The blood that flows from Iwein's wound when he falls on his sword has a motivational function in prompting the faithful lion to believe that Iwein is dead (Yv 3496–3507; Iw 3944–52). The reference to the bleeding wounds inflicted on captive knights by the scourge of a giant's dwarf (Yv 4109, Iw 4926) follows the patterns we saw in *Erec*, with Hartmann omitting references to bloodshed in knightly combat, but more ready to speak of non-knightly figures shedding blood. Finally Hartmann follows Chrétien to refer to bloodstains caused by the combatants beating at each other's helms in the combat between Iwein and Gawein (Yv 6128f.; Iw 7230f.). This is the only occurrence of the word 'blood' in a combat description in Hartmann's *Iwein*. The fact that this reference applies equally to both combatants blocks out the possibility of the reader's constructing an aggressor – victim relation; and as if this were not enough to debrutalize this reference to bloodshed, Hartmann carefully adds that the wounds inflicted were no threat to life (Iw 7234: 'die niht ze verhe engiengen'). It is a remarkable trait that, despite strong leads from Chrétien, Hartmann never refers to bloodstained swords or lances in *Iwein*. Here again one senses an ideological motivation behind the stylistic fastidiousness, a legitimatory attitude towards the main symbols of chivalry which conditions the imagination and the selecting processes of the author and knight Hartmann.

The debrutalization of combat is only one aspect of a broader pattern in the portrayal of social interaction in Hartmann's *Iwein*. In a recent study of courtly forms in German narrative and didactic literature around 1200, Harald Haferland usefully defines 'courtly society' neither in purely abstract, moral terms, nor in purely institutional terms, but as a flexible configuration of forms of interaction which show the interplay of agonal and reciprocal structures in the individual's relation to the world around him.[56] The agonal dimension involves the competitive pursuit of honour and praise, and is evident above all in public combats. The reciprocal dimension of courtly interaction is the network of mutuality and acknowledgement between individuals which is expressed in greetings, hospitality, friendship, conciliation, requests, expressions of gratitude and other forms of politeness and obligation which form a basic tone of courtly narrative, and which receive a didactic expression with a view to real life in Thomasin von Zerklaere's book of manners. The forms of expression of this network of reciprocity have their roots to a large extent in the older feudal relation between lord and vassal which, in courtly society, was taken beyond its original, pragmatic context and extended in ever finer modulations to condition the behaviour of persons who were not bound to each other by actual

---

56   Haferland, *Höfische Interaktion*, pp. 28ff.

legal ties.[57] In passing from the sphere of feudal loyalty to that of courtly interaction the pattern of reciprocity thus broadened out from a predominantly utilitarian, military and material function to create a more generalized and finely modulated set of social relations. In addition to this source in feudal ties, interaction between persons in courtly literature also shows the impact of specifically Christian values, not least in an ethical concept of the *militia* and in the ethical and emotional themes of compassion and a more or less penitential introspection.

It was in the framework of this more generalized concept of reciprocity and these Christian values (perhaps also with some input from classical, Roman ethics) that the early medieval warrior gave place, in the literature of the twelfth century, to the new cultural model of chivalry, which can no longer adequately be described by reference solely to military values or to the relationship between lord and vassal, but which presupposes (and furthers) a broader concept of social and moral relations. It is important for an understanding of the social texture of Hartmann's works and his concept of chivalry that, of all the German authors of the period, precisely Hartmann tends to accentuate reciprocal forms in his romances. Already Chrétien's *Yvain* warns against an excessive concern with the competitive pursuit of glory in tournaments and shows the hero rehabilitating himself by entering into and meeting obligations towards other people in the second cycle of the romance. Hartmann preserves this basic pattern, and he also intensifies and enlarges the sphere of reciprocity, the network of fine modulations in relationships between people in adapting Chrétien's *Yvain* – which is to say that these 'civilized' social interactions were not merely taken over from the French source but were often independent contributions of the German, knightly author.[58]

This tendency is expressed in, for instance, Hartmann's frequent expansion of passages in Chrétien's text, or his addition of independent comments, which advocate restraint and conciliation rather than anger (Iw 869–78, 2026–29, 4136–45, 6278–82, 6834, 8092–96), or which reflect on the relations between host and guest (Iw 286–368, 2822–49, 4403–21, 5578–5604, 5806–11) or on the topic of gratitude or reward for favours shown or services rendered (Iw 1223, 2731–38, 3069–79, 3723–27, 4247–60, 4853–58, 6753–55). Characteristic of Hartmann's adaptation in this respect is his treatment of Arthur's reception at Laudine's court (Yv 2302–92; Iw 2653–2716). Here Chrétien presents a vivid, noisy and

---

57 Ibid. pp. 122–25.
58 This comparison of Hartmann and Chrétien gives further support to Haferland's comments on the importance of reciprocity in Hartmann's Arthurian romances (*Höfische Interaktion*, pp. 116–19 and often).

thronging image of a royal entry. Houses are decked with silk, streets covered with carpets and protected from the sun by canopies; bells, horns and trumpets sound in the castle; girls dance to the music of flutes, pipes and drums; youths perform acrobatics; and Laudine emerges wearing 'imperial' dress (Yv 2360: 'un drap anperial') and surpassing a goddess in beauty, whilst Arthur is greeted with cries of jubilation as the greatest of all rulers. Hartmann omits all this colourful, dynamic physical detail, he refers in merely brief and unspecific terms to the good treatment extended to Arthur (Iw 2653–62), and he replaces Chrétien's lavish evocation of the external trappings of a great lordly festivity with an independent passage in which he records Laudine's thoughts and words of gratitude to Iwein for the honour he has brought her (Iw 2663–82), before reflecting in the narrator's voice on the importance of sincerity in a host's treatment of his guests (Iw 2683–94) and on the ethical value of friendship (Iw 2695–713). Characteristically in the comparison of Chrétien and Hartmann, it is the German, knightly author who shows the greater inwardness and reflectiveness. Chrétien writes as a clerically trained poet who has both intimate knowledge of great courts and the detachment needed to present the secular aristocracy as an unfolding panoply. Hartmann writes from more of an inside perspective, showing more identification with the feelings of his characters than Chrétien and a less detailed visualization of the outside world.

What we see in Hartmann's adaptation of Chrétien's *Yvain* is a tendency of major significance for the course of German literature around 1200: a reduction in the realm of physical violence, and an expansion of the inner, subjective realm of moral and emotional experience – an expansion too and a more explicit articulation of interpersonal relations based on reciprocity. Nor is this shift simply a matter of applied doctrine, rather it has an aesthetic dimension that reaches, as we have seen in various ways in this chapter, into the very detail of Hartmann's literary style.

In broad historical terms the chivalry presented in the second cycle of *Iwein*, as in the later parts of *Erec*, shows some impact of the debate about the ideal functions of the *militia* emanating from church sources.[59] We have seen that the internal dynamics of Hartmann's romances bear a structural resemblance to the contrast between an 'old' and a 'new' *militia* that was elaborated in crusading propaganda.[60] However, it is important to distinguish between different strands of thinking about Christian chivalry in the twelfth century. A further parallel to the ethical

---

[59]  See Endres, 'Die Bedeutung von *güete*', pp. 607f.; Sieverding, *Der ritterliche Kampf*, pp. 155, 278–284.
[60]  See above, p. 138.

content of Hartmann's concept of chivalry is provided by John of Salisbury, philosopher, historian, diplomat, and holder of high ecclesiastical office. John of Salisbury's *Policraticus*, completed in 1159, reflects in part John's experience of the Plantagenet court circles which were an important matrix for the formation of a chivalric ideology in the mid- and later twelfth century.[61] This work contains the most detailed discussion of the *militia* to emerge from the theoretical treatises of churchmen in the eleventh and twelfth centuries. The view of the *militia* in John's *Policraticus* has a different cultural focus from the Church's crusading propaganda, it shows a strong coloration of classical Roman ideas and of the political ideas of twelfth-century statecraft, and it has parallels with Hartmann's literary portrayal of knighthood on important social, ethical and religious points.

With regard to social status John describes the *milites* as being freer than other men and enjoying more immunities, for example immunity from base services (*Policraticus*, VI, 10). The *milites* form the armed hand of the commonwealth (ibid., VI, 1), and are set above the multitude of those who labour in menial occupations as superiors are placed above inferiors, though both are bound in reciprocity into the greater whole (ibid., VI, 20). This view of the social hierarchy is reminiscent of the privileged position of *ritter* in German society and in Hartmann's works. However, whilst knightly families in Germany and elsewhere in feudal Europe were trying to establish their social privileges as a matter of hereditary right during the twelfth century, John of Salisbury firmly ascribes a professional and ethical basis to these privileges. The professional basis of knighthood is military competence which derives from training and toil (ibid., VI, 2, 4, 8), and which earns honour. Also John's description of the name of *miles* as one of honour as it is of toil (ibid., VI, 8: 'Miles namque sicut laboris ita et honoris nomen est') foreshadows Hartmann's recurrent linking of knightly effort (*arbeit*) with honour (*êre*), and the pursuit of ease (*gemach, verligen*) with shame.[62] The ethical basis of the *militia* is, in the *Policraticus*, obedience to the law. The true *miles* serves the law on which human society is based, whilst those who use arms against the law are not true *milites* (ibid., VI, 8). Thus the military profession serves not the individual's private self-will but equity and the public good (ibid., VI, 8). This ethical justification of the *militia* has evident parallels with Hartmann's presentation of the knight as a defender of just causes in the later stages of *Iwein*. In explicitly religious terms of the relationship between man and God,

---

[61] See Flori, *L'essor*, pp. 280–89, 304–18; two other important observers of chivalry, Etienne de Fougères (see above, pp. 65f., 230f.) and Walter Map (see below, p. 266), were also connected to the Plantagenet court under Henry II.

[62] Er 2966–73; Gr 1677–720; Iw 76, 2791–97, 7175–80, 7209–13; see also Fischer, *Ehre*, p. 158.

John defends the *militia* as an institution akin to the clergy and pleasing to God, who ordained it (ibid., VI, 5). There is no question here of moral sanction being given only to a narrow crusading concept of chivalry, for John explicitly states that the *miles* may serve an infidel master so long as he does so without violating his own faith (ibid., VI, 9) – a position which throws interesting light on the figure of Gahmuret in Wolfram's *Parzival*. John goes so far as to state that *milites* who perform their office of protection are indeed 'saints' (*Policraticus*, VI, 8: 'Nam et haec agentes milites sancti sunt'). This religious legitimation has its echo in Hartmann's works when the young Gregorius defends *ritterschaft* as a way of life pleasing to God (Gr 1531–35), and when knights are described as having God's special protection in their performance of acts of rescue and help.

Hartmann's romances thus have strong affinities with John of Salisbury's treatise on statesmanship in their provision of a professional and ethical sanction for the *militia*. Indeed, of all the clerical voices on the *militia* in the twelfth century, John of Salisbury has perhaps most in common with Hartmann, and the parallels may be more than fortuitous, for the Plantagenet circles around Henry II of England, with which John was familiar, also exercised an influence (though just how directly and strongly we do not know) on the mental world of Hartmann's French sources, the romances of Chrétien de Troyes.[63] Nevertheless, the parallels are not complete, and the theme of knighthood in Hartmann's works cannot be interpreted merely as a versified rendering of John's theory of the *militia*. John's concept of the *militia* is philosophically grounded in an overall theory of the commonwealth, and the *milites* are seized in their military capacity and delineated, with much reference to Roman concepts of army discipline (one notes again the importance of Roman antiquity especially in scholarly theorizing on the *militia* in the twelfth century), as armed servants of the commonwealth. John's scheme has no room for the subtly modulated social interactions of courtliness which are essential to Hartmann's portrayal of knighthood.[64] John's ethically normative concept of the *militia* also excludes the dimension of love and the inner life of the emotions which have a paradigmatic value in Hartmann's works and elsewhere in the secular literature of the period as expressions of an essential degree of emancipation of secular culture from the Church's ideals of knighthood. John agrees with Hartmann in warning youth against neglecting military duty in pursuit of sensual pleasure – *Policraticus*, VI, 6 is a close parallel to Hartmann's account of Erec's *verligen*. But John does not bring the compensating affirmative portrayal of human love which is so

---

63  See above, pp. 14f.
64  See also Haferland, *Höfische Interaktion*, pp. 209ff.

important in the poetic legitimation of knighthood in secular literature. John of Salisbury, as an educated cleric with a profound interest in the affairs of state, and Hartmann von Aue, as a knight with an unusually high degree of literacy and learning, both testify to the importance of the intermingling of clerical learning and the culture of the lay nobility for the development of concepts of knighthood in the twelfth century, and both, in different ways, betray the influence of a great secular ruling house, a court – for John primarily as the seat of government, of princely power, for Hartmann more as a focus of sociability. But John, for all his respect for the *militia*, remains a clerical philosopher commenting on knighthood from the outside, whilst Hartmann, for all his absorption of clerical teaching, remains a knightly poet articulating – and shaping – the values of his own class from an inside perspective.

The knightly hero no longer lives entirely in his external, physical actions in *Iwein*, as may be said more justly of the warriors of the heroic tradition. Rather he has acquired a degree of autonomy of the inner emotional life and of moral experience which is expressed in the second cycle of the romance especially in his inner monologues and in his experience of compassion. In terms of genre, this introspective and moral dimension in *Iwein* shows Hartmann applying to the genre of romance constitutive features of his religious 'Legenden', *Gregorius* and particularly *Der arme Heinrich*.[65] However, a brief consideration of the motif of compassion shows that the relation between courtly romance and religious narrative in Hartmann's *œuvre* is more complex than this one-directional line of influence might suggest. For, whilst it is true that the theme of compassion links *Iwein* to *Der arme Heinrich*, this theme is firmly established already in Chrétien's *Yvain*, as 'pitiez' moves Yvain to help the lion (Yv 3373), and 'pitiez' remains an important motive in his later combats (Yv 3942, 4070, 5682, 5951). Thus in departing from older secular warrior traditions to delineate a compassionate image of knighthood in *Iwein*, Hartmann drew on Chrétien's courtly romance *Yvain* as well as on the experience of his own religious narratives.

Moreover, Hartmann attributed compassion to his knightly hero already in his account of the sad plight of the eighty widows in the 'Joie de la curt' episode in *Erec* (Er 8334–42; 9785–802). Hartmann was perhaps prompted by Chrétien's *Yvain* to add this quality of compassion to his *Erec*,[66] thus it may well have been largely his reading of a French courtly romance that led to Hartmann's first modifying the warrior ideal in the direction of gentler emotional and moral, even Christian qualities. In other words, not only religious literature, but also the courtly

---

[65] See Cramer, ' "Sælde und êre"', p. 46; Erben, 'Zu Hartmanns *Iwein*', p. 346; Hahn, '*güete* und *wizzen*', p. 196.
[66] See above, p. 132.

romance transmitted and developed moral values already in the twelfth century. Indeed the expansion of the moral and the emotional at the expense of the military is a fundamental tendency in the origin and the development of the courtly romance as a genre. This tendency is present at the birth of the genre if we compare Chrétien's *Erec et Enide* with the tradition of heroic warrior poetry. In Hartmann's adaptations of Chrétien's romances combats are still essential to the compositonal framework. But Hartmann's reduction of violence and his expansion of the moral sphere in his treatment of chivalry, especially in *Iwein*, foreshadows the importance of non-military, moral issues in Wolfram's *Parzival*, just as Iwein's asking the beleaguered lord what troubles him (Iw 4435f.: 'saget mir, herre, / durch got waz iu werre') anticipates the famous compassionate question with which Parzival will release Anfortas from his suffering (*Parzival* 795,29: 'œheim, waz wirret dier?').

### âventiure, *trial by combat and the role of courtliness*

Three controversial topics remain to be discussed in order to gain a better understanding of knighthood in *Iwein*, and the place of *Iwein* within Hartmann's *œuvre* and within the broader history of chivalry: *âventiure*, trial by combat, and the relation of knighthood to courtly values.

The theme of *âventiure* again raises the ethical question of the role of personal glory in the practice of arms. Harald Haferland maintains that 'truly courtly combats' are undertaken in romances around 1200 solely in pursuit of glory, and he cites Wolfram von Eschenbach for support: 'Die wirklich höfischen Kämpfe, wie die höfische Epik sie konzipiert, entstehen "niwan durch prîses hulde" (*Parzival* 538,4)'.[67] Praise is indeed an important spur to combat in courtly literature. But Haferland's comment gives a misleading impression of the moral status of combats undertaken for the sake of personal glory alone precisely in the works of the knightly authors Wolfram and Hartmann. For one thing, the line which Haferland quotes to illustrate the nature of such combats is itself only part of a passage in which Wolfram in the narrator's voice criticizes these combats (*Parzival* 538,1–8: 'Wer solte se drumbe prîsen, / daz di unwîsen / striten âne schulde, / niwan durch prîses hulde? / sine heten niht ze teilen, / ân nôt ir leben ze veilen. / ietweder ûf den andern jach, / daz er die schulde nie gesach'). Wolfram affirms the knight's use of force if there is a necessity or reason, grounds (*nôt, schulde*), but here and elsewhere he distances himself from fighting

---

[67] Haferland, *Höfische Interaktion*, p. 126.

which takes place merely for the sake of renown and without necessity or legitimate cause.[68]

Hartmann is less explicit in his criticism on this point. But he showed doubts as to whether the pursuit of personal honour alone was sufficient legitimation for serious combat (tournaments were, of course, a different matter) already in *Erec*.[69] His reservations on this score are if anything stronger in *Iwein*. Even Iwein's battle with Askalon has a previous objective cause in the shame done to Iwein's relative by Askalon (Iw 805–07), so that Wolfram of all authors, with his strong sense of kinship, would hardly have classed this as a combat without reason, (although, as we saw earlier in this chapter, it is indeed the consideration of personal honour that seems to dominate Iwein's subjective thoughts in this combat). More importantly, none of Iwein's combats in the second cycle of the romance, when Hartmann is clearly elaborating an ethically exemplary concept of chivalry, could remotely be described as being fought without good reason and for the sake of personal glory alone. Rather these combats are characterized by a heaping of legitimatory circumstances of obligation, aid, rescue and defence of justice which clearly set them apart from combats *âne schulde*.

By contrast Hartmann's use of the concept *âventiure* suggests reservations about combats which lack such external legitimation. We have seen that the term *âventiure* entered German literature, in Eilhart's *Tristrant*, as a form of combat practised by Arthur's knights in which the sole motive was pursuit of glory.[70] *Âventiure* remains closely associated with military chivalry in Hartmann's works, appearing only in *Erec* and *Iwein*, not in his other works, in which military chivalry plays at most a subordinate part. Further, a comparison of *Iwein* with *Erec*, especially in the light of Hartmann's reception of Chrétien, shows a retreat in the narrative prominence of the word *âventiure* and an increased independence and selectivity in Hartmann's use of the word in his later work.

The term *âventiure* is well established in relation to knightly combat in Chrétien's *Erec et Enide*, and knightly combat is also the most frequent association of *âventiure* in Hartmann's works.[71] In *Erec*, Hartmann follows Chrétien to present *âventiure* in a primarily laudatory sense. The positive connotations of *âventiure* in Hartmann's first romance are indicated in the fact that, like Chrétien, he applies it not only to Erec's initiatory combat against Iders (EeE 1482f.; Er 221, 492, 1528), but also to the climactic, ethically integrative 'Joie de la curt' encounter (e.g. EeE 5431, 5437, 5445, 5464, 5873; Er 7962, 7975, 7999, 8384, 8398, 8414), so that Erec's pursuit of *âventiure* clearly brings benefit to aristocratic

---

68   See Green, 'Homicide', pp. 61–66.
69   See above, pp. 122f., 131f.
70   See above, p. 122.
71   For what follows in this paragraph see Oettli, *The Concept of Âventiure*, pp. 10–117.

society within the romance, as well as asserting Erec's own warrior prestige. Chrétien continues the practice of his *Erec et Enide* in writing *Yvain*, that is to say he applies the term *avanture* not only to Calogrenant's dubious enterprise in his encounter with Esclados (Yv 177, 260, 362, 366), but also to Yvain's later deeds of aid and compassion (Yv 3934, 3945), which are described in general as 'Les avantures au lion' (Yv 6471). Hartmann uses the word *âventiure* less often in *Iwein* than in *Erec* (10 occurrences against 21). More importantly, in *Iwein* Hartmann differs from Chrétien, and from his own usage in *Erec*, in that he now applies *âventiure* far less often to his hero and uses the term far less often (if at all) in a commendatory sense. Of the ten occurrences of *âventiure* in *Iwein*, one has the literary sense of 'source' or 'story' (Iw 3026) and nine have a knightly sense. Of these nine, seven appear in Calogrenant's account of his ignominious enterpise (Iw 261, 372, 377, 525, 527, 549, 631). Only one occurrence relates to Iwein, when he is described in general terms as riding 'nâch âventiure' (Iw 3918). Apart from this one at best indirect allusion, Hartmann never associates the term *âventiure* with any of the combats of aid undertaken by Iwein after his awakening.

The remaining one occurrence of *âventiure* in *Iwein* (Iw 6331) relates to the disastrous undertaking of a young lord, who rides out in search of *âventiure* simply out of a youthful desire (Iw 6330: 'niuwan von sîner kintheit'), is taken captive and has to give thirty maidens into drudgery each year as tribute to buy his freedom. Chrétien uses the expression 'por aprandre noveles' (Yv 5258) to describe the young lord's journeying, not *avanture*, so that in this situation, where an enterprise with no socially useful cause leads to captivity for innocent people, Hartmann independently adds the term *âventiure*, just as he omits it from the combats in which Iwein's chivalry is placed in the service of women, justice and threatened lordship.[72] The only two encounters which are directly described as 'adventures' in *Iwein* thus involve disastrous failure for a young knight. Further, Hartmann was probably prompted by the folly of the young lord's enterprise in *Yvain* to point to the potentially tragic consequences of the search for *âventiure* already in *Erec*, when he has the lord of Brandigan refer to the many knights who have been killed because they were rash enough to seek adventure (Er 8479–81:

---

[72] Interestingly, this young lord is described specifically as a king by Chrétien (Yv 5257: 'li rois de l'Isle as Puceles'; compare Yv 5275), whilst Hartmann uses a less specific term of lordship: 'des [. . .] landes herre' (Iw 6328). The German term *des landes herre* need not imply royal status, but merely lordship over lands – for instance Hartmann himself describes Count Galoain as 'des landes herre' (Er 3479). It is worth noting that, when Chrétien shows a young king in an irresponsible light, Hartmann alters the text so as to apply a less specific lordship term to the man; too much should not be made of this detail, but it is in line with Hartmann's tendency to portray kingship in a positive light, and it does not fit easily with the view that *Iwein* represents a standpoint of non-royal, territorial lordship.

'die des niht wolden haben rât / von tumbes herzen stiure, / sine suochten âventiure'). The 'foolish hearts' of the knights in *Erec* echo the youthful folly of the young lord in *Iwein*: *tump* can of course combine folly and youth. This intertextual link further supports the view that Hartmann's shaping of the 'Joie de la curt' episode in *Erec* may have been influenced by his reading of *Yvain*. With regard to the concept of chivalry, it seems that Hartmann drew on this reading to project a negative connotation of *âventiure* into the primarily laudatory deployment of the term in *Erec*, as well as to add the quality of compassion to Erec's chivalry.

Hartmann has Kalogrenant provide the wild herdsman, who is ignorant of knightly ways, with a definition of the word *âventiure* (Iw 529-37). Kalogrenant's definition echoes the concept of *âventiure* in Eilhart's *Tristrant*, for Kalogrenant describes *âventiure* as a form of knightly combat where the only issue at stake is the personal glory of the victor (534: 'daz prîset in, und sleht er mich'). This definition of *âventiure* perfectly matches the combats 'without reason' (*âne schulde*) which Wolfram criticizes in his *Parzival*. As with the evaluation of Iwein's killing Askalon, the lack of consensus about central ethical aspects of chivalry in *Iwein* is reflected in an unresolved critical controversy in which Kalogrenant's concept of *âventiure* appears across a whole range as a programmatic affirmation, an ethically neutral expression or a comically burlesque criticism of the knight's pursuit of personal glory.[73] Some of the critical readings have perhaps attributed too aggressive a cutting edge to Hartmann's style here. But more surely the unproblematically affirmative readings fail to take account of the real reservations implied in Hartmann's attitude towards *âventiure* in *Iwein*, especially in view of his independently selective use of the term and its restriction almost entirely to the disastrously unsuccessful and merely self-seeking undertakings of Kalogrenant and the young lord.

The retreat of *âventiure* throws further light on the social ideology of Hartmann's *Iwein*. The knight's pursuit of 'adventure', involving as it did the search for armed combat, stood in a problematical relation to the maintenance of peace and order which was the highest aim of kingship.[74] Indeed there is a strand in the history of 'adventure' in the Middle Ages which links the concept explicitly with breach of the law. In thirteenth-century England royal decrees prohibited knights from

[73] For earlier critics see Voß, *Artusepik*, p. 190, n. 28. The controversy continues: Voß himself (*Artusepik*, pp. 24-30) and Fischer, *Ehre*, pp. 19-28 see *âventiure*, as defined by Kalogrenant, as a positive expression of the aristocratic ethos in *Iwein*, whilst Green, *Irony*, pp. 79-83, Ranawake, 'Zu Form und Funktion', pp. 102f., and Borck, 'Über Ehre', pp. 5f. see Kalogrenant's definition as morally deficient.
[74] See also Morris, *The Character of King Arthur*, p. 81: 'a realm teeming with adventure cannot be peaceful and orderly; and peace and order are – in theory at least – the ultimate aim of every king'.

'seeking adventures', holding tournaments or otherwise exercising arms without royal permission;[75] in the German *Karlmeinet* (ca. 1320) robber knights are described as living by 'adventure' (*Karlmeinet* 376,51: 'Den de leuent der ouenturen'; compare 375,24; 381,38); and in the didactic treatise on knighthood written ca. 1416 by Johannes Rothe, the epithet 'adventurously' (*Ritterspiegel* 960, 1168: 'ebinturlichin') is applied to robber knights (ibid. 935–76) and to sinful, arrogant knights who trust too much in their own youth, strength and arms and too little in God (ibid. 1165–68). Rothe was a priest, sometime town clerk of Eisenach and connected with the ruling landgraves of Thuringia. Rothe has strong legal interests, and his treatise draws heavily on the Roman military authority Vegetius and on the Christian concepts of the protective function of the *militia* which were propagated during the peace movements from the eleventh century onwards.[76] It is typical of a broader trend that the pursuit of 'adventure' should be seen from this administratively schooled perspective, which combined ecclesiastical, urban and politically centralizing interests, as arrogant and destructive wilfulness.

Hartmann does not go as far as these later sources in criminalizing 'adventure', but his restrained use of the term does suggest a more (or an even more) sceptical attitude towards the pursuit of glory in combat in *Iwein* than in *Erec*. Sociologically the treatment of the concept *âventiure* suggests a shift in narrative sympathy away from bachelor knight errantry and towards the realm of settled lordship, peace and order in Hartmann's last romance. This retreat of 'adventure' is reflected in an illuminating alteration of Hartmann's in his account of Kalogrenant's reception by an unnamed host, a settled minor lord, during his search for *âventiure*, for whereas the noble host in Chrétien says he has received many an errant knight seeking *avanture* (Yv 256–62), Hartmann alters this to have the host express surprise at Kalogrenant's undertaking and say that he has never received a guest who claimed to be searching for *âventiure* (Iw 369–77). The search for 'adventure' seems a less self-evident activity of knighthood in *Iwein* than it was in *Erec*, it arouses surprise even in the aristocratic world.

Given the importance of law and combat in *Iwein*, it is fitting that these two themes should come together in the last public scene of the romance, which is a formal trial by combat, in which Iwein and Gawein champion opposing parties. The trial by combat, or judicial duel, was part of the broader system of ordeals, that is to say an ancient mode of

---

75  *Calendar of the Patent Rolls 1232–1247*, pp. 20, 62, 148, 188 ; ibid., *1258–1266*, p. 227; Denholm-Young, 'The Tournament', p. 252. The phrase *aventuras quaerere* (= MHG *âventiure suochen*: Er 4340, 8481; Iw 6331) appears frequently in English royal prohibitions (Rymer, *Foedera*, II, p. 4; III, p. 258).
76  See Petersen, *Das Rittertum*, pp. 58–78.

trial in which a judgement was to be found by means of some physical test fraught with danger, for example plunging a hand into boiling water, holding a hot iron, walking barefoot over hot ploughshares or, as in the present case, an armed combat.[77] Such ordeals reach far back into pre-Christian times. They rested on the belief that the magic of the elements, then later God as the lord of justice, would indicate guilt or innocence by the outcome of the test. The ordeals were thus an attempt to bring about supernatural intervention in human affairs, in Christian times in the form of a judgement of God (*iudicium dei*). The attitude of the Church towards ordeals was mixed. But particularly the judicial duel was repeatedly (though not uniformly) condemned in ecclesiastical sources from the sixth century onwards as a detestable temptation of God and a superstitious and sinful shedding of Christian blood in peacetime.[78] An emerging rational tendency which was fortified by the renewal of study of Roman law led to intensified criticism of ordeals, and especially of the trial by combat, in the second half of the twelfth century. And the fourth Lateran Council (1215) formed a turning point in the history of the *iudicium dei* by seeking to ban the judicial duel altogether as well as forbidding the co-operation of priests in other forms of ordeal.[79]

The belief that God manifested his will, and that truth and justice could be revealed in passages of arms provided, however, a powerful legitimatory ideology and an impressive public ritual for the practice of arms, and the secular aristocracy clung to the judicial duel as a legal right against these critical voices throughout the twelfth century and beyond as tenaciously as it asserted its right of feud. Indeed there are close links between the attempts of centralizing monarchical authorities to curtail the feud and to control 'war's symbolic sister, the judicial duel';[80] and when reference is made to combat as a judgement of God in medieval secular literature, the concern of the text may be less to provide a truly Christian interpretation than to provide support for a controversial privilege of the secular aristocracy. The judicial duel was a valid procedure in German secular law in the twelfth and thirteenth centuries, appearing for instance in Barbarossa's peace ordinances of 1152 and 1179, and in the vernacular law books of the thirteenth century.[81] The weighty importance of these duels is indicated in a

---

[77] On ordeals, and especially the trial by combat, see Nottarp, *Gottesurteilstudien*, passim; Bloch, *Medieval French Literature and Law*, esp. pp. 13–28, 119–21; Green, *Irony*, pp. 83–90; Jillings, 'Ordeal by Combat', passim.
[78] On the mixed views in Church sources see Nottarp, *Gottesurteilstudien*, pp. 317–68.
[79] Ibid., p. 347.
[80] Bloch, *Medieval French Literature and Law*, p. 119.
[81] MGH Const., I, no. 140, cc. 3, 10 (pp.. 196f.); no. 277, cc. 6, 7 (pp. 381f.); *Sachsenspiegel, Landrecht*, I, 39, 43, 48, 63, 65 and often.

judgement presided over by Emperor Henry VI. In 1191 Henry's marshal had legitimately challenged a Strassburg knight to a judicial combat. The challenged person failed to appear, whereupon the emperor summoned him again, to his court in Hagenau. On this occasion (29. December 1191) the emperor and his court sat in the open from morning until sundown to await the man who had been summoned, and when he again failed to appear he was declared a proscribed man and stripped of his honour, his lands and his wife.[82] Finally, the judicial duel was an important focus for the interpenetration of combat, legal custom and social status, for as a general rule a person of superior condition of birth need not accept a challenge from someone of inferior status.[83] The challenge to combat was an occasion for demonstrating noble status, and this hierarchical function doubtless encouraged the survival of the judicial duel long after doubts about its religious legitimacy had become widespread.

In presenting the trial by combat Hartmann was thus not only following a literary lead from Chrétien but also, as often in his treatment of knighthood, reflecting on a matter of direct concern to the real life of the German aristocracy in his own day. Furthermore, in his treatment of combat as a judgement of God, Hartmann exploits the motif of divine assistance in combat as a means of invoking metaphysical support for the profession of arms which was the class privilege of knighthood, but he also, in *Iwein*, shows incipient reservations about the validity of the judicial duel as a legal process.

The belief that the outcome of a combat shows divine intervention is especially clear when, following the biblical example of David's battle against Goliath, victory goes to the combatant who is disadvantaged in human terms, and Hartmann draws on this biblical precedent when he speaks of God aiding Erec in his victory over the two giants (Er 5558–68).[84] In *Iwein* the hero himself expresses confidence that God will aid the cause of innocence and truth when he champions Lunete (Iw 5169: 'got und ir unschulde'; 5275: 'got gestuont der wârheit ie'). These references to God, innocence and truth are not merely fictional, literary devices, but elements drawn from the practice of judicial duels, before which the accused party averred his innocence and called on God's support in the combat.[85] However, if these instances suggest an

---

[82] *La Chronique de Gislebert de Mons*, pp. 214f., 268; Nottarp, *Gottesurteilstudien*, pp. 174f.

[83] *Sachsenspiegel, Landrecht*, I, 63: 'Itlich man mag kamphes weigeren deme, der snoder geboren iz, denne her'. Significantly this passage goes on immediately to state that a person of inferior status was not allowed to reject a challenge from a person of superior status on the grounds of this difference of birth: 'Der abir baz geboren iz, den en kan der snode geborne niht verlegen mit der bezzeren gebort, ab her en anspricht'; the rules of combat were thus calculated to protect the interests always of the higher status of birth.

[84] See also Green, *Irony*, p. 85.

[85] *Sachsenspiegel, Landrecht*, I, 63; Nottarp, *Gottesurteilstudien*, pp. 173, 276f.

unbroken faith in combat as a judgement of God, the judicial duel between Iwein and Gawein brings a more problematical view.

The circumstances of this combat show an attempt to abuse the judicial duel, as the grasping elder sister seeks a champion not in order to defend justice and truth, but in an attempt to deprive her innocent and good-hearted sister of the inheritance which should rightfully (Iw 5638, 7658f.) serve them both.[86] This contrast between the two parties also throws light on their respective champions. The knightly ethic of rendering service had of necessity, if it was to claim moral legitimacy and social usefulness, to distinguish between causes which merited aid and those which did not. That is to say that the readiness to provide military aid had to be backed up by an ethical judgement involving reflection. Again on this point the mingling of clerical and secular interests at the English Plantagenet court provides a revealing illustration, as Walter Map tells approvingly of the knight (*miles*) Grado (or Gado), who took part in military contests throughout the world, 'always weighing the claims of both sides so as to redress wrong and uphold justice'.[87] Specifically in judicial duels champions were expected to be confident of the rightfulness of the case they were representing.[88] Hartmann takes up this question of discrimination in the lending of aid when he has Iwein, in the lead-up to the final combat, say that he will offer aid to 'any good person' who seeks it (Iw 6002–04: 'swem mîns dienstes nôt geschiht / und swer guoter des gert, / dern wirt es niemer entwert'). These lines are Hartmann's independent addition, and they are a key expression of his mature knightly idealism. The generality of Iwein's offer of aid suggests a sense of the knight's obligation towards a far larger community than the kinship group which Iwein invoked as an ethical ground for the pursuit of retribution in the opening cycle (Iw 805–07). In their personnel Hartmann's romances remain within the confines of aristocratic society. However, the generality of Iwein's readiness to aid also establishes a tacit link with the broader view of the *militia* as the armed hand of the commonwealth as a whole; and Iwein's condition that his service will be granted only to a good cause gives his attitude (and Hartmann's mature idealism) the discriminating edge which lifts it above a naively unselective proferring of aid.

Gawein, by contrast, fails in this task of discrimination and champions the unjust cause of the elder sister. Whereas Hartmann expands in detail

[86] Mertens misinterprets when he claims that both sisters have a sound legal claim, that indeed the claim of the elder sister is legally perhaps stronger than that of the younger (*Laudine*, pp. 100–04); Schnell, 'Abaelard's Gesinnungsethik', p. 49, n. 75 rightly criticises Mertens on this point.

[87] Walter Map, *De Nugis Curialium*, II, 17.

[88] Nottarp, *Gottesurteilstudien*, p. 305; Bloch, *Medieval French Literature and Law*, p. 26.

on the circumstances of Iwein's offering aid for the innocent younger sister (Iw 5971–6072), he passes over the grasping elder sister's request and Gawein's offer of aid in a few lines (Iw 5663–77), saying nothing about her arguments or Gawein's thoughts, and providing the barest minimum of information needed for the action. This lack of comment does not imply approval or even neutrality in the evaluation of Gawein's position. Rather it should be seen in the light of an important stylistic feature of Hartmann's romances which should always be borne in mind when assessing the author's ethical sympathies – namely his tendency to expand and elaborate on actions which command his ethical approval and to abbreviate or pass over in silence non-exemplary actions. Hartmann's romances do not pretend to tell the whole ethical truth even-handedly and explicitly, as in a moral treatise. They have, as well as an ethically discriminating tone, a rhetoric of politeness which means that praise is direct and explicit, whilst criticism is often indirect, implicit or muted, as it might be in a polite conversation. Paradoxically it is Keii the mocker who expresses this rhetoric of politeness, in a comment which has no precedent in Chrétien's romance (Iw 2491–94: 'wan ich einem iegelîchen man / sîner êren wol gan: / ich prîs in swâ er rehte tuot, / und verswîge sîn laster: daz ist guot'). With regard to the task of literary interpretation, this attitude means that the reader should not take what is stated explicitly in the narrator's comments as the whole truth of the author's position, but has to listen to the voices of the characters and to significant silences, to gaps in the text, again as in a diplomatically polite conversation, where what remains unspoken can be just as revealing as what is said. Of all Hartmann's works, *Iwein* is most informed by this rhetoric of politeness, and the current controversies surrounding this work stem, in part at least, from the interpretative difficulties caused by the tension in the work between this rhetoric which tends to veil unpleasant truths, and a moral thrust which has a more critical edge. In the case of Gawein's defence of an unjust cause the position is clarified when one of Hartmann's favourite exemplary mechanisms comes into play: the fictional character's self-indictment. For Gawein himself concedes after the combat that he has been defending an unjust cause (Iw 7624: 'mîn unreht'; 7625f.: 'Diu juncvrouwe hât rehtes niht / vür die man mich hie vehten siht'). The contrast between Iwein's discretion and Gawein's lack of discretion in offering aid makes a typically Hartmannesque point of practical morality to a contemporary audience about the need for judgement in the exercise of arms.

Hartmann's account of the actual combat between Iwein and Gawein suggests that the duel has defects as a judicial process and no longer carries the wholehearted support of the author or of the society presented in the action.[89] It lies in the nature of the trial by combat that it can lead to death. However, the spectators at the combat, clearly with the author's sympathy, regret this possibility and look for other means of settling the dispute than a battle that might lead to the death of a fine knight (Iw 6908–38, 7273–81, 7323–32). Long before the combat the younger sister expressed a readiness to accept an amicable solution to the dispute if only her elder sister would show some accommodation and sense of justice (Iw 5729–34). Immediately before and during the combat Arthur himself and onlookers try to bring about a peaceful settlement without the duel running its course, but these founder on the obduracy of the elder sister's insistence on the right of combat (Iw 6918–28, 7273–90), and finally Arthur is so angered by this intransigence that he refuses to attempt further conciliation and insists on protecting the rights of the younger sister (Iw 7333–41). The account of the disputed inheritance is indeed characterized by two different concepts of justice, two opposed ways of settling disputes.[90] On the one hand there is the ancient, formalized, inflexible custom of the judicial duel, in which the parties face each other in enmity, in which there can only be a winner and a loser, and in which the role of the judge is merely to watch over the formal process. On the other hand there are attempts at conciliation and arbitration, which aim to settle the dispute peacefully, without the grim ritual of a possibly fatal combat, which look for a mutually acceptable solution rather than a confrontation of winner and loser, and in which the judge, as arbitrator, conciliator or referee has a far more active role than he has in the judicial duel. The opposition is also one between a legal process resting on the belief that justice will be revealed by supernatural means (by the judgement of God revealed in victory at arms), and a more rational view that human insight, reflection and discretion are needed in the finding of justice.

The narrator and Arthur's court show much sympathy with the more human, peaceful and conciliatory way of finding justice in this key episode. For one thing, the combat itself fails to produce a result. After a day's fearful battle-toil the combat remains undecided (Iw 7349ff.), the duel has not produced a judgement. It is as if God had withdrawn his judicial sanction from the combat and left it as a purely human contest between the two finest knights. The legal dispute is then not settled by a passage of arms, but placed in the competence of the human judge, Arthur (Iw 7648–52). And Arthur brings about a resolution by peaceful, human means, first eliciting a public confession from the elder sister that

---

[89] See also Fehr, 'Das Recht im Iwein', p. 97; Milnes, 'The Play of Opposites', p. 248; Hagenguth, Hartmanns 'Iwein', p. 151; Green, Irony, pp. 86f.; Schnell, 'Abaelards Gesinnungsethik', p. 67.

[90] For what follows in this paragraph see Schnell, 'Abaelards Gesinnungsethik', pp. 54–56.

her claim lacks justice (Iw 7655–70), and then, in an act of arbitration, obtaining her consent to a partition of the inheritance (Iw 7688–721), so that the dispute ends not with a polarization of winner and loser, but in reconciliation and a fair distribution of the contested lands. What began as a judicial duel in which truth and justice should be revealed by supernatural means in a victory at arms, so that knightly combat is sanctioned as God's way of passing judgement, thus ends with the king as judge establishing the truth and finding justice by the exercise of human intelligence and human judgement. This narrative sequence is not a purely fictional, poetic structure lacking contact with pragmatic reality, rather the sequence of an inconclusive trial by combat giving place to a royal judgement using peaceful means encapsulates an important trend in the history of medieval law.

From the twelfth century onwards inquisitional procedures (trial by inquest) gained ground in French courts, that is to say legal processes which involved the testimony of witnesses as a basis for the judge to reach a decision.[91] These more rational, human procedures at first existed side by side with the ancient aristocratic right of judicial duel, but gradually they suppressed and replaced the duel. In Germany legal processes aiming at peaceful conciliation and arbitration between contesting parties appear in increasing frequency from the middle of the twelfth century onwards.[92] These processes sought largely to restrict feuding and to replace it by peaceful methods of settling disputes. Both these forward-looking approaches to legal disputes are expressed in the way Arthur finds justice in *Iwein*, for his eliciting of an involuntary self-indictment from the elder sister by an intelligent question is in the spirit of the inquisitional process, which gathered and weighed the evidence of testimonies, whilst his wise procurement of an agreed settlement is in the conciliatory spirit of processes of arbitration. The inquisitional and the conciliatory approaches to justice were both part of the broader peace movements of the twelfth century, and with their propagation of these tendencies Chrétien and Hartmann (we may say: yet again) take their place in this larger historical development, which sought to replace the use of arms by peaceful means in settling disputes.

Further, the more rational processes of law that were set against the judicial duel in the settlement of actual disputes in the twelfth century were also favourable to the central authority of the king as supreme judge.[93] In the field of law as in other areas of social and political activity the extension of peace in the twelfth and thirteenth centuries tended to

---

91  Bloch, *Medieval French Literature and Law*, pp. 119–27.
92  Schnell, 'Abaelards Gesinnungsethik', pp. 54–60.
93  See also Bloch, *Medieval French Literature and Law*, p. 127: 'Substitution of inquest for combat was, of course, part of a general trend towards centralization of royal power [. . .]'.

promote the authority of the ruler. Seen in this light it is a gesture of considerable symbolic significance when the king takes the task of finding justice out of the arena of battle and into his own hands (Iw 7648f.: 'er sprach "ir müezent an mich / den strît lâzen beide" '); and finally, Hartmann's positive portrayal of Arthur in his capacity as arbitrator-judge yet again suggests a respectful rather than a critical attitude towards royal power.

The concept of 'adventure' and the trial by combat have played an important part in the continuing critical debate about the status of the court and courtly values in *Iwein*. We have seen that the court has a positive function in Hartmann's portrayal of knighthood in *Erec* in that it is an affirmed goal of the narrative and a measure of the hero's progress.[94] The court appears in a more problematical light in *Iwein*, and controversy continues in Hartmann studies as to whether *Iwein* maintains the affirmative integration of chivalry and courtly values which characterized *Erec*, or whether in Hartmann's last romance the hero's rehabilitation as 'the knight with the lion' somehow takes him beyond the courtly world, that is to say whether Hartmann adumbrates in *Iwein* a concept of chivalry that criticizes and transcends courtly values.[95] The controversy is important for an understanding of Hartmann's knightly idealism, and it is a further indicator of the complex nature of this idealism. The debate has focused largely on the portrayal and the role of Arthur's court and its relation to Laudine's realm and to Iwein's chivalry. I shall consider this complex first, then turn to the meaning and function of the vocabulary of courtliness in *Iwein*.

In a quite pragmatic sense Arthur's court is clearly not the final goal of the narrative in *Iwein*, since Iwein leaves this court to be reunited with Laudine at the end of the romance. What is not sufficiently noted in *Iwein* scholarship is that this pattern is present already in Hartmann's (though not in Chrétien's) *Erec*, for Hartmann's Erec too leaves Arthur's court to return to his homeland at the end of the romance.[96] Indeed Hartmann may well have been encouraged by his reading of *Yvain* to make his much discussed alteration to the end of Chrétien's *Erec* and have the hero return to his own land – yet again the closing stages of

---

94  See above, pp. 126–30.
95  For integrative views of the relation of Iwein's chivalry to courtly values see e.g. Ragotzky / Weinmayer, 'Höfischer Roman', p. 239; Zutt, *König Artus*, p. 53; Fischer, *Ehre*, pp. 156f.; Voß, *Artusepik*, pp. 53–55, 144–46. More critical views e.g. W. Ohly, *Die heilsgeschichtliche Struktur*, pp. 121–23, 131; Sacker, 'An Interpretation of Hartmann's *Iwein*', p. 10; Milnes, 'The Play of Opposites', p. 254; Carne, *Die Frauengestalten*, p. 108; Schweikle, 'Zum *Iwein* Hartmanns von Aue', pp. 10–21; Pütz, 'Artus-Kritik', p. 197; Selbmann, 'Strukturschema', pp. 77–82; Kraft, *Iweins Triuwe*, p. 166; Hahn, '*güete* und *wizzen*', p. 201.
96  See above, p. 29.

Hartmann's *Erec* seem to be coloured by his knowledge of *Yvain*. Erec's kingdom of Karnant and Laudine's realm form the territorial base of the hero's lordly existence, his *lant* (Er 2864, 2879, 2919, 9971, 9976, 10055, 10083; Iw 2420, 2437, 2615, 2728, 2748, 2782, 2880, 3528). The prominence of this motif of *lant* in Hartmann's romances and elsewhere in the literature of the period reflects the growing importance of territorial rule in the gradual transition of political authority from lordship over persons to rule over a territorial state.[97] Arthur's court, by contrast, is primarily the place of bachelor knighthood in Hartmann's works.[98] As such Arthur's court is a transitional stage, not the final goal in the biographical structure of Hartmann's romances. Both these romances suggest that the values of bachelor knighthood are an essential preliminary to secular lordship, but that these values are not in themselves sufficient to form the basis of a full individual life, let alone a society. This combination of affirmation and qualification with regard to bachelor knighthood largely accounts for the controversial status of Arthur's court in Hartmann studies, for this court, as the main forum of knightly 'youth', has an inherently ambivalent position, is both an affirmed focus of aristocratic values and also a stage in life which the hero has to leave behind him in order to become husband and ruler.

Within the fundamental ideological similarity of *Erec* and *Iwein*, Arthur's court is subject to more qualification in the later work. More precisely Hartmann still presents the king, Arthur, in a positive light in *Iwein*.[99] Consequently the opening encomium of 'künec Artûs der guote' (Iw 1–20) should be read quite unironically. But the presentation of the knights at Arthur's court is less consistently favourable in *Iwein* than it was in *Erec*.[100] It is thus not so much the role of kingship that becomes more problematical as we move from *Erec* to *Iwein*, but rather that of knighthood. The knights at Arthur's court have the reputation of providing help for those in need in *Iwein* (Iw 4510–19, 5659–62), but Iwein and Gawein are the only knights in the romance who actually give aid to those who ask for it from outside the Arthurian court. Further, Gawein's aid is given to an unjust cause (Iw 7625–27), and none of the parties who deservedly seek help from the knights at court – Lunete, the lord oppressed by Harpin, and the innocent younger sister – actually

---

97  On the historical dimensions of this process see now Arnold, *Princes and Territories*, passim.
98  See above, p. 235.
99  See above, pp. 20–24.
100  W. Ohly, *Die heilsgeschichtliche Struktur*, p. 97 and Schweikle, 'Zum *Iwein* Hartmanns von Aue', p. 17 both adopt a critical reading of Hartmann's portrayal of the Arthurian company, but also point out that Hartmann seems to shield specifically the king, Arthur, from this criticism; this is an important distinction, and the interpretation of Hartmann's *Iwein* (and of the author's sympathies) might be much helped if it were more widely recognized.

finds it there (Iw 4165–68, 4510–25, 5699–721). The failure of Arthur's knights to provide aid to those who seek it from outside the court contrasts with their readiness to act as a body when the interests of the Round Table are involved, as when the knights are eager to journey to the spring after hearing Kalogrenant's story (Iw 905f.: 'daz dûhte si rîterlich und guot, / wan dar stuont ir aller muot') and to engage in combat to rescue their own abducted queen (Iw 4620 ff.). The knights of the Round Table (with the exception of Iwein) show a certain aristocratic disdain in failing to greet Lunete (Iw 1183–95). They also seem too uncritically ready to believe the best of one of their own class when they urge Arthur, against his better (kingly) judgement, to grant the unspecified request of the strange knight (Iw 4569–78) which then threatens the honour of the court. Compositionally Arthur's court is no longer as important a point of reference for the action as it was in *Erec*. Whereas Erec brought the widows of the 'Joie de la curt' adventure to Arthur's court (Er 9826–75), Iwein merely brings the women released from captivity in the *Pesme Avanture* episode 'to safety' (Iw 6857: 'an ir gewarheit'). Similarly, in *Erec* the hero sends his defeated opponent to Arthur's court, where Iders becomes a new member of the retinue (Er 1022ff., 1279–83), and the knight Cadoc travels with his lady to gain recognition at Arthur's court (Er 5649–53, 5676–705), whilst there is no such enlargement of the Round Table in *Iwein* – the Arthurian company is still expanding, still open to new blood in *Erec* but seems more static and closed-off in *Iwein*.

The Round Table still has a high reputation in *Iwein*, but the actual performance of the knights does not live up to this reputation. In other words, Arthurian knighthood is no longer presented in a purely idealizing light in *Iwein*, rather the Round Table company is portrayed with a note of realism as a body in which only exceptional individuals live up to the ethic of providing aid for those in distress. The ethos of Arthurian knighthood no longer seems to permeate the narrative of *Iwein* to the same extent as it did in *Erec*. Like the retreat of *âventiure* this shift of emphasis suggests a further objectivization and relativization of the values of bachelor knighthood in comparison with the more subjective and enthusiastic attitude of the author in *Erec*. The element of caste-like exclusiveness of Arthur's knights in *Iwein* reflects the sharpening class distinctiveness which characterizes the social history of German knighthood around 1200 and which we have seen elsewhere in Hartmann's works, not least in the scene of Iwein's awakening.[101] Indeed precisely Hartmann's more detached presentation of Arthurian knighthood in *Iwein* brings its underlying social ideology into a sharper focus than was the case in *Erec*.

[101]  See above, pp. 215–17.

The reservations on the score of Arthurian knighthood do not imply such a general detachment of the author from the courtly world as has at times been suggested. The view that Iwein in the second cycle of the romance progresses beyond courtly values is based largely on the portrayal of Arthurian knighthood, which is thus tacitly accepted as the chief, practically the only focus of courtliness. However, the relation of Iwein's chivalry to courtliness can only be properly understood in the light of Hartmann's own use of the evaluative terminology of courtliness, particularly the terms *hövesch* and *hövescheit*.

We have seen that this evaluative terminology emerged in German vernacular sources during the second half of the twelfth century as an expression of the growing cultural importance of courts, and that its rise and crystallization paralleled the growing social distinctiveness of knightly vocabulary in these decades. Hartmann's own usage marks a key stage in the rise of courtly vocabulary, for his works show a symptomatic chronological development in this regard: of the 18 occurrences of *hövesch* in Hartmann's works, one figures in the *Klage* (817), one in *Erec* (5517), one in *Der arme Heinrich* (74) and 15 in *Iwein*; of the 7 occurrences of *hövescheit*, one figures in *Erec* (3461) and 6 in *Iwein*; and the negative *unhövescheit* appears twice in all, both times in *Iwein* (1189, 4919). Given the important role of the court in *Erec* it is hardly likely that Hartmann's sparse use of the term 'courtly' in this early work sprang from deliberate avoidance of the word, far more likely that the word *hövesch* was only just becoming firmly established and that the increased frequency of the term in *Iwein* actually reflects its key breakthrough in wider usage.[102] With his increasing usage of the terminology of courtliness, as with his decreasing use of *guoter kneht*, Hartmann appears as a valuable indicator of changes of usage in aristocratic circles at the end of the twelfth century.

As to social range, the term *hövesch* (or *hövescheit*) is applied to Gawein, the foremost Arthurian knight (Iw 2699, 2714, 3037), to Kalogrenant's host (Iw 788) and his daughters (Iw 932), to Lunete (Iw 1417, 5894), to Askalon (Iw 2195), to a lady in the retinue of the lady of Narison (Iw 3387, 3492), and to Iwein himself (Iw 1040, 3356, 3521, 3752, 4813, 6055, 6856). The concept of 'courtliness', in Hartmann's usage, relates not only to Arthur's court but just as freely to other courts, including that of Laudine and that of a local lord to whom the pursuit of

---

[102] Unfortunately Schrader, *Studien*, did not publish a complete list of occurrences of the terms *hövesch* and *hövescheit* in the works he studied, so that it is not possible to reconstruct an exact chronology of the spread of the terms on the basis of his work. This gap, together with the deficiencies of Schrader's semantic analysis, make a fresh collection and study of the material essential (see also Ganz, *'curialis / hövesch'*, p. 40). From the reading of other literature one has the impression that the last two decades of the twelfth century were a crucial breakthrough period for this terminology in the vernacular – but the point would need to be established objectively.

*âventiure* is an unusual undertaking. Consequently Walther Ohly interprets against the text when he restricts the concept of courtliness to Arthur's realm and describes Laudine's world as 'eine außerhöfische und unterhöfische Instanz'.[103] The position is rather that Hartmann presents courtliness as a quality that is potentially present, and certainly desirable throughout the aristocratic world, of which Arthur's court is only a part. It follows from this that it is not sound to draw from a note of reserve in Hartmann's portrayal of Arthurian knighthood the conclusion that Hartmann is expressing a general criticism of what he would regard as 'courtly' values. One rather has to ask after the meaning of the concept in Hartmann's view.

In terms of the social composition of the aristocratic world, courtliness applies to the sphere of lordship as well as to that of bachelor knighthood, to Laudine's realm as well as to Arthur's, and to lesser houses as well as to great courts. In behavioural and ethical terms courtliness spans a remarkably wide range in *Iwein*, for it is connected with the wearing of fine and expensive clothes (Iw 2195), the modest avoidance of boasting (Iw 1040), politeness of manners (Iw 116 – here used ironically), sparing the feelings of a person in a disadvantaged position (Iw 788, 3492), compassion (Iw 3387), and help given by the knight to a person in need (Iw 5653, 6055).[104] 'Courtliness' in Hartmann's usage thus stretches from matters of dress and social etiquette through personal tact, modesty and kindness up to the qualities of goodness, pity and the rendering of aid which are topmost in Hartmann's scale of ethical values and which are associated with Iwein's chivalry in the second cycle of the romance.[105] The term *hövesch* / *hövescheit* thus provides in *Iwein* a generalizing concept for the various attitudinal and ethical aspects of the enlarged ideal of chivalry (enlarged, that is, beyond the purely military) which Hartman explored already in the 'Joie de la curt' episode of *Erec*.[106] From the close of the twelfth century onwards, courtliness kept its place as a criterion of exemplary knighthood, appearing for instance as a key concept in the education of young nobles in Thomasin von Zerklaere's book of manners.[107] Indeed the progressive conceptualization of courtliness as we move from Hartmann's *Erec* through *Iwein* to Thomasin's didactic treatise provides

---

[103]  W. Ohly, *Die heilsgeschichtliche Struktur*, p. 111.
[104]  On the wide range of connotations of *hövesch* in *Iwein* see also Heinen, 'The Concepts *hof, hövesch*', p. 49.
[105]  For a positive view of courtliness in *Iwein* see also Jaeger, *The Origins of Courtliness*, pp. 244–46; Heinen, 'The Concepts *hof, hövesch*', p. 49 (with qualifications).
[106]  See above, pp. 129–33.
[107]  Thomasin himself states that the first section of his treatise teaches 'zuht und hüfscheit' to the young (*Der wälsche Gast* 1708f.), and that he has written an earlier 'book of courtliness' in the Romance tongue (ibid. 1174f.: 'an mîm buoch von der hüfscheit / daz ich welhschen hân gemacht').

insight into the civilizing function of courtly values, at least at the level of ideology and advocated behaviour, in the key decades around 1200.

Nevertheless, despite the positive connotations of *hövescheit* in *Iwein*, the association of chivalry with the court remains more problematical in Hartmann's last romance than it was in his earlier *Erec*. For one thing, the quality of 'courtliness' (*hövescheit*) itself is not so emphatically affirmed in an ethical sense, and not so central to Hartmann's ethical thinking in *Iwein* as are the values *triuwe, güete*, compassion and help. Of the 24 occurrences of the concept of courtliness in Iwein (including the negative *unhövescheit*), only one or two are linked directly to compassion (Iw 3387–91), or to Christian aid for the needy (Iw 6051–55); and when Hartmann as narrator, or one of his characters, appeals to ultimate ethical values, the concept 'courtly' plays little, if any part – Lunete, for instance, never mentions 'courtliness' in her indictment of Iwein, but reiterates the concept *triuwe* (Iw 3167–96). Courtliness is thus presented in *Iwein* as a desirable form of aristocratic behaviour, and is occasionally linked with high ethical values, but it is not in itself presented as the ultimate virtue.[108]

Moreover, at an institutional level, the portrayal of the court as the main focus of aristocratic sociability is more muted in *Iwein* than it was in *Erec*. A key feature of *Erec* is the fusion of personal and communal joy at court, so that joy appears as a socially cohesive force closely related to knightly activity. Such fusion of personal and communal joy figures only briefly and in a minor key in *Iwein*.[109] Communal joy is muted and fragile at courts in *Iwein*. It leads to quarrels in the opening scene at Arthur's court (Iw 108ff.), it sets the scene for personal disaster when Lunete accuses Iwein amid festive joy (Iw 3059ff.), and it masks deep suffering when a whole retinue merely pretends joy out of politeness to a guest (Iw 4413: 'trügevreude'). On the other hand the inner life of the hero is treated in more detail and more explicitly in *Iwein* than in *Erec* so that a gap opens up between personal and communal experience, and the concern of the text shifts towards the personal and subjective.

The end of each of Hartmann's two romances is significant in this respect, for whilst Erec's victory in his final combat restores joy to a court, and the work ends in a threefold apotheosis of communal joy at the court of Brandigan, at Arthur's court and in Erec's homeland,[110] Iwein's last combat remains undecided, the resolution of the conflict between Iwein and Laudine is brought about by Lunete's diplomacy and by the personal, mutual begging for forgiveness of the couple (Iw 8097–136), and the joy which this reconciliation brings is presented as a

---

[108]  See also Heinen, 'The Concepts *hof, hövesch*', p. 54.
[109]  See also Eroms, '*Vreude*', pp. 155–57.
[110]  See above, p. 129.

personal one, with no public celebration. It is appropriate to the personal quality of Iwein's and Laudine's reconciliation that the couple employ 'the language of repentance and forgiveness' in meeting each other.[111] This speaking in terms of 'sin', 'contrition', 'guilt', 'grace' and 'forgiveness' (Iw 8102–29) again brings something of the tone of Hartmann's religious legends into the romance *Iwein*, and it is on this note of contrition and personal joy that the romance ends, without the opening out to a public realm of the court that was so marked in the closing stages of *Erec*. Courtliness, as an affirmed quality of personal interaction, is indeed more highly developed and more explicitly articulated in *Iwein* than in *Erec*, but the court as a collective institution no longer has so commanding and pervasive a presence in Hartmann's last romance as it did in his first. In this sense, as in other features of style, there is a particular affinity between Hartmann's *Iwein* and *Der arme Heinrich*. It is not at all clear whether *Der arme Heinrich* preceded or followed *Iwein*, and indeed Hartmann could have been working on both at the same time. But whatever the chronological relation of *Iwein* and *Der arme Heinrich*, and despite the very real differences of theme, neither has such an enthusiastic apotheosis of chivalric sociability as that which figures in the closing stages of Hartmann's *Erec*, rather both tend towards a more reflective and personal inwardness.

*Chivalric values, aesthetic form and the historical situation of Hartmann's Iwein*

In broad terms, much the same could be said about the relation of chivalric values, aesthetic form and the historical situation with regard to *Iwein* as to *Erec*: both works have a pattern of success, crisis and reintegration within the secular world which involves a critical and legitimizing discussion of knighthood in the context of aristocratic society in south-west Germany towards or around the end of the twelfth century.[112] But there are also shifts of emphasis between the two works which call for interpretation.

In terms of social structure, both Hartmann's romances are addressed to the entire range of the aristocratic hierarchy. As the son of a king but also, for most of the romance, a knight wandering without retinue, Iwein, like Erec, could invite identification at the topmost and at the lowest levels of the aristocracy. Iwein's winning of a wife and lands by his own military prowess is also a fantasy of success capable of appealing to all who carried the sword. There is in *Iwein* little indication

---

[111]  McFarland, 'Narrative Structure', p. 154; compare Pérennec, *Recherches*, I, p. 176.
[112]  On *Erec* see above, pp. 135–46.

of a division of ethos between lesser and higher nobility. The vernacular term for *ministerialis* is used only once in *Iwein*, and then not in a technical sense, when Iwein declares himself to be Gawein's true 'dienestman' (Iw 7477). Indeed *Iwein* lends itself if anything even less well than *Erec* to a sharply profiled ministerial interpretation of its social function.[113] Rather the concept of knighthood's protective role provides in *Iwein* and in Erec an integrative ideology that is common to ministerial knights and the old nobility.[114]

*Iwein* does differ from *Erec* in providing more explicit signs of knighthood as an aristocratic status distinct from the rest of society, and in portraying the class mentality of knighthood with a hint of critical objectivity. Hartmann also shows a wider perspective and more social objectivity in *Iwein* than in *Erec* in his explicit linking of knighthood with youth and early manhood, and in his lively and original account of the tension between bachelor knighthood and married, landed lordship in Gawein's advice to Iwein.[115] This tension was bedded into the structure of aristocratic society in the central Middle Ages, it seems more constitutive for the world of Hartmann's romances than any rivalry between *ministeriales* and *nobiles*, and in explicitly treating it Hartmann again shows his sensitivity to the social realities which underlay the poetic world of romance.

With regard to the ethical legitimation of knighthood, Hartmann affirms the use of force as a class characteristic of the *militia* in his romances, but his affirmation is, decisively, a qualified one. In *Iwein*, Hartmann develops the tendency which informed his treatment of combat already in *Erec* by further meshing the knight's use of force into a network of legal, ethical and behavioural norms which tone down and harness the aggressively self-assertive warrior drive in chivalry. The political ideology of the peace laws is expressed from the outset of *Iwein*, as the first combat in the romance is prefaced in paradigmatic fashion by a ruler (Askalon) who charges an adventure-seeking knight (Kalogre-nant) with breach of the peace.[116] Even more pervasively in *Iwein* than in *Erec* the knight's use of force is bound into a legal and ethical framework.

However, Hartmann's concern was not merely to advocate obedience to external, objective laws (though the importance of this he took for granted), but also to cultivate inner curbs on aggressiveness by urging the importance of subjective intentions and inner moral reflection in the knighthood. This cultivation of the inner life links Hartmann's presentation of military chivalry in his romances in two directions – with

---

[113]  For reservations about this line of interpretation see also above, pp. 81f.
[114]  See also Mertens, *Laudine*, pp. 66f.
[115]  See above, pp. 219–26.
[116]  See above, p. 238.

the religious themes of his *Legenden* and with the subjective, emotional and moral reflection on love in his *Klage* and his lyric poetry. The dual structure of the romance has an ethical dynamic in *Erec* and in *Iwein*, as the hero's ethically oriented chivalry in the second cycle surpasses his more self-assertive and retributive use of force in the first cycle.[117] This pattern too is intensified in *Iwein*, as the retreat of *âventiure*, and the strong contrast between the self-orientation of Iwein's thoughts in the first cycle (his fear of being deprived of 'mîn rîterschaft', Iw 912) and his compassionate readiness to offer help in the second cycle, cast a critical light on chivalry which is based solely, or primarily, on the pursuit of personal glory. Similarly, the advocacy of peaceful conciliation in Arthur's royal judgement and in the reunion of Iwein and Laudine at the end of the work suggests a tacit reservation about the ethic of vengeance, the ethic of the feud, which underlies the events of the opening cycle. This is not to suggest that, after all, Hartmann presents Iwein as a murderer in the opening cycle, but to argue that the values which prompt action in the opening cycle are relativized and shown to be limited by the later action, and that the very composition of Hartmann's (and of Chrétien's) romances implies a subtle form of ethical criticism as well as celebration of the contemporary *militia*.

Hartmann's Arthurian romances both belong in the wider context of the peace movements of the eleventh through to the thirteenth century.[118] More precisely they share in large measure the concerns of the peace laws of the twelfth century. Like these laws, Hartmann's romances show knighthood as a privileged social status, and they confirm the knights' right to use armed force. However, in the romances as in the legal texts this right is also circumscribed, and affirmed only within a larger framework of justification. A leading authority on the German peace laws comments that they called for a change of heart in knighthood, because the warrior class was called on to give up traditional customs of feud in favour of an expansion of peace.[119] This change of heart receives an aesthetic expression in the changing, more ethically oriented nature of the hero's chivalry in Hartmann's narratives. A major tendency of the peace laws was to introduce mechanisms which delayed and restricted the use of military force in favour of peaceful means of settling quarrels: already Barbarossa's ordinance of 1186 formally required advance notice of feud, and by the 1230s the feud was relegated to a secondary position, and self-help with the use of armed force was sanctioned only after the party had

---

[117] On this aspect of *Erec* see above, pp. 137f.
[118] See also Sieverding, *Der ritterliche Kampf*, pp. 281–84; Schnell, 'Abaelards Gesinnungsethik', pp. 59f.
[119] Gernhuber, *Landfriedensbewegung*, pp. 21–23, 115.

attempted to gain satisfaction by peaceful legal means.[120] These delaying and restricting mechanisms have their poetic analogies in the network of limiting factors, including the moral reflectiveness of the hero, which circumscribe the legitimate use of force in Hartmann's romances.

The alignment of chivalry in Hartmann's romances with the peace laws again suggests the possibility of some impact of the Hohenstaufen court on Hartmann's literary production, for peace legislation was closely associated with the Hohenstaufen imperial court in Hartmann's time.[121] Moreover, developments in the Hohenstaufen ruling family and in their sphere of interest in Swabia in the 1180s and 1190s might throw some light on shifts of emphasis in Hartmann's portrayal of military chivalry and of the court as we move from *Erec* to *Iwein*.

The 1180s were a decade of achievement, relative peace and grounds for optimism in Hohenstaufen circles. At the level of imperial politics, the fall of Henry the Lion in 1180 and the attendant reorganization of relations between the crown and the imperial princes gave hope of long-term stability.[122] There was promise too in the personal composition of the Hohenstaufen family, for Frederick Barbarossa had five surviving legitimate sons, all of whom reached or approached the transition from youth to early manhood in the decade from about 1180. In 1180 Henry became fifteen, Frederick thirteen, Otto ten, Conrad eight, and Philip, the latecomer on whose shoulders such a heavy burden was to fall after Henry VI's death in 1197, three.[123] The great Whitsun festival at Mainz in 1184, when the emperor's two eldest sons were knighted, suggests that these were years apt for the promotion of knighthood not only for its military and political significance, but also as a form of sociability capable of enhancing the well-being of the court in peacetime.[124] Evidence of new forms of sociability and self-understanding involving youth and the emotions is provided by the cultivation of the new courtly lyric as a social art in Hohenstaufen circles in the 1180s, perhaps more in the entourage of the young King Henry than around his ageing father.[125] This cultural complex is highly suggestive for an author like Hartmann, who shows great interest, especially in his early works, in the emotional life of aristocratic youth and in the relation of knighthood and the court. Wherever Hartmann was working in south-west

---

[120] See above, pp. 91, 114.

[121] Thus the two great peace ordinances of this period, the Rhenish Franconian peace of 1179 and the constitution against arsonists of 1186, both open with an expression of Barbarossa's imperial majesty: 'Fridericus, dei gratia Romanorum imperator et semper augustus' (MGH Const., I, no. 277, p. 381; no. 318, p. 449).

[122] Munz, *Frederick Barbarossa*, p. 357.

[123] Ages based on Assmann, 'Friedrich Barbarossas Kinder', passim.

[124] See Fleckenstein, 'Friedrich Barbarossa und das Rittertum', pp. 1024–32.

[125] See above, pp. 186f.; on Henry VI as the likely focus of the Hohenstaufen poets see Bumke, *Mäzene*, p. 150.

Germany, it is hardly conceivable that he could have been ignorant of, or uninterested in, affairs at the imperial court. If he was in some way attached to the household of Berthold IV of Zähringen or Welf VI in the 1180s, news of, for example, the Mainz festivities of 1184 could easily have reached him, because Berthold and Welf both attended the imperial court on this occasion.[126] Hartmann's independent shaping of the close of *Erec* conveys a view of kingship that may well suggest sympathy to Hohenstaufen rule;[127] and in general the upbeat political and cultural atmosphere of the Hohenstaufen court in the 1180s, however directly or indirectly Hartmann may have experienced it, may well have provided a public motivation for the enthusiastic merging of knighthood, youth and kingship with the collective joy of the court in his adaptation of Chrétien's *Erec*.

The decade in which *Iwein* was written (ca. 1192–ca. 1203) brought darker tones in the history of Swabia and the Upper Rhein, and in the nexus of Hohenstaufen, Zähringen and Welf courts within which Hartmann's literary activity seems most likely to have taken place. Barbarossa and his son Frederick, duke of Swabia, both died on crusade, in 1190 and 1191 respectively. The young Hohenstaufen Conrad took over the Welf lands in Swabia after the death of Welf VI in 1191. Conrad led a bold but undisciplined life. He entered into a feud against Berthold V of Zähringen, which ended when he (Conrad) was killed in August 1196, allegedly whilst attempting to seduce another man's wife.[128] His elder brother Otto, count palatine of Burgundy, is credited with greed and faithlessness in his political dealings in these years.[129] In 1197 he murdered a relative of the Zähringen family, and this amongst other provocations caused Berthold of Zähringen to join an alliance of lords in a war of vengeance against Otto.[130] Berthold had joined a Saxon and Rhenish alliance against Emperor Henry VI in 1192, but he seems to have had closer relations with the emperor by 1195/1196. The fact that neither Henry VI nor the youngest Hohenstaufen brother, Philip, took up the feuds of their brothers Conrad and Otto against Berthold indicates that these feuds did not necessarily involve a fundamental rift between Berthold and the crown. The death of Henry VI in September 1197 produced a disputed succession to the crown which led to civil war and a serious weakening in the position of the crown. Berthold of Zähringen was approached to be a candidate for the crown in 1198, but

---

[126] *La Chronique de Gislebert de Mons*, p. 159; Mertens, 'Das literarische Mäzenatentum der Zähringer', p. 17 speculates that Hartmann may have accompanied Berthold to the Mainz court.

[127] See above, pp. 143–45.

[128] Freed, *The Counts of Falkenstein*, p. 66.

[129] Van Cleve, *The Emperor Frederick II*, p. 29.

[130] For what follows in this paragraph see Heyck, *Geschichte der Herzöge von Zähringen*, pp. 437–48.

after weighing the opposition he declined, and supported the candidature of the Hohenstaufen Philip against the Welf Otto.

Bernd Thum hypothetically locates Hartmann's works in the Altdorf Welf context, and he suggests that *Iwein*, which is dated by common consent after the death of Duke Welf VI in 1191, may have been intended partly as a reminder to the young Hohenstaufen lords of the duties of keeping peace and order in their lands.[131] In other words, the concern with peace-keeping in *Iwein* may reflect unease among the Welf knighthood, who had passed into Hohenstaufen service on the death of Welf VI, at the way the young Hohenstaufen Duke Conrad was running, or neglecting, their affairs in Swabia. Volker Mertens, arguing for a Zähringen context, points to the time of troubles throughout the empire after the death of Henry VI as the backcloth to *Iwein*.[132] Indeed at whatever stage in the decade up to ca. 1203 Hartmann was working on *Iwein*, and whatever specific audience he had in mind, political tensions and recurrent feuding involving the leading powers in south-west Germany, and consequently the foremost courts, meant that the historical situation was no longer as conducive to an optimistic idealization of youthful knightly adventure, or to an unproblematical projection of the court as a place of collective stability and joy, as it had been in the 1180s, the decade which left its mark on his *Erec*.

However, as well as springing from a changed historical situation, Hartmann's *Iwein* also exhibits, not least in the treatment of chivalry, a maturer authorial voice than his *Erec*, and the passage from *Erec* to *Iwein* may reflect biographical change in the life of Hartmann himself. The interplay of authorial voice and historical situation will be discussed in a brief concluding chapter, which will also draw together some of the main threads of our topic of knighthood in Hartmann's works.

---

[131]   Thum, 'Politische Probleme', pp. 60, 67–69.
[132]   Mertens, *Laudine*, p. 68.

# 9

# Conclusions

The works of Hartmann von Aue document key features of knighthood as a military and a social order, and of chivalry as an ethical, ideological and behavioural complex. In turn the history of knighthood illuminates key features of Hartmann's *œuvre*.

Knighthood was still, in the German empire around 1200, a military function, intimately connected with mounted warfare. This function is amply documented in the knight's use of force in Hartmann's works, and in Hartmann's presentation of shield, sword and lance as the characteristic military attributes of knighthood. Knighthood also acquired broader connotations of a prestigious social nature during the twelfth century, in a gradual redefinition of the upper levels of German society which involved movements in two directions: on the one hand a downward percolation of aristocratic principles and lifestyle from the old, free nobility into the expanding category of *ministeriales*, and on the other hand an expansion and an upward movement of the term *ritter*, 'knight', as it spread beyond its early sense of professional warrior, including serving vassal, to be accepted as an honouring term by great nobles.[1] It is an oversimplification to locate the origins of German knighthood exclusively either in the old, free nobility or in the newer category of *ministeriales*, rather the new order drew elements from both sources. As a result of these movements, knighthood was often viewed in the twelfth century as a military and social community, an *ordo*, that included the high nobility and the lesser *ministeriales*.[2] Moreover, precisely the period of Hartmann's literary activity, the last two decades of the twelfth century, formed an important transitional stage in the history of the German nobility, as these decades brought a spread of

[1] See above, pp. 63–72.
[2] See above, pp. 71f.

*miles* and *ritter* terminology in high noble circles in Germany, and a strengthening of the aristocratic principle of birth at the lower end of the knightly hierarchy.[3]

All these social tendencies are expressed in Hartmann's works. Indeed, it is a central conclusion of this study that Hartmann, in all the genres in which he worked, and with whatever degree of aesthetic stylization or narrative fictionality, remained attentive to the here and now of his German social environment, and that his works express, in various ways and at various levels, tensions and movement in the German aristocracy of his day. The speech and thoughts of Hartmann's characters reflect the sharpening class divisions between knighthood and peasantry,[4] and the application of the term *ritter* to serving knights and to sons of kings conveys knighthood as an order which embraced great nobles and *ministeriales*, whilst the anxious concern expressed by some figures about different degrees of nobility amongst knights expresses the hierarchical rifts that continued to exist within knighthood as a social order.[5] There are touches in Hartmann's works which suggest a particular sympathy for the lesser reaches of knighthood, but Hartmann's chivalric ideology remains socially more integrative than disjunctive, reaching out to the old free nobility as well as to the newer class of *ministeriales*.

The increasing social pre-eminence of knighthood was accompanied in the twelfth century by the development of a legitimatory ideological framework, that is to say by the crystallization of chivalry as an ethical and social ideal. Chivalry was less a matter of absolute moral thinking than a product of historical and social circumstances, and as such it brought together strands from widely differing directions. Hartmann was the first author in the history of German literature to include all the main components of this ideal in his works: warrior courage tempered with prudence; the Christian chivalry specifically of crusading warfare; a broader view of the knight as compassionate helper of the weak and defender of justice; and, reaching out from the military sphere, the qualities of love and decorous behaviour in peaceful social contexts. This amalgam of cultural values in Hartmann's presentation of knighthood expresses a tension which is central to chivalry as a historical phenomenon, a tension between warrior self-assertiveness and the view that armed force is fully legitimate only in the service of some broader cause. On this important issue Hartmann's treatment of knighthood seems again to be less the reflection of a society in calm stasis than a product of and a processing of social transition, in this case the long

[3]  See above, pp. 68–71.
[4]  See above, pp. 150f., 215f.
[5]  See above, pp. 73–83.

transition from a more clannish warrior ethos of the early Middle Ages, which claimed the use of force as an inherent right of the aristocracy, to the more pacified gentry class of the early modern period.[6]

The affinities between the chivalric ethos of Hartmann's romances and the provisions of the German peace laws, which also recognized the aristocracy's right of arms, but sought to limit this right and subordinate it to peaceful processes of law, confirm the transitional nature of this ethos, its balancing act, which verges on the paradoxical, involving warrior self-assertion and social control. The very composition of Hartmann's Arthurian romances has an ethical dynamic which, in the qualifications set upon the knight's use of force, reflects a major development in the broader legal and social history of the medieval aristocracy. The pondering of rights and wrongs in combat situations, the advocacy of restraint and conciliation, the attention paid to gestures of reciprocity and to courteous and considerate behaviour, all these features of a civilized ethos, which inform the social fabric of Hartmann's romances, and which counterpoint the praise of warrior values in *Erec*, and even more pervasively in *Iwein*, are not solely matters of internal literary style, but also reflexes of the broader historical dynamic of the peace movements, as this dynamic was experienced by a literate and thinking knightly author in the specific context of south-west Germany in the last decades of the twelfth century.

Hartmann was well equipped by chronology, and by what little we can gather about the social circumstances of his life, to provide a literary self-interpretation of knighthood. Knighthood, as a mark of social status and a cluster of ethical and behavioural values, has roots that reach back in different directions and to various depths of history. However, diverse as the origins of knighthood were, the second half of the twelfth century was a period of decisive importance, when the various strands came together to form the social and cultural ideology of chivalry which appears in the decades between 1160 and 1190 in the great princely courts of northern France.[7] The study of Hartmann's works in their social context has shown that much the same period was decisive for the history of chivalry in the German empire too, for it was in these decades that knighthood emerged ever more clearly as a social category in German historical sources, that the term *ritter* effected its crucial breakthrough in vernacular texts, and that the two poetic genres which were to be the main aesthetic vehicles for the ideology of chivalry – the courtly lyric and the courtly romance – emerged in German literature.

---

[6]   Compare Borst, 'Das Rittertum im Hochmittelalter', p. 229: 'Nur in der Zwischenlage zwischen Herrschaft und Dienst blühte das Rittertum, nur in der Epoche zwischen Adelswillkür und Staatsmacht [. . .]'.

[7]   See also Duby, review of Keen, *Chivalry*, in *Times Literary Supplement*, 29 June 1984, p. 720; Flori, *L'essor*, pp. 329f. and often.

Hartmann's use of French literary sources shows the indebtedness of the German empire to French culture in this key period. Indeed at one level, Hartmann's adaptations of French works are part of a broader reception of French aristocratic culture, which included styles of dress and forms of social behaviour, and which has recently been well surveyed in its historical context.[8] However, the early occurrence of important aspects of knightly ideology in religious and secular spheres in German sources that were independent of French literature,[9] and indeed the very vigour of Hartmann's own adaptation of French works, indicate that chivalry, far from being a purely literary import from France, also had roots in the social life of the German aristocracy.

The relation of Hartmann's literary presentation of knighthood to the social reality of his own day has emerged in this study as less simple than has at times been suggested. Hartmann's works reflect in part a pre-existing mentality of knighthood as a military and social grouping – but they also sought to shape this mentality. Chivalry was not yet, in the last decades of the twelfth century, a static and rigidly defined code of conduct, rather it was still in a process of formation, which is expressed, for instance, in the chronological changes in Hartmann's usage in the vocabulary of knighthood and of courtliness.[10] Hartmann's works do not stand, as it were, outside history, rather they were themselves part of the historical reality of chivalric values, as these were developing; they provided a repository of thoughts, feelings, ethical ideals, modes of behaviour which could influence the mentality of readers and hearers. This function of proposing models of feeling and conduct (*Leitbilder*) for aristocratic society is marked by the frequent references to Hartmann in later authors in medieval Germany, and, in the case of *Iwein*, by pictorial representations of the action which indicate its culturally normative resonance in the life of the German aristocracy.[11]

The precise conditions in which Hartmann's works were produced, and the location, or locations, of their primary reception, remain elusive. We do not know the identity of the lord whose death Hartmann mourns in his lyrics, or of any patron who promoted his literary activity, nor do we know whether lord and patron were one and the same person. Whatever the standing of Hartmann's lord, and the place of origin of his own family, his work presupposes the interest and encouragement of a

8   Bumke, *Höfische Kultur*, I, pp. 83–133.
9   See above, pp. 41, 48, 52f., 58–60, 171f.
10  See above, pp. 53f., 273–75.
11  On literary references to Hartmann, and on the pictorial representations of figures from *Iwein* see Cormeau / Störmer, *Hartmann von Aue*, pp. 23–25, 227–31, with further bibliography; on the Iwein murals at Rodenegg castle see now Curschmann, '*Der aventiure bilde nemen*', passim. For a historian's view of courtly literature as a means of shaping people's feelings in the twelfth century see Gillingham, 'Love, Marriage and Politics', pp. 298–300.

court, which could provide an audience, and access to the French works which he adapted. The three most prominent Swabian dynasties of Hartmann's day, the Hohenstaufen, the Welfs and the Zähringer, could each have met these conditions. Moreover, whilst it is plausible to look to these greatest dynasties, the possibility of a slightly lesser lordly household should not be excluded in the search for the primary reception of Hartmann's works.[12] The theme of knighthood does not yield evidence as to which court, or courts, formed Hartmann's target audience, since the mixed aristocracy of free nobles and *ministeriales*, which is implied in Hartmann's treatment of knighthood, was common throughout Germany in the late twelfth century. With regard to the political focus of Hartmann's work, Hartmann's adaptations of Chrétien's romances seem not to suggest an ideology which is more favourable to the German territorial princes than to the king. Rather, Hartmann shows respect for kingship by omitting, or toning down, criticisms of kings in adapting Chrétien – a feature in which he differs from his near contemporary, Wolfram von Eschenbach. Indeed, there is much in Hartmann's works that could have been looked on with favour in a Hohenstaufen context, or that could suggest at least an interested acquaintance with the Hohenstaufen sphere of influence.[13] This tendency of adaptation is not, in turn, an argument against the possibility that Hartmann worked with an eye on a princely, ducal (perhaps even the Zähringen) court; it may rather reflect the German political situation of the twelfth century, when, in spite of frequent conflicts between the king and disaffected princes, as there were frequent conflicts between the magnates themselves, 'nevertheless, the sources reveal an extraordinary degree of interdependence and cooperation between king and princes'.[14]

Whilst our ignorance about any patronage of Hartmann's works is regrettable, the importance of this information gap should not be overestimated. It remains significant that Hartmann, although he often reflects on the process of composition, never mentions a specific patron. Nor do his works suggest some underlying tension between the voice of the author and the wishes of a patron. However, they do convey a close and lively sense of communication (though varying in style from work to work) between poet and audience. Hartmann's *œuvre* as a whole is characterized by a high degree of authorial self-consciousness, a strong sense of the author as a poetic personality.[15] Moreover, this poetic

---

[12] See the perceptive comments of Boesch, 'Mittelhochdeutsche Dichtung am Oberrhein', pp. 88f.

[13] See above pp. 31–35, 142–46, 186f., 232, 269f., 279–81.

[14] Arnold, *Princes and Territories*, p. 11.

[15] See also Seiffert, 'Hartmann and Walther', p. 86; Reusner, 'Anhang', p. 167: 'Hartmann von Aue erscheint als eine für das deutsche Mittelalter ungewöhnlich klar faßbare Dichterpersönlichkeit'.

personality has knightly contours and shows some development in the course of the works, so that Hartmann's presentation of himself in the first person, and the image of the 'implied author' which we gain as we read him, also contribute to our perception of knighthood in his works.[16]

The chronology of Hartmann's songs is too uncertain to allow safe conclusions about a linear development of the poetic *persona* in these works. However, the emotional and moral sensitivity, and the broad range of the knightly voice in Hartmann's lyrics, from the lover's self-accusation, through criticism of lack of reciprocity in love, to the penitence and self-confidence of the crusader, make this small corpus into an impressive document of the cultural self-understanding of a German knight. The relative chronology of Hartmann's *Klage* and his narrative works, whilst posing some problems, is clearer than that of his lyric output; and these works exhibit not only a broad cultural range, but also some chronological development in the self-presentation of the author/narrator Hartmann, and in his concern with knighthood. In the early works, the *Klage* and *Erec*, Hartmann appears as a youth, or at least an inexperienced person (Kl 7: 'jungelinc'; Er 1603, 7480: 'tumber kneht'), and in both works there is a high degree of authorial identification with the young protagonist. Indeed the learning experiences of the protagonists in these two works seem to be, in part, poetic projections of the talented and self-conscious young knightly author Hartmann at the beginning of his literary career. Hartmann's empathy with chivalric youth continues in *Gregorius*, especially in his independent account of the young Gregorius's knightly ambitions, which echo the chivalric enthusiasm of hero and narrator in *Erec*, and the idealistic advice of the heart in the *Klage*. However, the ethos of knightly youth is also explicitly qualified in *Gregorius* by the narrator's penitential warnings against youthful over-confidence in the prologue (Gr 1–34), and by the larger framework of sin, penance and divine grace in the story itself, though a religious qualification of the young knight's pursuit of honour was adumbrated already at the end of Hartmann's *Erec*.

The handling of vocabulary, rhyme and rhythm, direct speech and descriptive passages all show *Der arme Heinrich* and *Iwein* to be later works than *Erec* and *Gregorius*.[17] The poetic *persona* of Hartmann also undergoes some change with the passage of time, as the qualities of youth and inexperience which are attributed to the figure Hartmann in the *Klage*, *Erec* and *Gregorius* give place in the later narratives to firm statements of the author's adult social standing as knight (AH 1; Iw 21) and 'dienstman' (AH 5). Hartmann is less intrusive, as narrator, in *Der*

---

16  The term 'implied author' is taken from Booth, *The Rhetoric of Fiction*, p. 151 and often.
17  See Wolff, 'Vom *Büchlein*', passim; Cormeau / Störmer, *Hartmann von Aue*, p. 26.

*arme Heinrich* and *Iwein* than he was in *Erec* and *Gregorius*.[18] His more restrained presence does not indicate a fading of authorial interest, rather it suggests the experience and discrimination of a mature author, who can search for material in various books (AH 6–15), can read and compose poetry in his leisure hours (Iw 21–30), and can look back on, and quote, his own earlier work, as a moral example of proper chivalric conduct, in the voice of no less a figure than Gawein, the foremost Arthurian knight (Iw 2791–98). With regard to the theme of knighthood within the narrative action, a more youthfully optimistic, even exuberant identification of the author with the chivalric pursuit of honour in combat in *Erec* gives way to a more qualified, less enthusiastically committed note in *Iwein*. Thus Erec's remarkable affirmation of the pursuit of honour in combat as a gamble sanctioned by God (Er 8521–75) suggests the author's identification with this wager of chivalry, whilst Hartmann's greater detachment from the self-assertive ethos of knightly youth is finely expressed in *Iwein* when this ethos, with its active pursuit of glory, an heiress and lands, recedes into the deceptive world of a dream experience at the moment of Iwein's awakening (Iw 3509–93).

The fading of indications of youth and inexperience in the poetic *persona* of Hartmann in the transition from the early to the later works may well reflect biographical change in the life of the historically real person Hartmann. It could be that the increasingly troubled historical context of Hartmann's literary activity as we move from the 1180s through the 1190s[19] coincided with the passage from knightly youth, or early manhood, to more settled responsibilities in Hartmann's own life, so that the greater concern with the social and moral obligations of chivalry, indeed a certain shift of social focus towards settled lordship, peace and order in *Iwein* by comparison with *Erec*, may reflect the impact on Hartmann's adaptation of Chrétien's work not only of a broader German historical situation, but also of Hartmann's own experience of mature social responsibilities.

There is, however, too much that is sure about Hartmann's authorial and historical position for this study to end on a speculatively biographical note which could take us outside the texts and into conjecture about the possible accidents of an individual life. What is clear, and of decisive importance for a literary and a historical understanding of Hartmann's works is Hartmann's unusual, but historically deeply significant position as an educated knight, a position which connects his works both to the world of the secular aristocracy and to that of clerical learning and spirituality. The interaction of these two spheres produced some of the most dynamic cultural developments

---

[18] Arndt, *Der Erzähler*, pp. 185f.
[19] See above, pp. 280f.

of the high Middle Ages, and this is nowhere more richly documented than in the history of chivalry, as critical voices within the Church urged an increase of moral awareness on the secular aristocracy, while clerical learning also provided the aristocracy with the intellectual and literary equipment which enabled it to articulate, in the literary theme of knighthood, a new, self-legitimizing ideology which enjoyed considerable independence from official Church thinking. Hartmann's involvement with both the cultural world of the lay nobility and that of clerical learning is a major factor contributing to the existential vigour and the cultural breadth of his work.

The courts of the twelfth century were, in historical reality, a major focus for the interaction of knights and clerics which so strongly influenced the development of a knightly ideology, and of a courtly culture.[20] Hartmann's works, too, testify to the importance of the court as a place of aristocratic sociability and a centre of values. However, Hartmann's independent elaboration of the debate between the young Gregorius and the abbot in *Gregorius*, and his sympathetic presentation of peasant life in *Der arme Heinrich*, also point towards a socially less prestigious, more local interplay of knighthood and religious values than the world of the great courts, and this more local experience is a further factor in the cultural complexity of Hartmann's situation. The unusually wide range of genres in his works – secular love lyrics, crusading songs, a didactic treatise on love, two chivalric romances, two religious narratives – is an appropriate expression of his key location at the meeting of various cultural traditions, and at an important stage in the social and ideological history of knighthood. Moreover, it is a mark of Hartmann's poetic achievement that his works of different genre, whilst remaining in a creative tension to each other, are not entirely different in ethos, rather there are cross-influences between the genres, for instance as a religious coloration enters his romances, and elements of chivalry and courtliness are taken up in his religious works. Recent scholars have rightly pointed to the importance of transgeneric features and intertextual links in Hartmann's works, and this study amply confirms that the creative stretching of the limits of different genres, which characterizes Hartmann's poetic activity, is connected not least with his position as an educated knight.[21]

Finally, the self-consciousness of Hartmann as author, which forms a flexibly cohesive link in the diversity of his works, is also, in large measure, a product of that interaction of different cultural values which led to the formation of chivalry as a broader ideology, and which called for an enhanced reflectiveness and interpretative activity on the part of

---

[20]  See Fleckenstein, 'Miles und clericus', passim.
[21]  McFarland / Ranawake (eds), *Hartmann von Aue*, pp. viiif.

authors, particularly in the formative period of the decades around 1200. Hartmann's works provide a literary self-interpretation of knighthood which was unprecedented for its range in Germany, and which forms an important document in the history of knighthood at a European level, and this act of self-interpretation also marks an important stage in the emergence of authorial self-consciousness in medieval literature. The juxtaposition of authorial voice and historical context is a fitting note on which to leave a poet in whose presentation of knighthood the two entered into such a creative relationship.

# Bibliography

## 1. Primary Sources

The Anglo-Saxon Chronicle, see The Peterborough Chronicle.

Annales Aquenses, ed. G. Waitz, MGH Scriptores, 24 (Hanover, 1879), pp. 33–39.

Das Annolied, ed. and transl. Eberhard Nellmann (Stuttgart, 1975).

The Archpoet, Die Gedichte des Archipoeta, ed. Heinrich Watenphul and Heinrich Krefeld (Heidelberg, 1958).

Arnold of Lübeck, Chronica Slavorum, ed. J.M. Lappenberg, MGH Scriptores rerum Germanicarum (Hanover, 1868).

Bernard of Clairvaux, De laude novae militiae, MPL, 182, cols 921–40.

Berthold of Zwiefalten, see Zwiefalter Chroniken.

Bouquet, Martin, Recueil des Historiens des Gaules et de la France, new edn, vol. XV (Paris, 1878; reprint Farnborough, 1968).

Caesarius of Heisterbach, Dialogus Miraculorum, ed. J. Strange (Cologne, 1851).

Calendar of the Patent Rolls 1232–1247 (London, 1906), 1258–1266 (London, 1910).

Chrétien de Troyes, Christian von Troyes. Sämtliche erhaltene Werke, ed. Wendelin Foerster. I: Cligés (Halle, 1884); II: Der Löwenritter (Yvain) (Halle, 1887); III: Erec und Enide (Halle, 1890); IV: Der Karrenritter (Lancelot) und das Wilhelmsleben (Guillaume d'Angleterre) (Halle, 1899); all 4 vols reprinted Amsterdam, 1965.

——, Erec et Enide = Kristian von Troyes. Erec und Enide. Textausgabe mit Variantenauswahl, ed. Wendelin Foerster, Romanische Bibliothek, 13, 3rd edn (Halle, 1934).

——, Erec und Enide, transl. and intr. Ingrid Kasten, Klassische Texte des romanischen Mittelalters, 17 (Munich, 1979) [Foerster's text of 1934 edn, with modern German translation].

——, Kristian von Troyes. Yvain (Der Löwenritter). Textausgabe mit Variantenauswahl, ed. Wendelin Foerster, Romanische Bibliothek, 5, 4th edn (Halle, 1912).

——, Yvain (Le chevalier au Lion), ed. T.B.W. Reid (Manchester, 1942; frequently reprinted) [reproduces Foerster's text of 1912].

——, Yvain, transl. and intr. Ilse Nolting-Hauff, Klassische Texte des romanischen Mittelalters (Munich, 1962) [Foerster's text of 1912, with modern German translation].

——, Perceval (Le Conte du Graal), ed. William Roach, TLF, 71, 2nd edn (Geneva and Paris, 1959).

(Note. In the present study references to Chrétien's Erec et Enide and Yvain are to Foerster's texts as established in the Romanische Bibliothek editions).

Eilhart von Oberg, *Tristrant*, ed. Franz Lichtenstein, QF, 19 (Straßburg, 1877).

——, *Tristrant*, ed. and transl. into modern French by Danielle Buschinger, GAG, 202 (Göppingen, 1976).

Ekkehard of Aura, *Chronica*, in *Frutolfs und Ekkehards Chroniken und die anonyme Kaiserchronik*, ed. Franz-Josef Schmale and Irene Schmale-Ott, FSGA, 15 (Darmstadt, 1972), pp. 122–208, 267–376.

*Eneas* see *Roman d'Eneas*.

Etienne de Fougères, *Le Livre des Manières*, ed. R. Anthony Lodge, TLF, 275 (Geneva and Paris, 1979).

Geoffrey of Monmouth, *The Historia Regum Britannie of Geoffrey of Monmouth. I: Bern, Burgerbibliothek, MS. 568*, ed. Neil Wright (Cambridge, 1984).

——, *The History of the Kings of Britain*, transl. Lewis Thorpe (Harmondsworth, 1966).

*Gereint, Son of Erbin*, in *The Mabinogion*, transl. Gwyn Jones and Thomas Jones, Everyman's Library, 97 (London and New York, 1949), pp. 229–73.

Gerhoh of Reichersberg, *De aedificio Dei*, MPL, 194, cols 1187–1336.

Gislebert of Mons, *La Chronique de Gislebert de Mons*, ed. Léon Vanderkindere (Brussels, 1904).

Gottfried von Straßburg, *Tristan*, ed. and transl. Rüdiger Krohn, 6th edn, 3 vols (Stuttgart, 1993).

*Grégoire*, see *La Vie du Pape Saint Grégoire*.

Guibert of Nogent, *Gesta Dei per Francos*, in *Recueil des Historiens des Croisades. Historiens occidentaux*, vol. IV (Paris, 1879), pp. 113–263.

Hartmann von Aue, Lyrics in *Des Minnesangs Frühling*, pp. 404–30.

——, *Lieder*, ed. and transl. Ernst von Reusner (Stuttgart, 1985) [texts based on *Des Minnesangs Frühling*].

——, *Die Klage – Das (zweite) Büchlein. Aus dem Ambraser Heldenbuch*, ed. Herta Zutt (Berlin, 1968).

——, *Erec*, ed. Albert Leitzmann, rev. Ludwig Wolff, ATB, 39, 6th edn, prepared by Christoph Cormeau and Kurt Gärtner (Tübingen, 1985).

——, *Gregorius*, ed. Hermann Paul, ATB, 2, 13th edn, prepared by Burghart Wachinger (Tübingen, 1984).

——, *Der arme Heinrich*, ed. Hermann Paul, ATB, 3, 15th edn, prepared by Gesa Bonath (Tübingen, 1984) [edition cited].

——, *Der arme Heinrich und die Büchlein von Hartmann von Aue*, ed. Moriz Haupt, 2nd edn (Leipzig, 1881).

——, *Der arme Heinrich von Hartmann von Aue*, ed. Erich Gierach, 2nd edn (Heidelberg, 1925).

——, *Iwein*, ed. G.F. Benecke and K. Lachmann, 7th edn, rev. Ludwig Wolff (Berlin 1968).

Hefele, C.J. and Leclercq, H., *Histoire des Conciles*, vol. V, 2 parts (Paris, 1912, 1913).

Heinrich von Melk, *Erinnerung an den Tod*, ed. Richard Kienast (Heidelberg, 1946).

Heinrich von Veldeke, *Sente Servas – Sanctus Servatius*, ed. Theodor Frings and Gabriele Schieb (Halle / Saale, 1956).

——, *Eneide*, ed. Gabriele Schieb and Theodor Frings, DTM, 58–59, 2 vols (Berlin, 1964–65).

Helmold of Bosau, *Chronica Slavorum*, ed. Heinz Stoob, FSGA, 19 (Darmstadt, 1973).

Herbort von Fritzlar, *Liet von Troye*, ed. G. Karl Frommann, BDNL, 5 (Quedlinburg and Leipzig, 1837; reprint Amsterdam, 1966).

Hermann von Sachsenheim, *Die Mörin*, ed. Horst Dieter Schlosser, Deutsche Klassiker des Mittelalters, N.F., 3 (Wiesbaden, 1974).

*Herzog Ernst*, ed. Karl Bartsch (Vienna, 1869).

*L'Histoire de Guillaume le Maréchal*, ed. Paul Meyer, Société de l'Histoire de France, 3 vols (Paris, 1891, 1894, 1901).

*Historia Welforum*, ed. Erich König, Schwäbische Chroniken der Stauferzeit, 1 (Stuttgart, 1938; reprint Sigmaringen, 1978).

Honorius Augustodunensis, *De imagine mundi*, MPL, 172, cols 116–87.

Hugo von Trimberg, *Der Renner*, ed. Gustav Ehrismann, 4 vols (Tübingen, 1908–11; reprint, with additions by Günther Schweikle, Berlin, 1970).

John of Salisbury, *Policraticus*, ed. Clemens C.J. Webb (Oxford, 1909).

——, *The Statesman's Book: Policraticus*, transl. John Dickinson (New York, 1963).

*Joufroi de Poitiers*, ed. Percival B. Fay and John L. Grigsby, TLF, 183 (Geneva and Paris, 1972).

*Karlmeinet*, ed. Adalbert von Keller, BLVS, 45 (Stuttgart, 1858; reprint Amsterdam, 1971).

*Die Kaiserchronik*, ed. Edward Schröder, MGH Deutsche Chroniken, I,1 (Hanover, 1892; reprint Berlin, 1964).

*König Rother*, ed. Theodor Frings and Joachim Kuhnt, Altdeutsche Texte für den akademischen Unterricht, 2 (Halle, 1954).

Lambert of Ardres, *Historia Comitum Ghisnensium*, ed. Johannes Heller, MGH Scriptores, 24 (Hanover, 1879), pp. 550–642.

Lampert of Hersfeld, *Annales*, ed. O. Holder-Egger and Wolfgang Dietrich Fritz, FSGA, 13 (Darmstadt, 1962).

Leitzmann, Albert (ed.), *Kleinere mittelhochdeutsche Lehrgedichte*, Erstes Heft, ATB, 9, 2nd edn (Halle, 1928).

*Lucidarius*, ed. Felix Heidlauf, DTM, 28 (Berlin, 1915).

*Das Ludwigslied*, in Wilhelm Braune (ed.), *Althochdeutsches Lesebuch*, 16th edn by E.A. Ebbinghaus (Tübingen, 1978), XXXVI.

Map, Walter, *De Nugis Curialium*, ed. and transl. M.R. James, rev. C.N.L. Brooke amd R.B. Mynors (Oxford, 1983).

*Des Minnesangs Frühling*, ed. Karl Lachmann et al., 36th edn, rev. Hugo Moser and Helmut Tervooren (Stuttgart, 1977).

Neidhart von Reuental, *Die Lieder Neidharts*, ed. Edmund Wießner, ATB, 44, 4th edn, rev. Paul Sappler (Tübingen, 1984).

*Das Nibelungenlied*, ed. Karl Bartsch, rev. Helmut de Boor, 21st edn (Wiesbaden, 1979).

Otto of Freising, *Chronica, sive historia de duabus civitatibus*, ed. Walther Lammers, FSGA, 16 (Darmstadt, 1961).

—— and Rahewin, *Gesta Frederici*, ed. Franz-Josef Schmale, FSGA, 17 (Darmstadt, 1965).

*The Peterborough Chronicle*, ed. Cecily Clark, 2nd edn (Oxford, 1970).

*Reinfried von Braunschweig*, ed. Karl Bartsch, BLVS, 109 (Tübingen, 1871).

*Die Reinhardsbrunner Briefsammlung*, ed. Friedel Peeck, MGH Epistolae selectae, 5 (Weimar, 1952).

*Der Reinhart Fuchs des Elsässers Heinrich*, ed. Klaus Düwel, ATB 96 (Tübingen, 1984).

Reinmar von Zweter, *Die Gedichte Reinmars von Zweter*, ed. Gustav Roethe (Leipzig, 1887; reprint Amsterdam, 1967).

Roger of Hoveden, *Chronica*, ed. William Stubbs, Rolls Series, 51, 4 vols (London, 1868-71).

*Das Rolandslied des Pfaffen Konrad*, ed. Carl Wesle, Altdeutsche Texte für den akademischen Unterricht, 3 (Halle, 1955).

*Roman d'Eneas*, ed. J.J. Salverda de Grave, Classiques Français du Moyen Age, 44, 62 (Paris 1925-29).

Rothe, Johannes, *Der Ritterspiegel*, ed. Hans Neumann, ATB, 38 (Halle, 1936).

Rudolf von Ems, *Willehalm von Orlens*, ed. Victor Junk, DTM, 2 (Berlin, 1905; reprint Dublin and Zürich, 1967).

*Ruodlieb*, ed. and transl. Fritz Peter Knapp (Stuttgart, 1977).

Rymer, Thomas, *Foedera, conventiones, litterae, et cujuscunque generis acta publica inter reges Angliae et alios quosvis imperatores, reges, pontifices, principes, vel communitates*, 4 vols (London, 1816-1869).

*Sachsenspiegel, Landrecht*, ed. Cl. Frhr. von Schwerin and Hans Thieme (Stuttgart, 1969).

*Seifried Helbling*, ed. Joseph Seemüller (Halle, 1886).

*Speculum ecclesiae. Eine frühmittelhochdeutsche Predigtsammlung (Cgm. 39)*, ed. Gert Mellbourn, Lunder Germanistische Forschungen, 12 (Lund / Copenhagen, 1944).

Thomasin von Zerklaere, *Der wälsche Gast*, ed. Heinrich Rückert, BDNL, 30 (Quedlinburg, 1852) [edition cited].

——, *Der welsche Gast*, ed. F.W. von Kries, GAG 425, 4 vols (Göppingen, 1984-85).

*Tirol und Fridebrant*, in A. Leitzmann (ed.), *Kleinere mittelhochdeutsche Lehrgedichte*, pp. 1-18.

Ulrich von Lichtenstein, *Frauendienst*, ed. Reinhold Bechstein, Deutsche Dichtungen des Mittelalters, 6-7, 2 vols (Leipzig, 1888).

Ulrich von Zatzikhoven, *Lanzelet*, ed. Karl A. Hahn (Frankfurt, 1845; reprint Berlin, 1965).

*La Vie du Pape Saint Grégoire. Huit versions français de la légende du bon pécheur*, ed. Hendrik Bastien Sol (Amsterdam, 1977).

*Vita Heinrici IV. imperatoris*, in Franz-Josef Schmale and Irene Schmale-Ott (eds), *Quellen zur Geschichte Kaiser Heinrichs IV*. FSGA, 12 (Darmstadt, 1963), pp. 407-66.

*Vorauer Alexander*, in Karl Kinzel (ed.), *Lamprechts Alexander*, Germanistische Handbibliothek, 6 (Halle, 1885), pp. 26-172.

Wace, *Le Roman de Brut*, ed. Ivor Arnold, Société des Anciens Textes Français, 2 vols (Paris, 1938-40).

Weinrich, Lorenz (ed.), *Quellen zur deutschen Verfassungs-, Wirtschafts- und Sozialgeschichte bis 1250*, FSGA, 32 (Darmstadt, 1977).

Wernher der Gartenaere, *Helmbrecht*, ed. Friedrich Panzer, ATB, 11, 8th edn, rev. Kurt Ruh (Tübingen, 1968).

William of Newburgh, *Historia Rerum Anglicarum*, in Richard Howlett (ed.), *Chronicles of the Reigns of Stephen, Henry II and Richard I*, Rolls Series, 82, 4 vols (London 1884–89), I, pp. 1–408; II, pp. 409–500.

*Winsbecke*, in A. Leitzmann (ed.), *Kleinere mittelhochdeutsche Lehrgedichte*, pp. 19–39.

Wirnt von Gravenberg, *Wigalois*, ed. J.M.N. Kapteyn, Rheinische Beiträge und Hilfsbücher zur germanischen Philologie und Volkskunde, 9 (Bonn, 1926).

Wolfram von Eschenbach, *Parzival* and *Willehalm*, in Karl Lachmann (ed.), *Wolfram von Eschenbach*, 6th edn (Berlin and Leipzig, 1926; reprint Berlin, 1965).

*Die Zwiefalter Chroniken Ortliebs und Bertholds*, ed. Luitpold Wallach, Erich König, Karl Otto Müller, Schwäbische Chroniken der Stauferzeit, 2, 2nd edn (Sigmaringen, 1978).

## 2. Secondary Literature

Aarburg, Ursula, 'Melodien zum frühen deutschen Minnesang', in Hans Fromm (ed.), *Der deutsche Minnesang. Aufsätze zu seiner Erforschung*, WdF, 15 (Bad Homburg, 1961), pp. 378–423.

Anderson, William, *Castles of Europe from Charlemagne to the Renaissance* (London, 1980).

Angermeier, Heinz, 'Landfriedenspolitik und Landfriedensgesetzgebung unter den Staufern', in Josef Fleckenstein (ed.) *Probleme um Friedrich II*, Vorträge und Forschungen, 16 (Sigmaringen, 1974), pp. 167–86.

Anglo, Sydney, 'How to Win at Tournaments: the Technique of Chivalric Combat', *The Antiquaries Journal*, 68 (1988), 248–64.

Arentzen, Jörg and Uwe Ruberg, *Die Ritteridee in der deutschen Literatur des Mittelalters. Eine kommentierte Anthologie* (Darmstadt, 1987).

Arndt, Paul Herbert, *Der Erzähler bei Hartmann von Aue. Formen und Funktionen seines Hervortretens und seiner Äußerungen*, GAG, 299 (Göppingen, 1980).

Arnold, Benjamin, *German Knighthood 1050–1300* (Oxford, 1985).

——, *Princes and Territories in Medieval Germany* (Cambridge, 1991).

Ashcroft, Jeffrey, '*Miles Dei – gotes ritter*: Konrad's *Rolandslied* and the Evolution of the Concept of Christian Chivalry', in W.H. Jackson (ed.) *Knighthood in Medieval Literature*, pp. 54–74.

——, 'Fürstlicher Sex-Appeal. Politisierung der Minne bei Tannhäuser und Jansen Enikel', in Ashcroft et al. (eds) *Liebe in der deutschen Literatur des Mittelalters*, pp. 91–106.

——, '*Als ein wilder valk erzogen*. Minnesang und höfische Sozialisation', *LiLi*, 19 (1989), 58–74.

——, Dietrich Huschenbett, William H. Jackson (eds), *Liebe in der deutschen Literatur des Mittelalters. St. Andrews-Colloquium 1985* (Tübingen, 1987).

Asmus, Herbert, *Rechtsprobleme des mittelalterlichen Fehdewesens* (dissertation, Göttingen, 1951).

Assmann, E., 'Friedrich Barbarossas Kinder', *DA*, 33 (1977), 435–72.

Barber, Richard, *The Knight and Chivalry* (London, 1974).

—— and Juliet Barker, *Tournaments: Jousts, Chivalry and Pageants in the Middle Ages* (Woodbridge, 1989).

Barker, Juliet, *The Tournament in England 1100-1400* (Woodbridge, 1986).

—— and Maurice Keen, 'The Medieval English Kings and the Tournament', in J. Fleckenstein (ed.), *Das ritterliche Turnier*, pp. 212-28.

Bayer, Hans, *Hartmann von Aue. Die theologischen und historischen Grundlagen seiner Dichtung sowie sein Verhältnis zu Gunther von Pairis*, Beihefte zum Mittellateinischen Jahrbuch, 15 (Kastellaun, 1979).

——, *'bî den liuten ist sô guot. Die meine des Erec* Hartmanns von Aue', *Euphorion*, 73 (1978), 272-85.

Bennet, Matthew, 'The Status of the Squire: the Northern Evidence', in C. Harper-Bill and R. Harvey (eds), *The Ideals and Practice of Medieval Knighthood*, I, pp. 1-11.

Benson, Larry D., 'The Tournament in the Romances of Chrétien de Troyes and *L'Histoire de Guillaume le Maréchal*', in id. and John Leyerle (eds), *Chivalric Literature. Essays on the Relation between Literature and Life in the Later Middle Ages*, Studies in Medieval Culture, 14 (Michigan, 1980), pp. 1-24.

Bertau, Karl, *Deutsche Literatur im europäischen Mittelalter*, 2 vols (Munich, 1972-73).

Beyerle, Franz, 'Der *Arme Heinrich* Hartmanns von Aue als Zeugnis mittelalterlichen Standesrechts', in *Kunst und Recht. Festgabe für Hans Fehr* (Karslruhe, 1948), pp. 28-46.

Beyschlag, Siegfried, *Die Lieder Neidharts. Text und Übertragung. Einführung und Worterklärungen. Konkordanz* (Darmstadt, 1975).

Bezzola, Reto R., *Le sens de l'aventure et de l'amour (Chrétien de Troyes)* (Paris, 1947).

Blair, Claude, *European Armour circa 1066 to circa 1700*, 3rd edn (London, 1979).

Blattmann, Ekkehard, *Die Lieder Hartmanns von Aue*, PhStQ, 44 (Berlin, 1968).

Bloch, Marc, *Feudal Society*, transl. L.A. Manyon, 2nd edn., 2 vols (London, 1965, reprint 1967).

Bloch, R. Howard, *Medieval French Literature and Law* (Berkeley, California, 1977).

Boesch, Bruno, 'Mittelhochdeutsche Dichtung am Oberrhein zur Zeit der Staufer – staufische Dichtung?', *Alemannisches Jahrbuch* (1979/80), pp. 69-98.

Boggs, Roy Amos, *Hartmann von Aue. Lemmatisierte Konkordanz zum Gesamtwerk*, Indices zur deutschen Literatur 12/13, 2 vols (Nendeln, 1979).

Boon, Pieter, 'Die Ehe des "Armen Heinrich" ', *Neophilologus*, 66 (1982), 92-101.

de Boor, Helmut, *Geschichte der deutschen Literatur von den Anfängen bis zur Gegenwart*, volume II, *Die höfische Literatur: Vorbereitung, Blüte, Ausklang 1170-1250*, 3rd edn (Munich, 1957).

Booth, Wayne C., *The Rhetoric of Fiction* (Chicago, 1961).

Borck, Karl Heinz, 'Adel, Tugend und Geblüt. Thesen und Beobachtungen zur Vorstellung des Tugendadels in der deutschen Literatur des 12. und 13. Jahrhunderts', *PBB* (Tübingen), 100 (1978), 423-57.

——, ' "Nû ist si vrî als ich dâ bin". Bemerkungen zu Hartmanns *Armen Heinrich*, v. 1497', in D. Huschenbett et al. (eds), *Festschrift für Kurt Ruh*, pp. 37-50.

——, 'Über Ehre, Artuskritik und Dankbarkeit in Hartmanns *Iwein*', in August Obermayer (ed.), *Die 'Ehre' als literarisches Motiv. E.W. Herd zum 65. Geburtstag*, Otago German Studies, 4 (Otago, 1986), pp. 1-18.

Borst, Arno, 'Das Rittertum im Hochmittelalter. Idee und Wirklichkeit', *Saeculum*, 10 (1959), 213-31.

—— (ed.), *Das Rittertum im Mittelalter*, WdF, 149 (Darmstadt, 1976).

——, *Mönche am Bodensee* (Sigmaringen, 1978).

——, *Lebensformen im Mittelalter* (Vienna, 1979).

Bosl, Karl, *Die Grundlagen der modernen Gesellschaft im Mittelalter. Eine deutsche Gesellschaftsgeschichte des Mittelalters*, Monographien zur Geschichte des Mittelalters, 4, 2 vols (Stuttgart, 1972).

Bradler, Günther, *Studien zur Geschichte der Ministerialität im Allgäu und in Oberschwaben*, Göppinger Akademische Beiträge, 50 (Göppingen, 1973).

Brall, Helmut, 'Imaginationen des Fremden. Zu Formen und Dynamik kultureller Identitätsfindung in der höfischen Dichtung', in Gert Kaiser (ed.), *An den Grenzen höfischer Kultur. Anfechtungen der Lebensordnung in der deutschen Erzähldichtung des hohen Mittelalters*, FGädL, 12 (Munich, 1991), pp. 115-65.

Brandt, Wolfgang, 'Die Entführungsepisode in Hartmanns *Iwein*', *ZfdPh*, 99 (1980), 321-54.

Braun, Werner, *Studien zum Ruodlieb. Ritterideal, Erzählstruktur und Darstellungsstil*, QF, N.F., 7 (Berlin, 1962).

Brinkmann, Hennig, 'Der Prolog im Mittelalter als literarische Erscheinung', *WW*, 14 (1964), 1-21.

Brogsitter, Karl Otto, '*Miles, chevalier* und *ritter*', in Herbert Kolb et al. (eds), *Sprachliche Interferenz. Festschrift für Werner Betz zum 65. Geburtstag* (Tübingen, 1977), pp. 421-35.

Broich, Ulrich, 'Heinrich II als Patron der Literatur seiner Zeit', in Walter F. Schirmer and Ulrich Broich, *Studien zum literarischen Patronat im England des 12. Jahrhunderts* (Cologne and Opladen, 1962), pp. 24-216.

Brooke, Christopher N.L., 'Geoffrey of Monmouth as a Historian', in id. et al. (eds), *Church and Government in the Middle Ages* (Cambridge, 1976), pp. 77-91.

Brooks, N.P., 'Arms, Status and Warfare in Late-Saxon England', in David Hill (ed.), *Ethelred the Unready. Papers from the Millenary Conference*, British Archaeological Reports, 59 (Oxford, 1978), pp. 81-103.

Brown, R. Allen, *The Normans and the Norman Conquest* (London, 1969).

Brunner, Otto, *Land und Herrschaft. Grundfragen der territorialen Verfassungsgeschichte Österreichs im Mittelalter*, 6th edn (Darmstadt, 1970).

Buck, Timothy, 'Heinrichs Metanoia: Intention and Practice in *Der arme Heinrich*', *MLR*, 60 (1965), 391-94.

Bumke, Joachim, *Ministerialität und Ritterdichtung. Umrisse der Forschung* (Munich, 1976).

——, *Studien zum Ritterbegriff im 12. und 13. Jahrhundert*, Beihefte zum *Euphorion*, 1, 2nd edn (Heidelberg, 1977).

——, *Mäzene im Mittelalter. Die Gönner und Auftraggeber der höfischen Literatur in Deutschland 1150-1300* (Munich, 1979).

——, *Höfische Kultur. Literatur und Gesellschaft im hohen Mittelalter*, 2 vols (Munich, 1986).

Busby, Keith, *Gauvain in Old French Literature*, Degré Second, 2 (Amsterdam, 1980).

Carne, Eva-Maria, *Die Frauengestalten bei Hartmann von Aue. Ihre Bedeutung im Aufbau und Gehalt der Epen*, Marburger Beiträge zur Germanistik, 31 (Marburg, 1970).

*Chanson de Geste und höfischer Roman*. *Heidelberger Kolloquium 30. Januar 1961*, Studia Romanica, 4 (Heidelberg, 1963).

Clark, Cecily, 'Studies in the Vocabulary of the *Peterborough Chronicle*, 1070–1154', *English and Germanic Studies*, 5 (1952/53), 67–89.

van Cleve, Thomas Curtis, *The Emperor Frederick II of Hohenstaufen* (Oxford, 1972).

Clifton Everest, J.M., 'Ritter as "rider" and as "knight". A Contribution to the Parzival-Gawan Question', in Werner Schröder (ed.), *Wolfram-Studien*, 6 (1980), 151–66.

Cormeau, Christoph, *Hartmanns von Aue 'Armer Heinrich' und 'Gregorius'. Studien zur Interpretation mit dem Blick auf die Theologie zur Zeit Hartmanns*, MTU, 15 (Munich, 1966).

——, 'Joie de la curt. Bedeutungssetzung und ethische Erkenntnis', in Walter Haug (ed.), *Formen und Funktion der Allegorie. Symposion Wolfenbüttel 1978* (Stuttgart, 1979), pp. 194–205.

—— and Wilhelm Störmer, *Hartmann von Aue. Epoche – Werk – Wirkung* (Munich, 1985).

Cowdrey, H.E.J., 'The Peace and the Truce of God in the Eleventh Century', *Past and Present*, 46 (1970), 42–67.

Cramer, Thomas, ' "Sælde und êre" in Hartmann's *Iwein*', *Euphorion*, 60 (1966), 30–47.

——, 'Soziale Motivation in der Schuld-Sühne-Problematik von Hartmanns *Erec*', *Euphorion*, 66 (1972), 97–112.

Csendes, Peter, *Heinrich VI* (Darmstadt, 1993).

Curschmann, Michael, '*Der aventiure bilde nemen*: The Intellectual and Social Environment of the Iwein Murals at Rodenegg Castle', in M. Jones and R. Wisbey (eds), *Chrétien de Troyes and the German Middle Ages*, pp. 219–27.

Curtius, Ernst Robert, 'Das "ritterliche Tugendsystem" ', in G. Eifler (ed.), *Ritterliches Tugendsystem*, pp. 116–45.

Dannenbauer, Heinrich, 'Adel, Burg und Herrschaft bei den Germanen', in Hellmut Kämpf (ed.), *Herrschaft und Staat im Mittelalter*, WdF, 2 (Darmstadt, 1964), pp. 66–134.

Davis, R.H.C., *The Medieval Warhorse. Origin, Development, Redevelopment* (London, 1989).

Delort, Robert, *Life in the Middle Ages*, transl. Robert Allen (London, 1974).

Denholm-Young, Noel, 'Feudal Society in the Thirteenth Century: the Knights', *History*, 29 (1944), 107–19.

——, 'The Tournament in the Thirteenth Century', in R.W. Hunt et al. (eds), *Studies in Medieval History presented to F.M. Powicke* (Oxford, 1948), pp. 240–68.

Dittmann, Wolfgang, *Hartmanns Gregorius. Untersuchungen zur Überlieferung, zum Aufbau und zum Gehalt*, PhStQ, 32 (Berlin, 1965).

Dopsch, Heinz, 'Probleme ständischer Wandlung beim Adel Österreichs, der Steiermark und Salzburgs vornehmlich im 13. Jahrhundert', in J. Fleckenstein (ed.), *Herrschaft und Stand*, pp. 207–53.

Douglas, David C., *William the Conqueror. The Norman Impact upon England* (London, 1969).

Duby, Georges, 'Dans la France du Nord-Ouest au XIIe siècle: les "jeunes" dans la société aristocratique', *Annales ESC*, 19 (1964), 835–46.

——, 'Lignage, noblesse et chevalerie au XIIe siècle dans la région mâconnaise. Une révision', *Annales ESC*, 27 (1972), 803–23.

——, 'Les laïcs et la paix de Dieu', in id., *Hommes et structures*, pp. 227–40.

——, 'La vulgarisation des modèles culturels dans la société féodale', ibid., pp. 299–308.

——, 'Les origines de le chevalerie', ibid., pp. 325–41.

——, *Hommes et structures du moyen âge. Recueil d'articles*, Le savoir historique, 1 (Paris, 1973).

——, *Medieval Marriage. Two Models from Twelfth-Century France*, Johns Hopkins Symposia on Comparative History, 11 (Baltimore and London, 1978).

——, *Le chevalier, la femme et le prêtre. Le mariage dans la France féodale* (Paris, 1981).

——, review of M. Keen, *Chivalry*, in *Times Literary Supplement*, 29 June 1984, p. 720.

——, *Le dimanche de Bouvines. 27 juillet 1214*, 2nd edn (Paris, 1985).

Duckworth, David, *Gregorius. A Medieval Man's Discovery of his True Self*, GAG, 422 (Göppingen, 1985).

Edwards, Cyril, 'Die Erotisierung des Handwerks', in J. Ashcroft et al. (eds), *Liebe in der deutschen Literatur des Mittelalters*, pp. 126–48.

——, ' "Nur ein fahrender, als er unterwegs war"? Zu Rang und Reisen Walthers von der Vogelweide', in Dietrich Huschenbett and John Margetts (eds), *Reisen und Welterfahrung in der deutschen Literatur des Mittelalters. Vorträge des XI. Anglo-deutschen Colloquiums* (Würzburg, 1991), pp. 96–109.

Ehrismann, Otfrid, 'Höfisches Leben und Individualität – Hartmanns *Erec*', in Walter Tauber (ed.), *Aspekte der Germanistik. Festschrift für Hans-Friedrich Rosenfeld zum 90. Geburtstag*, GAG, 521 (Göppingen, 1989), pp. 99–122.

Eifler, Günter, *Ritterliches Tugendsystem*, WdF, 56 (Darmstadt, 1970).

Elias, Norbert, *Über den Prozeß der Zivilisation. Soziogenetische und psychogenetische Untersuchungen*, suhrkamp taschenbuch wissenschaft, 158/159, 2 vols (Frankfurt a. M., 1976).

Emmel, Hildegard, *Formprobleme des Artusromans und der Graldichtung. Die Bedeutung des Artuskreises für das Gefüge des Romans im 12. und 13. Jahrhundert in Frankreich, Deutschland und den Niederlanden* (Bern, 1951).

Endres, Rolf, 'Die Bedeutung von *güete* und die Diesseitigkeit der Artusromane Hartmanns', *DVLG*, 44 (1970), 595–612.

Erben, Johannes, 'Zu Hartmanns *Iwein*', *ZfdPh*, 87 (1968), 344–59.

Erdmann, Carl, *Die Entstehung des Kreuzzugsgedankens* (Stuttgart, 1935, reprint Darmstadt, 1965).

Ernst, Ulrich, 'Der Antagonismus von *vita carnalis* und *vita spiritualis* im *Gregorius* Hartmanns von Aue', 2 parts, *Euphorion*, 72 (1978), 160–226 and 73 (1979), 1–105.

Eroms, Hans-Werner, *'Vreude' bei Hartmann von Aue*, Medium Aevum. Philologische Studien, 20 (Munich, 1970).

Evans, Dafydd, 'Wishfulfilment: the Social Function and Classification of Old French Romances', in Glyn Burgess (ed.), *Court and Poet. Selected Proceedings of the Third Congress of the International Courtly Literature Society* (Liverpool, 1981), pp. 129–34.

Faral, Edmond, *La Légende arthurienne. Études et documents*, Bibliothèque de l'École des Hautes Études, 255–57, 3 vols (Paris, 1929).

Fechter, Werner, *Lateinische Dichtkunst und deutsches Mittelalter. Forschungen über Ausdrucksmittel, poetische Technik und Stil mittelhochdeutscher Dichtungen*, PhStQ, 23 (Berlin, 1964).

Fehr, Hans, 'Das Waffenrecht der Bauern im Mittelalter', *Zeitschrift für Rechtsgeschichte, Germ. Abt.*, 35 (1914), 111–211

——, 'Das Recht im Iwein', in *Festschrift für Ernst Mayer* (Weimar, 1932), pp. 93–110.

Feldbauer, Peter, *Herren und Ritter*, Herrschaftsstruktur und Ständebildung. Beiträge zur Typologie der österreichischen Länder aus ihren mittelalterlichen Grundlagen, 1 (Vienna, 1973).

Fenske, Lutz, 'Soziale Genese und Aufstiegsformen kleiner niederadliger Geschlechter im südöstlichen Niedersachsen', in Fenske et al. (eds), *Festschrift Fleckenstein*, pp. 693–726.

——, 'Der Knappe: Erziehung und Funktion', in J. Fleckenstein (ed.), *Curialitas*, pp. 55–127.

——, Werner Rösener, Thomas Zotz (eds), *Institutionen, Kultur und Gesellschaft im Mittelalter. Festschrift für Josef Fleckenstein zum 65. Geburtstag* (Sigmaringen, 1984).

Fischer, Hubertus, *Ehre, Hof und Abenteuer in Hartmanns 'Iwein'. Vorarbeiten zu einer historischen Poetik des höfischen Epos*, FGädL, 3 (Munich, 1983).

Fisher, Rodney, 'Räuber, Riesen und die Stimme der Vernunft in Hartmanns und Chrétiens *Erec*', *DVLG*, 60 (1986), 351–74.

Fleckenstein, Josef, 'Friedrich Barbarossa und das Rittertum. Zur Bedeutung der großen Mainzer Hoftage von 1184 und 1188', in *Festschrift für Hermann Heimpel zum 70. Geburtstag*, vol. II, VMPIG, 36, 2 (Göttingen, 1972), pp. 1023–41.

——, 'Zum Problem der Abschließung des Ritterstandes', in Helmut Beumann (ed.), *Historische Forschungen für Walter Schlesinger* (Cologne and Vienna, 1974), pp. 252–71.

——, 'Zur Frage der Abgrenzung von Bauer und Ritter', in Beinhard Wenskus et al. (eds), *Wort und Begriff 'Bauer'*, Abhandlungen der Akademie der Wissenschaften in Göttingen, phil.-hist. Klasse, Folge 3, 89 (Göttingen, 1975), pp. 246–53.

——, 'Die Entstehung des niederen Adels und das Rittertum', in id. (ed.), *Herrschaft und Stand*, pp. 17–39.

— (ed.), *Herrschaft und Stand. Untersuchungen zur Sozialgeschichte im 13. Jahrhundert*, VMPIG, 51 (Göttingen, 1977).

——, 'Das Rittertum der Stauferzeit', in *Die Zeit der Staufer. Geschichte – Kunst – Kultur* (Katalog der Ausstellung, Stuttgart, 1977), vol. III, pp. 103–09.

——, 'Vom Rittertum der Stauferzeit am Oberrhein', *Alemannisches Jahrbuch* (1979/80), pp. 21–42.

——, 'Das Turnier als höfisches Fest im hochmittelalterlichen Deutschland', in id. (ed.), *Das ritterliche Turnier*, pp. 229–56.

— (ed.), *Das ritterliche Turnier im Mittelalter. Beiträge zu einer vergleichenden Formen- und Verhaltensgeschichte des Rittertums*, VMPIG, 80 (Göttingen, 1985).

——, 'Miles und clericus am Königs- und Fürstenhof', in id. (ed.), *Curialitas*, pp. 302–25.

—— (ed.), *Curialitas. Studien zu Grundfragen der höfisch-ritterlichen Kultur*, VMPIG, 100 (Göttingen, 1990).

Flori, Jean, 'Les origines de l'adoubement chevaleresque. Étude des remises d'armes et du vocabulaire qui les exprime dans les sources latines jusqu'au début du XIIIe siècle', *Traditio*, 35 (1979), 209–72.

——, *L'idéologie du glaive. Préhistoire de la chevalerie*, Travaux d'histoire éthico-politique, 43 (Geneva, 1983).

——, *L'essor de la chevalerie. XIe–XIIe siècles*, Travaux d'histoire éthico-politique, 46 (Geneva, 1986).

Fossier, Robert, *La terre et les hommes en Picardie jusqu'à la fin du XIIIe siècle*, 2 vols (Paris and Louvain, 1968).

Foulon, Charles, 'Le rôle de Gauvain dans *Erec et Enide*', *Annales de Bretagne*, 65 (1958), 147–58.

Fourrier, A., 'Encore la chronologie des œuvres de Chrétien de Troyes', *BBSIA*, 2 (1950), 69–88.

Frank, Istvan, *Trouvères et Minnesänger. Recueil de textes pour servir à l'étude des rapports entre la poésie lyrique romane et le Minnesang au XIIe siècle* (Saarbrücken, 1952).

Frappier, Jean, *Chrétien de Troyes. L'homme et l'œuvre*, Connaissance des Lettres, 50 (Paris, 1957).

Freed, John B., 'The Origins of the European Nobility: The Problem of the Ministerials', *Viator*, 7 (1976), 211–41.

——, *The Counts of Falkenstein: Noble Self-Consciousness in Twelfth-Century Germany*, Transactions of the American Philosophical Society, 74, Part 6 (Philadelphia, 1984).

Freytag, Hartmut, 'Ständisches, Theologisches, Poetologisches. Zu Hartmanns Konzeption des *Armen Heinrich*', *Euphorion*, 81 (1987), 240–61.

Freytag, Wiebke, '*rehte güete* als wahrscheinlich *gewisse lêre*: Topische Argumente für eine Schulmaxime in Hartmanns *Iwein*', in M.H. Jones and R. Wisbey (eds), *Chrétien de Troyes and the German Middle Ages*, pp. 165–217.

Friedemann, Käte, *Die Rolle des Erzählers in der Epik* (Berlin, 1910; reprint Darmstadt, 1969).

Fromm, Hans, 'Doppelweg', in Ingeborg Glier et al. (eds), *Weg – Typ – Situation. Studien zu poetologischen Bedingungen in der älteren deutschen Literatur. H. Kuhn zum 60. Geburtstag* (Stuttgart, 1969), pp. 64–79.

Fuhrmann, Horst, *Deutsche Geschichte im hohen Mittelalter: von der Mitte des 11. bis zum Ende des 12. Jahrhunderts* (Göttingen, 1978).

Gamber, Ortwin, 'Die Bewaffnung der Stauferzeit', in *Die Zeit der Staufer. Geschichte – Kunst – Kultur* (Katalog der Ausstellung, Stuttgart, 1977), vol. III, pp. 113–18.

Ganshof, F.L., *Feudalism*, transl. Philip Grierson (London, 1952).

Ganz, Peter F., 'Dienstmann und Abt. *Gregorius Peccator* bei Hartmann von Aue und Arnold von Lübeck', in E.J. Schmidt (ed.), *Kritische Bewahrung. Festschrift für Werner Schröder* (Berlin, 1974), pp. 250–75.

——, '*curialis / hövesch*', in G. Kaiser and J.-D. Müller (eds), *Höfische Literatur*, pp. 39–55.

——, '*hövesch / hövescheit* im Mittelhochdeutschen', in J. Fleckenstein (ed.), *Curialitas*, pp. 39–54.

Gärtner, Kurt, 'Der Text der Wolfenbütteler Erec-Fragmente und seine Bedeutung für die Erec-Forschung', *PBB* (Tübingen), 104 (1982), 207–30, 359–430.

——, 'Stammen die französischen Lehnwörter in Hartmanns *Erec* aus Chrétiens *Erec et Enide*?', *LiLi*, 21 (1991), Heft 83, 76–88.

Gernhuber, Joachim, *Die Landfriedensbewegung in Deutschland bis zum Mainzer Reichslandfrieden von 1235*, Bonner Rechtswissenschaftliche Abhandlungen, 44 (Bonn, 1952).

Gerould, G.H., 'King Arthur and Politics', *Speculum*, 2 (1927), 33–51.

Gewehr, Wolf, *Hartmanns 'Klage-Büchlein' im Lichte der Frühscholastik*, GAG, 167 (Göppingen, 1975).

Giffin, Mary E., 'Cadwalader, Arthur and Brutus in the Wigmore Manuscript', *Speculum*, 16 (1941), 109–20.

Gillies, John R., *Youth and History. Tradition and Change in European Age Relations 1770–Present* (London and New York, 1974).

Gillingham, John, 'Love, Marriage and Politics', *FMLS*, 25 (1989), 292–303.

——, 'The Context and Purposes of Geoffrey of Monmouth's *History of the Kings of Britain*', *Anglo-Norman Studies*, 13 (1990), 99–118.

Giloy-Hirtz, Petra, 'Der imaginierte Hof', in G. Kaiser and J.-D. Müller (eds), *Höfische Literatur*, pp. 253–75.

Goez, Werner, *Gestalten des Hochmittelalters. Personengeschichtliche Essays im allgemeinhistorischen Kontext* (Darmstadt, 1983).

Gottzmann, Carola L., *Deutsche Artusdichtung, Bd. I. Rittertum, Minne, Ehe und Herrschertum. Die Artusepik der hochhöfischen Zeit*, Information und Interpretation, 2, 2nd edn (Frankfurt a.M., 1986).

Green, Dennis H., 'Hartmann's Ironic Praise of Erec', *MLR*, 70 (1975), 795–807.

——, 'The King and the Knight in the Medieval Romance', in A. Stephens et al. (eds), *Festschrift for Ralph Farrell*, Australian and New Zealand Studies in German Language and Literature, 7 (Bern, 1977), pp. 175–83.

——, 'Homicide and *Parzival*', in D.H. Green and L.P. Johnson, *Approaches to Wolfram von Eschenbach*, pp. 11–82.

——, 'The Concept *âventiure* in *Parzival*', ibid., pp. 83–161.

——, *Irony in the Medieval Romance* (Cambridge, 1979).

——, *The Art of Recognition in Wolfram's 'Parzival'* (Cambridge, 1982).

——, 'The Reception of Hartmann's Works: Listening, Reading, or Both?', *MLR*, 81 (1986), 357–68.

— and L.P. Johnson, *Approaches to Wolfram von Eschenbach. Five Essays*, Mikrokosmos, 5 (Bern, 1978).

Grimm, Jacob, *Deutsche Rechtsaltertümer*, 4th edn, prepared by Andreas Heusler and Rudolf Hübner, 2 vols (Leipzig, 1922).

Gross, Hedwig, *Hartmanns Büchlein, dargestellt in seiner psychologischen, ethischen und theologischen Bezogenheit auf das Gesamtwerk des Dichters* (Würzburg, 1936).

Grubmüller, Klaus, 'Nôes Fluch. Zur Begründung von Herrschaft und Unfreiheit in mittelalterlicher Literatur', in D. Huschenbett et al. (eds), *Festschrift für Kurt Ruh*, pp. 99–119.

Gürttler, Karin R., '*Künec Artûs der guote*'. *Das Artusbild der höfischen Epik des 12. und 13. Jahrhunderts*, SGAK, 52 (Bonn, 1976).

Haase, Gudrun, *Die germanistische Forschung zum 'Erec' Hartmanns von Aue*, Europäische Hochschulschriften, Reihe I, 1103 (Frankfurt a. M., 1988).

Haferland, Harald, *Höfische Interaktion. Interpretationen zur höfischen Epik und Didaktik um 1200*, FGädL, 10 (Munich 1988).

Hagenguth, Edith, *Hartmanns 'Iwein'. Rechtsargumentation und Bildsprache* (dissertation, Heidelberg, 1969).

Hahn, Ingrid, *'güete* und *wizzen*. Zur Problematik von Identität und Bewußtsein im *Iwein* Hartmanns von Aue', *PBB* (Tübingen), 107 (1985), 190–217.

Hanning, Robert W., *The Vision of History in Early Britain from Gildas to Geoffrey of Monmouth* (New York and London, 1966).

——, 'The Social Significance of Twelfth-Century Romance', *Medievalia et Humanistica*, New Series, 3 (1972), 3–29.

Harper-Bill, Christopher and Ruth Harvey (eds), *The Ideals and Practice of Medieval Knighthood*, vols I–III (Woodbridge, 1986, 1988, 1990).

Harvey, Ruth, *Moriz von Craûn and the Chivalric World* (Oxford, 1961).

Harvey, Sally, 'The Knight and the Knight's Fee in England', *Past and Present*, 49 (1970), 3–43.

Haubrichs, Wolfgang, '*Reiner muot* und *kiusche site*. Argumentationsmuster und situative Differenzen in der staufischen Kreuzzugslyrik zwischen 1188/89 und 1227/28', in R. Krohn et al. (eds), *Stauferzeit*, pp. 295–324.

——, 'Deutsche Lyrik', in *Neues Handbuch der Literaturwissenschaft*, ed. Klaus von See, vol. VII: *Europäisches Hochmittelalter*, ed. Hennig Krauß (Wiesbaden, 1981), pp. 61–120.

Haug, Walter, *Literaturtheorie im Mittelalter. Von den Anfängen bis zum Ende des 13. Jahrhunderts. Eine Einführung* (Darmstadt, 1985).

Haupt, Jürgen, *Der Truchseß Keie im Artusroman. Untersuchungen zur Gesellschaftsstruktur im höfischen Roman*, PhStQ, 57 (Berlin, 1971).

Heger, Hedwig, *Das Lebenszeugnis Walthers von der Vogelweide. Die Reiserechnungen des Passauer Bischofs Wolfger von Erla* (Vienna, 1970).

Heinen, Hubert, 'The Concepts *hof, hövesch* and the Like in Hartmann's *Iwein*', in Edward R. Haymes (ed.), *The Medieval Court in Europe*, Houston German Studies, 6 (Munich, 1986), pp. 41–57.

Hempel, Wolfgang, *Übermuot diu alte. Der superbia-Gedanke und seine Rolle in der deutschen Literatur des Mittelalters*, SGAK, 1 (Bonn, 1970).

Henne, Hermann, *Herrschaftsstruktur, historischer Prozeß und epische Handlung. Sozialgeschichtliche Untersuchungen zum 'Gregorius' und 'Armen Heinrich' Hartmanns von Aue*, GAG, 340 (Göppingen, 1982).

Hennig, Ursula, 'Herr und Mann – Zur Ständegliederung im *Nibelungenlied*', in Achim Masser (ed.), *Hohenemser Studien zum Nibelungenlied*, Montfort Vierteljahrsschrift für Geschichte und Gegenwart, Heft 3/4, 1980 (Dornbirn, 1981), pp. 175–185.

Herlem-Prey, Brigitte, *Le Gregorius et la Vie de Saint Grégoire. Determination de la source de Hartmann von Aue à partir de l'étude comparative intégrale des textes*, GAG, 215 (Göppingen, 1979).

——, 'Schuld oder Nichtschuld, das ist oft die Frage. Kritisches zur Diskussion der Schuld in Hartmanns *Gregorius* und in der *Vie du Pape Saint Grégoire*', *GRM*, N. F. 39 (1989), 3–25.

Heyck, Edouard, *Geschichte der Herzöge von Zähringen* (Freiburg i. Br., 1891).

Hofer, Stefan, *Chrétien de Troyes. Leben und Werk des altfranzösischen Epikers* (Graz and Cologne, 1954).

Hoffmann, Hartmut, *Gottesfriede und Treuga Dei*, MGH Schriften, 20 (Stuttgart, 1964).

Holmes, Urban T., 'The Arthurian Tradition in Lambert d'Ardres', *Speculum*, 25 (1950), 100–03.

Hölzle, Peter, *Die Kreuzzüge in der okzitanischen und deutschen Lyrik des 12. Jahrhunderts*, GAG, 278, 2 vols (Göppingen, 1980).

Homberger, Dietrich, *Gawein. Untersuchungen zur mittelhochdeutschen Artusepik* (dissertation, Bochum, 1969).

Huby, Michel, *L'adaptation des romans courtois en Allemagne au XIIe et XIIIe siècles* (Paris, 1968).

——, 'L'interpretation des romans courtois de Hartmann von Aue', *CCM*, 22 (1979), 23–38.

Hunt, Tony, 'The Emergence of the Knight in France and England 1000–1200', in W.H. Jackson (ed.), *Knighthood in Medieval Literature*, pp. 1–22.

——, 'Beginnings, Middles and Ends: Some Interpretative Problems in Chrétien's *Yvain* and its Medieval Adaptations', in Leigh A. Arrathon (ed.), *The Craft of Fiction. Essays in Medieval Poetics* (Rochester, Michigan, 1984), pp. 83–117.

——, *Chrétien de Troyes: Yvain (Le chevalier au Lion)* (London, 1986).

——, '*Iwein* and *Yvain*: Adapting the Love Theme', in M. H. Jones and R. Wisbey (eds), *Chrétien de Troyes and the German Middle Ages*, pp. 151–63.

Huschenbett, Dietrich, 'Minne als Lehre. Zur Bedeutung der "Vorläufer" der Minnereden für die Literaturgeschichte des 12. und 13. Jahrhunderts', in J. Ashcroft et al. (eds), *Liebe in der deutschen Literatur des Mittelalters*, pp. 50–6.

——, et al. (eds), *Medium Aevum deutsch. Beiträge zur deutschen Literatur des hohen und späten Mittelalters. Festschrift für Kurt Ruh* (Tübingen, 1979).

Jackson, Timothy R., 'Paradoxes of Person: Hartmann von Aue's Use of the *Contradictio in Adiecto*', in T. McFarland and S. Ranawake (eds), *Hartmann von Aue*, pp. 285–311.

Jackson, William H., '*prison et croisié*. Ein Beitrag zum Begriff *arme ritter*', *ZfdA*, 101 (1972), 105–17.

——, 'Ulrich von Zatzikhoven's *Lanzelet* and the Theme of Resistance to Royal Power', *GLL*, 28 (1975), 285–97.

——, 'Friedensgesetzgebung und höfischer Roman. Zu Hartmanns *Erec* und *Iwein*', in Volker Honemann et al. (eds), *Poesie und Gebrauchsliteratur im deutschen Mittelalter. Würzburger Colloquium 1978* (Tübingen, 1979), pp. 251–64.

——, 'Knighthood and Nobility in Gislebert of Mons's *Chronicon Hanoniense* and in Twelfth-Century German Literature', *MLR*, 75 (1980), 797–809.

——, 'The Concept of Knighthood in Herbort von Fritzdar's *Liet von Troye*', in id. (ed.), *Knighthood in Medieval Literature*, pp. 39–53.

— (ed.), *Knighthood in Medieval Literature* (Woodbridge, 1981; reprinted from *FMLS*, 17, 1981, no. 2).

——, 'The Tournament in the Works of Hartmann von Aue: Motifs, Style, Functions', in T. McFarland and S. Ranawake (eds), *Hartmann von Aue*, pp. 233–51.

——, 'Knighthood and the Hohenstaufen Imperial Court under Frederiak Barbarossa (1152–1190)', in C. Harper-Bill and R. Harvey (eds), *The Ideals and Practice of Medieval Knighthood*, III, pp. 101–20.

——, 'Zum Verhältnis von *ritter* und *kneht* im 12. und 13. Jahrhundert', in

Wolfgang Dinkelacker et al. (eds), *'Ja muz ich sunder riuwe sin'. Festschrift für Karl Stackmann zum 15. Februar 1990* (Göttingen, 1990), pp. 19–35.

——, 'Aspects of Knighthood in Hartmann's Adaptations of Chrétien's Romances and in the Social Context', in M. H. Jones and R. Wisbey (eds), *Chrétien de Troyes and the German Middle Ages*, pp. 37–55.

Jaeger, C. Stephen, *The Origins of Courtliness. Civilizing Trends and the Formation of Courtly Ideals 939–1210* (Philadelphia, 1985).

Jillings, Lewis, 'Ordeal by Combat and the Rejection of Chivalry in *Diu Crône*', *Speculum*, 51 (1976), 262–76.

Johrendt, Johann, *'Milites' und 'militia' im 11. Jahrhundert. Untersuchungen zur Frühgeschichte des Rittertums in Frankreich und Deutschland* (dissertation, Erlangen-Nürnberg, 1971).

Jones, Martin H., 'Chrétien, Hartmann and the Knight as Fighting Man: On Hartmann's Chivalric Adaptation of *Erec et Enide*', in id. and R. Wisbey (eds), *Chrétien de Troyes and the German Middle Ages*, pp. 85–109.

Jones, Martin H. and Roy Wisbey (eds), *Chrétien de Troyes and the German Middle Ages*, Arthurian Studies, 26; Publications of the Institute of Germanic Studies, 53 (Cambridge and London, 1993).

Jordan, Karl, *Henry the Lion. A Biography*, transl. P.S. Falla (Oxford, 1986).

Jungbluth, Günther, 'Das dritte Kreuzlied Hartmanns. Ein Baustein zu einem neuen Hartmannbild', *Euphorion*, 49 (1955), 145–62.

Jusserand, J.J., *Les sports et les jeux d'exercice dans l'ancienne France* (Paris, 1901).

Kaiser, Gert, *Textauslegung und gesellschaftliche Selbstdeutung. Die Artusromane Hartmanns von Aue*, 2nd edn (Wiesbaden, 1978).

——, 'Minnesang – Ritterideal – Ministerialität', in H. Wenzel (ed.), *Adelsherrschaft und Literatur*, pp. 181–208.

—— and Jan-Dirk Müller (eds), *Höfische Literatur, Hofgesellschaft, höfische Lebensformen um 1200*, Studia humaniora, 6 (Düsseldorf, 1986).

Kaufmann, E, 'Acht', *HRG*, I (Berlin, 1971), cols 25–32.

Keen, Maurice, *Chivalry* (New Haven and London, 1984).

Kellermann, Wilhelm, 'L'adaptation du roman d'Erec et Enide de Chrétien de Troyes par Hartmann von Aue' , in *Mélanges de langue et de littérature françaises du Moyen Age et de la Renaissance offerts à Jean Frappier*, 2 vols (Geneva, 1970), I, pp. 509–22.

Kern, Fritz, *Gottesgnadentum und Widerstandsrecht im frühen Mittelalter. Zur Entwicklungsgeschichte der Monarchie*, 3rd edn (Darmstadt, 1962).

Kern, Peter, 'Interpretation der Erzählung durch Erzählung. Zur Bedeutung von Wiederholung, Variation und Umkehrung in Hartmanns *Iwein*', *ZfdPh*, 92 (1973), 338–59.

Knight, Stephen, *Arthurian Literature and Society* (London, 1983).

Kohler, Erika, *Liebeskrieg. Zur Bildersprache der höfischen Dichtung des Mittelalters*, Tübinger Germanistische Arbeiten, 21 (Stuttgart and Berlin, 1935).

Köhler, Erich, *Ideal und Wirklichkeit in der höfischen Epik. Studien zur Form der frühen Artus- und Graldichtung*, Beihefte zur *ZfrPh*, 97 (Tübingen, 1956).

——, 'Die Rolle des niederen Rittertums bei der Entstehung der Trobadorlyrik', in id., *Esprit und arkadische Freiheit. Aufsätze aus der Welt der Romania* (Frankfurt and Bonn, 1966), pp. 9–27.

——, 'Vergleichende soziologische Betrachtungen zum romanischen und zum deutschen Minnesang', in Karl Heinz Borck and Rudolf Henß (eds), *Der Berliner Germanistentag 1968. Vorträge und Berichte* (Heidelberg, 1970), pp. 61–76.

Kraft, Karl-Friedrich O., *Iweins Triuwe. Zu Ethos und Form der Aventiurenfolge in Hartmanns 'Iwein'. Eine Interpretation*, Amsterdamer Publikationen zur Sprache und Literatur, 42 (Amsterdam, 1979).

Kratins, Ojars, *The Dream of Chivalry. A Study of Chrétien de Troyes's 'Yvain' and Hartmann von Aue's 'Iwein'* (Washington, 1982).

Krohn, Rüdiger, Bernd Thum, Peter Wapnewski (eds), *Stauferzeit: Geschichte, Literatur, Kunst*, Karlsruhe Kulturwissenschaftliche Arbeiten, 1 (Stuttgart, 1978).

Krüger, Sabine, 'Das Rittertum in den Schriften des Konrad von Megenberg', in J. Fleckenstein (ed.), *Herrschaft und Stand*, pp. 302–28.

——, 'Das kirchliche Turnierverbot im Mittelalter', in J. Fleckenstein (ed.), *Das ritterliche Turnier*, pp. 401–24.

Kuhn, Hugo 'Erec', in id., *Dichtung und Welt im Mittelalter* (Stuttgart, 1959), pp. 133–50.

——, 'Minnesang als Aufführungsform. Hartmanns Kreuzlied MF 218,5', in id., *Text und Theorie* (Stuttgart, 1969), pp. 182–90.

Kühnel, Jürgen, 'Zum *Reinhart Fuchs* als antistaufischer Gesellschaftssatire', in R. Krohn et al. (eds), *Stauferzeit*, pp. 71–86.

Laurie, Helen C.R., *Two Studies in Chrétien de Troyes*, Histoire d'Idées et Critique Littéraire, 119 (Geneva, 1972).

Lehmann-Langholz, Ulrike, *Kleiderkritik in mittelalterlicher Dichtung*, Europäische Hochschulschriften, Reihe I, 885 (Frankfurt a. M., 1985).

Lewis, Robert E., *Symbolism in Hartmann's 'Iwein'*, GAG, 154 (Göppingen, 1975).

Leyser, Karl, 'Early Medieval Canon Law and the Beginnings of Knighthood', in L. Fenske et al. (eds), *Festschrift Fleckenstein*, pp. 549–66.

Liebertz-Grün, Ursula, *Zur Soziologie des 'amour courtois'. Umrisse der Forschung*, Beihefte zum *Euphorion*, 10 (Heidelberg, 1977).

——, *Das andere Mittelalter. Erzählte Geschichte und Geschichtserkenntnis um 1300. Studien zu Ottokar von Steiermark, Jans Enikel, Seifried Helbling*, FGädL, 5 (Munich, 1984).

Linke, Hans-Jürgen, *Epische Strukturen in der Dichtung Hartmanns von Aue. Untersuchungen zur Formkritik, Werkstruktur und Vortragsgliederung* (Munich, 1968).

Lofmark, Carl, 'The Advisor's Guilt in Courtly Literature', GLL, 24 (1970/71), 3–13.

Luttrell, Claude, *The Creation of the First Arthurian Romance. A Quest* (London, 1974).

Maddox, Donald, *Structure and Sacring. The Systematic Kingdom in Chrétien's 'Erec et Enide'*, French Forum Monographs, 8 (Lexington, 1978).

Matthias, Anna-Susanna, 'Yvains Rechtsbrüche', in Kurt Baldinger (ed.), *Beiträge zum romanischen Mittelalter*, ZfrPh Sonderband (Tübingen, 1977), pp. 156–92.

——, 'Ein Handhaftverfahren aus dem Perceval/Parzivalroman', GRM, 34 (1984), 29–43.

Maurer, Friedrich, *Leid. Studien zur Bedeutungs- und Problemgeschichte, besonders in den großen Epen der staufischen Zeit*, Bibliotheca Germanica, 1 (Bern, 1951).

McCann, William J., 'Gregorius's Interview with the Abbot: A Comparative Study', *MLR*, 73 (1978), 82–95.

McDonald, William C., with the collaboration of Ulrich Goebel, *German Medieval Literary Patronage from Charlemagne to Maximilian I. A Critical Commentary with Special Emphasis on Imperial Promotion of Literature*, Amsterdamer Publikationen zur Sprache und Literatur, 10 (Amsterdam, 1973).

McFarland, Timothy, 'Narrative Structure and the Renewal of the Hero's Identity in *Iwein*', in id. and S. Ranawake (eds), *Hartmann von Aue*, pp. 129–57.

—— and Silvia Ranawake (eds), *Hartmann von Aue. Changing Perspectives. London Hartmann Symposium 1985*, GAG, 486 (Göppingen 1988).

Meng, Armin, *Vom Sinn des ritterlichen Abenteuers bei Hartmann von Aue* (Zürich, 1967).

Mertens, Volker, 'Kritik am Kreuzzug Kaiser Heinrichs? Zu Hartmanns 3. Kreuzlied', in R. Krohn et al. (eds), *Stauferzeit*, pp. 325–33.

——, *Gregorius Eremita. Eine Lebensform des Adels bei Hartmann von Aue in ihrer Problematik und ihrer Wandlung in der Rezeption*, MTU, 67 (Munich, 1978).

——, *Laudine. Soziale Problematik im 'Iwein' Hartmanns von Aue*, Beihefte zur ZfdPh, 3 (Berlin, 1978).

——, 'Iwein und Gwigalois – der Weg zur Landesherrschaft', *GRM*, 31 (1981), 14–31.

——, 'Kaiser und Spielmann. Vortragsrollen in der höfischen Lyrik', in G. Kaiser and J.-D. Müller (eds), *Höfische Literatur*, pp. 455–69.

——, 'Das literarische Mäzenatentum der Zähringer', in Karl Schmid (ed.), *Die Zähringer* (Sigmaringen, 1986), pp. 118–34.

——, ' "Factus est per clericum miles cythereus". Überlegungen zu Entstehungs- und Wirkungsbedingungen von Hartmanns *Klage-Büchlein*', in T. McFarland and S. Ranawake (eds) *Hartmann von Aue*, pp. 1–19.

Milnes, Humphrey, 'The Play of Opposites in *Iwein*', *GLL*, 14 (1960/61), 241–56.

Misrahi, Jean, 'More Light on the Chronology of Chrétien de Troyes?', *BBSIA*, 11 (1959), 89–120.

Mitteis, Heinrich, *Der Staat des hohen Mittelalters. Grundlinien einer vergleichenden Verfassungsgeschichte des Lehnszeitalters*, 7th edn (Weimar, 1962).

——, *Deutsche Rechtsgeschichte. Ein Studienbuch*, 15th edn, rev. Heinz Lieberich (Munich, 1978).

Mohr, Wolfgang, 'Landgraf Kingrimursel. Zum VIII. Buch von Wolframs *Parzival*', in Werner Kohlschmidt and Paul Zinsli (eds), *Philologia Deutsch. Festschrift zum 70. Geburtstag von Walter Henzen* (Bern, 1965), pp. 21–38.

——, 'arme ritter', *ZfdA*, 97 (1968), 127–34.

Morris, Colin, *The Discovery of the Individual 1050–1200* (London, 1972).

Morris, Rosemary, *The Character of King Arthur in Medieval Literature*, Arthurian Studies, 4 (Woodbridge, 1982; reprint, 1985).

Mortimer, Richard, 'Knights and Knighthood in Germany in the Central Middle Ages', in C. Harper-Bill and R. Harvey (eds), *The Ideals and Practice of Medieval Knighthood*, I, pp. 86–103.

Müller, Ulrich, 'Tendenzen und Formen. Versuch über mittelhochdeutsche Kreuzzugsdichtung', in Franz Hundsnurscher and U. Müller (eds),

'Getempert und gemischet' für Wolfgang Mohr zum 65. Geburtstag, GAG, 65 (Göppingen, 1972), pp. 251–80.

Munz, Peter, Frederick Barbarossa. A Study in Medieval Politics (London, 1969).

Naumann, Hans, 'Die Hohenstaufen als Lyriker und ihre Dichterkreise', Dichtung und Volkstum, 36 (1935), 21–49.

Nayhauss-Cormons-Holub, Hans Christoph, Graf von, Die Bedeutung und Funktion der Kampfszenen für den Abenteuerweg der Helden im 'Erec' und 'Iwein' Hartmanns von Aue (dissertation, Freiburg, 1967).

Nellmann, Eberhard, 'Ein zweiter Erec-Roman? Zu den neugefundenen Wolfenbütteler Fragmenten', ZfdPh, 101 (1982), 28–78.

Niedner, Felix, Das deutsche Turnier im 12. und 13. Jahrhundert (Berlin, 1881).

Nitze, William A., 'The Character of Gauvain in the Romances of Chrétien de Troyes', Modern Philology, 50 (1952/53), 219–25.

Nottarp, Hermann, Gottesurteilstudien, Bamberger Abhandlungen und Forschungen, 2 (Munich, 1956).

Oettli, Heinz, The Concept of 'Âventiure' in Hartmann and Wolfram (dissertation, Cambridge, 1971).

Oexle, Otto Gerhard, 'Tria genera hominum. Zur Geschichte eines Deutungsschemas der sozialen Wirklichkeit in Antike und Mittelalter', in L. Fenske et al. (eds), Festschrift Fleckenstein, pp. 483–500.

——, 'Deutungsschemata der sozialen Wirklichkeit im frühen und hohen Mittelalter. Ein Beitrag zur Geschichte des Wissens', in Frantisek Graus (ed.), Mentalitäten im Mittelalter. Methodische und inhaltliche Probleme, Vorträge und Forschungen, 35 (Sigmaringen, 1987), pp. 65–117.

Ohly, Friedrich, 'Vom geistigen Sinn des Wortes im Mittelalter', ZfdA, 89 (1958), 1–23.

Ohly, Walter, Die heilsgeschichtliche Struktur der Epen Hartmanns von Aue (dissertation, Freie Universität Berlin, 1958).

Öhmann, Emil, 'Der romanische Einfluß auf das Deutsche bis zum Ausgang des Mittelalters', in Friedrich Maurer and Heinz Rupp (eds), Deutsche Wortgeschichte, 3rd edn, vol. I (Berlin and New York, 1974), pp. 323–396.

Oman, Charles W.C., The Art of War in the Middle Ages. AD 378–1495, 2 vols (London, 1924; reprint Ithaca, 1960).

Opll, Ferdinand, Friedrich Barbarossa (Darmstadt, 1990).

Orme, Nicholas, From Childhood to Chivalry. The Education of the English Kings and Aristocracy 1066–1530 (London and New York, 1984).

Otto, Eberhard F., 'Von der Abschließung des Ritterstandes', Historische Zeitschrift, 162 (1940), 19–39.

Pähler, Heinrich, Strukturuntersuchungen zur 'Historia Regum Britanniae' des Geoffrey of Monmouth (Bonn, 1958).

Painter, Sidney, French Chivalry. Chivalric Ideas and Practices in Mediaeval France (Baltimore, 1940; reprint Ithaca, 1957).

Parisse, Michel, La Noblesse Lorraine. XIe–XIIIe siècle, 2 vols (dissertation, Université de Nancy II, Lille and Paris, 1976).

Parry, John Jay and Robert A Caldwell, 'Geoffrey of Monmouth', in Roger Sherman Loomis (ed.), Arthurian Literature in the Middle Ages. A Collaborative History (Oxford, 1959), pp. 72–93.

Paterson, Linda, 'The Occitan Squire in the Twelfth and Thirteenth Centuries', in C. Harper-Bill and R. Harvey (eds), *The Ideals and Practice of Medieval Knighthood*, I, pp. 133–51.

Payne, Ann, *Medieval Beasts* (London, 1990).

Pérennec, René, 'Adaptation et société: l'adaptation par Hartmann d'Aue du roman de Chrétien de Troyes, *Erec et Enide'*, *Etudes Germaniques*, 28, (1973), 289–303.

——, *Recherches sur le roman arthurien en vers en Allemagne aux XIIe et XIIIe siècles*, GAG, 393, 2 vols (Göppingen, 1984).

Pernoud, Régine, *Aliénor d'Aquitaine* (Paris, 1965).

Peters, Ursula, 'Niederes Rittertum oder hoher Adel? Zu Erich Köhlers historisch-soziologischer Deutung der altprovenzalischen und mittelhochdeutschen Minnelyrik', *Euphorion*, 67 (1973), 244–60.

——, 'Artusroman und Fürstenhof. Darstellung und Kritik neuerer sozialgeschichtlicher Untersuchungen zu Hartmanns *Erec'*, *Euphorion*, 69 (1975), 175–96.

——, 'Von der Sozialgeschichte zur Familienhistorie. Georges Dubys Aufsatz über die Jeunes und seine Bedeutung für ein funktionsgeschichtliches Verständnis der höfischen Literatur', *PBB* (Tübingen), 112 (1990), 404–36.

Petersen, Julius, *Das Rittertum in der Darstellung des Johannes Rothe*, QF, 106 (Strassburg, 1909).

Pitt-Rivers, Julian, 'Honour and Social Status', in J.G. Peristiany (ed.), *Honour and Shame* (London, 1965), pp. 19–77.

Pratt, Karen, 'Adapting Enide: Chrétien, Hartmann and the Female Reader', in M. H. Jones and R. Wisbey (eds), *Chrétien de Troyes and the German Middle Ages*, pp. 67–84.

Pütz, Horst-Peter, 'Artus-Kritik in Hartmanns *Iwein'*, *GRM*, 22 (1972), 193–97.

Ragotzky, Hedda and Barbara Weinmayer, 'Höfischer Roman und soziale Identitätsbildung. Zur soziologischen Deutung des Doppelwegs im *Iwein* Hartmanns von Aue', in Christoph Cormeau (ed.), *Deutsche Literatur im Mittelalter. Kontakte und Perspektiven. Hugo Kuhn zum Gedenken* (Stuttgart, 1979), pp. 211–53.

Ranawake, Silvia, 'Mehrschichtigkeit des Erzählerkommentars bei Hartmann von Aue', in Leonard Forster and Hans-Gert Roloff (eds), *Akten des V. Internationalen Germanisten-Kongresses Cambridge 1975*, Heft 2, Jahrbuch für internationale Germanistik, Reihe A, vol. II (Bern and Frankfurt a. M., 1976), pp. 414–24.

——, 'Zu Form und Funktion der Ironie bei Hartmann von Aue', in Werner Schröder (ed.), *Wolfram-Studien*, 7 (Berlin, 1982), 75–116.

——, 'Erec's *verligen* and the Sin of Sloth', in T. McFarland and S. Ranawake (eds), *Hartmann von Aue*, pp. 93–115.

Reusner, Ernst von, 'Kreuzzugslieder: Versuche, einen verlorenen 'Sinn" wiederzufinden', in R. Krohn et al. (eds), *Stauferzeit*, pp. 334–47.

——, 'Hartmanns Lyrik', *GRM*, 65 (1984), 8–28.

——, 'Anhang' = the commentary and afterword section of Hartmann von Aue, *Lieder. Mittelhochdeutsch / Neuhochdeutsch*, ed., transl. and with commentary by Ernst von Reusner (Stuttgart, 1985).

Reuter, Hans Georg, *Die Lehre vom Ritterstand. Zum Ritterbegriff in Historiographie und Dichtung vom 11. bis zum 13. Jahrhundert*, Neue Wirtschaftsgeschichte, 4, 2nd edn (Cologne and Vienna, 1975).

Rickard, Peter, *Britain in Medieval French Literature, 1100–1500*, (Cambridge, 1956).

Rieckenberg, Hans-Jürgen, 'Leben und Stand des Minnesängers Friedrich von Hausen', *Archiv für Kulturgeschichte*, 43 (1961), 163–76.

Riley-Smith, Jonathan, *The Crusades. A Short History* (London, 1987; reprint, 1990).

Robertshaw, Alan, 'Ambiguity and Morality in *Iwein*', in T. McFarland and S. Ranawake (eds), *Hartmann von Aue*, pp. 117–28.

Rocher, Daniel, 'Lateinische Tradition und ritterliche Ethik', in G. Eifler (ed.), *Ritterliches Tugendsystem*, pp. 452–77.

Rösener, Werner, 'Ritterliche Wirtschaftsverhältnisse und Turnier im sozialen Wandel des Hochmittelalters', in J. Fleckenstein (ed.), *Das ritterliche Turnier*, pp. 296–338.

——, 'Bauer und Ritter im Hochmittelalter', in L. Fenske et al. (eds), *Festschrift Fleckenstein*, pp. 665–92.

Rosenhagen, Gustav, 'Beiträge zur Charakteristik Hartmanns von Aue', *Zeitschrift für den deutschen Unterricht*, 28 (1914), 94–110.

Roßbacher, Roland, '*Lanzelet*. Artusritter, Königssohn und gewählter König. Ulrichs von Zatzikhoven politische Stellungnahme', *Jahrbuch der Oswald von Wolkenstein Gesellschaft*, 3 (1984/85), 187–201.

Ruh, Kurt, 'Zur Interpretation von Hartmanns *Iwein*', in Werner Kohlschmidt and Paul Zinsli (eds), *Philologia Deutsch. Festschrift für Walter Henzen zum 70. Geburtstag* (Bonn, 1965), pp. 39–51.

——, *Höfische Epik des deutschen Mittelalters*, Grundlagen der Germanistik, 7, 25, 2 vols (Berlin 1967, 1980).

Runciman, Steven, *A History of the Crusades*, 3 vols (Cambridge, 1951–54).

Sacker, Hugh, 'An Interpretation of Hartmann's *Iwein*', *GR*, 36 (1961), 5–26.

Le Sage, David, ' "Ane zuht" or "âne schulde"? The Question of Iwein's Guilt', *MLR*, 77 (1982), 100–13.

Salmon, Paul, *The Works of Hartmann von Aue in the Light of Medieval Poetics* (dissertation, London, 1956).

——, 'The Underrated Lyrics of Hartmann von Aue', *MLR*, 66 (1971), 810–25.

——, ' "Ane zuht". Hartmann von Aue's Criticism of Iwein', *MLR*, 69 (1974), 556–61.

Scheunemann, Ernst, *Artushof und Abenteuer. Zeichnung höfischen Daseins in Hartmanns 'Erec'* (Breslau, 1937).

Schindele, Gerhard, '*Helmbrecht*. Bäuerlicher Aufstieg und landesherrliche Gewalt', in Dieter Richter (ed.), *Literatur im Feudalismus*, Literaturwissenschaft und Sozialwissenschaften, 5 (Stuttgart, 1975), pp. 131–211.

Schirmer, Walter F., *Die frühen Darstellungen des Arthurstoffes* (Cologne, 1958).

Schmidt, Klaus, 'Das Herrscherbild im Artusroman der Stauferzeit', in R. Krohn et al. (eds), *Stauferzeit*, pp. 181–94.

Schmolke-Hasselmann, Beate, *Der arthurische Versroman von Chrestien bis Froissart. Zur Geschichte einer Gattung*, Beihefte zur ZfrPh, 177 (Tübingen, 1980).

Schnelbögl, Wolfgang, *Die innere Entwicklung der bayerischen Landfrieden des 13. Jahrhunderts*, Deutschrechtliche Beiträge, 13, Heft 2 (Heidelberg, 1932).

Schnell, Rüdiger, review of K.-E. Geith, *Carolus Magnus*, in *ZfdPh*, 99 (1980), 433–41.

——, 'Abaelards Gesinnungsethik und die Rechtsthematik in Hartmanns *Iwein*', *DVLG*, 65 (1991), 15–69.

Schönbach, Anton E., *Über Hartmann von Aue. Drei Bücher Untersuchungen* (Graz, 1894).

Schottmann, Hans, 'Gregorius und Grégoire', *ZfdA*, 94 (1965), 81–108.

Schrader, Werner, *Studien über das Wort 'höfisch' in der mittelhochdeutschen Dichtung* (Würzburg, 1935).

Schreiner, Klaus, ' "Hof" (*curia*) und "höfische Lebensführung" (*vita curialis*) als Herausforderung an die christliche Theologie und Frömmigkeit', in G. Kaiser and J.-D. Müller (eds), *Höfische Literatur*, pp. 67–139.

Schröder, Edward, 'Die Datierung des deutschen Rolandsliedes', *ZfdA*, 65 (1928), 289–96.

Schröder, Richard and Eberhard von Künßberg, *Lehrbuch der deutschen Rechtsgeschichte*, 7th edn (Berlin and Leipzig, 1932).

Schröder, Werner, 'Zum *ritter*-Bild der frühmittelhochdeutschen Dichtung', *GRM*, 53 (1972), 333–51.

Schulte, Aloys, 'Eine neue Hypothese über die Heimat Hartmanns von Aue', *ZfdA*, 41 (1897), 261–82.

——, *Der Adel und die deutsche Kirche im Mittelalter. Studien zur Sozial-, Rechts- und Kirchengeschichte*, 3rd edn (Darmstadt, 1958).

Schultz, Alwin, *Das höfische Leben zur Zeit der Minnesinger*, 2nd edn, 2 vols (Leipzig, 1889).

Schulze, H. K., 'Meier', *HRG*, III (Berlin, 1984), cols 439–42.

Schulze, Ursula, '*âmis unde man*. Die zentrale Problematik in Hartmanns *Erec*', *PBB* (Tübingen), 105 (1983), 14–47.

Schupp, Volker, 'Kritische Anmerkungen zur Rezeption des deutschen Artusromans anhand von Hartmanns *Iwein*. Theorie – Text – Bildmaterial', *Frühmittelalterliche Studien*, 9 (1975), 405–42.

Schweikle, Günther, 'Zum *Iwein* Hartmanns von Aue. Strukturale Korrespondenzen und Oppositionen', in Fritz Martini (ed.), *Probleme des Erzählens. Festschrift für Käte Hamburger zum 75. Geburtstag* (Stuttgart, 1971), pp. 1–21.

——, *Die mittelhochdeutsche Minnelyrik, I: Die frühe Minnelyrik. Texte und Übertragungen, Einführung und Kommentar* (Darmstadt, 1977).

——, 'Der Stauferhof und die mittelhochdeutsche Lyrik, im besonderen zur Reinmar-Walther-Fehde und zu Hartmanns *herre*', in R. Krohn et al. (eds), *Stauferzeit*, pp. 245–59.

Schwietering, Julius, *Die Demutsformel mittelhochdeutscher Dichter*, Abhandlungen der königlichen Gesellschaft der Wissenschaften Göttingen, phil.- hist. Klasse, N.F., 17,3 (Berlin, 1921).

Seiffert, Leslie, 'Hartmann von Aue and his Lyric Poetry', *OGS*, 3 (1968), 1–29.

——, 'Hartmann and Walther: Two Styles of Individualism. Reflections on *armiu wîp* and *rîterlîche vrouwen*', *OGS*, 13 (1982), 86–103.

Selbmann, Rolf, 'Strukturschema und Operatoren in Hartmanns *Iwein*', *DVLG*, 50 (1976), 60–83.

Shaw, Frank, 'Die Ginover-Entführung in Hartmanns *Iwein*', *ZfdA*, 104 (1975), 32–40.

Sieverding, Norbert, *Der ritterliche Kampf bei Hartmann und Wolfram: Seine Bewertung im 'Erec' und 'Iwein' und in den Gahmuret- und Gawan-Büchern des 'Parzival'* (Heidelberg, 1985).

Sinka, Margit M., ' "Der höfschste man": An Analysis of Gawein's role in Hartmann von Aue's *Iwein*', *MLN*, 96 (1981), 471–487.

Southern, R. W., *The Making of the Middle Ages* (London, 1953).

Sparnaay, Hendricus, *Hartmann von Aue. Studien zu einer Biographie*, 2 vols (Halle/ Saale, 1933, 1938).

Stengel, Edmund E., 'Die Entstehung der Kaiserchronik und der Aufgang der staufischen Zeit', *DA*, 14 (1958), 395–417.

Tatlock, J.S.P., *The Legendary History of Britain. Geoffrey of Monmouth's Historia Regum Britanniae and its Early Vernacular Versions* (Berkeley and Los Angeles, 1950).

Tax, Petrus W., 'Studien zum Symbolischen in Hartmanns *Erec*. Erecs ritterliche Erhöhung', *WW*, 13 (1963), 277–88.

Thomas, Heinz, '*Ordo equestris* – *ornamentum Imperii*. Zur Geschichte der Ritterschaft im *Moriz von Craûn*', *ZfdPh*, 106 (1987), 341–53.

——, 'Nationale Elemente in der ritterlichen Welt des Mittelalters', in Helmut Beumann and Werner Schröder (eds), *Ansätze und Diskontinuität deutscher Nationsbildung im Mittelalter*, Nationes, 8 (Sigmaringen, 1989), pp. 345–76.

——, 'Matière de Rome – matière de Bretagne. Zu den politischen Implikationen von Veldekes *Eneide* und Hartmanns *Erec*', *ZfdPh*, 108 (1989), Sonderheft, pp. 65–104.

Thompson, James W., *The Literacy of the Laity in the Middle Ages*, 2nd edn (New York, 1960).

Thum, Bernd, 'Politische Probleme der Stauferzeit im Werk Hartmanns von Aue: Landesherrschaft im *Erec* und *Iwein*. Mit einem Anhang: Hartmann von Aue, *Augia Minor* und die Altdorfer Welfen', in R. Krohn et al. (eds), *Stauferzeit*, pp. 47–70.

——, *Aufbruch und Verweigerung. Literatur und Geschichte am Oberrhein im hohen Mittelalter. Aspekte eines geschichtlichen Kulturraumes* (Karlsruhe, 1980).

Topsfield, L.T., *Chrétien de Troyes. A Study of the Arthurian Romances* (Cambridge, 1981).

Turner, Ralph V., 'The *miles literatus* in Twelfth- and Thirteenth-Century England: How Rare a Phenomenon?', *American Historical Review*, 83 (1978), 928–45.

Ullmann, Walter, *The Individual and Society in the Middle Ages* (London, 1966).

——, *Medieval Political Thought* (reprint Harmondsworth, 1979).

Voß, Rudolf, *Die Artusepik Hartmanns von Aue. Untersuchungen zum Wirklichkeitsbegriff und zur Ästhetik eines literarischen Genres im Kräftefeld von soziokulturellen Normen und christlicher Anthropologie*, Literatur und Leben, N.F., 25 (Cologne and Vienna, 1983).

——, ' "Sunder zuchte". Ulrich Füetrers Rezeption des *Iwein*-Verses 1056', *ZfdA*, 118 (1989), 122–31.

Wapnewski, Peter, *Hartmann von Aue*, Sammlung Metzler, 17, 6th edn (Stuttgart, 1976).

Warlop, E., *The Flemish Nobility before 1300*, 4 vols (Kortrijk, 1975–76).

Warren, W.L., *Henry II* (London, 1973).

Wattenbach, Wilhelm and Franz-Josef Schmale, *Deutschlands Geschichtsquellen im Mittelalter: Vom Tode Kaiser Heinrichs V. bis zum Ende des Interregnums*, vol. I (Darmstadt, 1976).

Wehrli, Max, 'Iweins Erwachen', in id., *Formen mittelalterlicher Erzählung. Aufsätze* (Zürich, 1969), pp. 177–93.

Wells, David A., 'The Medieval Nebuchadnezzar. The Exegetical Tradition of Daniel IV and its Significance for the Ywain Romances and for German Vernacular Literature', *Frühmittelalterliche Studien*, 16 (1982), 380–432.

——, 'Gesture in Hartmanns *Gregorius*', in T. McFarland and S. Ranawake (eds), *Hartmann von Aue*, pp. 159–86.

Wentzlaff-Eggebert, Friedrich Wilhelm, *Kreuzzugsdichtung des Mittelalters. Studien zu ihrer geschichtlichen und dichterischen Wirklichkeit* (Berlin, 1960).

Wenzel, Horst, *Höfische Geschichte. Literarische Tradition und Gegenwartsdeutung in den volkssprachigen Chroniken des hohen und späten Mittelalters*, Beiträge zur älteren deutschen Literaturgeschichte, 5 (Bern and Frankfurt a. M., 1980).

—— (ed.), *Adelsherrschaft und Literatur*, Beiträge zur älteren deutschen Literaturgeschichte, 6 (Bern and Frankfurt a. M., 1980).

Wiegand, Herbert Ernst, *Studien zur Minne und Ehe in Wolframs Parzival und Hartmanns Artusepik*, QF, 49 (Berlin and New York, 1972).

Wiehl, Peter, *Die Redeszene als episches Strukturelement in den Erec- und Iwein-Dichtungen Hartmanns von Aue und Chrestiens de Troyes*, Bochumer Arbeiten zur Sprach- und Literaturwissenschaft, 10 (Munich, 1974).

Wießner, Edmund and Harald Burger, 'Die höfische Blütezeit', in Friedrich Maurer and Heinz Rupp (eds), *Deutsche Wortgeschichte*, 3rd edn, vol. I (Berlin and New York, 1974), pp. 187–253.

Willson, Harold Bernard, 'Sin and Redemption in Hartmann's *Erec*', GR, 33 (1958), 5–14.

——, '*Amor inordinata* in Hartmann's *Gregorius*', *Speculum*, 41 (1966), 86–104.

——, 'Kalogrenant's Curiosity in Hartmann's *Iwein*', GLL, 21 (1967/68), 287–96.

van Winter, Johanna Maria, 'Die mittelalterliche Ritterschaft als "classe sociale" ', in A. Borst (ed.), *Rittertum*, pp. 370–91.

Wisniewski, Roswitha, 'Hartmanns *Klage*-Büchlein', *Euphorion*, 57 (1963), 341–69.

Woledge, Brian, 'Bons vavasseurs et mauvais sénéchaux', in *Mélanges offerts à Rita Lejeune*, 2 vols (Gembloux, 1969), II, pp. 1263–77.

Wolff, Ludwig, 'Vom *Büchlein* und *Erec* bis zum *Iwein*', DU, 20 (1968), Heft 2, 43–59.

Wünsch, Marianne, 'Allegorie und Sinnstruktur in *Erec* und *Tristan*', DVLG, 46 (1972), 513–38.

Zink, Georges, '*Geburt* bei Chrétien und bei Hartmann', in Rainer Schönhaar (ed.), *Dialog: Literatur und Literaturwissenschaft im Zeichen deutsch-französischer Begegnung. Festgabe für Josef Kunz* (Berlin, 1973), pp. 22–31.

Zotz, Thomas, 'Städtisches Rittertum und Bürgertum in Köln um 1200', in L. Fenske et al. (eds), *Festschrift Fleckenstein*, pp. 609–38.

Zutt, Herta, *König Artus, Iwein, der Löwe. Die Bedeutung des gesprochenen Worts in Hartmanns 'Iwein'*, Untersuchungen zur deutschen Literaturgeschichte, 23 (Tübingen, 1979).

# Index

abduction 57, 89, 117
Adelger, Bavarian duke 58
Albrecht von Johansdorf 185
*Anglo-Saxon Chronicle* 2, 50
*Annales Aquenses* 70 n. 122
*Annolied* 50 n. 47
Archpoet 169 n. 6
*armiger* 52
Arnold of Guines 18 n. 59
Arnold of Lübeck, *Chronica Slavorum*
   190; Latin transl. of Hartmann's
   *Gregorius* 53 n. 57, 155, 190 n. 78
arrogance, pride 100–02, 151f., 183,
   263
Arthur, king 1f.; in HRB 3–9; in
   Chrétien 9–16, 20, 30f., 145; in
   Hartmann 19f., 36; in Hartmann's
   *Erec* 19f., 23, 25–30, 128f.; in
   Hartmann's *Iwein* 19–24, 196, 232,
   268–72; in Wolfram's *Parzival* 31,
   231; *see also* court(s)
*âventiure (aventura, avanture)*: rise of
   121f.; in Eilhart's *Tristrant* 122; in
   Harmann's *Erec* 122f.; in Chrétien
   260f.; in Hartmann's *Iwein* 238,
   260–63; and glory 122, 262; and
   breach of the peace 262f.

Baldwin V, count of Hainault 6 n.
   21, 70, 155, 226
Baldwin VI, count of Hainault 70f.,
   155
barons 9, 11–13, 15f., 21–25, 31, 144f.
belt, military (*cingulum*) 69f., 229–31
Bernard of Clairvaux 18 n. 59, 87,
   132 n. 150, 151 n. 10; *De laude*
   *novae militiae* 88 n. 15, 138, 183
Bernard II, count of Lippe 195
Bernger von Horheim 180, 187
Berthold IV, duke of Zähringen 30f.,
   188, 280

Berthold V, duke of Zähringen 30f.,
   246, 280
Berthold of Zwiefalten, chronicler 40,
   117 n. 108, 215 n. 15
Bligger von Steinach 187
Burggraf von Regensburg 171
Burggraf von Rietenburg 172

Caesarius of Heisterbach, *Dialogus*
   *Miraculorum* 106 n. 78
captives, captivity 17, 91, 109, 115,
   179, 247
castles 92, 101, 117
Celestine III, pope 188
*chanson de geste* 10
Charlemagne, emperor 59f.
*chevalier*: Chrétien's heroes as 18f.,
   equestrian connection of 43;
   equivalent of *cniht, miles, ritter* 50;
   linked with robbery 110; and
   *serjant/escuiier* 52; *see also* chivalry;
   knighthood
chivalry (ethics, ideology, mentality,
   practices of knighthood) passim;
   and the Church 40f., 80, 82–88,
   105f., 114, 133, 138, 151–53, 165,
   185, 192f., 229–31, 255–58;
   complexity of values in 96, 100,
   130–34, 136f., 139–42, 283f.;
   criticisms of 86, 100, 105, 130,
   151f., 162, 166, 184, 208, 278;
   group identity of 7f., 16, 28, 40f.,
   82f., 86, 93, 115, 142, 173f., 192f.,
   220f., 277, 282f.; historical roots of
   1f., 6–8, 41f., 84–96, 114f., 134,
   148 n. 2, 171f., 229–32, 284f.; and
   justice 91f., 102f., 109f., 116, 142,
   245–49, 256, 283; justifications of
   86–88, 96, 102f., 106, 115f., 137f.,
   152f., 157, 173f., 189, 192f., 245–
   53, 255–59, 277, 289; as a moral

314

Henry I, king of England 2, 4, 6, 17
Henry II, king of England 14f., 17,
145, 230, 256f.
Henry, the Young King, son of
Henry II 6, 15, 17
Henry the Lion, duke of Saxony and
Bavaria 279
Henry the Liberal, count of
Champagne 18 n. 59
Henry, son of Henry the Liberal of
Champagne 18 n. 59
Henry of Huntingdon 3
Herbort von Fritzlar, *Liet von Troye*
61f., 75 n. 139
Hermann von Sachsenheim, *Die
Mörin* 222 n. 38
Hermann of Thuringia, landgrave 25,
31
*Histoire de Guillaume le Maréchal* 17,
18 n. 59
*Historia Welforum* 28 n. 86, 32 n. 102,
35 n. 114, 206 n. 41
Hohenstaufen, dynasty of 32–34,
143f., 232, 286; *see also* court(s),
Hohenstaufen; Conrad, duke of
Franconia; Conrad, duke of
Swabia; Frederick I Barbarossa;
Frederick I, Frederick II, Frederick
IV, Frederick V, dukes of Swabia;
Henry VI, emperor; Otto, count
palatine of Burgundy; Philip of
Swabia
homicide 89, 237f., 240–42
Honorius Augustodunensis, *De
imagine mundi* 52, 67
honour 26, 85, 105–08, 122–26, 128f.,
131f., 135f., 138f., 152, 157f., 162–
64, 189f., 201f., 215, 221–26, 228,
235, 239f., 242–45, 247f., 251, 256,
259f., 262, 288
household, duties of 218, 221–26, 235
*hövesch/hövescheit* 92f., 126, 199,
273–75
Hugo von Trimberg, *Der Renner* 136,
203
humility 86, 114, 139, 164, 201, 205

Innocent II, pope 105
introspection 94, 102, 119f., 125,
165f., 173f., 180f., 191f., 200f.,
209, 233, 236, 250f., 255, 258,
275f., 277f.

irony 17, 107, 113, 211, 223
*îsenhuot* 45, 111

John, king of England 11
John of Salisbury 151 n. 10;
*Policraticus* 230, 256–58
*Joufroi de Poitiers* 222
joust, lance charge 8, 104f., 111, 154,
157, 174
joy 127–29, 131f., 133f., 180, 275f.
judicial duel (*iudicium Dei*) 263–70;
Church's attitude towards 264; in
secular law 264f.; as
demonstration of social status 265;
replaced by peaceful processes
268–70

*Kaiserchronik* 3, 24, 55, 57–61, 75 n.
139, 92f., 171f., 218f.
*Karlmeinet* 263
kingship 10–14, 19f., 24f., 143–45,
261 n. 72, 269f., 286; theocratic
and feudal concepts of 10f.; *see
also* Arthur
*knabe* 45, 52
*kneht* 35f., 50–53, 56, 119, 219; *guoter
kneht* 50f., 53f., 273; *tumber kneht*
35f.
knighthood, passim; aristocratic
tendencies in 1f., 7, 16f., 40, 47,
64, 68f., 150f., 216f., 231, 272,
282f.; and classical antiquity 34,
80, 95 n. 50, 219 n. 24, 230, 257,
263; and kingship 9, 11f., 16–19,
25–27, 32–34, 87, 114, 120f., 133f.,
143, 232, 249, 268–70; material
cost of 7, 27, 40, 46f., 156, 218,
221–23; and merchants 59–61; as
military function 1, 7, 16, 39, 43–
47, Chapter 3 passim, 148, 154,
156, 192, 237–70, 282; and
*ministeriales* 64–69, 71f., 74–77, 83,
142, 170, 282; and nobility 63–83,
216f., 142, 170, 282; and peasantry
40, 58–61, 68f., 148, 150f., 202–08,
215–17, 283; regional variations in
2, 7f., 16f., 64–66, 69–71, 77–79,
154–56; and serfdom 67; and
service 47, 49f., 66f., 171f., 188f.,
248, 266; statistics of 46f., 49, 65;
terminology of 41–43, 48, 50–61,
69–71, 73–77; *see also* chivalry;

# ARTHURIAN STUDIES